Visible Minorities and Multiculturalism: Asians in Canada

Edited by

K. Victor Ujimoto

and

Gordon Hirabayashi

*With the
Assistance of
P.A. Saram*

Butterworths

Toronto

© 1980 Butterworth and Company (Canada) Limited
      2265 Midland Avenue
      Scarborough, Ontario, Canada M1P 4S1
All Rights Reserved.
Printed and Bound in Canada.

The Butterworth Group of Companies:

Canada: Butterworth & Co. (Canada) Ltd., Toronto, Vancouver

United Kingdom: Butterworth & Co. (Publishers) Ltd.,
              London, Borough Green

Australia: Butterworth Pty. Ltd., Sydney, Melbourne, Brisbane

New Zealand: Butterworth of New Zealand, Ltd., Wellington

South Africa: Butterworth & Co. (South Africa) Pty. Ltd., Durban

United States: Butterworth Inc., Boston
              Butterworth (Legal) Inc., Seattle

Canadian Cataloguing in Publication Data

Main entry under title:

Visible minorities and multiculturalism

Papers originally prepared for presentation and discussion at the
Learned Societies Meetings of 1977 and 1978, held at the University
of New Brunswick and the University of Guelph, respectively,
as part of the sessions of the Canadian Asian Studies Association.

ISBN 0-409-87435-3

1. Asians in Canada — Congresses.   2. Multiculturalism — Canada —
Congresses.*   I. Ujimoto, K. Victor, 1935-   II. Hirabayashi, Gordon, 1918-
III. Canadian Asian Studies Association.

FC106.06V58   971.00495   C80-094010-5
F1035.06V58

Preface

The papers in this book were originally prepared for presentation and discussion at the Learned Societies Meetings of 1977 and 1978, held at The University of New Brunswick and The University of Guelph, respectively. As part of the sessions of the Canadian Asian Studies Association (CASA) these meetings opened a new area of scholarly pursuit, the Asians in Canada. Heretofore, the established areas of Asian Studies were East Asia, South Asia and Southeast Asia.

The emergence of Asian Canadians as an area of research and discussion had at least a two-pronged beginning. On the one hand there has been a growing interest in research on ethnic groups and an increasing number of studies on Asian Canadians. As well, teachers of Multiculturalism and Canadian Studies, not to mention Ethnic and Minority Group courses, have begun to call for materials on Asians in Canada in order to fill an important gap in the study of Canada and intergroup relations in Canada.

From quite a different perspective the Canadian Asian Studies Association, in looking for support of its growing programs, began to explore beyond the usual sources of Social Sciences and Humanities Research Council, Department of External Affairs, Canadian International Development Agency (CIDA), and International Development Research Centre (IDRC), and consulted the Multicultural Directorate of the Secretary of State. Here, it was told that it is outside the terms of reference for the Multicultural Directorate to support programs outside of Canada. Well then, what about Asians in Canada? And so there developed a close-working relationship between CASA and the Multicultural Directorate, and a program of theory, research and applied concerns dealing with the varied experiences of Asians in Canada became a reality.

Planning of the conference and the selection of papers were done by a steering committee of Victor Ujimoto, P. A. Saram and Gordon Hirabayashi, with the active cooperation of Richard Young of the Multicultural Directorate. Participants in the first conference represented not all but a wide sampling of Asians in Canada; they reported on the settlement experiences of their respective ethnic groups. Other papers dealt with historical controversies and current issues. In the second conference, papers began to reflect some comparative perspectives and the thoughts and expressions of Asian Canadian writers, who demonstrated they were neither white Canadian nor Asian; they had distinctive Asian Canadian viewpoints and perspectives.

From the papers and discussions at the first two conferences, certain objectives appeared to shape up. The state of knowledge in the field, a primary problem, began to be clarified — from descriptive accounts of settlement experiences (case studies) to searching for common generalizations and patterns; from single group studies to inter-group relations; from interpretation of Asian experiences via assimilation perspective to one utilizing a more pluralistic model; from the exclusively social sciences to some creative arts, writing and music contributions.

As a by-product some kind of a community of Asian scholars have emerged, not in a clannish sense, but with a creative springboard toward shared Canadian scholarly experiences and insights. This may flower into more creative enterprises.

As part of this endeavour it was decided by the conference organizers that the papers of the first two conferences be published. Accordingly, authors were asked to revise their original presentations, and the editors have attempted to organize the collection. Because there was unevenness in the early programs, a balanced presentation is not possible. However, this book is hoped to provide the foundation for a better-balanced next book.

Acknowledgements

We wish to express our sincere gratitude to Dr. Richard Young, Multiculturalism Directorate, Secretary of State, Ottawa, for his continued encouragement, patience, and understanding in our effort to prepare this book. The financial support provided by the Secretary of State, Ottawa, is gratefully acknowledged.

The technical advice and administrative assistance provided by Dr. Elliot L. Tepper, Executive Secretary, and Erna Stark, Office Manager, Secretariat, Canadian Asian Studies Association, are gratefully acknowledged. We also wish to express our gratitude to our publishers, especially Peter Horowitz and Sherry Henderson, for their constructive comments and editorial suggestions.

None of this would have come to fruition without the secretarial assistance of the Asian Canadian Research Project, University of Guelph, and we wish to express our deep appreciation and sincere thanks to Barbara Nicol, Esther Cockburn, Dina Forner, Fran Reinders, and Mutsuko Ujimoto for their patience and skilled efforts in typing the manuscript.

K. Victor Ujimoto
Gordon Hirabayashi
July 30, 1979.

Table of Contents

1

Asian Immigrants and Canadian Multiculturalism: Current Issues and Future Opportunities

Brenda E. F. Beck
Department of Anthropology and Sociology
University of British Columbia

The field of Asian ethnic studies in Canada is just beginning to blossom. The following series of papers, presented at the 1977 and 1978 Meetings of the Canadian Asian Studies Association, represent a new trend. The CASA has, in previous years, been mainly concerned with Asia itself. But during the past two years, it welcomed a series of panels on Asians in Canada, the results of which appear in this volume. As well as suggesting a growing field of scholarly interest, these papers also point out some of the difficulties inherent in such research work. Both the positive results and some obvious gaps are discussed below.

The new attention being paid to the Asian communities in Canadian society finds the researcher faced with the same problems that vex the humanities and social sciences at large. Should efforts focus on pro-ducing descriptive reports about specific Asian groups or should we attempt broad comparative surveys that can encompass immigrants from a wide variety of countries and social origins? Should we concentrate on ethnographic work, or do we need to focus more directly on the cultural adjustment processes which underlie current and past events? And finally, are we to study the individual immigrant or should we focus on "group" phenomena? If the latter, we face yet one more dilemma: how to adequately demarcate a group's boundaries.

Clearly historians, sociologists, psychologists and anthropologists (to name but a few of the disciplines concerned) need to cooperate in charting this new research territory. Immigration involves a complex set of interaction effects, both for newcomers and for the host society. There is little room in this field for isolating simple cause and effect relationships. The task is enormous. Furthermore, research results in this field can be critically important. They can contribute both to policy formulation and to the pride, identity and well-being of Canadian society at large. Sensitivity to cultural variation, a cooperative spirit, and innovative research designs, however, will be required before a useful outcome can be obtained.

The substantive papers which follow represent initial efforts by a large range of scholars to study Asian immigrant reactions and contributions to Canadian society. Each one focuses on a specific topic. Many are defined by a concern to describe the adjustment experience of one particular group (Pakistani; Korean; Vietnamese; East Indian; Chinese; and Japanese). Several others deal with early community structures and organizations. Lai's paper, taking a rather innovative tack, illustrates how Chinese overseas records can be used as a source of data to reconstruct the population structure of Chinatown in Victoria, B.C. Wickberg provides an overview of early Chinese associational development. In contrast, Chan examines the myth of the Chinese "sojourner" in Canada.

Another group of papers deal with more "official" reactions by the host community, as gleened from newspaper commentaries, speeches by politicians, and various government legislation. Contributions by Bhatti, Raj, Roy, and Sunahara deal with the early "exclusionist" attitudes of many Anglo-Canadians. Each describes the fears of many Anglo-Canadian residents that an Asian presence could contaminate their "white" society and/or undermine their "parliamentary" institutions. Buchignani, Groberman, and Indra take a somewhat different look at this issue. They attempt to describe the instrumental and economic "causes" behind official immigration decisions. Bowerman and Buchignani focus specifically on the contemporary situation. They bring the volume up to date by discussing current Human Rights policies and pending immigration legislation.

In addition, two contributors, Naidoo and Kim, examine role-perceptions and self-perceptions. Naidoo is interested in the sense of accomplishment and achievement aspirations of East Indian women and she makes a comparative analysis with a sample of Anglo-Saxon women. Kim takes a psychological approach and uses attitude scaling techniques. He asks newly arrived Koreans to distinguish between their own attitudes and perceived parental ones. With such data, Kim then attempts to measure the development of a new sense of identity experienced by Koreans in the Canadian context. This paper is especially innovative when viewed from a methodological perspective since it contrasts results obtained from a group tested in Korea with those obtained from a group of "host" Canadians. In this way we can begin to see how the speed and direction of changes occuring in the immigrant context may be precisely studied.

Figure 1 locates some of the articles in this volume inside a single, rather general, framework. This is done for the following reasons: 1) such a chart can guide a reader towards papers that may be of special personal interest; 2) such a framework can help to relate these contributions to each other by indicating some of the crucial dimensions of this new research area; and 3) the blanks which remain in the chart draw attention to certain issues which have been sorely neglected to date.

A preliminary discussion of the rationale and terminology employed in this chart are needed before tackling the "blank areas" within it. The terms "host" and "immigrant" were chosen to avoid definitional problems. Going back far enough in time one might speak of the several Indian and Eskimo groups of Canada as the original "hosts."[1] But, for the papers contained in this volume "resident in Canada before 1900" provides an adequate definition of this term. The term "immigrant" is used to refer to those who arrived after this same point in time. Figure 1 is structured by four main quadrants. A horizontal axis separates the subjects studied into host and immigrant categories; a vertical axis divides the responses to a given subject group into own and other. The same responses are also subdivided into perceptions of a respondent's "own" category and perceptions of them by an outside group. Country of birth, ethnic and linguistic background, or religious affiliation are only a few of many further delimitations individual authors have made to narrow this definition of "immigrant" to a select group for study.

The framework we propose is structured around a concept of "perception" because of the great importance this issue seems to have, both for the individual immigrant, and for cultural adjustment processes in general. The host group's perception of the immigrant's qualities, and the assessment immigrants have of their own needs and abilities to cope, together shape the new life these two groups will have in

Figure 1

The Substantive Papers: Classification of Some Private Attitudes and Group Perceptions of Persons Studied

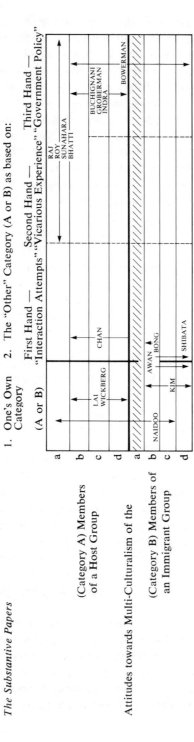

The Substantive Papers

1. One's Own Category (A or B)
2. The "Other" Category (A or B) as based on:

First Hand — "Interaction Attempts" Second Hand — "Vicarious Experience" Third Hand — "Government Policy"

(Category A) Members of a Host Group

Attitudes towards Multi-Culturalism of the

(Category B) Members of an Immigrant Group

Key: Definition of the Horizontal Subdivisions.

    a) Prevent contact: Keep out of (a country or region)
    b) Encourage "separate but equal" status in (a country or region)
    c) Encourage institutional integration in (a country or region)
    d) Encourage cultural assimilation in (a country or region)
    ///// Category not relevant to the present set of papers but included for logical consistency.

Definition of the Individual Spaces

AB ... YZ = Name of the author of a given paper (placed so as to indicate, in rough terms, the nature of the data reported)

    ⟶ = Range of attitudes or perceptions probably incorporated in a given author's sample.

relation to each other. Unfortunately, most of the contributions in this volume do not go very far towards addressing this fundamental issue. What images of "own" and "other" groups in Canada have people developed? Furthermore, the great range of sources for these concepts (first, second and third hand input) remains largely unexplored. The fact that so few horizontal arrows are needed in Figure 1 to describe individual papers shows up this lacune clearly. Awan's essay goes the furthest, perhaps, as it deals with some details concerning the interface between the "own" and "other" columns. Awan discusses the Pakistani concern with fostering an "Islamic identity," as well as this group's market institutional successes in the areas of Canadian schooling and employment. The other five "ethnographically" oriented papers deal with this question briefly. Such a classification is necessarily rough, but it does help to point out the differing emphases present in different essays.

In the further exploration of this problem of "mutual perceptions," it is hoped that the layered and complex concept of "host group" can also be tackled more directly. Clearly, what the host group defines itself to be, and what the immigrant group believes itself confronted with, are both important determinants of potential interaction patterns. There are some obvious pitfalls, however, in defining the "hosts." Regional and even local patterns (rather than national ones) seem to be the relevant units to explore. Who are the "locals" for a given immigrant group? French/English differences are clearly important in this regard, but more detailed variation should also be studied. There are vast provincial contrasts, for example, in the importance of persons of German ancestry as a third local community. In the 1961 census almost 10% of the population of Manitoba claimed a German ethnic background, while only slightly over 1% made such a claim in New Brunswick, and still fewer did so in Prince Edward Island. Similar differences are important at the city level. Over three-quarters of the non-English and non-French population of Montreal continue to use a non-official language on a daily basis, while less than half of the equivalent population groups of other cities do so (O'Bryan, et al., p. 134). High concentrations of certain immigrant groups in given areas clearly have a major effect on host/immigrant perceptions (O'Bryan, et al., p. 133).

Less obvious perhaps, but equally important is the attitude that each group or person studied has toward more general processes of culture contact. Such attitudes can exist, both on a group level and as attributes of individuals. The government's non-official languages study of 1974, for example, asked each respondent about attitudes toward multiculturalism. The authors reported an important finding:

the recency of immigration, the sex, and the ethnic origin of a person each appear to have very little effect on the response. There was also remarkably little variation by region (O'Bryan, et al., pp. 159-63). Such findings suggest that we should treat multicultural attitudes as an independent variable in future studies. Instead, we should begin to ask what effect a given position on multiculturalism has on other aspects of immigrant/host perceptions.

In line with the above discussion, Figure 1 has been sub-divided into several rows, according to whether the view of a given respondent (or sub-group) thinks that: a) contact between ethnic groups should be prevented; b) "separate but equal" statuses within a contact framework should be encouraged; c) institutional or public "integration" (only) is desirable; or d) "cultural assimilation" to some set of common (private) standards is wanted. None of the papers published here deal directly with such a breakdown of study samples, but this strategy should be suggested to future researchers. In the figure, the vertical arrows simply mean that finer distinctions cannot be made on this basis of present work. A "prevention of contact" option is also included for immigrant groups, since such persons could opt to emigrate back to a non-ethnically mixed homeland in some cases. The shading suggests that this situation is not depicted by any of the papers in the present collection.

Two other "blank areas" depicted by the chart indicate a particularly neglected area in current research efforts. We have in mind the images of "self" and of "other" that constantly reach one through the public media. As was pointed out in discussion following the formal paper presentations, media reports on the political and economic state of a particular immigrant's homeland have much to do with forming "host" images of that immigrant group's background. These may be largely irrelevant to the immigrant situation. Still, there can be no doubt of the influence of international events and power relationships on the immigrant experience. We need to study both how this process works, and how to counteract its (frequently) pernicious impact on the Asian immigrant to Canada.

Beyond the "special reports" of the media on given Asian countries, there lies a much vaster field in need of study; namely, the role that the press and television have in conveying more subtle messages about Canada's host society. It would seem reasonable that many recently arrived immigrants (especially women) receive a great proportion of their early ideas about their Canadian hosts from these sources. The simple absence of most ethnically and culturally distinctive sub-sections of the population in roles of media leadership provides a very unreal picture of the homogeneity of Canadian society. At the same time, this phenomena may provide a rather realistic image of the kinds of people who actually wield power. Also important is the very distorted picture the media provide of Canadian home life, family values, societal violence, and material consumption patterns. We have very little knowledge about what the media convey to all of us. The CBC, for example, has yet to do any extended content analysis of its programming with regard to basic values of any kind. Thus, work on how host and immigrant preceive themselves and each other through the media is urgently needed. The role of the ethnic press can also constitute a valuable line of inquiry here. What do the various "ethnic" publications excerpt from the official language media? And what special "slants" do they provide with their "Ann Landers" column equivalents, advertising choices, etc? The chart points up the present lack of research in this whole area.

The fact that ethnic awareness seems to vary independently of the degree of "objective" distance between the cultural traditions of given groups should also be a subject for study. The unusually negative attitudes towards multiculturalism displayed by Canadians with French, Ukrainian or Russian backgrounds (Berry, et al., p. 161) for example, are certainly significant. This data (also from the 1974 non-official languages study) suggests that a heightened awareness of one's ethnicity can be expressed as a response to (as well as the cause of) other social phenomena (Breton, et al., p. 197). Even attitudes of exclusiveness are always part of a large bundle of "we"/"they" relationships. Thus such patterns of action and reaction concerning perceived identities should be amenable to study within this same framework. One does not need to limit the definition of such "perceptions," furthermore, to those of the host and the immigrant. A study of (French/English) subdivisions within the host community, or of the interrelations between two immigrant groups could be assessed using a similar format.

The main point of the chart then, is to encourage the reader to think in terms of relationships, rather than to reason about each ethnic group individually. The fact that such social units (real or perceived) find themselves reacting to one another lies at the heart of all culture contact. It seems best to admit this fact in our basic formulation of the research arena. Furthermore, any study of immigrant adaptation must concern itself with the question of change. In the social sciences this topic has always been bedeviled by the problem of identifying "end points." One can only speak of change relative to some given or "fixed" state and then provide a description of a vectoral movement away from that point in a specific direction. It is only by the comparison of groups at different points in the history of their contact that one can begin to identify these vectors. Perhaps a series of charts, such as the one described above, depicting the same groups at different points in time (or space), can eventually help us produce such "vectoral" maps.

We now move to a brief survey of some points that several of these papers have in common. A topic stressed by at least one author (Awan) is the importance of a network of kin ties in helping the immigrant adapt to a new context. Family loyalty and the sharing of opportunities and resources amongst a wide circle of kinsmen provides the newly arrived with a sense of security, as well as with a set of ready-made (if second-hand) contacts with the larger society. On the other hand, such "buffer networks" may be counter productive and even exploitative in the long run. Immigrants who remain within a mental or spatial "ghetto" of like-minded persons may suffer a handicap in the acquisition of needed new skills. They may also become dependent on better-positioned members of their own group. Striking out on their own in the new environment might be more desirable. A study designed to investigate these issues is badly needed.

A question raised by several authors also relates to the topic of "ethnic enclaves." Does the spatial spreading of a "visible" ethnic group throughout a region, or a given metropolis, help or hinder its acceptance by the wider society? Awan argues that a thin distribution is desirable, while others argue that it can hinder a positive response. At the core of this debate are two issues, neither of which has a clear answer at present. Firstly, does geographic spread increase or decrease a group's "visibility"? And secondly, does such "visibility" ultimately speed or retard positive acceptance on the part of a host community? No doubt the problem has a complex solution, heavily dependent on the economic position of the newcomers and on the extent to which the host society finds their superficial characteristics (dress, demeanour) attractive. Certainly more understanding of these processes is needed. As Bowerman suggests, unfavorable "visibility" leads rapidly to discriminatory perceptual habits on the part of the host community.

The role of the children, for first generation immigrants, is also an important aspect of immigrant adjustment (Shibata). A child can often take on the task of "interpreter," becoming the first truly bilingual member of the family unit. He may also be in an advantageous position to enter the homes of members of the host community. A surprising, but especially important, finding (Kim) also points to the critical role of the immigrant wife. A study of a Korean-Canadian sample suggests that these women tend to adopt the values of the host society more quickly than do their husbands. This may be explained in part by the greater gains a woman stands to make in self-identity vis-a-vis a traditionally marginal public role. If this work stands up to further inquiry it could prove extremely significant. Perhaps women, and not men, are the prime persons to take on the role of cultural "go-betweens" in immigrant life. This same finding also fits nicely with Lévi-Strauss' theoretical predictions about women. He predicted as early as 1949 that women would serve as "mediators" by virtue of their marginal social and political position (Lévi-Strauss, pp. 568-9).

Despite these various "convergences" between papers, there are also some surprising gaps. Particularly, we may note that the more ethnographically oriented papers fail to set their work in the context of a growing array of statistical data on Canadian immigration. No one has mentioned the report of the Second Canadian Conference of Multiculturalism or the excellent summaries of two major government studies contained within it. Similarly, no mention is made of the 1976 *Report of the Royal Commission on Bilingualism and Biculturalism*, which contains over a hundred pages of statistical tables, and a summary of much detailed historical and ethnographic material. References to a fine summary of contemporary research issues contained in the back of Volume V (1976) of the Canadian Ethnic Studies Association are also lacking. Individual studies of specific ethnic groups certainly have their place, but we need to work towards "framing them" within the larger context of immigration history and of broader contributions to the field.

Some of the major issues contained within the broad framework of studies just mentioned can be cited in conclusion. First of all, none of the ethnographic papers published here attempt any systematic examination of the effects of age on arrival (or of current age) upon attitudes or experiences relating to cultural adjustment. Yet general intuition, plus recent research work on expectation theory (Kim), lead us to speculate that youthfulness can be an important factor in facilitating creative "adjustment" patterns. If nothing else, it is certainly clear that being young is a great advantage in second-language learning. None of the other "obvious" factors in the acculturation situation such as level of education, a rural versus an urban setting, or religious background, are systematically treated. One study, especially where a small sample is combined with intensive informal interviewing, can never deal with all of these issues. But we must begin to design our studies so that at least some of these "obvious" factors are held constant.

Perhaps the most absorbing and significant question of all, however, remains to be asked. We are always speaking of the "cultural" differences which people of various social and ethnic backgrounds carry with them. But it is still quite unclear what constitutes a "cultural factor." As one friend has aptly put it, "culture is just another term for a mystery factor: it is what is left over after all controllable variation has been factored out." The *Report of the Royal Commission on Bilingualism and Multiculturalism* has called culture: "a driving force animating a significant group of individuals" (Volume 1, p. 38) or "a style of living made up of many elements that colour thought, feeling and creativity, like the light that illuminates the design of a stained glass window" (Volume 4, p. 11). Such quotations make the "mystery" of culture quite clear.

What culture consists of is something that has troubled the social sciences, particularly scholars working in anthropology, for more than a century. Somehow, the discipline whose raison d'etre is to grapple with this issue is still 'at sea' in its attempts to define what their basic subject matter consists of. Modern-day immigration and the multicultural environments which such population movements create, provide an ideal setting for future work on this problem. Only in such a context, where we can see various forms of this "mystery factor" in action and in reaction, can we begin to sort out where the essence of the matter lies.

Let us now go one step beyond this to venture a few bold suggestions. Where should we begin to look in more depth? For one, culture seems to lie in the expressive domain more than in a realm of logic or of absolutes. Two cultures may well share certain fundamental values. For example, two groups may both rate the importance of close family bonds, personal honesty, and productive skills very highly. Yet the way those personal bonds are expressed, the context in which honesty is thought appropriate, and the nature of the skills which are honored, may vary greatly. Cultural assumptions about interaction expectations, about settings, and about appropriate manipulative means are usually not consciously held. Yet they are critical to successful social outcomes. We know that actors who approach a situation without such common ground often fail to adequately "understand" one another.

It seems, then, that we must probe the area of mutual (unspoken) expectations more deeply in future multicultural research. Needless to say, questions and observations designed to explore these expectations will have to be cleverly worked out. It would seem that research work on concepts of exchange (Mauss, Kapferer) is also quite relevant. And a final direction in which to expand our current inquiries may be in the direction of metaphor.[2] Metaphor is the expressive side of verbal logic, just as contextual expectations and body gestures provide an expressive dimension to given role and status structures. The content and situational use of metaphors varies significantly from culture to culture. It may well be that to understand another culture, we do not need a new set of ultimate values so much as we need to learn new ways of expressing (basically) familiar ideas.

This focus on "culture as a set of collective habits of expression" has the further advantage of merging descriptive content with the study of process. Research designs, clearly, must fit the phenomena studied. In this case, (as in the initial chart) the problem is one of mutuality. Each person and each sub-group in a multicultural setting is constantly seeking to understand an "other" and to redefine the "own self" in that light.[3] The genius behind good research on this topic will lie in finding a way to simplify the complex dimensions of this basic process; at the same time, using penetrating new techniques to focus on certain aspects of that wider problem in special depth.

NOTES

1. There are certain interesting historical ironies in this area, of course. Many Frenchmen, for example, defined themselves as the "host" group upon their arrival in North America, treating native Indians as people to be proselytized and brought into the fold of the greater Catholic church (Isajiw, xii).

2. Raj's paper is rather innovative here. His detailing of (negative) metaphors used by the host community towards East Indians early in the 20th century is quite informative. Although he does not analyze his material from this perspective, this data clearly points to certain core images having to do with "Asian history," "disease theory" and concepts of the "primitive."

3. I acknowledge a debt to G. H. Mead (1934) in stimulating my attempt to formulate the problem in this way.

BIBLIOGRAPHY

Berry, John, Kalin, Rudolf, and Taylor, Don.
    1976. "Summary — Multiculturalism and Ethnic Attitudes in Canada" pp. 149-68. in the Canadian Consultative Council on Multiculturalism's Report entitled *Multiculturalism as State Policy*. Ottawa, Department of the Secretary of State.

Breton, R., Burnet, J., Hartman, N., Isajiw, W., and Lennards, J.
    1977. "The Impact of Ethnic Groups on Canadian Society: Research Issues" pp. 191-213. in W. Isajiw (ed.) *Identities: The Impact of Ethnicity on Canadian Society*. Toronto, Peter Martin Associates.

Canadian Consultative Council on Multiculturalism,
    1976. *Multiculturalism as State Policy* (Report of the Second Canadian

Conference on Multiculturalism). Ottawa, Department of the Secretary of State.

Isajiw, Wsevolod.
    1977. *Identities: The Impact of Ethnicity on Canadian Society*. Toronto, Peter Martin Associates.

Kapferer, Bruce (ed.)
    1976. *Transaction and Meaning*. Philadelphia, Institute for the Study of Human Issues.

Levi-Strauss, Claude.
    1967. *Les Structures Elementaires de la Parente*. Paris, Mouton (reprint of the 1949 edition).

Mauss, Marcel.
    1970. The Gift (I. Cunnison, Trans.) London, Routledge and Kegan Paul.

Mead, George Herbert.
    1934. *Mind, Self and Society*. Chicago, University of Chicago Press.

O'Bryan, Ken, Reitz, J. G., and Kuplowska, O.
    1976. *Non-Official Languages Study: A Review of the Principle Results*. pp. 131-45. in the Canadian Consultative Council on Multiculturalism, Report entitled *Multiculturalism as State Policy*. Ottawa, Department of the Secretary of State.

Royal Commission on Bilingualism,
    1967, 1970. *Report: Volumes I and IV*. Ottawa, King's Printer.

2

The Population Structure of North American Chinatowns In The Mid-Twentieth Century: A Case Study*

Chuen-yan David Lai
University of Victoria

One of the major problems in the study of urban ethnicity is a scarcity of information. The elements of population composition such as sex, age, and marital status usually appear in national censuses but they are rarely broken down according to ethnic groups in individual cities. Demographic data about an ethnic urban enclave are seldom collected or published officially. For example, a study of the population structure of a Chinatown has to rely much more on field surveys than on official data. The purpose of this paper is twofold; first, to reveal that many overseas Chinese records can be utilized as a source of demographic data, and second, to reconstruct the population composi-

* Grateful acknowledgment is given to the Canada Council for its financial support in this research, and to the Chinese Consolidated Benevolent Association in Victoria for its permission to use its archives.

tion of a Canadian Chinatown in 1939, which was very characteristic of the demographic structures of many other contemporary North American Chinese urban enclaves.

NATURE OF DATA

The source of data used in this paper is the three volumes of the Chinese government bonds sale records which are kept by the Chinese Consolidated Benevolent Association in Victoria, Canada. After the outbreak of the Sino-Japanese War in 1937, the Chinese government attempted to raise a war fund by issuing the Chiu-kuo Kung-chai (the Bonds for Rescuing the Motherland) and urged the overseas Chinese to purchase them. In response to the call from China, the Chinese in Canada immediately set up the Chinese Liberty Fund Association for promoting the sale of government bonds. The branch of the Association in Victoria succeeded in raising nearly Can. $69,000 within sixteen months from January 1938 to April 1939. The amount of bonds promised for purchase by the twenty-three voluntary associations and 2,579 individual Chinese in Victoria were recorded in three thick volumes of register. According to the old-timers, nearly every Chinese in the city had bought the bonds. It was said that a certain man surnamed Teng who had not made a contribution to the war fund, was later punished by being tied to a pole in Chinatown by some infuriated patriots.[1] The purchasers of the bonds represented over eighty percent of the Chinese living in Victoria in 1939.[2] The register records each purchaser's full name, address in Victoria, home county and village origins, sex, age, occupation, number of bonds promised for purchase and the amount of payment. An example is shown in Figure 1. From this information it is possible to study the demographic composition of the Chinese in Victoria in 1939.

THE SEX AND AGE RATIO

The unbalanced distribution of sex and age is readily visible from a population pyramid. Nearly ninety-five per cent of the Chinese in Victoria were males and about half of them were in the age groups between 50 and 69 years of age.[3] This is illustrated in Figure 2. This situation is accounted for by two major factors, namely the traditional Chinese attitude toward emigration and the exclusion of Chinese immigration after 1923. The Chinese normally did not dream of emigration because of their traditionally strong tie with their families.

Figure 1

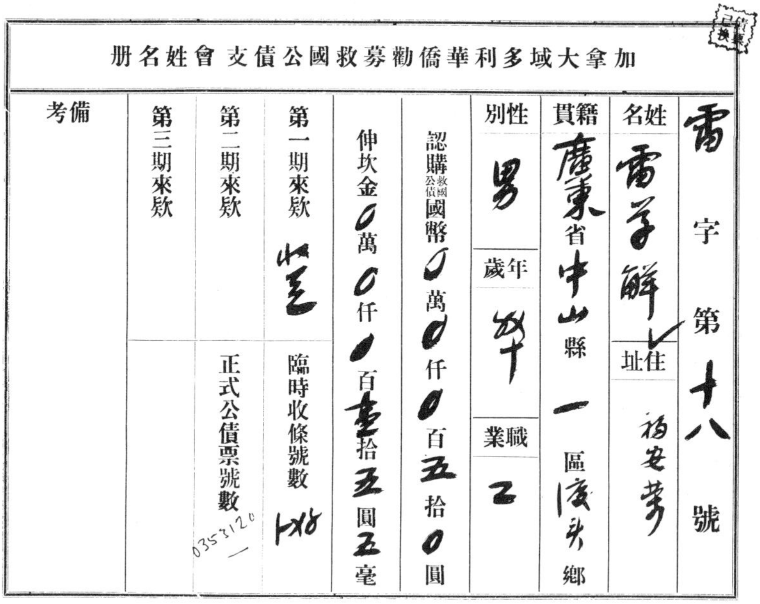

A Page from the Bonds Sale Record (It lists demographic data such as sex, age, and occupation of purchaser.)

However, rural unemployment, famine, poverty and civil war in China together with economic opportunities abroad induced some to leave home.[4] Most of the early emigrants were single young men. After they had laboured for many years in Canada and had saved some money, they would return home to get married. When they came back to Canada again, they would leave their families behind, partly because they had no intention of settling down permanently in a foreign country, and partly because they could not afford to bring their families with them even if they wanted to. Moreover, they were excluded from entering Canada after 1923 by the Chinese Immigration Act which even prevented those Chinese with Canadian domicile or citizenship from bringing their wives and children to Canada.[5] Until the Act was repealed in 1947, most of the married men in Victoria's Chinatown had lived a life similar to that of a bachelor for over two decades. By the 1930s, many of them had reached an age in the late forties and above. The population pyramid which was indicative of the predominance of elderly males and scarcity of females, was very typical of the demographic composition of many other North American Chinatowns from the 1930s through the early 1960s.

Figure 2

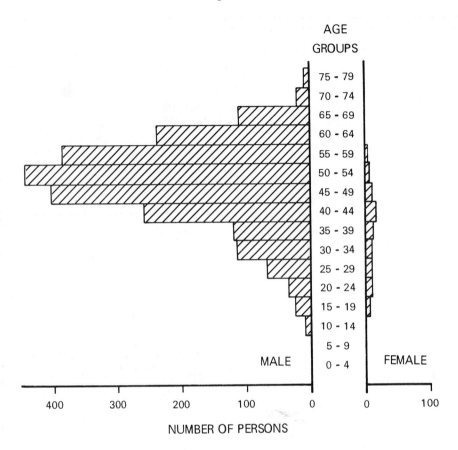

The Age and Sex Pyramid of the Chinese Population in Victoria,
1938 to 1939
N.B. The pyramid excludes 288 miles and 24 females whose ages were
not recorded in the register.

Figure 3

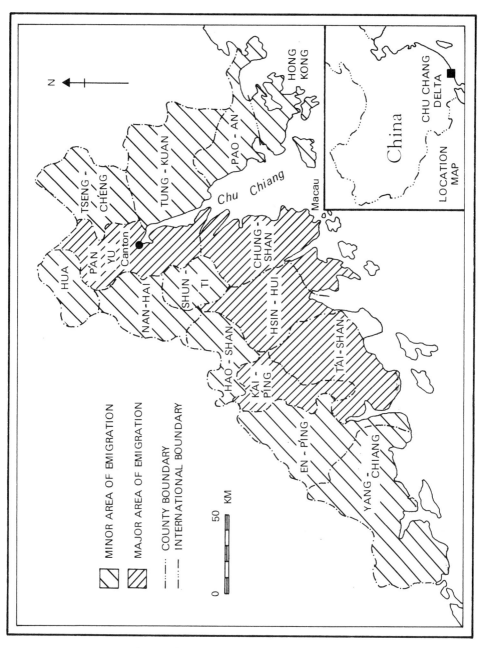

Areas of Chinese Emigration to Canada

Provenance By Home Country

An overseas Chinese community can be sub-divided into segments according to the place of origin of the inhabitants or by their surnames. The home county origins of the Chinese immigrants are an important element in the population structure of a Chinatown. All the Chinese in Victoria, for example, had originally come from Kwantung Province in South China. The data in Table 1 reveals that nearly ninety per cent of the Chinese in Victoria originally came from five counties, namely T'ai-shan, Hsin-hui, K'ai-ping, P'an-yu, and Chung-shan. The locations of these counties are shown in Figure 3. Other studies have indicated that in many other North American cities such as New York, San Francisco, and Vancouver, an over-whelming majority of the Chinese residents had also originated from these same counties.[6] Hitherto, no research has been conducted on the provenance of the Chinese in North America based on their home village origins mainly because such information is rarely available. However, from the information given in the government bonds sale records, it is possible to identify the home villages of the Chinese residents in Victoria. Most of them were found to have come from a few villages in a county. For instance, as shown in Table 2, of the approximately four hundred Chinese in Victoria who belonged to P'an-yu county, over three-quarters of them had in fact come from four villages and the remainder came from over

TABLE 1

Classification of the Chinese Population in Victoria According to Their Home County Origins, 1939

| Home County | No. of Persons | | | |
	Male	Female	Total	% of Total
T'ai-shan	585	44	629	24.4
Chung-shan	556	14	570	22.1
Hsin-hui	439	21	460	17.8
P'an-yu	388	10	398	15.4
K'ai-p'ing	225	12	237	9.2
Tseng-ch'eng	90	—	90	3.5
En-p'ing	54	5	59	2.3
Shun-te	24	16	40	1.6
Nan-hai	11	2	13	0.5
Other Counties	175	8	83	3.2
	2,447	132	2,579	100.0

TABLE 2

Distribution of the Immigrants from P'an-yu County
According to Their Home Village Origins, 1939

Home Village	No. of Persons	% of Total
Nan-ts'un	168	42.2
Pei-ts'un	80	20.1
Pang-hu	52	13.1
Ya-hu	39	9.8
27 other villages	59	14.9
	398	100.0

twenty-seven other villages in that county. This phenomenon reveals not only the effect of chain migration but also the fact that chain migrants were related more strongly to a small village base rather than to a county base.

Clan Origins

The similarities in one's surname was another very important factor to consider when examining the origin of inhabitants of the overseas Chinese community. The overseas Chinese assumed that all those who had the same surname were the offsprings of the same patrilineal ancestors and that they would thus belong to the same "clan." Based on this assumption, there were all together eighty one surnames or "clans" in Victoria's Chinatown. Eleven large clans, which had over fifty members each, accounted for about two-thirds of the Chinese population in the city. This is shown in Table 3. Most of the members in each clan had come from one or two counties. For example, about seventy percent of the Chinese surnamed Li had originally come from T'ai-shan and Chung-shan counties, whereas ninety-five percent of the people surnamed Chou were natives of P'an-yu and K'ai-p'ing counties. Nearly all those surnamed Kuan or Hsu had originated from one county. When the members of each clan are grouped according to their home villages instead of counties, most of them are found to be from relatively few villages. For example, nearly sixty percent of the Chou people in Victoria had come from one village, namely Nan-ts'un (South Village) as indicated in Table 4. It can be deduced that Nan-ts'un was one of the typical South China villages which was habitated by one or two lineages.[7] In this case, people bearing the surname Chou

TABLE 3

The Home County Origins of the Members of the Eleven Larger Clans, 1939

Clan	T'ai-shan	Chung-shan	Hsin-hui	P'an-yu	K'ai-p'ing	Others	Total
Li	129	103	72	2	—	29	335
Chou	1	1	1	172	88	10	273
Huang	96	20	39	3	19	36	213
Ch'en	88	18	61	2	—	37	206
Lui	51	71	10	2	—	41	175
Lin	36	36	86	1	1	3	163
Liang	5	46	17	1	3	10	82
Ma	72	8	—	—	—	1	81
Kuan	—	3	2	—	61	7	73
Hsu	1	—	—	66	—	1	68
Lei	3	60	—	—	—	—	63
Others	147	204	172	149	65	110	847
Total	629	570	460	398	237	285	2579

TABLE 4

Distribution of the Chou Clansmen According to Their Home County and Village Origins, 1939

Home County	Village	No. of Persons	% of Total
P'an-yu	Nan-ts'un	162	59.3
	Other villages	10	3.7
K'ai-p'ing	Mao-kang	45	16.5
	Other villages	43	15.8
Tseng-ch'eng	Tao-ch'i-ling	4	1.5
	Unspecified	1	0.4
Chung-shan	Lung-t'ou-huan	1	0.4
Hsin-hui	Ta-tse	1	0.4
T'ai-shan	Unspecified	1	0.4
Unspecified	Unspecified	5	1.8
Total		273	100.0

TABLE 5

The Occupational Distribution of the Chinese in Victoria, 1939

Occupation	No. of Persons	% of Total
Working Class		
Labourers	1636	63.4
Cooks	116	4.5
Vegetable Pedlars	49	1.9
Washermen	42	1.6
Tailors	12	0.5
Sailors	10	0.4
Barbers	9	0.4
Fish hands	9	0.4
Gardeners	6	0.2
Boot workers	3	0.1
Driver	1	0
Non-Working Class		
Students	23	0.9
Clergymen	3	0.1
Teachers	3	0.1
Insurance Agents	2	0.1
Reporter	1	0
Newspaper Manager	1	0
Doctor	1	0
Occupation Not Specified		
Farming	157	6.1
Commerce	131	5.1
Housewives	55	2.1
Restaurant	22	0.9
Greenhouse	16	0.6
Grocery	9	0.4
Watch shop	1	0
Hotel	1	0
Unemployed	2	0.1
Unspecified	258	10.0
Total:	2579	100.0

were predominant in the village. Once the migrants were in Canada, they began to sponsor their own clansmen and maintained their genealogical relationship in the foreign country.

OCCUPATIONS

The classification of occupations based on the government bonds sale records is not very satisfactory because many purchasers wrote down words such as "farming," "commerce," and "restaurant" which did not clearly specify their occupations. Most of the people in these categories were, in fact, wage earners rather than owners of farms, shops or restaurants. The working class far outweighed the non-working class in terms of the number of persons in the various occupations as shown in Table 5. For instance, over seventy percent of the Chinese were cooks, pedlars, workers and labourers of other trades.

There was also occupational specialization. As illustrated in Table 6, most of the cooks and washermen, for example, were the natives of Tai-shan county, but farm labourers and vegetable pedlars were from Chung-shan county. When the cooks are grouped according to their surnames, over half of them bear the surnames of Huang, Ch'en, Kuan or Ma. The monopoly of some occupations by certain clans or county people in Chinatown was mainly due to jobs being given to relatives, fellow clansmen, fellow-villagers or close friends in preference to outsiders. This resulted in the congruence between occupation and like origin in terms of provenance and surnames.

TABLE 6

Home County Origins of Workers in Seven Selected Occupations, 1939

Occupation	Total No. of Persons	Home County Origins of Workers							
		T'ai-Shan	K'ai-p'ing	Hsin-hui	En-p'ing	P'an-yu	Chung-shan	Tseng-ch'eng	Other counties
Cook	116	58	17	28	4	1	4	1	3
Washermen	42	33	—	7	—	—	—	1	1
Restaurant	22	14	7	—	1	—	—	—	—
Greenhouse	16	7	1	5	—	—	3	—	—
Vegetable pedlars	49	—	—	3	—	—	46	—	—
Farming	157	12	7	22	—	7	78	28	3
Grocery	9	1	1	—	—	—	7	—	—

CONCLUSIONS

The demographic structure of Victoria's Chinatown in the late 1930s was characterized by an imbalance of the predominance of elderly males, who were wage earners and who had come from relatively few villages in China. This structure was typical of many other North American Chinatowns during the mid-twentieth century although its elements may vary slightly in different cities. Empirical research in some North American Chinatowns today may reveal that this lopsided population pattern still exists and can be used as a generalized model to describe some existing Chinatowns. There are many Chinese archives which have not yet been explored or fully utilized by researchers. For example, records, such as burial permits and donation receipts, kept by many overseas Chinese voluntary associations may contain population data which are not available in official censuses. A collection of these records will be an invaluable source of research materials for comparative studies of the overseas Chinese communities in the world.

NOTES

1. David T. H. Lee, *Chia-na-ta Hua-ch'iao-shih*, (A History of Chinese in Canada), (Freedom Publisher, Victoria, 1967), p. 463.

2. According to the 1941 Census, the Chinese population in Victoria stood at 3,037 (2,549 males and 488 females) *Census of Canada, 1941,* Vol. 4, p. 535.

3. Unless stated otherwise, all the data are based on the records of the government bonds sale in 1938-39.

4. Sendou Chang, "The Distribution and Occupations of Overseas Chinese," *Geographical Review,* Vol. 58, 1968, p. 104.

5. *Statutes of Canada,* 1923, 13-14 George V. Chap. 38, pp. 301-315.

6. B. L. Sung, *The Story of the Chinese in America,* (Collier Books, New York, 1967), p. 13 and T. W. Chinn (ed.), *A History of the Chinese in California,* (Chinese Historical Society of America, San Francisco, 1969), p. 20.

7. In Hong Kong, for example, there are twenty-six single-surname and eighteen multi-surname villages in the Sha Tau Kok area. See Maurice Freedman, "Chinese Lineage and Society: Fakien and Kwangtung," (The Athlone Press, London, 1966), p. 17.

3

Chinese Associations in Canada, 1923-47

Edgar Wickberg
University of British Columbia

Several years ago the late Maurice Freedman proposed a general theory of associational development among overseas Chinese. "General" is the proper word, since the theory was so general as to be almost commonsensical and unexceptional. Simply stated, Freedman argued that the greater the size and complexity of the overseas Chinese community, the larger the number and the greater the diversity in its associations.

It seems to me that the Freedman model takes us only part way along the road towards understanding overseas Chinese associational development. Even if we add related work by Crissman and by Willmott, there remain some unanswered questions. Some of these questions have come forward as I have researched, as well as several other people, the history of the Chinese in Canada. Here are some examples. Why, in a community seemingly large enough and complex enough to have a community-wide mediating association, such as a Chinese Benevolent Association or a Chamber of Commerce, will there occasionally *not* be such an organization, while in another community of somewhat less size and complexity such an association may exist?

Why, in the Canada of the 1920s and 1930s, is there a great proliferation of Chinese schools, although the school age population in the Chinese communities is very small compared to that of the Chinese population as a whole? Why, despite the stability in size and general composition of Canadian Chinese communities during the 1920s and 1930s, do theatrical groups proliferate, even in small Chinese communities? And finally, why, despite stability in size and composition during the 1920s and 1930s, do associations continue to develop numerically as well as in terms of variety? By the Freedman model, stability in size and composition should be accompanied by stability in the number and kind of associations. Indeed, in earlier research, Graham Johnson and I assumed a general stability in the number and kind of associations in Vancouver's Chinese community between 1923 and the early 1960s. We noted that the number and character of associations in the early 1960s was roughly comparable to those believed to exist in 1923. Without closely investigating the intervening period, and conscious of the *major* associational development that has occurred since the early 1960s, we assumed stability over four decades. The Freedman model suggested it and our general knowledge of the demography of those decades reinforced this assumption.

Upon closer examination, it appears that there was a considerable amount of associational development during the 1920s and 1930s. In light of this discovery and further thinking about the problem, I would like to address the questions raised above. I will deal generally with Chinese communities, but will present specific examples for comparison from Vancouver, Toronto and Calgary.

The typology, or classification I will use is an expanded version of one used earlier by Willmott. The categories are these:

(1) The community-wide, or "umbrella" association. This is typically a Chinese Benevolent Association (or CBA). It is at least nominally representative of the entire local Chinese community, and its functions include mediation of disputes within the community and articulation of the community's interests to the host society. In fact, the CBA-type organization is most often given official or unofficial status by host governments as the sole spokesman of Chinese community interests.

(2) The clan association. These are organizations of people of the same surname. Their major functions are concerned with social service and the welfare needs of members.

(3) The district association. These associations are made up of persons from the same home district in China. Their functions overlap those of the clan association. They are especially important for persons whose surname is not one of the more prominent ones

and who, therefore, may have either no clan association they can join, or at best a weakly developed one.

(4) The fraternal-political association. The two major ones, historically, were the Chee Kung Tong (or Chinese Freemasons, under its various names) and the Kuomintang (or KMT). Their interests during 1923-47 were politics in China and in local China-towns, and the welfare of their members in Canada.

(5) Trade associations. These may include anything from a general chamber of commerce to labour unions to special occupational associations.

(6) Youth organizations. These are usually YMCA-type bodies or Boy Scouts and Girl Guide troops, but may also include sports associations.

(7) Chinese theatrical groups, which often overlap youth groups and other categories.

(8) Chinese schools.

(9) Chinese churches, usually Protestant and Catholic.

(10) Chinese newspapers.

Before presenting our information on associations in Canada and attempting to address the questions mentioned above, let us briefly summarize some relevant aspects of the history of the Chinese in this country. After an early period of almost unrestricted Chinese immigration, government policy began to apply checks, first in the form of a headtax payment, which reached the level of $500 per person by 1900, and was required of all Chinese on arrival. Although this measure briefly checked the flow, events and conditions in China and Canada, and loopholes in the law, quickly encouraged resumption of a considerable flow of Chinese immigrants into Canada between 1901 and 1921. In 1923 a Chinese Immigration Law effectively banned most new immigrants. For the next 25 years, until that law was replaced by new legislation in 1947, there were, for all practical purposes, no more new immigrants from China. Natural increase of the population already here provided for some growth during the 1920s, but in the 1930s deaths, retirements to China, and depression conditions were not balanced by natural increase, and the overall Chinese population decreased. The figures are: 1901: 17,000; 1911: 28,000; 1921: 40,000; 1931: 47,000; 1941: 35,000.

Between 1921 and 1941 the broad geographical distribution of the Chinese remained generally stable. Sixty percent were found in British Columbia. A much smaller number (about 12% of the total) were in Ontario. Alberta came next, then Manitoba. The number of Chinese in the Maritimes was always small. Ever since 1901 the majority of the Chinese in Canada have been urban dwellers, and the general trend in this century has been towards an even larger urban percentage. Using the Census figures, in 1921 Vancouver's Chinese population was about 6,000; Victoria's about 3,000; Toronto had about 2,100; Montreal about 1,700. No other community numbered over 1,000. Calgary, to be discussed briefly below, had about 650. In 1941, Vancouver's Chinese population had increased to about 7,000; Victoria was similar to 1921, at 3,000; Toronto stood at 2,300; Montreal, as before, was about 1,700. Calgary now had about 800 Chinese. In all these cities there had been some growth of Chinese population during the 1920s, followed by decline in the 1930s.

The final point about population shows that throughout the period prior to 1947, families were relatively scarce in the Chinese communities of Canada. Although most Chinese men in Canada were married, Chinese emigration practices and Canadian government immigration laws and policies made it unusal for them to have their families with them. Typically the family remained in China. Hence, Canadian Chinese communities were made up largely of single males. In 1921, on the eve of the Chinese Immigration Law that froze further Chinese immigration to this country, the ratio between males and females was very high. Even in B.C., where the largest number of Chinese women were found, the male-female ratio ranged from 5 to 1, to 17 to 1. In Toronto it was 17 to 1; in Montreal, 15 to 1; in Winnipeg, 33 to 1; in Calgary, 16 to 1. By 1941, the ratios were somewhat lower everywhere, but there is no major city where the ratio was any lower than 5 to 1. Under these circumstances, and with a moderate number of children per family, the size of the "second generation," or "native-born" generation that emerged in the 1920s and 1930s was small. In fact, the Chinese population was always one of the oldest in Canada. As late as 1941, 60% of its members were over 45 years of age, and 85% were over 20 years of age. The small size of the "native-born" generation is important in associational terms. We would assume that native-borns growing up in families in Canada would have somewhat different associational needs and interests from those of aging single men whose interests still centered largely on China. Accordingly, a large native-born generation might produce many new associations, but we might expect a small one to produce very few associations. In fact, the picture is more complicated than that.

Let us now briefly outline associational development in three cities between 1923 and early 1937. Vancouver was the largest, most diverse Chinese community in Canada during that period. Toronto was the largest Chinese settlement in Eastern Canada. Calgary represents one of the largest Chinese communities on the Prairies. The three may

1923

	Vancouver	*Toronto*	*Calgary*
CBA	1	(substitute organ.)	0
Clan Assns.	26	10	6
District Assns.	12	2	1
Fraternal-political			
Freemasons	1	1	1
KMT	1	1	1
Trade Assns.	5	1	0
Youth	3	2	0
Theatrical	2 or 3?	1	0
Schools	2	1	1
Churches	4	2	1
			(YMCA may also be counted above)
Newspapers	2	1	0
	(counting Victoria)		

1937

	Vancouver	*Toronto*	*Calgary*
CBA	1	0	1
		(as before)	(Edmonton CBA)
Resistance Organization	1	1	
Clan	46	16	11
District	17	4	1
Fraternal-political			
Freemasons	1	1	1
KMT	1	1	1
Trade	12	2	0
Youth	7	2	0
Theatrical	5 or 6	4	3
Schools	13	2	1
Churches	4	2	1
Newspapers	2	2	0
	(a 3rd in 1920s only)		

therefore be taken as representative, in a general way, of major Chinese communities in three regions of the country.

It must be noted that because of incomplete information and the prevalence of organizations that exist in name only or alternate in and out of existence, these figures must be treated as rough approximations only.

For the purposes of this paper, I would like to leave aside any discussion of district and clan associations. Let us turn to the questions presented at the outset. First, concerning the existence of a CBA, Vancouver had one in 1923, Calgary did not, and Toronto had a substitute organization. If size and complexity are the determining factor Freedman says they are, it is no surprise that Vancouver, the largest and most complex community, had a full complement of associational types, represented at the apex by a CBA. Calgary, with a Chinese population of only 600 and a simple associational structure, apparently reflecting a relatively homogenous community, had no CBA. Surprisingly, when a CBA is established in Alberta during the early 1930s, it is at Edmonton, not Calgary. Edmonton's Chinese population was smaller than Calgary's and apparently even more homogenous. Yet Edmonton established a CBA which attempted to claim responsibility for Calgary as well. Equally surprising is the absence of a broadly-based full-fledged active CBA in Toronto both in 1923 and in early 1937. The substitute organization that performed some of the functions of a CBA was the Chinese Young Men's Christian Institute (YMCI), a group made up of Protestant Christian Chinese, which, under various names, attempted to represent the Toronto community on specific issues. Toronto's Chinese community was the third largest in Canada in 1923, following Vancouver and Victoria. At 2,100 persons it was larger than Montreal, with 1,700 members; yet Montreal, in 1914, had formed the Chinese Association of Montreal, as a broadly based representative body. Even Winnipeg, a community about the size of Calgary, had a CBA by 1923. Why not Toronto?

It has been said that political divisions were the reason. It is certainly true that politics — and that meant, up to 1947, primarily China-oriented politics — were a great divisive force in many Canadian Chinese communities. It will be noticed that the major political-fraternal associations, the KMT and the Freemasons, had already established branches in all three of these cities. In fact, even small Chinese communities without any other organizations would often have either a Freemason branch or a KMT branch, or both. The KMT-Freemason rivalry was a major historical force in the Canadian Chinese communities throughout the period we are discussing.

Perhaps a CBA that represented the whole community could best be formed only when the community was homogenous and simple, quite contrary to Freedman's model. In Montreal, almost all Chinese were in the laundry business in 1914 and they formed their CBA because of a proposed city bylaw that would have threatened laundry interests. But on the other hand, Winnipeg, plagued by political discord, was able, after a struggle, to establish a CBA. And Vancouver and Victoria, the most complex and diverse communities, full of varying interests and political rivalries that led to spectacular violence, established CBAs early and maintained them somehow, although not without controversy. In other words, neither size nor degree of complexity or simplicity, nor political homogeneity seems to account for the existence of a CBA.

The second question concerns the proliferation of Chinese schools far beyond what appear to be the needs of a small "younger generation." This phenomenon is noticeable in Vancouver, and, in fact, may be restricted to Vancouver. Toronto established a second school; this one under Freemason auspices. Since the Freemasons were also beginning a newspaper in Toronto at about the same time, it would appear that their Toronto school was part of an effort to strengthen their Eastern Canada operations in a city where their competitor, the KMT, was already very strong. Chinese schools in Canada were often associated with political groups and viewpoints and, in fact, the promotion of a given group's views might be the major reason for a school's existence. The explosion of schools in Vancouver (not all of which lasted) was no doubt partly a reflection of the larger number of children there than anywhere else, except perhaps Victoria. But the supply clearly exceeded the demand, and many schools had only a few students. Other than politics, there were two major influences on the formation of schools. One was cultural and educational trends in China. The other was government policy and social discrimination in Canada. In China great changes and experiments took place in education during the 1920s and 1930s, at least in the coastal cities. Much of the classical language and learning were replaced by a simplified modern written language and literature with a focus on modern problems. The Chinese in Canada were divided over how traditional or how modern their schools should be. Thus, schools proliferated in part because of competition among various philosophies and attitudes towards teaching materials and methods. Regarding social discrimination in Canada, one factor that helped maintain Chinese schools was practical need. As long as young Chinese could find few jobs outside of Chinatown, they needed the language skills appropriate to Chinatown employment.

The third question is: why did theatrical groups proliferate? Again, the likely answer is: "because of China's cultural influence." In all three cities there were more theatrical groups in 1937 than in 1923. Such groups could also be found by the late 1930s, in small towns in B.C. and perhaps in minor communities elsewhere. There had been theatrical performances and resident troupes in major communities since 1900 or earlier. Besides pure entertainment they had furnished occasions and vehicles for fund-raising for various causes. In China during the 1920s and 1930s, performances on contemporary themes using colloquial Chinese and Western dramatic conventions began to develop. These were often used for political purposes, to dramatize domestic political struggles or resistance to Japanese invasion. Similar plays were performed in Canada, with similar political uses. Canadian influences were present: some plays were in English and were influenced by the plays given in English language public schools, to which Chinese students were exposed. But the initiative and the uses came from China.

The expansion of youth associations in Vancouver should be noted in passing. There is an overlap here with theatrical groups since many of the latter were related to Chinese youth groups. Again, both Chinese and Canadian influences seem to exist. YMCA-type organizations, scouting groups, soccer clubs and the like were clearly part of Canada. *But* such groups had become an important part of the middle class life of Chinese in the modernizing coastal cities of China, which served as a partial model for the urbanized Chinese of Canada.

Finally, the general question arises: why, despite stability in size and composition do Chinese communities in Canada during the 1920s and 1930s, contrary to the Freedman prediction, not remain stagnant in terms of associational development, but continue creating new groups? Some possible answers have already been suggested, but let us consider the category of trade associations, which we have not mentioned up to now. Again, the real action occurs in Vancouver, but the difference may be more apparent than real. If we had, for Toronto and Calgary, the kind of day-to-day information over several years that we have for Vancouver, the picture might be very different. In Vancouver, Chinese labour unions are formed because of discriminatory practices in shingle and pulp mills, or perhaps, to protect the employment or welfare needs of Chinese workers during the Depression. When white opposition to Chinese activities in the produce business developed, the Chinese protected their interests by forming various associations during the 1920s and 1930s. At one time, in the 1930s, there were five Chinese associations in Vancouver that were related to one or another aspect of the vegetable growing and selling business. Proposed legislation or policies against the interests of Chinese owners of Western-style restaurants led to the creation of Chinese restaurant owners associations in Toronto and elsewhere. Trade associations were probably most common in B.C. because of the diverse occupations pursued by the B.C. Chinese. In Eastern and Central Canada, laundry and restaurant operations tended to dominate. I suspect, however, that if we had the information for other cities that we have for Vancouver we would find that there were laundry associations, restaurant associations, and others in many parts of Canada; some of them short-lived, lasting only through a period of crisis, but nonetheless in existence and viable for a time. Trade associations, in other words, reflect Chinese employment patterns and white resistance to those patterns. The persistence of legislation, actual or only threatened, and agitation, against specific business interests of the Chinese, throughout the period 1923-1947, accounts for the continued development of new trade associations.

What generalizations can we now make about the Freedman model? Size and complexity, clearly, do not explain everything. Bill Willmott has already warned, with reference to the Freedman model, that government policy is an important consideration. When the government of a host society recognizes a given Chinese organization as the legitimate spokesman for all Chinese interests, for example, it alters the development possibilities of all Chinese associations. Furthermore, when a government, like the Canadian government, cuts off all Chinese immigration as it did in 1923, it appears to freeze the Chinese communities in their present shape, especially if the natural increase of those already here will, inevitably, be slight. But there are other important forces at work, such as specific policies of governments at *all levels* affecting *specific* Chinese business interests, *or* the general reaction of white Canadians to Chinese business and occupational opportunities. We have noted the effects of these forces on school and trade association development. Perhaps, most of all, we need to keep in mind the timing, or the historical context in which these Canadian Chinese communities matured — not merely in terms of Canadian history, but particularly in terms of Chinese history. As long as the majority of politically-minded Chinese were concerned with the politics of China, and as long as Chinese and white attitudes encouraged continued Chinese preoccupation with Chinese culture, then political and cultural trends in China would have a major role in shaping associational development overseas. Canada's Chinese in the 1930s may have been the *heirs* of *nineteenth* century Chinese *peasant* culture but they were also the *affiliates* of *early twentieth* century Chinese *urban* culture — in touch with Hong Kong, Canton, Shanghai and even Peking. Unless we recognize that, we shall get nowhere in attempting to understand their cultural life and their associational development.

4

The Myth of the Chinese Sojourner in Canada

Anthony B. Chan
East Asian Studies Programme
York University

In the study of the Chinese experience in Canada, one of the most enduring features generally taken at face value and essentially untested is the assumption that the Chinese immigrant who came to Canada perceived his experience in North America as an interlude in his career in China. Articulated in learned journals, graduate theses, and community reports, the Chinese as a transient figure in Canadian history has become almost a venerable construct because of its widespread acceptance. William Willmott stated that the Chinese "left to sojourn elsewhere with the clear intention of returning to his home (China), of supporting it in the meantime, and of eventually being buried in his village."[1] Edgar Wickberg, in a recent book review, remarked that the Chinese were also influenced by the "existence of access to China and the possibility of realizing there the immigrants' dream of returning with the wealth to buy land and to retire amid comfort and local esteem."[2] Paul S. Levine, in a thesis, agreed that the "first Chinese came to Canada with the intent of staying for a short time because of the desire to gain wealth."[3] In two reports sponsored by the Ontario Ministry of Culture and Recreation, Multi-cultural Development Branch, Wesley Lore commented that the Chinese "planned to work hard, earn a fortune, and return rich to China."[4] The vice-president of Toronto's Mon Sheong Foundation (home for elderly Chinese Canadian citizens) in 1976, Dr. S. F. Liu, concurred that the Chinese

> who came to Canada looking for a better life were not allowed to bring their wives and families. Many never meant to stay permanently in Canada, but to return to their homeland, hopefully with a bag of gold.[5]

The classic statement on the Chinese as a sojourner is Paul C. P. Siu's "The Sojourner." Referring to the Chinese laundry owner and worker, especially in Chicago, Illinois, Siu stated that the:

> essential characteristic of the sojourner is that he clings to the culture of his own ethnic group .... . Psychologically he is unwilling to organize himself as a permanent resident in the country of his sojourn. . . .
> It is convenient, therefore, to define the "sojourner" as a stranger who spends many years of his lifetime in a foreign country without being assimilated by it. The sojourner is par excellence an ethno-centrist.[6]

In the context of the Chinese "sojourner" society in Canada, such descriptions as "predominantly male" and "bachelor" were made by politicians, journalists and authors of the time, and contemporary writers.[7] Because of the "sojourner's" desire to return to China once wealth was attained, such other features as "inclined towards monetary wants" and therefore, "economic self-aggrandizement" and "individual selfishness" could be implied.

While there is almost always some mention of the Chinese as a "sojourner" in scholarly papers and community studies on the Chinese in Canada, there has never been an examination of the validity of this assumption. In this paper, examination will be made concerning: 1) the origin of the term *huā qiáo* (华 侨) in Chinese history, 2) the historical development of the Chinese as "sojourner" in Canada, and 3) the myth of the Chinese "sojourner" in Canada.

Overseas Chinese have usually been referred to as Chinese sojourner, especially in North America. But the term *huā qiáo,* translated as overseas Chinese, has never been referred to as Chinese sojourner in the People's Republic of China or Taiwan. *Huā qiáo* has always been designated as overseas Chinese.[8] The term "sojourner" has been trans-lated as *lǚjú de rén* (旅 居 的 人) or *dòuliú de rén* (逗 留 的 人) In the context of the translation of the term "sojourner," no reference was made to the Chinese. Furthermore, during the Eastern Jin dynasty (东 晋 , 317-420 A.D.), commanderies and districts were established as local administrative boundaries between the northern and southern regions. The term *qiáo* was used to denote that there was a movement of people from the north of the Changjiang (Yangtze River) to the southern area. *Qiáo* indicated migration rather than temporary existence.[9] References to the Chinese by most Chinese writers always contained the term *huā qiáo,* never *lǚjú de rén* or *dòuliú de rén.*[10]

Since the Chinese did not refer to themselves as "sojourners," when indeed did the assumption of the Chinese as a "sojourner" originate and how did it develop? The earliest documented official reference describing the Chinese as a "sojourner" in Canada was made by John A. Macdonald in 1882. As Prime Minister in his second term of office (1878-1891), he stressed that after the Canadian Pacific Railway was built, the Chinese would return to China. After all, they had not brought women with them and, thus were unlikely to be permanent settlers.[11] Ignoring the fact that the Chinese railway workers were brought to Canada on a contract basis as labourers,[12] Macdonald either overlooked the fact or was unaware that women immigrants accompanying their male counterparts was highly unlikely. From the outset, economic considerations prevented the entrance of Chinese women and families from coming to Canada. Indeed, because of the need for Chinese male workers in agricultural, public works, coal mining, and salmon canning enterprises shortly after the first arrival of Chinese immigrants to the gold fields of the Cariboo in 1858,[13] the demand was not for Chinese women or children. Since the Chinese labourers contracted for railway work, for example, sold their labour to the Canadian Pacific Railway, as well as the fact that these workers were usually poor peasants, the presence of women would have been an awesome economic burden. Who would pay for their passage and sustenance? Neither the male labourers could, nor the contractors, if they were willing. While Macdonald's argument proved to be faulty, his comments were the first political indications that the Chinese were in Canada to be exploited when the economic need arose. Since white politicians and business people later viewed them as an expedient, sometimes necessary, but always a temporary source of labour, the myth of the sojourner was born. In the context of the Chinese sojourner in the United States, which is applicable to the Canadian situation in terms of myth making, Frank Chin argued that:

> The logic of the myth of the Chinese Sojourner duplicates the logic Nazi's used to justify anti-Semitism in Europe. We came to America

without our women (a sign we had no intention of settling here), refused to assimilate, were alien and incapable of accommodating the democratic, individualistic manly ideals that throbbed in the guts of every American word, breath and deed, established our own clannish social structures in defiance of the laws of the land, robbed America of her wealth and took it home to China and our women; therefore, we deserved the exclusion laws, the anti-Chinese riots, the lynchings to stop the drain of America's wealth.[14]

In Canada, the situation was, unsurprisingly, almost completely similar. The Chinese came to Canada without their women, appeared to refuse to assimilate, formed clannish organizations such as the Chinese Benevolent Association and *Hongmen* (Triad) societies among others, and appeared only to desire material wealth which was sent to China. The latter belief was succinctly stated by Amor De Cosmos in 1879. He attributed the economic loss to Canada to the presence of the Chinese. Estimating that 6,000 Chinese lived in British Columbia, De Cosmos placed their average earnings at $300 annually thus making the aggregate income $1,800,000. Deducting $360,000. ($60 per person) as the cost of living, he surmised that the net of $1,440,000. was sent back to China. If the 6,000 people were Canadians who earned $400 per year, the $2,400,000. total earning would remain in Canada.[15]

While the Chinese in Canada were usually male and, therefore, lived in a bachelor community demonstrating once again that they were in Canada temporarily, there were other indicators of the Chinese as a "sojourner." The fact that the Chinese were engaged in the laundry or restaurant business also indicated their desire to return to China once their fortunes were made. Because of the limited capital involved, these businesses could be easily liquidated. Thus, their investments were easily turned over. A factor not considered was that institutional racism forced many Chinese into these ethnic enterprises.[16]

According to the Sessional Papers of the British Columbia Legislature of 1902, there was a time when the Chinese were engaged in other occupations. The industry of market gardening was monopolized by the Chinese, about 600 were employed in the coal mines on the coast, 1,000 were working in placer mines of whom about 100 worked for themselves either on royalty or under lease, and 183 were in the shingle and bolt business. There were Chinese workers in the salmon canning industry, as well as 14 Chinese tailor shops with 83 employees, of which 12 shops made clothes for white Canadians and the rest for Chinese customers. Cordwood cutting was taken over by the Chinese, but was later monopolized by the Japanese. There were approximately 1,000 persons engaged in the laundry business and a few Chinese were also in the production of footwear and cigars among other small trades.[17] Many Chinese, therefore, were engaged in financially reward-ing enterprises. But it was because of their competitiveness that white Canadians sought to deprive them of a productive living and, at the same time, relegating them to such menial service employment as washing and cooking.[18] Institutional racism through the passage of specific acts prevented or hindered the Chinese from engaging in parti-cular occupations and participating fully in Canadian society. While some acts were overturned by Ottawa, others prevented the Chinese from buying land or diverting water for agricultural purposes, as well as imposing a $15. licence fee to deter the Chinese from mining for gold in 1884. Two years later, the British Columbia government added a clause in every private act prohibiting the employment of any Chinese for any labour that was authorized in the head tax act of 1885.[19] Attempts by labour unions, politicians, and the media were also made to systematically exclude the Chinese from certain occupa-tions and from Canadian society.[20]

In 1903, the head tax was increased to a high of $500. effective January 1, 1904. While it effectively destroyed the contract system of employing Chinese workers, those in Canada were able to receive better wages because of the demand for Chinese labour caused by tax. To counteract this unexpected circumstance, Ottawa passed a law stipulating that every Chinese must possess $200 before landing in Canada.[21] In June 1917, another law was passed which stated that any Chinese could be arrested without a warrant if suspected of illegal entry. In 1919, the first step to the eventual 1923 Exclusion Act was imposed by Ottawa. Any potential immigrant could now be denied entrance to Canada as a result of his customs, habits, mode of life, style of property holding, or the inability to become readily assimi-lated.[22] This was directly aimed at the Chinese immigrant. The Chinese were denied the right to vote in federal elections in 1920. Early exclusion in provincial elections was made in British Columbia (1875) and Saskatchewan (1909). Since they were not voting citizens, the Chinese were excluded from such professions as law, teaching, and pharmacy. Moreover, laws were enacted to prevent white women from being employed by Chinese businesses, especially in restaurants. Beginning in 1908, schools were segregated in British Columbia.[23] In 1925, a male minimum wage act was passed in British Columbia attempting to replace "cheap" Chinese workers with white labourers.[24]

The impact of institutional racism on the myth of the Chinese sojourner was far reaching because it made scapegoats of the Chinese for Canada's economic ills. It was not surprising that being excluded from certain occupations, exposed to violence, especially in 1907, assessed head taxes, denied the franchise, and segregated in schools, the Chinese were "virtually unassimilable." No wonder the Chinese were accused of "living in seclusion and (eating) strange foods;" they made little effort to make friends among the local population — their inability to speak English made associations difficult.[25] Indeed, institutional racism forced the Chinese to live in Chinatowns and to establish such institutions as the Chinese Benevolent Association for their own protection and survival. Most of the local population were not inclined to have a Chinese friend. It was, in effect, not the Chinese who were entirely at fault for not assimilating into Canadian society. They were unwelcomed as members of the human race since white Canadians perceived the Chinese as inferior species. The Chinese were, in the words of Mr. Justice Gray, merely "living machines."[26]

White Canada's perception of the Chinese in strictly economic terms and its denial of the right to vote ended any potential interest on the part of the Chinese in the workings of Canadian "democracy." All focus on the political situation in China, from the fall of the Qing dynasty to the establishment of the Republic of China in 1912 and the rise to power of the *Guomindang* (Nationalist party) of Sun Wen (Sun Yatsen), was directly reinforced. The Chinese in Canada and in other *huá qiáo* communities played a significant monetary role in the revolutionary and reform efforts in China. In 1897, Sun was able to collect enough funds from the Chinese in Victoria and Vancouver that he could afford to change from an intermediate class to a state room on the *Empress of India* sailing out of Vancouver.[27] By the spring of 1911, HK $70,000 was subscribed by *Hongmen* members in Canada by mortgaging their clubhouses to buy bonds for the *Guomindang.* Compared to the HK $15,000 raised in Hawaii and the rest of the United States by another leader of the *Guomindang,* Huang Xing, the Chinese in Canada played a large role in aiding revolutionary activities in China. To help pay for the planned April 27, 1911 uprising in Guangzhou (Canton), a further HK $85,000 was raised in Canada. The Chinese Canadian contribution was considered the "greatest triumph" while there was only "fair success" in the United States.[28] In 1912, $150,000 was raised by Seto Maytong, an official of the Hongmen, by mortgaging society buildings in Victoria, Vancouver, and Toronto.[29]

While the Chinese in Canada were more interested in aiding Sun Wen's anti-Qing cause, there were also attempts to raise revenue for more conservative movements. A branch of the *Baohuanghui* (Protect the Emperor Society) was formed on July 20, 1899 by the famous Confucian reformer, Kang Youwei in Victoria. The *Baohuanghui* which came out of the ashes of the 1898 reform movement in China was able to raise $7,800 from the Chinese in Victoria and Vancouver.

Establishing an additional branch in Vancouver, Kang's society proved to be a formidable competitor for *huā qiáo* money to the anti-Qing revolutionary organizations.[30] The 1911 Revolution and the demise of the Qing dynasty, however, symbolized the collapse of this emperor's movement.

Interest in aiding Sun Wen and Kang Youwei's efforts at establishing change in China can be argued from the viewpoint that the Chinese in Canada were always preoccupied with conditions in China. This would, perhaps, provide further evidence of their status as sojourners in Canada. Taking this perception, however, avoids the realities of institutional racism. If the Chinese were indeed sojourners, their major objective, as politicians, scholars, and community observers have stated, would be to return to China with enough wealth to purchase land and live in ease with respect and esteem. By the stress on the monetary aspect, the Chinese, if they were sojourners, would be more interested in their own selfish ends of financial aggrandizement. Thus, interest in China's political situation would be maintained only as a passing interest, and only if it did not entail large financial donations. But this conflicts with the fact that the *huā qiáo* financial connections between China and Canada were highly successful for the Chinese revolutionaries and reformers. Patriotism certainly played a role in the Chinese Canadian remittances to China. In view of the prevailing conditions, patriotism to Canada would have been naive. Yet, because large sums were given freely to Sun Wen, in particular, with mortgages on buildings and land, the prevailing urge to return to China which almost all observers of the Chinese in Canada have noted was, however, subordinate to aiding less selfish ventures. Since many Chinese were willing to provide large sums of money to these causes rather than return swiftly to China once their fortunes were made, does provide credence to the contention that they desired to settle in Canada. Some, undoubtedly, wanted to return to China after attaining wealth. But the majority remained in Canada. In spite of the rampant racial discrimination as well as the attempt by the Chinese Benevolent Association to discourage immigration,[31] Canada was still attractive to the Chinese. Their willingness to endure all these negative forces succinctly demonstrated their commitment to making Canada their home. If there was a sojourner mentality, it would have cracked under such racial pressures.

From linguistic, historical, and political considerations, the Chinese sojourner in Canada was a myth perpetrated by politicians, scholars, students, and even members of the Chinese community. It was basically an economic image of the Chinese formulated by individuals for specific purposes. The sojourner myth also reflected the individualistic tendencies of observers with an essentially Western perception of historical and political realities. Ascribing Western assumptions of economics and, in turn, concepts of individualism and selfishness to a non-Western subject made the Chinese in Canada more comprehensible for white Canadians. Calling the Chinese sojourners, therefore, was an appropriate way of fitting them into a Western context. But the continued perception of the Chinese as a sojourner by contemporary writers also perpetuates distortions of history.

NOTES

1. William Willmott, "Some Aspects of Chinese Communities in British Columbia," *BC Studies,* no. 1 (Winter, 1968-69), p. 28.

2. Edgar Wickberg, Review of Ban Seng Hoe, *Structural Changes of Two Chinese Communities in Alberta, Canada* (Ottawa: National Museum of Man, Canadian Centre for Folk Culture Studies, Mercury Series Paper, no. 9, 1976) in *Journal of Ethnic Studies,* V (Winter, 1978), pp. 107-108. See also Howard Palmer, "Anti-Oriental Sentiment in Alberta, 1880-1920," *Canadian Ethnic Studies,* II (December, 1970), p. 31; Stanford M. Lyman, "Chinese Secret Societies in the Occident: Notes and Suggestions for Research in the Societies of Secrecy," *The Canadian Review of Sociology and Anthropology,* I (May, 1964), p. 93 among others.

3. Paul S. Levine, "Historical Documentation Pertaining to Overseas Chinese Organizations," (Unpublished M.Phil. thesis, University of Toronto, Toronto, 1975), p. 38, 43.

4. Wesley Lore, "The Chinese Communities," in George W. Bancroft (editor), *Outreach for Understanding* (Toronto: Ministry of Culture and Recreation, 1976), p. 47.

5. S. F. Liu, "The Elderly Chinese," in Bancroft, *Outreach,* p. 52.

6. Paul C. P. Siu, "The Sojourner," *American Journal of Sociology,* LVIII (July, 1952), p. 34.

7. John A. Macdonald, Debates, House of Commons, 1882, p. 1476; Hilda Glynn-Ward, *The Writing on the Wall: Chinese and Japanese Immigration to B.C.* (Toronto: University of Toronto reprint, 1974); see notes above.

8. See *A New English-Chinese Dictionary* (Shanghai, 1975), p. 930 and *A New Practical Chinese-English Dictionary* (Taibei: The Far Eastern Book Company, Ltd., 1971), p. 934.

9. Yan Gengwang, *Zhongguo difang xing zhengzhi dushi, History of the Regional and Local Administration in China,* part II, Volmue I (Taibei: Academiz Sinica Publications no. 45, 1963), Chapter I, p. 8.

10. See Li Donghai, *Jianada huaqiao shi, The History of the Overseas Chinese in Canada* (Taibei: Haidian, 1967); *Xiandai huaqiao renwu zhi, Biographies of Contemporary Overseas* Chinese (Taibei: Zhonghua chuban she, 1973). See also *Meiguo huaqiao Nianjian, Handbook of Overseas Chinese in America* (New York: People's Foreign Relations Association of China, 1946), among others.

11. John A. Macdonald, Debates, House of Commons, 1882, p. 1476.

12. Royal Commission on Chinese Immigration: Report and Evidence (Ottawa, 1885), p. 398.

13. Li, *Jianada*, p. 60; *San Francisco Globe*, May 16, 1858.

14. Frank Chin, "Confessions of the Chinatown Cowboy," *Bulletin of Concerned Asian Scholars*, IV (Fall, 1972), p. 63.

15. Amor De Cosmos, Debates, House of Commons, 1879, p. 1258. While some Chinese did indeed send part of their earnings to China, they were not the only ones. Henry F. Angus stated that "Canadians were none too popular in British Columbia before Confederation. They were often termed 'North American Chinamen'; the implication being that they saved their money and sent it back home to Canada". See his *British Columbia and the United States* (Toronto: Ryerson Press, 1942), pp. 192-193.

16. This argument follows Peter S. Li's critical study of "Ethnic Business in the U.S.," *Journal of Ethnic Studies*, IV (Fall, 1976), pp. 35-41.

17. British Columbia Legislative Assembly, Sessional Papers, 1902, Chapter 7-21.

18. The assumption that the Chinese were engaged primarily in washing and cooking enterprises is still prevalent among Chinese themselves. See Roxanna Ng, "The Vancouver Chinese Immigrant Community and Social Services," *Rikka*, IV (Autumn/Winter, 1977), p. 72. Ng also agreed with Karin Straaton that before 1885 that there was relatively little discrimination exercised toward the Chinese. Both Ng and Straaton are mistaken in view of the 1875 British Columbia act that denied the Chinese the right to vote.

19. British Columbia Legislative Assembly, Sessional Papers, 1886; p. 347.

20. In Hamilton, Ontario, for example, various municipal By-laws were passed to prevent economic growth by the Chinese. See Gao Wenxiong, "Hamilton: The Chinatown That Died," *The Asianadian: An Asian Canadian Magazine*, I (Summer, 1978), pp. 15-17.
The Canadian media, especially *Macleans Magazine* and *Saturday Night* also exhibited strong racism against the Chinese. See K. Paupst, "A Note on Anti-Chinese Sentiment in Toronto Before the First World War," *Canadian Ethnic Studies*, IX (1977), pp. 54-59.

21. Morris Davis and Joseph F. Krauter (editors), *The Other Canadians: Profile of Six Minorities* (Toronto: Methuen Pub., 1971), p. 62.

22. *Canada Year Book* (Ottawa, 1957-1958). p. 168.

23. See especially Mary Ashworth, "The Segregation of Immigrant Children in B.C.," *Working Teacher*, I (Winter, 1978), pp. 7-10.

24. W. A. Carrothers, "The Immigration Problem in Canada," *Queen's Quarterly*, (Summer, 1929), p. 521.

25. Palmer, "Anti-Oriental Sentiment," p. 31.

26. Cited in Persia C. Campbell, *Chinese Coolie Emigration* (Taibei: Cheng wen Pub., 1970, copyright, 1923), p. 45.

27. Harold Z. Schiffrin, *Sun Yat-sen and the Origins of the Chinese Revolution* (Berkeley: University of California, 1968), pp. 138-139.

28. C. Martin Wilbur, *Sun Yat-sen: Frustrated Patriot* (New York: Columbia University, 1976), pp. 42-43. See also Yen Ching-hwang, *The Overseas Chinese and the 1911 Revolution* (London: Oxford University, 1976), p. 238.

29. Lyman, "Chinese Secret Societies," p. 93.

30. Schiffrin, pp. 161, 183.

31. Lai Chuen-yan, "Chinese Attempts to Discourage Emigration to Canada: Some Findings from the Chinese Archives in Victoria," *BC Studies*, no. 18 (Summer, 1973), pp. 33-49. The Chinese Board of Trade in Vancouver also tried to stop the Chinese from going to Canada. It sent cables to the Hong Kong guilds and also printed 30,000 circulars to be distributed in Hong Kong and the Treaty Ports. The circular dated June 3, 1908 stated that: the Chinese immigrant "in spending so much money to come here (Canada), even if he should find work with ordinary wages, it would be several years before he could regain what he paid as head tax; so why not take that money and go into business in our own country (China) and earn a living." McInnes to Oliver, May 30, 1908, June 3, 1908. Great Britain Foreign Office Archives, FO 228/2237.

5

A Comparative Study of British and Canadian Experience With South Asian Immigration

F. M. Bhatti
Lansbury Institute, London

Indian immigration into Canada started with Sikh soldiers coming from parts of the Far East[1] outside India, and slowly extended to their friends and relatives in India. The rosy impression about Canada that the Indian soldiers acquired while returning from the Queen's Jubilee celebrations, or the visit by Indian soldiers to Canada, after their participation in the campaign against the Boxer Rebellion in China, might have been the starting point of this movement. After 1905 it made sudden strides, chiefly as a result of systematic exploitation by steamship companies for political and economic motives. Certain individuals[2] tried to exploit the situation for their personal benefit. Consequently, immigration accelerated with the letters (with money orders enclosed) sent home by fortunate first comers.

The gradual increase of Indian immigration into Canada coincided with a large influx of Japanese and Chinese. After the imposition of restrictions on Chinese immigration, the people of British Columbia did not consider their presence a threat because the Chinese did not claim a position of equality with the Europeans. They confined their activities to certain limited menial occupations, and were mostly employed as domestic servants, laundrymen, cooks and kitchen-help, labourers in clearing forest lands, inside workers at canneries and as above ground workers at collieries.[3] Japanese migration was at first to Hawaii and then to the U.S. mainland. However, under pressure from the Hawaiian Farmers' Association, the U.S. administration restricted this movement. Incidentally, at that time — January 31, 1906 — Japan and Canada concluded a treaty by which subjects of each power were granted "full liberty to enter, travel and to reside in any part of the dominions and possessions of the other contracting party."[4] The Japanese immigrants began to use British Columbia as a springboard to get into the U.S.[5] However, this practice seemed to have accelerated the rate of the very visible Oriental immigration into Canada.

By the end of the nineteenth century, Indians had also started going to such Western states as Washington, California and Oregon. But soon the growth of the Indian community was resented by the white workers, for the Indian infiltration of cheap labour had unfavourable repercussions for the U.S. labour organizations. In the year 1906-07 the United States of America was facing an economic crisis.[6] In order to cope with the situation, the employers demanded longer hours of work with lower wages. The only group of labourers who fell into line with their demands were Indians, to whom even those unpalatable terms were better than the ones obtainable at home in India. The Indians went to work when trade unions struck for higher wages and better conditions because they were not cognizant of the conflict between workers' organizations and the employers. Thus relations between them and other workers deteriorated, and Indians became unpopular as strike breakers and black-legs. They were ostracized by American labour groups and even subjected to intimidation and punishment. They were frequently beaten and in many cases kidnapped and put in cars which deposited them several miles away from the cities where they lived.[7]

As early as May 1905, an organization entitled "The Japanese and Korean Exclusion League" was formed in San Francisco. Its object was the total exclusion of Japanese and Koreans from the United States and its insular territory. The American Federation of Labour had taken up the matter of exclusion of the Chinese, Japanese and Koreans at its twenty-fourth session in November 1904.[8] In 1907, when the number of Indian immigrants into Washington, Oregon and California increased, it changed its name from "The Japanese and Korean Exclusion League" to the Asiatic Exclusion League.[9] Its leader, Olaf A. Tveitmoe, of the San Francisco Building Trades Council started a campaign against Orientals in his paper, the *Organized Labor*. He asserted that "the Asiatic would drag down white labor to his lower level."[10] In his address at the 'Labor Day' celebrations at San Francisco on September 2 — reported in the *Organized Labor* of September 7 — he emphasized that the mission of unionized labour was "to guard the gateway of Occidental Civilization (West Coast) against the Oriental invasion."

Anti-Asiatic rioting occurred in a few cities including Seattle, Everett and Bellingham. In the most publicised incident at Bellingham, in September 1907, six hundred lumberjacks herded some two hundred Indians out of town, with many immigrants suffering injuries.[11] A contemporary journalist delightfully reported that the "tawny subjects of Great Britain were as docile as cattle" and in one case, "a school boy drove in three of the timorous Asiatics who had once served in the soldiery of Great Britain."[12] Another magazine sarcastically entitled its account as "War with Great Britain."[13] The Asiatic Exclusion League held Indians responsible for the riots by declaring that their willingness to work for low wages, and their filthy and immodest habits invited reprisals.

Thus the Indians had to leave these states and they made their way to Canada. When this news appeared in the press, Lord Grey, the Governor General of Canada, asked Laurier, the Canadian Prime Minister, to make necessary arrangements for the reception of Indian evacuees from the United States because they were British subjects in need of the protection of the British Crown.[14]

The Asiatic Exclusion League had also been very active in the important cities of British Columbia during 1907. In September, Mr. Ishii, the Japanese Commissioner, arrived in Seattle, and believing that he would remain there for several days, the League had planned a hostile demonstration against the Asiatics in general and the Japanese in particular. But Mr. Ishii decided to leave for Vancouver before any demonstration could be carried out. However, upon learning of this, the Secretary of the Seattle Exclusion League (Mr. A. E. Fowler, who had led the attacks on Indians at Bellingham) boarded the same train for Vancouver. Acting upon Mr. Fowler's instructions, the Asiatic Exclusion League of Vancouver arranged for a parade followed by a public meeting in the City Hall on September 7, 1907. The City Hall was literally within a stone's throw of China Town and was not much removed from Powell Street where most of the Japanese resided at that time. Fowler proposed a march through the Chinese and Japanese quarters. Some boys, directed by Fowler, began to throw stones and then the crowd turned into a mob, invaded China Town and swept on to the Japanese quarters. At first the Japanese met the invading force with passive resistance, then, arming themselves with sticks, bottles and knives, they routed their persecutors. The following morning, Sunday, further trouble occurred. In the ensuing rioting the Japanese showed their fighting skill, turned upon their assailants and routed them. They patrolled the streets in their special quarters carrying revolvers and knives and did the job of the police.[15]

The Indians took refuge in their Gurdwaras (Sikh temple) and in the mills where they worked. They were mild-mannered and inoffensive, and did not carry any weapons as did the Japanese. They were fellow-subjects of Canadians under the British Crown and desired to live peacefully. They were, however, equally unacceptable because they appeared to be odd people who were unable to adapt themselves to their new situation: far less than the Chinese and Japanese did they attempt to make their customs and dress conform to Western ideas. Their turbans, flowing beards, and dark skins gave them an unkempt appearance, however clean they actually might have been.

The British Columbia government headed by Conservative Premier Sir Richard McBride, had already exploited the Oriental immigration question to full extent in the provincial election of February 1907.[16] Seeing the popularity of anti-Asiatic elements on the Pacific Coast, the government had publicized its strong opposition to Oriental immigration.[17] Two days prior to the general election in British Columbia, the *Province* (a Conservative paper) printed a sensational front page article declaring that Liberals had made a secret agreement with the Grand Trunk Railroad that in the case of a Liberal victory in the election, it would be allowed to import 50,000 Japanese workers.[18] The Liberal party was faced with the impossibility of replying to the Conservative charges at length, because the latter were made on the eve of the election.[19] In this way McBride very skillfully, through his criticism of the Dominion immigration policies, achieved the largest majority in the popular vote.[20] After the September riots, McBride took up his old uncompromising stance against the so-called 'Oriental' invaders. He was a witty politician with his finger on the popular pulse,[21] so his opposition to the Oriental immigration was quite vociferous.

The Canadian government hurriedly negotiated the "Gentlemen's Agreement"[22] with Japan, which restricted the number of immigrants coming direct from that country to 400 per year. There remained, however, the question of those Japanese who entered Canada from Hawaii, and that of Indians from the Far Eastern countries. These questions needed delicate handling. On the first issue, the Japanese government was unwilling that any of its subjects should be explicitly barred from Canada, and therefore the problem of Japanese immigrants from Hawaii must be carefully considered; on the second issue, the Canadian government, aware of its Imperial responsibilities, was unwilling to affront so important a member of the Imperial community as India. Direct representation to India on this matter had met little response.[23] The Indian government, already beset with the threat of insurrection, was unwilling to provoke domestic hostility by acting against the interests of its own people.[24]

The problem was solved by a stroke of superb diplomatic skill. Under Section 30 of the Immigration Act (Statutes of Canada, 1906),

> The Governor General in Council may by proclamation or order, whenever he considers it necessary or expedient prohibit the landing in Canada of any specified class of immigrants.[25]

The Canadian authorities had full power to take any action they thought fit to solve the immigration problem. Based on this, they passed, on January 8, 1908, an Order in Council to the effect that whenever the Minister of the Interior deemed it to be necessary, immigrants might be prohibited from landing in Canada unless they came from the country of their birth or citizenship by a continuous journey using through tickets purchased before leaving the country.

This immediately and effectively stopped the inflow of the Japanese and this "continuous passage regulation," as it came to be known, chanced to be so framed as to apply equal force against the Indian immigrants as well.

Then the Canadian government's representative — Mackenzie King — paid visits to London, England (March and December 1908), and India in January 1909. The Imperial Indian and Canadian governments agreed to the exclusion of Indian immigrants from Canada through the effective use of the "direct passage clause" and avoidance of any publicity on the subject.[26] This ban, however, was challenged and contested in Canadian law courts and even brought before the Imperial Conference in 1911.[27] But Indian migrants as well as wives and children of those already settled in Canada were still barred. The Indian migrants sent a deputation to Ottawa, London and India,[28] but the Canadian government refused to relax its policy. When these regulations proved insufficient and defective and could not be sustained in the law courts in 1913,[29] further restrictions were imposed.[30] Finally in 1914 the attempts of Indian migrants to enter Canada by chartering the *Komagata Maru* were frustrated to the extent of almost using the Canadian naval force.[31]

At this time British Columbia had only a small population; geographically, it was remote from Europe and its high mountain chain seemed to isolate it from the rest of Canada. It was the last choice for settlement of European migrants, and problems and insecurities facing workers there were enormous.[32] The entire economy of the province was based on specialized resources responsive to and dependent upon the vagaries of external markets. A much larger percentage of the wage income of British Columbians, as compared to Canada as a whole, derived directly from the export of goods and services, and as such was dependent upon the rise and fall of world prices. Large numbers of workers were employed in industries such as lumber, mining, long-shoring and maritime trades, which were plagued by harsh surroundings, a high accident rate, geographical and social isolation, a continuous turnover of manpower, and unstable family conditions. Workers in these outlying communities developed an intense group consciousness, and a cohesive isolation. Gradually, the western province developed large-scale industries, and out of this grew a new capitalist class. This industrialism produced a virile labour movement intent on maintaining its rights through a strong organization of workers. Inopportunely, this precarious labour situation was beset by waves of Oriental, Eastern European and American immigrant workers who were ready to give their services for relatively low wages, thus creating an unstable labour market[33] in the eyes of organized labour. Asian migrants in particular, with their coloured skins, different modes of dress and willingness to work more cheaply as labourers were perceived by the Canadian workers in British Columbia as a threat to their economic future. Organized workers began to unite against this invasion, and soon labour unions had a grip on all working classes.

Labour leaders were immediately interested in acquiring political importance. They were quick to realize that the authority of the labour unions as a strong pressure group in the working of the two democracies on either side of the border in North America could be strongly established by a well organized labour force.[34] Testing the full extent of their power, the labour leaders pointed out that the brunt of the impact of increased Oriental migration would fall not upon large property owners, capitalists or technical experts (who would, indeed, benefit), but upon the common labourer. Unions, therefore, included exclusion of Oriental workers as a part of their programme of labour welfare. Since the development of the West Coast of North America was in its early stages, it needed a large number of workers — who were not easily available from the eastern parts of Canada and the United States. Only truly working-class European migrants who were unable to establish themselves in the east made their way to the Pacific coast. Such settlers felt insecure about their abilities and their job security. Any competition, or even the possibility of such competition, from hard-working Asians naturally made them feel threatened.[35] Under such conditions, labour union leaders desiring to establish their own political influence were quick to make full use of Oriental immigrants as scapegoats.

On the other hand, the capitalist class, desiring to establish its industries, encouraged Oriental immigration,[36] and this fact was equally cited by the unions as an example of labour exploitation. Since Orientals, particularly Indians, were unfamiliar with the working of unions and hampered from learning about them by the language barrier and the hostility of the organized workers, they showed indifference to union membership and were absent from union strikes and lock-outs; because of this they were branded as blacklegs, strike-breakers and a menace.[37] The press reaction to Asiatics on the Pacific coast was equally hostile, and its sensationalism contributed to the feeling against Orientals. In British Columbia, the Conservative Party was able to win the election on the strength of its anti-Oriental slogans. Such was the feeling generated against the Asiatic immigrant at that time that soon both political parties (Conservative and Liberal) professed their support of anti-Asiatic hysteria, and the heated atmosphere resulted in anti-Oriental riots in September 1907.[38] Demands for a complete ban on Oriental immigration were a direct result of all this political manoeuvring and emotional blackmail.

In order to win labour votes in provincial and federal elections, both political parties had to become involved in this local immigration problem. Both parties, therefore, showed their enthusiasm in convincing the labouring classes that they were aiming to achieve immigration control, with the decrease and, ultimately, exclusion of Orientals as immigrants to Canada. The seeds of discrimination and exclusion were thus sown and fertilized, and everyone — labourers, labour leaders, politicians — hoped to benefit from the harvest. Thus, when South Asian migration began, the atmosphere in British Columbia was already hostile. Even though South Asians were British subjects and citizens of the British Empire, they were unwelcome. The Dominion government, its own racist views strengthened by the British Columbia attitude, adopted restrictive and discriminatory practices and policies towards Indians and tried to establish their effective exclusion. Their status as British subjects did not help them to enter Canada; rather, it led to a fear of inexhaustible numbers of Indian migrants coming to Canada and changing the Western cultural atmosphere of the country. The immigration question became an insoluble issue throughout the British empire, for it created a colour and race consciousness which had its repercussions in the politics of India, Britain and Canada. Unfortunately, the effective exclusion of Indians from Canada, which was the basic policy for the Dominion, had the tacit approval of the Imperial and Indian governments.[39] This, in turn, served as the greatest contributory factor to anti-British movements in the once loyal province of the Punjab during the First World War.

The Indians' exclusion was officially agreed upon under a diplomatic agreement made under the Reciprocity of Treatment resolution in the Imperial War Conference of 1918. This policy continued until 1947, when India and Pakistan became independent countries. At that time Canada sensed the urgency of coming to an understanding and arrangement with them. India might have used this excuse for leaving the Commonwealth.[40] In 1951, during the post-war period, the Dominion government replaced this policy of exclusion with an agreement to accept a small number of Indian migrants under a quota system. In 1967 Canada adopted a universal immigration policy, and by 1972, Canada accepted a reasonable number of Asians expelled from Uganda.

Given the world-wide economic recession over the past five years, Canada decided to review the entire immigration policy. It published the *Green Papers* in February 1975, and the immigration policy question was debated for nearly two-and-a-half years. In the meantime the Economic Council of Canada expressed its concern about the growing level of unemployment and Canada's inability to make full use of its labour force.[41] Canada had already become self-sufficient in meeting its needs with highly trained human resources.[42] In the light of changing demands, the Canadian Parliament passed the New Immigration Act under which the principles regarding admission to Canada remain unchanged. However, there are important changes in the overall administration of immigration policy. Immigration levels will be developed in consultation with provinces and other appropriate groups, to determine regional demographic and labour needs. Moreover the Act requires the Minister responsible for immigration to make an annual public announcement of the number of immigrants the federal government plans to admit during a given period. This number will be at a global level, not a country-by-country quota.[43] The emphasis is on employment and the name of the relevant department has been changed to Employment and Immigration in place of Manpower and Immigration.

According to the Census of Canada (1971), the number of South Asians in Canada was 52,100, and new immigrants from the Indian subcontinent numbered 6,281 in 1971, 6,239 in 1972, and 4,639 in 1973 (in all, 76,259).[44] The outstanding characteristics of the new migrants were their high educational qualifications, cosmopolitan outlook, and lack of permanence in any one country or locality. Canadian immigration policy, with its emphasis upon educational and occupational qualifications, attracted, and still attracts, such migration in increasing numbers. Under the new immigration policy, the number of migrants from South Asian countries began to increase, and the characteristics of this new group were quite different from those entering Canada in the earlier part of this century. Inter-group contact of immigrants and the host community can result either in conflict or in harmony, depending upon the situation and conditions under which it occurs. When the conflict situation involves a combination of equal status, common goals, no competition along group lines, and has the support of authorities, law and customs, as well as being free from the use of the scapegoat hypothesis, political exploitation, ignorance, and the fear of a sudden influx of aliens, improved group relations may be envisaged. Canada is trying the difficult experiment of building a multi-cultural society in which a myriad of cultural, economic, political, demographic and ecological factors interplay. However, there are still instances of racial discrimination in employment, housing and other services. Physical characteristics, such as skin colour, facial appearance, or hair texture, seem to be the main causes for such behaviour, even today.[45]

THE UNITED KINGDOM SITUATION

The decision to emigrate is based on a number of motives which differ according to individual need in individual cases. Nevertheless, the desire to become better off has always been a dominant factor in migration movements.[46] In the Indo-Pakistan subcontinent, agricultural over-population, poverty and unemployment have provided the major incentives for emigration. These push factors have been so strong that South Asians are willing to migrate for the sake of employment at very low remunerative levels.[47] Migrants in such circumstances are drawn to areas where economic opportunities are abundant and where they will receive relatively high pay for their work.[48] The push mechanism of acute pressures of one kind or another was always present in South Asia, and therefore the desire to emigrate was strong. This created administrative, diplomatic and political difficulties for the Indian government, and it tried to restrict emigration by the application of various regulations.

The situation in the United Kingdom regarding migration during British rule in India was a different matter. Every Indian was a British subject, and was therefore free to come to Britain. In the main, only educated Indians — such as students, professional men and politicians — came. They stayed for the duration of their studies and invariably returned home after training. In addition to these, numbers of Indian seamen also settled in port towns. The Second World War resulted in the tremendous loss of human resources and destruction of industries and economic institutions in Western Europe, and after the war the process of redevelopment and reconstruction required additional manpower. Thus, there was a boom in economic activities. In the meantime, British rule in India came to an end in 1947, but South Asians retained their status as British subjects.[49]

The South Asian subcontinent underwent a terrible upheaval during the process of acquiring independence, especially in the Punjab. When, in the 1950s, there was news of a demand for labour in the U.K., Sikh ex-soldiers from India and Punjab Muslims from Pakistan were the first to come to Britain. Emigration, unlike water, flows wherever possible from countries of a low standard of living to countries with better opportunities and a higher life style. Another major source of South Asian migration was Gujerat on the west coast of India. Like Punjabis, Gujeratis had suffered on account of pressure on land. Gujeratis were well known as migrating traders in the British colonies in Africa; it was, therefore, small wonder to find Gujeratis, like the Punjabis, moving to Britain when opportunity appeared. The third wave of migration came from Bengal, the most thickly populated part of the subcontinent. Through British-owned tea plantations, merchants and shipping companies, Bengalis came to know about the possible opportunities available in Britain. Bengali sailors often visited Britain and drifted ashore when their boats were in British harbours. Once a tradition of migration was established, it acted as a social force and many sections of the society which might not have an economic reason to migrate were drawn into it.[50] The process of this chain migration (prospective migrants learnt from the early arrivals about opportunities, transportation, employment, accommodation and above all, their success) began to reinforce the movement.[51]

Punjabis, Gujeratis and Bengalis were the three distinct groups of South Asian migrants who came to Britain. As the demand grew, news spread, and the fear of possible restrictive legislation to control migration from the new Commonwealth developed. Publicity along these lines from the South Asian travel agents worked; the number of South Asian migrants began to accelerate. Though only a small fraction of the Indo-Pakistani population had grasped the idea that Britain offered better economic prospects and opportunities for cultural development, this small percentage appeared as a flood to the British host community.

Officially, Britain was reluctant to recognize that it was a country which neded immigrants. Prior to the arrival of South Asians in substantial numbers, immigrants from the West Indies began to arrive in Britain. The unfavourable effects of emigration to the Old Dominions on the expanding post-war economy, together with a long-term decline in the British rate of natural population increase (especially during the war) had combined to produce a declining rate of growth in the labour force.[52] Firms had to recruit these new migrant workers because they could not get either British white workers or foreign white workers.[53] During the years 1955-60, the Home Office estimated that there had been an influx of 161,450 West Indians and 50,190[54] South Asians in Britain. New Commonwealth immigration started as a search for employment opportunities, and migrants began to concentrate where unskilled labour was reputed to be in short supply. They tended to gravitate towards those areas where not merely jobs existed, but housing was fairly freely available. Thus there was a rapid growth of immigrant enclaves, not in the New Town, for instance, but characteristically within declining twilight inner city areas whose native population was apparently already on the move out.[55] The rapid increase of coloured immigrants was resented by a section of the British population, and there were race riots in 1958. By 1961, the Conservative government passed the Immigration Act. The Home Secretary, R. A. Butler, explained that the "flood" of immigrants had necessitated controls. The new regulations came into operation in July 1962. Under this Act, immigrants from the Commonwealth countries were divided into three categories: Category A voucher immigrants had to have a definite offer of employment from a U.K. employer; Category B voucher immigrants had to possess particular skills or qualifications (for instance medical and nursing qualifications), and about half of those admitted under this category were doctors; Category C applications were for those without either specific job offers or specific qualifications. In the first three years of operation, admission quotas were filled entirely by immigrants in categories A and B, and Category C was discontinued in 1965 after a waiting list of 300,000 applicants had accumulated — some indication of the large number of immigrants who could well have arrived in the U.K. in the absence of any form of control. Besides, under the 1962 Act, all those who had served in the British armed forces could also come to the U.K. The Liberal and Labour parties opposed the Act and declared it would be repealed when they came to power. However, the Labour party came to power in 1964, and within a few months it changed its stance. In Spring 1965 it sent Lord Mountbatten on a tour of Commonwealth countries in order to seek their cooperation in restricting immigration into Britain.

New regulations were introduced in the summer by which the number of annual immigrants was fixed at 8500. Thus by 1965, there was no fundamental difference on this issue between the two main political parties in Britain. By 1968, another element came into the immigration debate; a substantial number of Asians had been given British passports because they were imported into parts of Africa by the British administrators. By 1968, the new African states began to impose restrictions on the economic activities of such Asians and they started coming to Britain in noticeable numbers. At this, the British government hurriedly imposed restrictions on the entry of such British passport holders. Then in early spring, Tory M.P. Enoch Powell made his controversial speech on immigration, predicting doom and gloom for British society if immigration continued. Though he had to resign, this brought a respectability to talks and speeches opposing immigration, and preaching repatriation. After winning the election of summer 1970, the Conservative Party brought in much tougher immigration restrictions in 1971. It virtually stopped primary immigration into Britain. Until the end of the sixties, however, dependents of settled migrants were allowed in without any formal entry visas, but subsequently, these were made compulsory. With tougher restrictions on immigration, the entry process was made more complicated and lengthy, resulting in long delays. Now the waiting period is about 26 months for the first interview at the British visa offices in the Indian subcontinent. The press reports about long waiting lists of dependents are exaggerated, however. In the recent past, the Conservative leadership has expressed strong fears about being "swamped" by the unending flow of migrants. These alarmist suggestions create an ill-informed sensationalism as well. Recently a prominent member[56] of the Commission for Racial Equality paid a visit to the South Asian subcontinent and the British visa offices there, and his estimate of total dependents applying to come to Britain was not more than 40,000 in all.

After the introduction of the voucher system in 1962, trends in migration began to change. The new arrivals came from different parts of the subcontinent and a majority of them were educated and professional men, whereas the majority of earlier South Asian migrants came from highly rural areas. A substantial number of these were ignorant of the English language, European ways of life, and urban society. But in spite of these basic handicaps most of them found employment, for a number of reasons: some companies and business organizations needed to recruit extra staff for shift work, or there was recruitment of an additional labour force owing to expansion; sometimes there was a demand for workers in certain areas, or unattractive working conditions and low wages made indigenous workers scarce. South Asians from the Punjab, Gujerat and Bengal might have been noted for their loyalty to the British Raj, but their unusual clothing, unshaven beards, coloured turbans, or ignorance of the English language created an unfavourable impression in the host community. Most of them were unaccompanied by their wives, and thus they did not have a normal family life. Usually, they began to live in groups of three to fifteen men and remained apart from the rest of the community. They were further isolated by their lack of education. Migrants who lack the skills or competitive qualifications to establish their economic and social position tend to become permanent inhabitants of ethnic concentrations in areas to which they first migrated. If many fail to move on, the social balance in such areas will be upset, and ghettoes and slums will develop, entailing much human misery in the long term.

South Asian migrants have tended to concentrate in certain areas, mostly large conurbations[57] where there were opportunities for employment, cheap accommodation, and the presence of friends and countrymen. Some have little education, others none at all — having never used pen, pencil, paper or book.[58] Their concentration in socially deprived areas and lack of communication skills allow them little chance to master the native tongue.

The age and sex distribution of South Asian migrants changed with the severe controls imposed in 1962, 1965, 1968 and 1971, as the families of settled migrants began to arrive, as well as professionals and their dependents. Some students also stayed on as migrants. The number of South Asian immigrants was 384,600 in 1971; and, if their British-born children are included in these calculations, the number totalled 652,800.[59]

THE CANADIAN AND BRITISH SITUATIONS: A COMPARISON

Successive governments in the U.K. have treated restrictions on immigration as matters of considered policy, and this has been reflected in a series of *White Papers,* 1961-1976. The curbs on migration from the new Commonwealth introduced in 1962 marked the beginning of this practice, whereas in the same year Canada tried to liberalize her immigration policy. Nevertheless, not many coloured immigrants entered Canada until the post-1967 period, in spite of positive migration attitudes and Canadian prosperity pre-1970. Though Britain was officially adopting a policy of restriction on immigration, in actual fact 30,710 South Asian migrants entered the country even in 1975,[60] and the number in the U.K. totalled 600,000 approximately; whereas, in Canada, in spite of an "open door" immigration approach, there were only 76,000. Britain, then, continued to receive the migrants, albeit under a system of control, in spite of almost continuous inflation and economic difficulty. Canada, too, began to experience recession in 1971, so that now it is difficult even for white professionals from the United States and Britain to gain posts, let alone the coloured migrant.

In Canada, the residence patterns of migrants are scattered, and there are few concentrations to be found; in the U.K. however, South Asians have experience of low quality housing, multi-occupations, and close proximity to other coloured immigrants. These factors, plus unfamiliarity with the language and discrimination in employment,[61] have resulted in the formation of South Asian enclaves, such as Southall and East London. Such concentrations sometimes become the target of adverse publicity and are compared with the black ghettoes in the U.S.: from these stem fears of social aggressiveness and racial trouble. However, it must not be forgotten that the coloured population of Britain *in toto* is only about 3 percent, whereas in the U.S. it is 11 percent. Besides, cleavages exist within the immigrant group in Britain: there are West Indians, Pakistanis, Bangladeshis, Cypriots, etc. Religiously and linguistically they differ.[62] Again, the bad housing conditions of many South Asians need not necessarily be a source of trouble. In Newcastle, for example, 6 percent of the population of Rye Hall (a twilight area) is South Asian, and they own 18 percent of the houses; they are not at all interested in being rehoused in council accommodation.[63]

In both the U.K. and Canada, adverse publicity through the press and the media has gone far in influencing public opinion on matters of migration and its control. Sensationalism makes news, and sometimes such practices are intentionally carried out for commercial gains, creating serious misunderstanding.[64] Such unfortunate practices are not confined to the English-speaking papers; the immigrant press itself can often be at fault.

In Britain during the last decade there has been a rise in extremist organizations like the National Front and National Party. A section of prominent politicians always try to fish in the troubled waters of British race problems; however, these extremist organizations have not been able to make any headway in local or national elections.

The central government is sensitive of the need to take positive remedial action in the deprived areas of inner cities where the main ethnic concentrations are. Similarly, the local authorities do their utmost. According to the Race Relations Act of 1976, it is the job of the local authorities to combat discrimination on racial grounds. In Canada, the multi-racial programme is opposed by a small but unpleasant organization called The Western Guard, which closely resembles Britain's National Front. Fascist tendencies, including anti-semitism and other forms of racism, have existed for a long time among a small percentage of the Canadian population and can be found in small sections of old-established ethnic groups. There are leaders here too, but they are less prominent and less tolerated than the British extremist and alarmist politicians are.

Adding to the confusion over immigration in Britain is the question of entry of dependents, whereas in Canada this red herring scarcely exists.

Immigration for Britain is an accidental process and for Canada it is a basic policy question. In Canada it involves the provinces and two/three departments of the federal government; being a federal system, sometimes lengthy delays result. On the other hand, Britain has no such active provincial governments; administration is centralised, and therefore should be more expeditious and less complex.

Although Britain has gone far to discourage migration in recent years, while Canada has encouraged it, once migrants have arrived in the U.K. much is done to help and advise them, if they care to seek out and use such assistance. There are community development projects, educational priority areas, regional offices of the Community Relations Commission, numerous welfare agencies, and adult and further education facilities. Britain, in fact, has shown that it is not necessary for a country to be rich to accommodate immigrants; on the contrary, it has been found that discriminatory legislation against Asiatics was most prolific in the United States and Canada between 1891 and 1920, when economic competition was least.[65]

South Asians have brought with them their religions, dress and a distinctive way of life. Both in Canada and Britain, temples, mosques and gurdwaras are seen to be established. The Sikh temple in Vancouver and the Central London mosque are added tourist attractions in both Canada and Britain. The popularity of Indian food has encouraged the setting up of South Asian restaurants in both countries.

The arrival of coloured migrants in Britain highlighted the gaps in the school curriculum, which was not geared to serve non-English speaking Oriental children. Similarly, the local authorities had to make provisions for teaching English as a Second Language to adults as well as children. At the same time, training colleges and universities had to adjust their progammes to include an element of Asian studies. Canada, however, had already adapted its system, especially in those provinces where South Asians and other Orientals had settled.

Britain's economic growth and development, as well as her imperial and industrial past were responsible for the mass immigration experiences and social policy expansion. Now the current prospect of nil economic growth makes the likelihood of any further mass immigration or any medium term social policy seem unlikely. Nevertheless, Canada has much better prospects for expansion and immigration will continue in substantial numbers without creating further problems.

Taken all in all, it would appear that South Asians in both Britain and Canada are unlikely to react in the violent manner usual for minorities in the United States to the problems of accommodation and adjustment which they find on arrival in an alien environment. Such reaction is improbable for the following reasons: there are too many ethnic/linguistic/religious divisions within the South Asian immigrant groups itself; family life is still close-knit, and influence of parents and senior members of the community over the young is still strong; and there is an overwhelming desire for education and training, and a propensity for hard work and the ambition to establish private businesses and other enterprises, which would be put most at risk at a time of violent and unruly reaction.

NOTES

1. Emigrant, *Indian Emigration*, Oxford 1924, p. 74.

2. Governor General of Canada to the Secretary of State for Colonies, April 27, 1908, C.O. 886/1.

3. Canada, House of Commons Debates, January 1908, 1649.

4. Ian H. Nish, *The Anglo-Japanese Alliance: the Development of Two Island Empires*, 1894-1907 (London 1966), p. 362.

5. Rodolphe Lemieux, Minister of Labour, Confidential Report of his Mission to Japan. . . . 1908, pp. 6-8, Lemieux Papers.

6. "There were signs of disturbance in the New York Stock Exchange". See M. P. Fairchild, "Immigration and Crises", *American Economic Review*, 1911, p. 757.

7. Press Report, September 1907, R.G.7, G 21, File 332, Vol. 199.

8. MacInnes to Oliver, Minister of the Interior, Ottawa, Feb. 13, 1908, C.O. 886/1.

9. Report by MacInnes, File 1371, L/P & J/6/864; and Jacobus ten Brock, Edward N. Barnhart and Floyd, W. Matson, *Prejudice, War and the Constitution* (Berkeley, 1958), pp. 34-35.

10. *Organized Labor* (San Francisco), Jan. 2, 1907.

11. Governor General, File G. 21, No. 332, Vol. 199, 1907.

12. W. D. Dodd, "Hindu in the North West", *World Today* XIII, 1907, pp. 1157-1160.

13. *Outlook*, LXXXVII, 1907,pp. 51-52.

14. Governor General of Canada to the Secretary of State for Colonies Sept. 24, 1907, C.O. 886/1.

15. *Colonist,* Sept. 8, 1907; *Seattle Post Intelligencer,* Sept. 8, 1907, *Canadian Annual Review,* 1907 (Toronto, 1908), p. 386; and *Province,* Sept. 9, 1907.

16. Brian Ray Douglas Smith, "Sir Richard McBride: A study in the Conservative Party of British Columbia, 1903-1916," M.A. Thesis (Queen's University, Kingston, 1959), p. 77.

17. Mary E. Hallett, "A Governor General's Views on Oriental Immigration to British Columbia, 1904-1911," *B.C. Studies,* No, 14, 1972, p. 56.

18. *Province,* Feb. 1, 1907.

19. Roman Hromnysky, "The Western Canadian Regional Governments and the Federal System 1900-1930," M.A. thesis (University of British Columbia, Vancouver, 1965), p. 87.

20. Roman Hromnysky and Martin Robin, *Canadian Provincial Politics* (Scarborough, 1972), p. 46.

21. *New York Evening Post,* Oct. 26, 1907.

22. The "Gentlemen's Agreement" was the result of a detailed discussion between Rodolph Lemieux, Canadian Minister of Labour and Postmaster General and Count Hayashi, Japanese Minister of Foreign Affairs. Lemieux Report on his Mission to Japan, Jan. 12, 1908, Lemieux Papers.

23. India Office Minutes, Nov. 18, 1907 and Governor General of Canada to Secretary of State for Colonies, tele., Nov. 11, 1907, File 3330 L/P & J/6/780.

24. Viceroy of India to Secretary of State for India, tele., Jan. 22, 1908, File 1371, L/P & J/6/864.

25. Revised Statutes of Canada, 1906, Vol. II, p. 1715.

26. MacKenzie King, Memo. on his Mission to England, May 2, 1908, Lemieux Papers; and Mackenzie King, Memo. re: Emigration from India to Canada, Feb. 5, 1909. King Papers.

27. Cd. 5741 Imperial Conference 1911, Precis of the Proceedings.

28. India Office to Colonial Office April 22, 1913, C.O. 42/975/13055; Hardinge, Viceroy of India to Sikh delegates, Dec. 20, 1913. Hardinge Papers.

29. "Re. Thirty Nine Hindus," *Dominion Law Reports* and "Re Narain Singh et al" *British Columbia Reports* Vol. XVIII (1912-13), p. 506.

30. P.C. 2642 December 1913 and P.C. 23 and 24, 1914.

31. Komagata Maru Committee of Enquiry Report 1914.

32. See Martin Robin, *Canadian Provincial Politics* (Scarborough, 1972).

33. P. Gladstone, "Unionism in the Fishing Industry in British Columbia," *Canadian Journal of Economics and Political Science,* XVI (February 1950), p. 2.

34. See Paul Phillips, *No Greater Power: a Century of Labour in British Columbia* (Vancouver, 1967).

35. *Organized Labor* (San Francisco), 2 Jan., 1907.

36. John Morley, Secretary of State for India, to Minto, Viceroy of India, 26 March 1908, Minto Papers, 1008.

37. Tom MacInnes (Secret agent for the Government of Canada for the Investigation of Reasons for Indian Immigration) to Oliver, Minister of the Interior, Ottawa, 10 Oct., 1907, CO 886/1.

38. *Colonist,* 8 Sept., 1907; *Seattle Post Intelligencer,* 8 Sept., 1907; *Canadian Annual Review,* 1907 (Toronto, 1908), p. 386; *Province,* 9 Sept. 1907 and 1 Feb., 1907; *New York Evening Post,* 26 Oct., 1907; Bethune, Mayor of Vancouver, to Laurier, Prime Minister of Canada, 11 Sept., 1907, CO 886/1.

39. Cd. 9177. Proceedings of the Imperial War Conference, 1918.

40. John D. Kearney, High Commissioner for Canada, in India, closely observed the attitude of the Indian government and the Indian Constituent Assembly towards future membership of the Common-wealth and the impact of the exclusion of Indians from Australia and Canada as immigrants. He personally discussed these matters with St. Laurent, Canadian Minister for External Affairs in Ottawa, and he had a long conservation with Sir Girja Shanker Bajpai, Secretary General, Department of External Affairs, Government of India. He also registered his concern about the right-wing stand of Sardar Patel, Indian Home Minister and Deputy Prime Minister. Full details of his interview with Sir Girja are available in his secret despatch to the Secretary of State for External Affairs, 27 May, 1948: File 536999, Vol. 18.

41. Economic Council of Canada, *People and Jobs. A Study of the Canadian Labour Market,* Ottawa 1976, p. 3.

42. M. Wisenthal, E. Rechnitzer and Z. Zsigmond, "Educational Attainment of Canadians: Looking Ahead," *The Canadian Business Review,* Vol. 1, no. 2, Spring 1974, pp. 20-23.

43. Statutes of Canada 1976-77. Chapter 52,

44. Breakdown of the number of South Asians settled in Canadian provinces: Newfoundland 305; Prince Edward Island 130; Nova Scotia 1165; New Brunswick 340; Quebec 5000; Ontario 22,455; Manitoba 1855; Saskatchewan 1250; Alberta 3215; British Columbia 16,350. *Census of Canada,* 1971

45. Kananur V. Chandra, *Racial Discrimination in Canada. Asian Minorities* (San Francisco, 1973).

46. See Julius Isaac, *Economics of Migration* (London, 1947), p. 3.

47. See UN, *The Determinants and Consequences of Population Trends* (New York, 1953), p. 113.

48. See Warrren S. Thompson, *Population Problems* (New York, 1965), p. 373.

49. British Nationality Act, 1948.

50. G. S. Aurora, *The New Frontiermen: A Sociological Study of Indian Migrants into the U.K.* (Bombay, 1971).

51. John MacDonald and D. MacDonald, "Chain Migration, Ethnic Neighbourhood Formation and Social Networks," *Social Research* 29, 4, 1962.

52. C. Senior, "Race Relations and Labour Supply in Great Britain," Paper for the American Sociological Society Race Relations Section, Detroit, 1956.

53. P. L. Wright, *The Coloured Worker in British Industry* (London, 1968).

54. E. J. B. Rose, *Colour and Citizenship: A Report on British Race Relations* (London, 1969).

55. K. Jones and A.D. Smith, *The Economic Impact of Commonwealth Immigration* (Cambridge, 1970).

56. B.B.C. Programme for Asian Viewers. Sunday, 7 May, 1978.

57. The numbers of South Asians in the following cities were: Greater London 136,515; Leicester 12,285; Birmingham 35,400; Walsall 12,120; Coventry 10,130; Bradford 17,045. See *Ethnic Minorities* (CRC, London, 1975), p. 11.

58. Patrick Sookhdeo, *Asians in Britain: a Christian Understanding* (London, 1972).

59. G. B. Billian Lomas, *Census 1971. The Coloured Population of Great Britain* (London, 1971).

60. Institute of Race Relations, *Prevention of Race Discrimination in Great Britain* (London, 1972).

61. *Ibid.*

62. Daniel C. Kramer, "White versus Coloured in Britain: an Explosive Confrontation," *Social Research,* 1969, 36:4, pp. 585-605.

63. See J. G. Davies and John Taylor, "Race, Community and Conflict," *New Society,* 9 July, 1970, pp. 67-69. See also Anthony H. Richmond, "Housing and Racial Attitudes in Bristol," *Race,* Vol. 12, 1970, pp. 49-58.

64. Christopher Bagley, "Race Relations and the Press: An Empirical Analysis," *Race,* Vol. 1, 1973, pp. 59-70.

65. Charles Price, "White Restrictions on Coloured Immigration," *Race,* Vol. 7, 1966, pp. 217-234.

6

Some Aspects of East Indian Struggle in Canada, 1905-1947

Samuel Raj
Ottawa, Ontario

A topic of this nature immediately poses the problem of objectivity to a writer of East Indian background. During the period under consideration, East Indians felt that they were unfairly excluded from gaining a share of the bounties of Canada. The few who managed to gain a foothold in Canada were hurt by constantly being subjected to humiliation, compounded by a sense of betrayal. Canada and India were part of the same British Empire, and Canadians and Indians served the same sovereign. The common sovereign had repeatedly promised Indians that they would not suffer any form of discrimination based on race, colour or religion in his global Empire.[1] Yet when a part of his Empire, Western Canada, was thrown open for settlement, strangers from different lands were invited to enter but they, the children of the Empire, were excluded from it: every ingenious means was adopted to keep them out of the coveted land. Further, the strangers within the gate were given free access to British rights and privileges, but the same were denied to the "Brown Children"[2] who had carried Britain's banner and fought her battles in many lands. The "Brown Children" felt that their common Father whom they had unswervingly

63

served, for whose glory they had often shed their blood, and in whose word they had implicitly placed their confidence allowed them to be mistreated by their naughty White brothers. Can a member of a race (incidentally, I am not a Sikh, neither am I an Aryan, but I would have been subjected to the same experience, had I been there) that felt excluded, humiliated, and betrayed assess its dark period objectively? That is the task of this paper.

I believe that any historical experience, however grim it might be, can be discussed objectively as long as one keeps in mind what Herbert Butterfield calls "man's universal sin."[3] Man's universal sin must be defined as self-regarding or self-orientedness, which is the dominant instinct of nature. No collective group (such as race or nation) is less self-regarding, self-oriented or selfish than another, although an individual may be less selfish than another. A nation or a race may be more intelligently selfish than another but never qualitatively less selfish. As a collective group, the victim is qualitatively no different from the villain. If circumstances had been reversed, the former's behaviour would not have been any different from the latter. If there had been any difference at all, it must have been because one was more intelligently selfish but not less selfish. The difference, then, is not moral (in Kantian sense[4]) but technical. In fact, collective groups (nations or races) seldom ever act on a moral plane, although they may never fail to portray their actions in moralistic terms. They respond to the call of morality only when they feel that their obedience would not seriously hurt their self-interest. Such obedience has no moral content at all.

Frequently intelligent selfishness is mistaken for morality. For instance, some have described the withdrawal of the United States from Southeast Asia as a moral act. Indeed, the United States was no more moral or no less selfish when she left Southeast Asia than when she went in. She intervened when she felt that her interest was at stake, and she left when she discovered her involvement was detrimental to her self-interest. One must not forget that the Anti-Vietnam War Movement gained momentum only when it became obvious that no American interest was involved in the Southeast Asian conflict.

One must also remember that Herbert Butterfield's "man's universal sin" includes the author as well. No one who is part of society and shares its basic instinct of self-orientedness is free from that description which every society is: self-regarding and sinful. Then every author who is a member of a society can relate to any and all historical persons not as a saint but as a sinner. He could approach historical persons not as a righteous judge with a verdict, but as a fellow sinner who himself is in need of understanding and forgiveness. It is in the recognition of this sinful identity with all historical persons, both villians and victims, I believe, that one's objectivity lies. I intend to approach this subject with the attitude of a fellow sinner, guilty of the same qualitatively, not to pass judgement but to understand the experience of the victim and the attitude of the villain.

The main struggle in which East Indians were involved stemmed from the attitude of the dominant society towards them. The dominant society wanted to keep Canadian soil free from another Asian "defilement," East Indians in this case. To achieve this objective, the dominant society, at first, tried to exclude East Indians from Canada. By 1914, it had effectively managed to close the door to East Indian immigration. Meanwhile the dominant society sought also to extinguish the East Indian presence in Canada by eliminating the possibility of its self-perpetuation. It tried to make it impossible for resident East Indian men to bring their wives to Canada. It was hoped that such an approach would make Canada free from the undesirable East Indian element within a generation. Further, the dominant society subjected East Indians to political disability. East Indians were perpetually reminded of their unwelcomed presence and their second-class status. The East Indian struggle was essentially to react against these measures of the dominant society and to obtain for themselves what they considered to be their legitimate rights as British subjects.

In this paper, we shall first discuss the unsuccessful attempt to keep Canada open for East Indians. Second, we shall concentrate on the struggle to gain admission into Canada for the wives and families of resident East Indian men. Third, we shall deal with the effort to gain political equality which became a reality only when the homeland of East Indian Canadians became free from foreign domination. Before we proceed with these areas of discussion, it may be essential to provide some relevant background.

The earliest East Indian immigrants to Canada perhaps arrived in the year 1899.[5] Some of these immigrants landed in Victoria and others in Vancouver, B.C.[6] After the turn of the century, a few more trickled into the province. The 1904 census record lists 258 East Indians in British Columbia,[7] and from 1905 onwards there is detailed information on the number of East Indians immigrated to Canada. The number of East Indians to Canada during the period 1904 to 1966 is shown in Table I.

Nearly all the early East Indian immigrants were Sikhs, natives of the Punjab and adherents of Sikhism, a reformed religion founded by Guru Nanak in the 15th century A.D. The beliefs and practices of Sikhs considerably differed from those of the Hindus. Although nearly all the early East Indian immigrants were Sikhs, the dominant society simply called them all Hindus, perhaps to differentiate them from

Table I

East Indian Immigrants to Canada 1904-1966

1904-05	45	1926	60	1947	167
1905-06	387	1927	56	1948	64
1906-07	2,124	1928	52	1949	54
1907-08	2,623	1929	58	1950	93
1908-09	6	1930	80	1951	99
1909-10	10	1931	47	1952	172
1910-11	5	1932	62	1953	140
1911-12	3 (?)	1933	33	1954	177
1913	5	1934	33	1955	249
1914	88 (?)	1935	21	1956	332
1915	nil	1936	13	1957	334
1916	1	1937	14	1958	459
1917	nil	1938	14	1959	741
1918	nil	1939	11	1960	691
1919	nil	1940	6	1961	744
1920	10	1941	3	1962	830
1921	13	1942	nil	1963	1,331
1922	21	1943	nil	1964	2,077
1923	40	1944	nil	1965	3,491
1924	46	1945	1	1966	4,094
1925	62	1946	8		

Source: Sushil Jain, *East Indians in Canada,* pp. 3, 8-9. The data presented above may not be absolutely correct but they do reveal some idea about the flow of East Indian immigration to Canada.

Amerindians. There was also a sprinkling of Hindus and Muslims among the early immigrants.[8]

The earliest immigrants were retired soldiers of the British Indian army. Their interest in Canada seemed to have risen at the occasion of Queen Victoria's diamond jubilee (1897) in London, England, when some of them made "friends with Canadian troops and exchanged notes."[9] Many of these soldiers were stationed in the Far East in places like Penang, Hong Kong, Shanghai, and Singapore. On their way home, they passed through Canada, and they became deeply impressed by the wide prairies and majestic mountains; they were also greatly touched by the reception which they received wherever they stopped on their journey across Canada. At the end of their term of service, instead of returning to India, they turned their faces towards the land that had greatly impressed them.[10] These early immigrants appeared to have done quite well, and they sent favourable and even glowing reports back to their families and friends in India and to their former mates in the Far East.[11]

About the same time, some steamship companies, particularly the CPR, carried a program of propaganda in some parts of North India, especially in the Punjab, to stimulate interest in emigration to Canada. The combination of these factors resulted in the sudden and explosive increase in the number of immigrants arriving in British Columbia in the year 1906.[12]

To this "apparently massive East Indian immigration," British Columbia's response was swift, violent and hostile. The press described the East Indian arrival as "Hindu Invasion." Frequently, it featured front page articles under captions such as "Invasion Threatened," "Hordes of Hungry Hindoos Invade Vancouver City," "Agent of Hindus is . . . Spying out the Land," "The Invasion of British Columbia," "Hordes of Hindus on Steamer Tartar," "Hindus Coming in Hundreds," "More are on the Way," "Many Thousands More Will Come," and "Hindus are Expected to Fight to Enter Canada." The press also portrayed the East Indian immigrants in the worst possible light. Captions such as "Hindus . . . Evade the Police," "Fiendish Crime Done by Hindus," "Hindoos Hold up Lonely Homes . . . Create a Reign of Terror in Suburbs," "Masked Hindoo Sandbags Vancouver Woman," "Hindus Revel in Litigation," "Hindu Quarters in Deplorable State . . . with Filth and Alive with Rats," "Get Rid of Hindus at Whatever Cost" and similar headlines were quite common.[13] At times the press carried front page cartoons portraying overwhelming waves of "Hindu immigration," foreboding the end of the White race in British Columbia and focussing on the need to stop the "Hindu menace."[14] The local politicians denounced the East Indian immigrants as a burden to the city, destructive to the British way of life in the province, and as breeders of disease. The labour groups accused them of presenting unequal competition and of subverting the interest of the working class.[15]

Ottawa's response to the East Indian immigration was slow but nevertheless decisive. Despite British Columbia's many demands, Ottawa did not act immediately. It had to consider the imperial interest as well.[16] However as it became obvious that the East Indian immigration would not stop unless acted decisively, Ottawa invoked the "Continuous Voyage" Order, an Order-in-Council which had been originally issued to keep away the Japanese emigrating from Hawaii. The Order-in-Council stated that

the Governor-General in Council may . . . prohibit the landing . . . of

> any immigrants who have come to Canada otherwise than by con-
> tinuous journey from the country of which they are natives . . .[17]

This meant no one could emigrate from India to Canada as there was
no direct steamship service between these two countries. Further, no
East Indians living abroad could immigrate to Canada since the Order
required the prospective immigrant to sail directly from the land of his
origin. The application of the "Continuous Voyage" Order effectively
arrested the flow of East Indian immigration.

Ottawa, suspecting that the "Continuous Voyage" Order might be
challenged in the courts, introduced a new Immigration Act in 1910.
The new act gave legislative sanction to the Order-in-Council and
expressly placed it beyond judicial interpretation or meddling.[18] The
same act also ordered all Asian immigrants, except Japanese and
Chinese who laboured under different laws, to be in possession of $200
upon landing in Canada. Three years later, perhaps to placate the
labour groups, Ottawa approved a regulation prohibiting the landing
of any labourer, skilled or otherwise for a certain period of time.[19] The
East Indians were never told explicitly that they were a prohibited
class of immigrants. They could still come if they would meet the
conditions. Canada undoubtedly adopted a "facetious" and "subter-
fuge" policy in her dealings with the East Indian immigration.[20]

The dominant society had several reasons for excluding East Indians.
It was feared that the admission of East Indians, even in small numbers, would be injurious to the advancement and preservation of Anglo-
Saxon civilization and pre-eminence. Among the English-speaking
people at that time, it was generally believed that they represented the
pinnacle of human evolution and achievement, and that they were
destined to reach greater heights during the course of the present
century. Canadians fondly hoped and some of them even firmly believed that the Anglo-Saxon genius would find its consummation in
"this broad and fair land." It was feared that the admission of the
"lesser breeds" into Canada would frustrate the realization of "this
noble destiny."[21] Furthermore, there was the fear (not just among the
Social-Darwinists) that unless "this western frontier of the Empire"
remained fully secure for Anglo-Saxons, in the "irrepressible conflict"
between races, they would lose their pre-eminent position in the world.[22]

If one would keep in mind these views of the dominant society,
nearly all the objections that the dominant society raised against the
admission of East Indians, whether sound or absurd, make sense.
Whether the dominant society alleged the East Indians to be "unassimilable," "filthy," "immoral," "treacherous," "lazy," "liars," and "hea-
thens," or eulogized them for their "vitality," "ingenuity," and "grati-

tude," and challenged them to be partners in developing "our common heritage" in the tropics, or resorted to stupid arguments that the good Lord had put the Pacific ocean between America and Asia to keep the Asians away,[23] the message was still the same: that Canada must be kept preserved for the unfolding of the Anglo-Saxon genius without let or hindrance and for the maintenance of its pre-eminence among the races.[24]

> ... the people of the Western races ... of this broad and fair land ... hope that civilization in the best and truest sense may advance and develope (sic) to a fuller degree than has yet been achieved. But the invitation or admission of these people, the Hindus, would threaten and even make impossible the realization of these hopes.[25]
> ... To prepare ourselves for the irrepressible conflict, Canada must be and remain a White Man's country. On this western frontier of the Empire will be the forefront of the coming struggle ... Therefore we ought to maintain this country for the Anglo-Saxon and those races which are able to assimilate themselves to them. If this is done, we believe that history will repeat itself and the supremacy of our race will continue. We believe that Canada holds in its hand to a large degree the future of Caucasian civilization.[26]

Besides the concern for the preservation and progress of the Anglo-Saxon race, a more mundane argument was often advanced to exclude East Indians. That the admission of East Indians was unfair to labour was constantly mentioned. It was stated that their presence would have the effect of lowering wages and destroying small businesses. Perhaps this economic argument stirred up more violent emotions among the masses than any other argument, including those of the preservation and "noble destiny of the Anglo-Saxon race."[27]

To a lesser extent, the dominant society did not approve the presence of East Indians in Canada because it could not envisage the possibility of a healthy pluralistic society composed of many diverse cultural, linguistic, religious and racial elements. It was thought that a homogeneous people was a prerequisite for the building of a sound democratic tradition, a vibrant society and a strong nation. That individual liberty and free institutions could exist in a society of heterogeneous people seemed impossible. There were good reasons for it. The history of the world had known many pluralistic societies, but, if I am not mistaken, it has never known a thorough-going one in which individual liberty flourished and free institutions functioned. The dominant society of early twentieth century Canada had come to terms with a degree of religious, linguistic, and cultural pluralism, but a pluralistic society of multi-culture, multi-language, multi-religion and multi-race was still beyond its dream.[28]

Initially East Indians reacted to Canada's resolution to exclude them with disbelief. They did not and would not believe that their presence was generally resented by Canadians although they knew that they were being denounced as "undesirables." The East Indians thought that the resentment against them was limited to a small group, largely to scheming union leaders, unscrupulous politicians and yellow journalists.[29] They did not believe that Canadians would ever become so un-imperial and un-British to shut their door against fellow British subjects. Should Canada ever act so unworthy of its British heritage and contrary to British character, they assumed Britain would intervene on their behalf. They believed that as British subjects they had the inalienable right to unrestricted travel and immigration throughout the Empire. They could not imagine that they would be shut out of a British territory while strangers from alien lands were permitted to enter the same.[30]

When the "continuous voyage" clause of the order-in-council was applied to exclude East Indians, their simple faith in the British character of Canadians received a rude shock, yet they did not lose confidence either in the Canadian public or in the essential "fairness and justice of the British race." They reacted by taking the trouble to explain their case to the Canadian public and to make appeals to the British authorities.

In presenting their case to the Canadian public,[31] they attempted to show how British they were and tried to answer the charges of their opponents. "Racially," said they, "the Hindus are no different from the Anglo-Saxons." To emphasize their racial identity with the dominant society, one of the East Indian leaders, Dr. Sunder Singh, called his paper the *Aryan*. They also claimed religious resemblance with the dominant society. Since most of the East Indians in Canada were Sikhs, with good reason, they described theirs as "a reformed religion," contemporaneous to Protestantism in Europe. In morals and discipline they went on to point out that they were similar to Oliver Cromwell's Puritans. They were also monotheists and monogamists, exactly like the members of the dominant society. Further, they went on to portray their fidelity to the British Crown and their devotion to the Empire. They had fought His Majesty's battles and carried his banners in many lands, and they were still more than willing to do the same. They also reminded their readers that it was their devotion to Britain that saved India for the Empire in the 1857 Rebellion.

In answering the charges of their enemies, they tackled them squarely. They did not deny that they were "unassimilable," but they argued that there already were many unassimilable groups in Canada.

Some friends put forward the argument that Hindus will not assimilate. But what is the case with Jews, Italians, Bulgarians, Ruthenians, Doukhobors and others? Do they assimilate with the Canadian society? Surely assimilation does not mean dull uniformity.[32]

Diversity, they insisted, would not weaken but strengthen and vitalize Canada. Furthermore, they denied that they were a menace to white labour. The class of East Indians who were in Canada, said they, were farmers, and if given an opportunity, they would clear and settle on the land. They would complement and never supplant white labour. They also denied that climatically and otherwise Canada, particularly Southern British Columbia, was unsuitable for them. The homeland of the Sikhs, the Punjab, they said, was often colder than Southern British Columbia. To counteract the charge of "filthiness," "immorality," and "laziness," they often published series of favourable testimonials from authorities whom the dominant society would respect. In denying the presence of paupers and indigents among them, they pointed to the temples, the Guru Nanak Land and Trust Company and the general prosperity of several of their numbers as proofs of their vitality, energy, and resourcefulness. They emphasized that very few other people had made comparable economic stride in such short time. Finally, they also sounded a mild warning that if their rights as British subjects were not respected, Canadians would be indirectly assisting the cause of "sedition" in India and thus responsible for destroying imperial unity.[33]

In all their appeals to the authorities, whether in Ottawa, London, or New Delhi, their argument was the same. They complained that their British rights were being violated and called for redress. In their memorials and delegations, they reminded the British authorities of Britain's pledge to the Indian people and asked that it might be kept faithfully.

With the passage of time, as it became obvious that the authorities had little or no concern for the grievances of East Indians, their initial disbelief turned into anger, and they decided to force the issue. They called upon the Indian National Congress to boycott British and, more particularly, Canadian goods. They also presented direct challenges to test the legality of Canada's restrictive immigration act. The first was Judge Hunter's verdict on Narain Singh's case (December, 1913). To the amazement of many British Columbians, Judge Hunter of the Supreme Court, when appealed, ordered the release of some 49 East Indian immigrants on the basis that the Immigration Act of 1910 was invalid on technical grounds. The second case was the heartbreaking *Komagata Maru* incident. The Province's Supreme Court unanimously ruled against the immigrants on board the *Komagata Maru* that they were illegal, and subsequently they were all forced to return to the East at gun point. The *Komagata Maru* incident effectively closed the door to East Indian immigration.[34]

The disillusionment of the East Indians was slow but real and bitter. It slowly dawned on them, almost like a man coming out of stupor, that Britain had little or no intention of fulfilling her pledge to the Indian people, and that she had been hypocritical all along. "British-ness" no longer stood for "justice and fairness" but for "hyprocisy and deceit." Perhaps the East Indians in Canada had no valid basis for their obstinate faith in Britain's justice and fairness. They had the examples of Australia and South Africa before their eyes.[35] In the study of imperial history, often it is sad but fascinating to observe the supreme but naive confidence that many Indians had in Britain's pledge to India, and then their gradual and at times sudden disillusion-ment that Britain never meant what she said. In defence of Britain, how-ever, one may point out that hyprocisy is a sin of the "saint" and not the "sinner," and morally speaking the "hypocrite" is on a higher plan than the "realist."[36]

The struggle to gain admission for the wives and families of the resident East Indians was just part of the wider campaign to keep Canada open for East Indians, but it was peculiarly intensive and highly emotional. The dominant society wanted to undo the "wrong" that had been already done. By keeping the women out, it hoped to purge Canada of the East Indian element within a generation. For "the comfort and happiness of the generations that are to succeed us," it was argued, "we must not permit their women to come in at all."[37] The exclusion of women, it was hoped, would induce many men to leave Canada and the ones who refused to leave would be prevented from "defiling the land" with their progeny.

Unlike the wider campaign, the struggle to obtain admission for the wives and children enjoyed a degree of support from the Canadian public. In fact, east of the Rockies, except for labour unions, nearly every other group favoured the admission of the "Hindu wives."[38] Even those who suggested repatriation to solve the "Hindu problem" conceded the East Indian men's right to bring their wives and children if they could not be repatriated.[39] To a certain extent it was this support that forced the Government to rescind the deportation order against the two women and their children who had arrived with their returning husbands in January, 1912, and permitted them to remain in Canada "as an act of grace . . . and without establishing a pre-cedent."[40]

This favourable response in the East was largely due to the effort of persons like Dr. Sunder Singh, Rev. Hall, and Isabella Ross Broad.

Singh was responsible for creating a favourable climate in university circles and clubs such as the Empire Club and the Canadian Club. Hall and especially Broad made considerable impact on the church-going Christians.[41] But, where it mattered most, west of the Rockies, even the Ministerial Association voted to keep the East Indian women out lest a "Hindu colony" emerge in a "Christian country."[42]

Final victory became a possibility as a result of the adjustment in the imperial relation caused by the pressure of the Great War. Indians now represented India in the Imperial Council. The Imperial Conference of 1917 intervened on behalf of the East Indians, and Ottawa agreed to give serious consideration to the matter, thus two years later in 1919, resident East Indian men were allowed to bring their wives and children under the age of 21. Data for 1920 to 1923 is shown in Table II.

TABLE II

East Indian Immigration to Canada:
Wives and Children

YEAR	WOMEN	CHILDREN
1920	—	—
1921	2	1
1922	4	4
1923	5	4

Source: Eric Morse, *Immigration and Status of British East in Canada.*

The struggle to gain political equality did not end until the time when the British East Indians ceased to be British. It began as soon as East Indians were denied the franchise. In the early days East Indians did exercise their political rights, since names of some of them appear on the voters' list.[43] The arrival of a large number of East Indians in 1906 and the possibility that they might participate in the forthcoming provincial election caused grave concern and there arose the cry that the polls were "unprotected against the Hindus."[44] The result was the Bowser amendment to the Election Act which simply added "Hindus" to other "Asian undesirables," Chinese and Japanese, who had already been disenfranchised.[45] In the following year (1908), the civic charter was also amended to exclude East Indians.[46] These amendments did not go without any protest. At least there was one protest march in Vancouver demanding re-enfranchisement of East Indians (1910). Prime Minister Laurier complained,

> These men have been taught by a certain school of politics that they were the equals of British subjects. Unfortunately, they are brought to face the hard fact when it is too late.[47]

However the agitation over disenfranchisement was neither popular nor permanent. The urgency to gain entry for the wives and children took precedence over the concern for political rights.

The denial of political rights was not without economic handicaps. As the provincial voters' list was the basis for both provincial and municipal government contracts, East Indians were prevented from bidding for them. They were also denied direct or indirect employment. East Indians, along with other Asiatics, were also excluded from the sale of Crown timber. Those professions which used the voters' list as the basis of admission, such as education, law and pharmacy, were also closed to them. East Indians could not serve as jurors as well. Admittedly, these disabilities made little or no difference to the first generation of East Indians, but it did have an effect on the second and succeeding generations. Above all, these were constant reminders of their second class status in the land of their adoption.[48]

Demands for political equality became increasingly loud after the Indians obtained seats at the Imperial Conference. The Indian representatives had the habit of reproving their Canadian colleagues for their failure to live up to imperial responsibilities.[49] The plight of the East Indians also invited criticism from successive distinguished Indian visitors to Canada, which was always an embarrassment to their hosts.[50] But Ottawa unfailingly pleaded provincial autonomy. Some British Columbian politicians, in private, admitted the unreasonableness of denying the franchise to the East Indians,[51] but no one dared to propose it in public until the C.C.F. came forward in the 1930s. Among the academics, H. F. Angus, professor at the University of British Columbia, pleaded the cause of the East Indians and other Asians, pointing out that British Columbia's treatment of them was both unjust and unwise.[52] In general, the East Indians themselves had become quite disillusioned with the futility of protests and appeals, yet the lamp of hope was kept alive by people like Kartar Singh, the Hundel Brothers, and Dr. D. P. Pandia.

The final thrust in the struggle to obtain political equality did not come until the Indian independence movement was in its final stage. In the early 1940s, the East Indian community had some strong leaders, and it also had the support of the C.C.F. The international climate was changing as a result of the Nazi ideology and the War. The myth of Aryan superiority, so long used to keep the non-whites in second-class status, had become an object of shame and remorse. Above all, there emerged the imminent prospect of an independent

India which might not remain indifferent in the plight of its emigrants in Canada. The combination of all these factors necessitated "a change of heart in B.C." and made possible the repeal of the discriminatory clause in the Election Act (1947). Within a short while, the East Indians were given the municipal franchise as well.[53]

The fortunes of East Indians in Canada were closely tied to the fate of their homeland, India. As long as India remained in the state of dependency, the appeals and remonstrances of East Indians in Canada went unheeded. Only as India was able to assert itself politically, the grievances of Indians in Canada were heeded and re-dressed. There is a lot of truth in Nkrumah's motto, the first President of Ghana, "Seek ye first the political kingdom and all these things shall be added to you." The day India became politically free, East Indians ceased to be second-class citizens in Canada. The tragedy of the East Indian experience in Canada is that the rights and privileges for which East Indians struggled for so long came to them only when the basis of their claims became obsolete: British rights and privileges were theirs only when they ceased to be British subjects and citizens.

NOTES

1. The Character Acts, The Queen's Proclamation etc.

2. The expression "Brown Children" was first used by Western educated Indians in the latter part of the 19th century.

3. Herbert Butterfield, *Christianity and History*, p. 86. London: G. Bell, 1954.

4. Immanuel Kant, *Groundwork of the Metaphysics of Morals*. New York: Harper and Row, 1964.

5. Jogesh C. Misrow, *East Indian Immigration to the Pacific Coast.* (Stanford, Calif., May, 1915), p. 2.

6. *Ibid.*

7. Quoted in I. M. Muthanna, *People of India in North America,* Vol. 1, Bangalore: Lotus Printing House, 1975, p. 3.

8. Saint N. Singh, a visiting journalist from the Punjab, stated in 1906 that to his knowledge all the East Indian immigrants were from the Punjab except one who was from Nepal. *The Daily Province,* November 14, 1906, p. 6. However, there were some Moslems and at least one Hindu among the early immigrants. Muhmad Khan was described as "a long time resident." *Ibid.,* May 21, September 19. There was also Imam Dhinn. Muthanna, *op. cit.,* pp. 134-135. The editor and publisher of *Free Hindustan* (Vancouver, 1908), the first Indo-Canadian paper, was a Bengali Hindu.

9. J. C. Misrow, p. 2.

10. *Ibid.*

11. *The Province,* November 14, 1906, p. 6, A Report by Saint N. Singh *The Colonist,* Sept., 1906, p. 3.

12. I. M. Muthanna, op. cit., pp. 21-22; R. A. Button, *Sikh Settlement in The Lower Mainland of B.C.,* p. 11; William Mackenzie King, *Report on His Mission to England . . . On the Subject of Immigration* (1908). Besides the retired soldiers, many who came from the Far East were ex-policemen or watchmen. The ones who came directly from India were "chiefly peasants and farmers, straight from their rural farms in the villages," Saint N. Singh's Report, *Ibid.* See also J. C. Misrow, *op. cit.,* pp. 2-3.

13. See the Four Victoria and Vancouver dailies, *The Colonist, The Times, The Province,* and *The World* for the years from 1906 to 1908. Among the four dailies, the *Province* appears to have been the most notorious in maligning the "Hindus." The *World* was very sensational, and not particularly vicious against the "Hindus." The earlier immigrants did not attract any attention as they came in small numbers. Saint N. Singh's Report, *Ibid.* The first complaint against East Indians was made in the winter of 1905-1906. A reference to this complaint is found in the issue of August 23, 1906 (p. 1), *The Province.*

14. See the March and November issues of the *Province,* 1908.

15. There are numerous references to these complaints in nearly all the periodicals of the time. Some labour spokesmen alleged the Oriental immigration to be a "capitalist plot." This accusation is interesting in view of the fact that so often today the leftists denounce racism as the product of a capitalist system. The capitalists never win!

16. W. L. Mackenzie King's Report. Earlier, the Indian Government was asked to legislate against Indians emigrating to Canada. The Indian Government politely declined to take any direct measures to prevent the emigration, but it offered otherwise to co-operate with the Canadian Government's request. The steamship companies which were involved in fostering interest in emigration to Canada were informed that their activities were not viewed "with favour" by any of the Governments concerned, British, Canadian or Indian. Further, prospective emigrants were told how dreadful life was in Canada for East Indians and warned that they might not be allowed to emigrate as the laws and other provisions in Canada were not sufficient for their protection and welfare. (The Indian Emigration Act, 1883, declared that a person would not be allowed to emigrate to any country whose laws and other provisions were not sufficient to the protection and welfare of Indians).

    The Canadian Government also asked the steamship companies not to sell tickets to East Indians if their destination was some point in Canada. In most cases, the companies agreed to co-operate with the Canadian Government.

17. Quoted in E. E. Smillie, "An Historical Survey of Indian Migration Within the Empire," *CHR*, IV, 3 (September, 1923), pp. 217-257.

18. The 23rd article of the Act stated, "No court, and no judge or officer thereof, shall have jurisdiction to review, quash, reverse, restrain or otherwise interfere with any proceeding, decision or order of the Minister or any Board of Inquiry, or officer in charge, had made or given under the authority and in accordance with the provisions of this Act relating to the detention or deportation of any rejected immigrant, passenger, or other person, upon any ground whatsoever unless such person is a Canadian citizen or has Canadian domicile." Quoted in Robie L. Reid, "The Inside Story of the 'Komagata Maru'," *The British Columbia Historical Quarterly*, V. 1 (January, 1942), 1-23.

19. *Ibid.*

20. Principal Mackey, "Problem of Immigration," *The Westminster Hall Magazine* (July, 1914), pp. 5-9.

21. Numerous references may be cited. Just few references are given. *House of Commons Debates* (1914), pp. 1220-1260; the *Province*, 17-6-1914, p. 6 (Editorial), 8-12-1914, p. (Editorial), 5-3-1912, p. 6 (Editorial-, 27-5-1914, p. 6 (Editorial); *The Westminster Hall Magazine* (July, 1914), pp. 5-9; W. L. Mackenzie King's Report; H. H. Stevens, Oriental Problem. Peter Ward, "White Canada Forever: British Columbia's Response to Orientals," 1858-1914 (Ph.D. Dissertation, Queen's, 1974), pp. 141-146, 190-192, 224-256.

22. The *Daily Colonist*, February 27, 1908, p. 4 (Editorial); See also Peter Ward, op. cit., pp. 259-260.

23. Those people who argued that "if the good Lord had intended Orientals and 'Whites' to live in the same country, He would not have put the Pacific ocean between them" quite conveniently failed to remember that the same good Lord had also put the Atlantic ocean between the Whites and the Reds to keep them apart.

24. Same as #21. K. K. Kawakami, "Canada as a White Man's Country," *Current History* (1924), p. 830; *The Monetary Times*, 17-2-1912, p. 719.

25. Quoted in Peter Ward, op. cit., p. 143 (A letter from Sivertz to Frank Oliver, 17-12-1906).

26. *The Colonist*, September 13, 1907, p. 4 (Editorial).

27. *The Western Methodist Recorder* (July, 1914), p. 12; *The Province*, December 8, 1914, p. 6 (Editorial); Jan. 5, 1912, p. 1; *House of Commons Debates* (1914), pp. 1251-1253; *Literary Digest*, August 8, 1914, p. 226. H. H. Stevens, Oriental Problem; *The Vancouver Sun*, June 17, 1913, p. 6. See also Peter Ward, *loc. cit.*

28. *The Province*, Feb. 12, 1912, p. 1; I. M. Muthanna, *op. cit.*, p. 154; Peter Ward, *op. cit.*, pp. 259-260. A letter from Dr. Scott to Prime Minister Borden, Jan. 5, 1912; *The Presbyterian Record* (September,

1906), p. 398; *The Vancouver Sun,* June 17, 1913, p. 6 (Editorial); James Woodsworth, *Strangers Within Our Gate,* Toronto: Methodist Church of Canada, 1909, p. 277.

29. Saint N. Singh's Report, *Ibid.*

30. This is the impression one forms in reading the relevant contemporary literature. See *India's Appeal to Canada:* Dr. Sunder Singh's addresses in the Empire and the Canadian Clubs; Quotes in I. M. Muthanna's, *op. cit.*

31. East Indian leaders presented their case to the Canadian public through the medium of pamphlets, university centres, service clubs, and church groups. They also had papers in English; this must have reached largely only the "converted."

32. A Hindu Canadian, *India's Appeal to Canada.*

33. For example see *India's Appeal to Canada:* Isabella Ross Broad, *The Sikhs in Canada* (a Pamphlet, 1915); also *The Province,* December 10, 1908, p. 1.

34. On May 23, 1914, the Japanese ship *Komagata Maru* anchored in Vancouver harbour. Its 376 East Indian passengers, including the leader Gurdit Singh, sought admission into Canada on the basis of their "citizenship" in the Empire. As expected, the vast majority of the people of Vancouver and the immigration authorities were determined to keep the passengers on board from landing. The dispute was taken by the Supreme Court of British Columbia, and later the Federal Government intervened. Only the returning passengers were allowed to land, and others on board were ordered home. When the immigration authorities tried to go aboard the vessel to implement the order, they were badly beaten up by the frustrated passengers. Subsequently, one-half of Canada's new navy was dispatched to execute the Government's order. On August 8, the *Komagata Maru* was escorted to the high seas. For a full discussion on the *Komagata Maru* incident see Ted Ferguson, *A White Man's Country* (An Exercise in Canadian Prejudice) Toronto: Doubleday Canada Ltd., 1975. See also Eric Morse, "Some Aspects of the Komagata Maru Affairs, 1914," *CHA Report,* 1936, pp. 100-108; Eric Morse, "Immigration and Status of British East Indians in Canada," M.A. Thesis, Queen's, 1936; I. M. Muthanna, *op. cit.*

35. Some pointed out that many of the East Indians in Canada were simple people, unfamiliar with the game of politics, and that is why they held on to their faith in Britain's fairness. (See *India's Appeal To Canada*)

36. "Realist" — defined as one who glorifies pragmatism and makes no pretension of moral or altruistic values or principles.

37. *The Vancouver Sun,* June 5, 1913; June 17, 1913; *The Province,* March 5, 1912.

38. I. M. Muthanna, op. cit., pp. 152-159, 183.

39. Ibid., p. 155 (Professor T. L. Walker of the University of Toronto suggested free passage and $500 cash compensation per person for voluntary repatriation.)

40. The two women, wives of Bhag Singh and Balwant Singh, and their children arrived in Vancouver on January 22, 1912, with their returning husbands. The husbands were allowed to return to their homes as they had Canadian domicile but the wives and children were detailed for deportation. They were freed on bail later. Their plight was taken up by the entire East Indian community and their sympathizers, and it became the object of many deliberations in several places in Canada as well as in London, England, and New Delhi, India. After several months of uncertainty, the families' nightmare came to an end with intervention by Parliament. I. M. Muthanna, *op. cit.*, pp. 147-159; House of Commons Debates (1912) N. 2457.

41. See Peter Ward, *op. cit.*, pp. 224-256; Also Isabella Broad, *op. cit.* for her moving appeal.

42. *The Province*, April 30, 1912.

43. *The Province*, October 22, 1906, p. 1 (e.g. Herman Singh, Bhola Singh).

44. *Ibid.*, October 17, 1906.

45. *Ibid.*, March 20, 1907.

46. I. M. Muthanna, op. cit., pp. 130-131. No specific reason was given at that time, but later the ones who were against the East Indian franchise said that East Indians were British subjects and not British citizens. H. H. Stevens was perhaps the originator of this view. *The Province* echoed Steven's view. But Stevens confessed that not many people accept his neat distinction between the citizen and the subject. *The Province*, 20-3-1907; 27-5-1914; *House of Commons* Debate (1914), 1237. It was also stated that franchise is a conferred right and not an inherent British right. See Eric Morse's M.A. thesis.

47. I. M. Muthanna, *op. cit.*, pp. 130-131.

48. Quoted in Eric Morse, *op. cit.*, p. 82.

49. H. F. Angus, "The Legal Status in British Columbia of Residents of Oriental Race and their Descendants," *The Canadian Bar Review*, IX, 1 (Jan. 1931), 1-12; "Underprivileged Canadians," *Queen's Quarterly*, 1931, pp. 445-460.

50. John Norris, *Strangers Entertained:* A History of the Ethnic Groups of British Columbia. Vancouver: Evergreen, p. 233. See Kar Singh's *Canada and India* (Monthly Journal); also Eric Morse's M.A. thesis.

51. "Asiatic Immigration into Canada," *The Round Table Conference*, March 1923.

52. See his many articles.

53. John Norris, op. cit., p. 233; *The Vancouver Sun*, 3-3-1943; 16-3-1944; 28-3-1945; 21-4-1948; April ?, 1947; see *The Province* on these days;

The Montreal Star, 6-2-1947; *Canadian Business,* 1952, p. 124; H. E. Angus, "East Indians in Canada," *International Journal* (Winter, 1946-1947); The repeal of the amendment was successful on the third attempt. The CCF was the force that was behind it, although it wasn't a party vote.

See also John F. Hilliker, "The War, The Vote and Canadian Relations With India, 1939-1945." A Paper Presented at the CSAS Meeting, 1976; James Eayrs, *In Defence of Canada: Peacemaking and Deterrence* (Toronto, 1972), pp. 226-242.

7

The Illusion of Toleration: White Opinions of Asians in British Columbia, 1929-37

Patricia E. Roy
University of Victoria

On the morning of November 27, 1929 — just a month after the Great Crash — about thirty men, including the president of the Union of British Columbia Municipalities who was chairman of the meeting, gathered at the Hotel Vancouver. Among those present were municipal politicians from the Fraser Valley and Vancouver Island, the provincial minister of agriculture, the president of the Vancouver Board of Trade and representatives of the Farmers' Institutes, the B.C. Fishermen's Protective Association, the Retail Merchants Association of B.C. and the Native Sons of B.C. Most of these organizations had been actively involved in anti-Asian agitation in the past; their objective that November day was to found yet another in the long line of anti-Asian groups in British Columbia. The White Canada Association sought legislation to "prevent further Oriental penetration in British Columbia, and reduce the present menace to our national life . . ."[1] Despite its auspicious beginning, its plans to establish a broadly-based organization, and the prolific pen of its secretary, C. E. Hope,[2] who claimed the presence

81

of Asians created unemployment among British Columbia whites,[3] the White Canada Association never became more than a small "research group."[4]

What does the failure of the White Canada Association to secure the support of either the provincial government or the public at large and the relative absence of public discussion of the "Oriental Question" during the early 1930s suggest? First, it tends to confirm a hypothesis that when British Columbians faced other unrelated crises, racial agitators had difficulty in attracting widespread attention. During the 1914-1918 war, for example, anti-Asian agitation was also sporadic and was confined to a few local areas. And, in the early 1930s, coping with the Depression was a more immediate problem than the "Oriental Question." Second, and this is the theme of this paper, it indicates that white British Columbians were beginning to tolerate their Asian neighbours. New immigration regulations and continued restrictions on the economic activities of Asians in the province relieved many British Columbia worries about an "Oriental Menace." Yet, while British Columbians seemed to forget their old hostilities, their prejudices were so deeply ingrained that Japan's endeavours to acquire a Greater East Asia Co-Prosperity Sphere revived old fears. Toleration proved to have shallow, illusory roots.

In contrast to earlier times and to the late 1930s, there was little reaction to incidents which, on other occasions, would have provoked widespread outbursts of anti-Asian feelings. Some examples will illustrate the point. In the federal election of 1921, the "Oriental Question" was widely discussed; in 1935, the Oriental franchise was an issue in several constituencies. In 1930, Asians were scarcely mentioned and then only in three constituencies.[5] Rumours of illegal Asian immigration were long part of the stock in trade of anti-Asian agitators; public reaction to 1937-8 rumours of illegal Japanese immigration forced the federal government to appoint a special board of inquiry to investigate. In 1931, the conviction of the Japanese interpreter of the Department of Immigration in Vancouver on charges of conspiracy to violate immigration laws stimulated little comment. Even before the First World War, stories of Japanese plans to attack the coast circulated;[6] in late 1937, allegations of Japanese naval officers disguising themselves as fishermen set off a new round of anti-Japanese agitation.[7] A pamphlet published in 1932 with the provocative title, *Japan: The Octopus of the East and It's [sic] Menace to Canada* received scant notice, and parliamentary references to Japanese spies by A. W. Neill (Independent, Comox-Alberni) and Thomas Reid (Liberal, New West-minster) elicited no comment in British Columbia.[8] In the 1920s, British Columbia Members of Parliament, such as H. H. Stevens

(Conservative, Vancouver City), successfully campaigned for Chinese exclusion legislation; in 1938, British Columbia M.P.s again ignored party allegiances and pressed for the extension of the Chinese Immigration Act of the Japanese. In 1931, Stevens urged Prime Minister Bennett to relax some provisions of the Chinese Immigration Act.[9] In the retail trade, white merchants were in the forefront of the agitation for restrictions on Asian immigration in the 1920s; in Vancouver, at least, they were among those most concerned with the Japanese presence in the late 1930s. Nevertheless, the representative of the B.C. Retail Merchants Association, who appeared before the Mass Buying Committee of the House of Commons in 1934, had only one objection to Asian merchants — their use of cut flowers as loss leaders![10]

There was considerable other evidence of the marketplace accommodating itself to the presence of Asians. In the late 1920s, socialists within the Vancouver Trades and Labour Council persuaded that body to accept some Japanese members, the Vancouver Camp and Mill Workers, to share in the common struggle against capitalist employers.[11] After a lively debate at the 1931 convention, the Camp and Mill Workers persuaded the Trades and Labour Congress of Canada to change its platform of Asiatic exclusion.[12] A better example of organized labour adjusting to Asian competition was the Vancouver-based Shingle Weavers Union. This union once tried to eliminate Chinese workers from shingle mills; in 1935, it increased its membership tenfold by granting an associate charter to Chinese workers and by discontinuing the "contract" system by which Chinese worked for substandard wages under the direction of a "boss."[13] White fishermen no longer unanimously opposed Japanese fishermen and, in several instances, actually urged a relaxation of license restrictions affecting Japanese fishermen.[14] Many farmers also began co-operating with their Chinese and Japanese neighbours. After the provincial government passed a new Natural Products Marketing Act in 1934, Asians and whites in several areas tried to make it work. At Vernon in the Okanagan Valley, Chinese and Japanese joined other vegetable growers in forming a local marketing board. So successful was this board in getting good prices, the *Vernon News* described the "Oriental brains" guiding the board as "the sensation of the marketing season thus far."[15] In the Fraser Valley, where Japanese produced about eighty-five percent of the berry crop, a small fruit and rhubarb marketing board formed by Japanese and white growers in 1935 worked well and, even after it fell apart, inter-racial co-operation continued.

Appearances of accommodation were deceiving; suggestions of toleration usually had a qualifier or explanation. The Trades and

Labour Congress only modified its stand on Asian immigration by substituting the phrase, the "exclusion of all races which cannot properly be assimilated into the national life of Canada" for the old term, "Asiatic exclusion."[16] This change demonstrated concern for Japanese sensitivities but, by not defining "assimilation," it satisfied those who feared an "open door" immigration policy. On the Fraser River, white fishermen called for a renewal of the federal programme reducing the number of fishing licenses issued to Japanese. Their member of parliament, Thomas Reid, claimed Japanese fishermen were building "up a part of Japan on the Canadian Pacific Coast."[17] In agriculture, Chinese potato growers were frequent scapegoats for problems with marketing laws and procedures. In the Vernon area, inter-racial co-operation failed when the Chinese complained the marketing board forced them to accept lower prices.[18] In the Fraser Valley berry industry, it succeeded only because the Japanese were so dominant, white growers had little choice but to co-operate.

And, the suggestion of H. H. Stevens and others that restrictions on Chinese immigration be relaxed were limited to regulations affecting merchant and student visitors, not to permanent immigrants. Canada's minister to Japan, Canadian delegates to the Kyoto conference of the Institute of Pacific Relations, and businessmen on a Chamber of Commerce tour of the Orient discovered that the Chinese Immigration Act insulted the Chinese people and, by deterring merchants and students, impeded trade. As the *Victoria Times* noted,

> If there is any disposition therefore to raise the Oriental exclusion cry now, it will be wise of those who raise it to bear in mind the important consideration . . . [of trade] . . . to remember that the unemployment problem — in fact our economic recovery — depends largely upon more commerce between the Dominion and the Orient.[19]

The desire for trade certainly contributed to the adjustments in the attitudes of white British Columbians towards the Chinese and Japanese, but the main reason for change was a reduction of cessation of many of the fears which had long underlain their hostilities to Asians. In the marketplace, the activities of Asians had been partially restricted. The fishing industry provides the best example. In 1923, the federal government, responding to British Columbia pressure, began reducing the number of fishing licenses issued to Japanese. The courts, after a Japanese challenge, eventually ruled against this policy. Nevertheless, the proportion of Japanese salmon fishermen declined from approximately thirty-eight percent in 1922 to approximately fourteen percent in 1931.[20] In addition, there was increasing recognition that by forcing Asians out of one industry, the government was merely moving them into another. "We haven't diminished their number," claimed the Vancouver *Province,* "we have simply pushed them about."[21] Although it was never explicitly stated, there was also recognition that the Depression was world-wide, that British Columbia was no worse off than areas which had no Asian competitors for jobs.[22]

The main reason for a change in attitude, however, was the fact that Asian immigration had all but stopped. While the number of Japanese in the province was increasing as the result of a high birth rate (there was little reaction to vital statistics reports of it),[23] revisions to the Gentlemen's Agreement in 1928 had reduced the number of Japanese immigrants to a maximum of 150 per year. The Chinese Immigration Act in 1923 virtually excluded Chinese. Since ninety-one percent of the twenty-seven thousand Chinese in the province were males, many of whom were elderly, the Chinese population was beginning to decline.[24] The New Westminster *British Columbian,* a newspaper traditionally hostile to the Asian presence, observed,

> There is not a burning hatred of the Chinese and the Japanese as such in the white breast. When these trans-Pacific voyagers are so reduced in number as to form only a small proportion of the population, when their presence does not endanger the white man's chance of earning a livelihood, they will be treated with equanimity.[25]

The nature of the "Oriental Problem" had also changed; a growing proportion of the Asians in the province, especially the Japanese, were Canadian-born. The Vancouver *Province* noted:

> It is becoming increasingly a problem of our own people of Chinese and Japanese born in Canada, educated in Canadian public and high schools, and in everything but descent more Canadian than Oriental. ... What are we going to do about them?[26]

Even A. W. Neill, no lover of the Japanese, after telling Parliament that "more trouble is caused by the stork than by the immigrant ship," quickly added, "we have them and we must put up with them."[27]

There are a number of examples of hesitant steps towards toleration of Canadian-born Asians who were still largely a youthful group[28] and whose presence was most evident in the schools. In the past, Victoria had attempted to establish segregated schools; later in the decade, Alderman Halford Wilson of Vancouver, and others, cited the existence of Japanese language schools as evidence of Japanese disloyalty. In contrast, in the early 1930s, the few comments on Asians in the school system suggested they were being accepted into Canadian society. Following inspection of cadets at Vancouver's Strathcona

School, Brigadier J. Sutherland Brown commented that "the orientals, particularly the Japanese were much smarter than others of the Company, particularly in physical training."[29] This multi-racial school regarded itself as a "melting pot" trying "to make good Canadian citizens" of its students.[30] The idea of assimilation was not confined to this unique school. Fraser Valley school trustees who had been concerned about Japanese language schools decided that Canadian-born Japanese would soon be "absorbed" into the Canadian race.[31]

Assimilation, however, did not extend to intermarriage. Although a discussion at a Student Christian Movement Conference, for example, concluded that intermarriage might solve the problem of the second generation Japanese, old ideas died hard. Rev. Hugh Dobson, chairman of the United Church's B.C. Conference on Racial Relations, agreed there had been many successful interracial marriages, but said he "would be offended by the entrance of an Oriental into his family."[32]

Nevertheless, church groups accepted Chinese and Japanese in their young people's activities.[33] In 1929, at the Christmas session of the Older Boys' Parliament, a United Church-sponsored group, a Chinese and a Japanese boy were present as elected delegates. Their presence scandalized some weekly newspaper editors. Yet, when C. F. Davie M.L.A. (Conservative, Cowichan-Newcastle) described their presence as a desecration of the Legislative Chamber, he aroused considerable anger rather than the widespread support he would have enjoyed a few years earlier. The Kamloops *Sentinel,* for example, welcomed the competition in the schools provided by Chinese and Japanese children, praised their manners and morals, and urged, "let us be fair and get rid of our racial prejudices."[34] Later, the presence of young Asians at the Older Boys' Parliament was cited as a precedent for admitting Asian girls to the nurses' training programme at the Vancouver General Hospital.[35]

The practical test of assimilation was the franchise. The 1931 decision of the Legislature, albeit by a single vote, to enfranchise about eighty Japanese veterans of the Canadian Expeditionary Force appeared to be the first step towards the elimination of barriers to Chinese and Japanese enjoying civil rights in British Columbia. It is an "act of justice," declared the Victoria *Times,* but then added, it does "not involve any fundamental departure from our electoral system."[36] A few voices did call for the extension of the franchise to all native-born Canadians.[37] The most outspoken of these was H. F. Angus, a professor of economics and political science at the University of British Columbia and an active participant in the Institute of Pacific Relations. By 1934, Professor Angus was speaking to service clubs and other groups as diverse as the W.C.T.U. and the Ad and Sales Bureau of the Vancouver Board of Trade. Some of these groups endorsed his arguments but others, such as the nativistic Native Sons of British Columbia, retained their rigid opposition to any idea of assimilation.[38]

The public might have continued to regard Angus as merely a voice from the ivory tower but in 1934, J. S. Woodsworth, the founder of the C.C.F., unwittingly revived old prejudices when he told Parliament he thought the "oriental ought to be able to vote in British Columbia."[39] Later, he told a Vancouver audience there was "no excuse in a civilized country" for refusing "fair play" to the Orientals within it.[40] The issue divided the C.C.F. and gave the Liberals and Conservatives plentiful ammunition to use in several constituencies against the newly-formed but popular C.C.F. during the 1935 federal election. Liberal and Conservative candidates warned that once the Orientals got the vote, they would be elected to the Legislature and to Parliament, would repeal laws (including those relating to immigration) designed to protect the white population and would appoint Orientals to important government jobs. In the course of the election, almost every old anti-Asian bogey was revived.[41] Once the election was over, anti-Asian agitation declined. The franchise issue had little effect in most constituencies but it reminded the electorate of old antagonisms.

External events then intruded. The Manchurian Affair had drawn little comment in British Columbia but by the summer and fall of 1937, regular newspaper reports of Japanese advances and atrocities in China revived anti-Asian agitation. First-hand accounts from white refugees who passed through Victoria and Vancouver en route to their Eastern Canadian or British homes, brought the matter close to home. As old fears of a Japanese attack re-appeared, British Columbians became especially responsive to rumours of Japanese spies and illegal immigrants.

The illusion of toleration which appeared at the beginning of the decade was rapidly being eroded by 1937. Those who favoured admitting the Canadian-born Asians into some privileges of citizenship faced bitter attack. Those who encouraged toleration for trade's sake were discouraged by serious disruptions in trade caused by the Sino-Japanese war. And, as farmers and merchants continued to suffer from the Depression, they again found the Chinese to be convenient scapegoats. Yet, even in 1935 and 1936, anti-Asian agitation was somewhat sporadic and tended to be confined to particular issues and particular areas of the province. There was one significant change. In the past, white British Columbians had attacked both Chinese and Japanese; now, they focussed their hostilities primarily on the Japanese who seemed to be a much greater threat. Despite talk of relaxing immigration restrictions, despite evidence of economic co-operation, and despite sympathetic consideration of the problems of Canadian-born Asians, toleration had been a fragile, illusory quality. It could exist only when white British Columbians felt free of any threat from Asians or from Asia.

NOTES

1. "Minutes of Meeting Held in the Hotel Vancouver, November 27, 1929," Copy in Provincial Archives of British Columbia (hereafter PABC), Premier's Official Correspondence, 1929, File 60, "Oriental Matters."

    The meeting called for provincial laws to prohibit Orientals from owning or leasing more land, for federal action to insure that Orientals were not included on the revised federal voters' lists and to check on alleged illegal Chinese immigration. Two weeks later, a White Canada Association delegation met the provincial cabinet to press their request for legislation against Oriental land ownership as the first step towards restricting the occupations in which Orientals could engage in British Columbia. (*Vancouver Daily Province*, 10 December 1929).

2. Born in England, Hope had resided in British Columbia since 1888. A sometime architect, land surveyor, realtor and farmer, he made the White Canada Association a retirement hobby. He had been speaking out against Asians in the province since at least 1914. During the 1930s he regularly wrote to the Department of Immigration in Ottawa reporting the presence of illegal Chinese and Japanese immigrants but, when questioned, could not provide precise details. (A. L. Joliffe, memo for T. A. Crerar, 23 September 1937, Public Archives of Canada (hereafter PAC), Department of Immigration Records, RG 76, Accn 69/17, File 462223).

    Hope also published several articles in the national press: "Canada's Oriental Province," *The Country Guide,* 1 November 1930; "British Columbia's Racial Problem," *McLean's* 1 and 15 February 1930; C. E. Hope and W. K. Earle, "The Oriental Threat," *McLean's* 1 May 1933.

3. C. E. Hope to W. A. Gordon, 3 September 1930, PAC, RG 76 Accn 69/17, File 462223; Hope to R. B. Bennett, 30 March 1931 and Hope to T. A. Crerar, 28 February 1936, *Ibid.*

4. Hope to Herbert Marler, 23 November 1935, PAC, Department of External Affairs Records, RG 25 G1, File 105-35.
    Hope attributed the absence of support for his Association to businessmen's fears of unspecified Japanese reprisals and to a "feeling of what's the use, Ottawa will do nothing." (Hope to W. A. Gordon, 5 June 1931, PAC, RG 76, Accn 69/17, File 462223.)

5. The Liberals apparently dropped plans to list the curtailment of Chinese immigration as one of their accomplishments before the 1930

federal election. "Memorandum on Liberal Action on Federal Labour Matters. Proposed, 1930." PAC, W. L. M. King Papers, Memorandum and Notes, File 785, #C81763. The advertisements of A. W. Neill, who usually supported the Liberals, boasted of having tackled the Oriental Question of ending Chinese immigration and of restricting Japanese immigration and fishing. (*Comox Argus*, 17 July 1930; *Port Alberni News*, 17 July 1930). The only other constituencies in which Asians were mentioned were New Westminster and Fraser Valley.

6.   See for example, a serial story "The Pacific War of 1910" by C. H. Stuart Wade which began in *Westward Ho Magazine*, Vol. IV (June 1909).

7.   On agitation in the 1920's and 1930's see Patricia E. Roy, "Educating the 'East': British Columbia and the Oriental Question in the inter-war Years," *BC Studies*, no. 18 (Summer 1973).

8.   F. Leighton Thomas, *Japan: The Octopus of the East and It's* (*sic*) *Menace to Canada* (Vancouver, n.p., 1932). In his pamphlet Thomas recited such tales as that of Takihashi, a high Japanese officer who, after working as bookkeeper and clerk at a small Vancouver Island hotel, returned to Japan to lecture the Japanese army on the ease of attacking British Columbia.

Canada, House of Commons, *Debates*, 28 April 1933, p. 4423; Reid's statement caused some diplomatic embarrassment when the Japanese government unofficially complained that no Canadian official challenged Reid's claim.

For Neill, see *Debates*, 29 May 1936, p. 3249 and *Comox Argus*, 17 October 1929.

9.   H. H. Stevens to R. B. Bennett, 15 January 1931, PAC, R. B. Bennett Papers, vol. 366, #241841.

10.   On the campaign of the merchants, see Patricia E. Roy, "Protecting their Pocketbooks and Preserving their Race: White Merchants and Oriental Competition," in *Cities in the West*, ed. by A. R. McCormack and Ian MacPherson (Ottawa, National Museum, 1975), pp. 116-138.

11.   See Paul Phillips, *No Power Greater: A Century of Labour in British Columbia* (Vancouver, B.C. Federation of Labour, 1967), p. 100. Phillips notes the divisive effect this had on the labour movement.

12.   *Vancouver Daily Province*, 24 September 1931.

13.   The United States National Recovery Act forced B.C. mills to maintain wages and working conditions in line with those in the United States if they wished to continue to export their products. Within the province, the Male Minimum Wage Act had been in effect in the lumber industry since 1925. See also Vancouver *News-Herald*, 15 August 1933 and *The Commonwealth*, 20 September 1935.

14.   For example, *The Commonwealth*, 28 December 1934; *Province*, 22 and 24 November 1932. See also Hozumi Yonemura, "Japanese

Fisherman in British Columbia and British Fair-Play," *Canadian Forum*, vol. X (July 1930), p. 367.

15. *Vernon News*, 12 July 1934.

16. *Province*, 24 September 1931.

17. Canada, House of Commons, *Debates*, 28 April 1933, p. 4423.

18. Kamloops *Sentinel*, 6 September 1935.

19. 31 March 1931.

20. See Yonemura, "Japanese Fishermen" and C. H. Young and Helen R. Y. Reid, *The Japanese Canadians* (Toronto, University of Toronto Press, 1938), p. 251.

21. *Province*, 29 April 1930. When the provincial government announced unemployed white miners from Nanaimo had replaced forty-one Chinese coal miners at Cumberland, the *Vancouver Star* observed the government had "only completed the easiest part of its task. It has still to see to it that the evicted Chinese do not create a new problem for white men elsewhere." (1 April 1930).

22. The administration of relief to unemployed Asians also shows an illusion of toleration. In the summer of 1931, the provincial cabinet committee on Unemployment Relief withdrew its decision not to register Orientals after several bodies including the Vancouver Trades and Labour Council protested. As the government backtracked, it explained the measure had been only a temporary expedient as relief officials had been overwhelmed with applications. Since their own benevolent associations traditionally looked after Chinese and Japanese in distress, the government believed Asians were the least desperate of the unemployed. (*Province*, 8 and 13 July 1931; *Star* 18 and 29 August, 1931; Circular, "To All Registrars from Committee of the Executive Council on Unemployment Relief August 19, 1931," PABC, Premier's Official Correspondence, 1930-3, File U-4-G (2) #11401; Chairman of the Committee of the Executive Council on Unemployment Relief to Hoiki Chow, Chinese Consul, Vancouver, 22 August 1931, *Ibid.*, #11398. A similar letter was sent to the Japanese consul.)

    By 1935, however, the persistence of unemployment rendered Asians less able to care for themselves and more vulnerable. In Victoria some indigent Chinese, several of whom had not eaten for three days, appealed directly to the provincial government when the city refused them aid. The province replied they were a civic responsibility. (It would be misleading to suggest this was the result of racial discrimination; the unemployed, especially single males, were often the victims of jurisdictional disputes.) In Vancouver, the city granted relief to indigent Chinese but, sticking to the old idea that Chinese could live for less than white men, gave it on a lower scale than to whites or Japanese. (*Province*, 9 January 1935; *The Commonwealth*, 5 April 1935 and 21 June 1935; J. H. McVety, General Superintendent, B.C. Office, Employment Service of Canada to Gordon Sloan, 15 April 1935, Copy in PAC, Ian Mackenzie Papers, vol. 19).

23. In 1933 the Registrar of Vital Statistics reported the Japanese birth rate in British Columbia was 36.4 per thousand in contrast to a rate of 14 per thousand among those of English descent (*Province*, 6 September 1933). I have not found any examples of adverse comment between 1930 and 1935. For an explanation of the Japanese birth rate see Young and Reid, *The Japanese Canadians*, pp. 25-33.

24. Calculated from 1931 census figures quoted in Young and Reid, *The Japanese Canadians*, p. 207.

25. 13 August 1930.

26. 14 March 1930.

27. House of Commons, *Debates*, 26 June 1931, p. 3122.

28. See tables, Young and Reid, *The Japanese Canadians*, p. 207.

29. Brown, D.O.C., M.D. #11 to Secretary, Department of National Defence, 11 March 1930, PAC, Department of National Defence Records, RG 25 D1, vol. 15.

30. See Arthur P. Woollacot, "Canadian-Born Orientals," *Canadian Forum* vol. XI (November 1930), pp. 52-4.

31. *Province*, 11 May 1934.

32. *Province*, 19 June 1931.

33. The ambivalent attitude of the Protestant Churches to Oriental Immigration is described in W. Peter Ward, "The Oriental Immigrant and Canada's Protestant Clergy, 1885-1925," *BC Studies*, no. 22 (Summer 1974), pp. 40-55.

34. 8 April 1930. See also *Province*, 14 March 1930.

35. *Province*, 2 March 1932. See also Nora Kelly, *Quest for a Profession: The History of the Vancouver General Hospital School of Nursing* (Vancouver, Vancouver General Hospital Alumnae Association, 1973), pp. 83-86.

36. 1 April 1931. See also *Province*, 2 April 1931.

37. Among them were S. S. Osterhout of the United Church of Canada in his book. *Orientals in Canada* (Toronto, 1929), p. 208 and the Trades and Labour Congress, *Report of Proceedings*, 1931, pp. 141-2.

38. H. F. Angus, "More than a Tenth of B.C. Is Asiatic and There's the Problem," *Province*, 1 September 1934; *News-Herald*, 19 June 1934; *Province*, 23 June 1934.

39. House of Commons, *Debates*, 22 June 1934, p. 4206.

40. *The Commonwealth*, 15 November 1934.

41. See H. F. Angus, "Liberalism Stoops to Conquer," *Canadian Forum*, vol. XV (December 1935), pp. 389-390.

8

Federal Policy and the Japanese Canadians: The Decision To Evacuate, 1942

M. Ann Sunahara*
University of Calgary

In the heat of the Second World War the Canadian government amended the Defence of Canada Regulations to grant the Minister of Justice the authority to arbitrarily remove "any and all persons" from any "protected area" in Canada and to detain such persons without trial.[1] That amendment was subsequently used to uproot the 23,000 men, women and children of Japanese race residing on or near the Pacific Coast and to exclude them from that coast for seven years. Past students of the evacuation of Canada's Japanese minority have been hampered by a lack of access to government documents. Accordingly, they have accepted and promoted the position of the federal government of the time that the evacuation resulted directly from the capitulation of the federal government to the demands of public

* The author wishes to acknowledge the valuable guidance and assistance of Dr. Howard D. Palmer, the University of Calgary, and Dr. Roger Daniels, the University of Cincinnati.

opinion from British Columbia. The war with Japan, they argue, aggravated existing inter-racial tensions in British Columbia producing intense and irresistable anti-Japanese sentiment. In the face of that sentiment, they conclude, the federal government resolved to defuse the situation by removing an unpopular minority, racially the same as a belligerent enemy.[2]

While this position conforms with the ideals of Canadian democracy and government responsiveness to public opinion, both good and bad, several factors undermine the all-encompassing power of public opinion in this instance. First, the decision to evacuate the Japanese Canadians was not taken in Victoria or Vancouver where anti-Japanese traditions and war hysteria were strongest, but in Ottawa where saner authorities opposed the demands of British Columbia's elected representatives. Second, the government which made this decision was not a minority government clinging to power and needing to bend at every blast of public opinion. Rather, the wartime King government was a sophisticated political machine capable of circumventing strong national public opinion when it felt the demands of the public to be unwise, as was amply demonstrated in the conscription crisis of the same year.[3] Third, the evacuation of the Japanese minority was not only a Canadian phenomenon, but a continental phenomenon. Historical studies of the parallel American experience have demonstrated that West Coast public opinion was only one factor among several in the American decision for evacuating the Japanese Americans.[4] Finally, the thesis that public opinion alone determined Japanese Canadian policy fails to explain the subsequent wartime behaviour of the federal government toward the evacuees. This situation particularly obtains in the 1945 decision to deport a large portion of the Japanese minority, a decision taken in the face of strong public support for moderation in that policy especially as it pertained to Canadian-born Japanese.[5]

The above factors suggest that other considerations prompted the government to support the demands of British Columbia's representatives in a manner contrary to all the liberal principles for which Canada was supposedly fighting. This paper explores three such considerations: federal attitudes toward the Asian minorities, the parallel American experience, and the conscription crisis of 1942.

Traditional federal attitudes toward Asian Canadians did not conform with the ideals of justice and equality for which Canada claimed to be fighting in Europe. Rather, the attitudes of both Cabinet members and the civil service reflected the middle-class notions on race extant in the prewar period. Social Darwinist doctrines which held that the "progressive" political, social and industrial development of the Caucasian nations was proof of the manifest superiority of the

Caucasian race and its "natural" obligation to rule "inferior," less capable, non-white peoples, were only beginning to be questioned in the 1920s and 1930s.[6] Among politicians, ever sensitive to sources of criticism and controversy, only the "socialist" C.C.F. Members of Parliament openly promoted the notion that non-white Canadians should receive the same rights and privileges as Caucasian Canadians. The vast majority of politicians, when they considered the matter at all, either quietly supported discriminatory legislation, or, in the case of British Columbian politicians, provincial or federal, exploited Social Darwinist doctrines to the hilt.[7]

The sympathy of the King government with these doctrines, and with British Columbia's anti-Asian lobby, is evident in prewar legislation affecting Asians. Prior to the 1920s, most anti-Asian legislation had been passed by the B.C. Legislature and had been promptly disallowed by the federal government, but, importantly, not on humanitarian or ethical grounds. Rather, in almost every case the grounds cited by the federal government, whether Liberal or Conservative, were that the legislation contravened the Anglo-Japanese treaty of 1894, and that Japan had taken it upon herself to object.[8] It was sympathetic, successive governments claimed, but was restrained from acquiescing to British Columbia's demands only because of considerations of Imperial policy.

Once relieved of those considerations in the 1920s and 1930s, the federal government readily joined British Columbia in enacting discriminatory legislation. In 1923, no longer constrained by Imperial trade agreements with a weak and divided China, the first Mackenzie King government introduced an immigration bill designed to exclude Chinese immigrants. At the same time, on-going negotiations with a strong, but no longer totally friendly, Japan combined with changes in Japan's own policies with respect to its population problems to further restrict Japanese immigration to Canada.[9] Similarly, in 1920, when the issue of enfranchising Asians arose with the introduction of a federal franchise act, the issue was quietly squelched at the request of politicians from British Columbia. Reconsidered again in 1936 at the urging of the C.C.F. party, the possibility was again rejected in a Liberal dominated Special Committee on the Election and Franchise Act, despite a well executed campaign by the Japanese Canadian Citizens' League, a second generation or *nisei* organization.[10]

The implementation of such legislation reflected the personal attitudes of Prime Minister William Lyon Mackenzie King. It would be simplistic to call King a racist, as his early writings give evidence of liberal ideals on racial matters. Indeed his revulsion at the treatment of Blacks in Toronto is cited as one factor inspiring his study of Toronto's slums.

In addition, throughout his entire lifetime, King's personal dealings with non-Caucasians were reportedly free of condescension and were marked by personal sympathy.[11] And yet as early as 1907, King had bowed to the prejudices of the anti-Asian lobby from British Columbia. Supporting the arguments of the anti-Asian racialists whose rantings had led to the Vancouver riots of that year, King counselled the Postmaster General, Rodolphe Lemieux, who was in Japan negotiating an immigration agreement, as follows:[12]

> Japan is a power greater than the people of this continent have ever dreamed and that as Canadians in dealing with the Orient, if true to our country, we will realize there is no strategy too subtle or diplomacy too fine for us to be prepared to meet. ... [Y]ou could not do better than to tell the people of British Columbia that on a great question of this kind there can be no diversity of interest as between any one part of the Dominion and the whole, and that their problem is Canada's problem and that in all your negotiations you have been mindful of this.

Government policy on racial issues, he had decided early, should be founded on the average prejudices extant at the time.[13] The role of government in such matters was to follow, not to lead.

This apparent ambiguity arises out of King's ability to formulate a rational solution to the ethical problems involved using what he interpreted as "scientific" criteria. Calling upon the general propositions concerning competition formulated by classical economists, King concluded that the introduction of Asian labour to the British Columbian labour force would undermine the standards of Caucasian labour, and decided that one of the roles of the state was to protect such standards, necessitating the exclusion of Asian labour.[14] Asians, he also argued, ought to be excluded because they came from climates dissimilar to Canada's, making their adjustment difficult, and because the split labour market[15] they produced was conducive to producing the conditions which promote socialism. The presence of an Asian labour force in British Columbia, he informed the British authorities in 1908, meant that the corporations employing them prospered while "the mass of men remain wage earners with no stake in the community" allowing socialism to make headway.[16] Such rationalizations provided King not only with an ethical and scientific justification for the actions of the Vancouver mob of 1907, but with a political justification which enabled him to put his humanitarian ideals in a remote second place in his priorities. By 1909 King could conclude that "it is in every way desirable that Canada should be kept for the white races and India for the black, as Nature seems to have decreed,"[17] while working out in his leisure time the details of an exclusion program based on passport controls.[18]

If King and most Members of Parliament felt that their role in racial matters was to follow the apparent consensus, others were more than willing to define that consensus. To the politicians from British Columbia, Asian Canadians were a British Columbian matter best left to the non-C.C.F. Members of Parliament from that province. Only people who had lived and worked in British Columbia, they argued, could really understand the "Oriental menace" and properly guide policy on Asian Canadian matters. By the late 1930s most of Ottawa concurred with this point.[19]

The most influential of the British Columbian Members was the Hon. Ian Alistair Mackenzie, the Minister of Pensions and Health in 1941. Mackenzie was a Highland Scot who after distinguished service in the First World War had entered law and politics in British Columbia where he had immigrated in 1914. Elected to the House of Commons in 1930 after ten years in the provincial legislature, Mackenzie was known for his political astuteness, his hard drinking, his allergy to hard work, and his anti-Asian posture. Like all B.C. Members of Parliament, except the C.C.F. members, Mackenzie commonly used an anti-Asian stance in his election campaigns. While for some, this stance was necessitated by the B.C. political tradition of paying lip-service to the anti-Asian attitudes of organized interest groups in the province, Mackenzie's support of the anti-Asian lobby went beyond the normal requirements of B.C. politics. His personal correspondence and his adherence to the issue long after it had ceased to be politically viable, both attest to the virulence of his sentiments. Asians, he believed, were a political, economic and strategic threat to British Columbian society. He held them responsible for the economic difficulties of B.C. labour and believed that the anti-Asian stance of non-C.C.F. politicians had contributed significantly to reducing C.C.F. support in British Columbia.[20]

Despite his obvious biases, however, as Minister for British Columbia in a Cabinet which regarded Asians as a British Columbian problem, policy decisions and appointments affecting Asians normally included consultation with Mackenzie. This tradition is evident in both the 1940 correspondence of the Fisheries Minister, Joseph E. Michaud, and the appointment of the Standing Committee on Orientals the same year. Writing Mackenzie as the Minister responsible for British Columbia, Michaud asked Mackenzie how many licences he, as Fisheries Minister, should issue to Japanese Canadian boat pullers in that year. Michaud wrote:[21]

I have always found it difficult to justify this arbitrary legislation against British Subjects of Japanese origin. This year in view of the reasons that we are giving for our participation in the European War, it would seem all more difficult to explain why we are adopting against these British Subjects of Japanese origin the technique that Hitler adopted against the Czechs, the Slovaks and the Poles.

Of course I am willing to be guided by your opinion with the assurance that when the time comes you will justify my arbitrary attitude.

While aware that the licencing policy of his government was contrary to Allied principles of justice and humanity, Michaud was content to continue the practice if Mackenzie would relieve him of the problem of justifying his actions. Similarly, when the federally appointed Special Committee on Orientals, which had been investigating illegal Asian immigration, recommended in its 1940 report that a federal Standing Committee on Orientals be appointed to advise the federal government on Asian Canadian policy, Mackenzie was consulted. The result was a five man committee of British Columbian residents of which only one, Professor H. F. Angus, openly favoured equality for Asians. Of the remainder, Assistant Commissioner F. J. Mead of the R.C.M.P. was considered officially neutral, while the rest, Mayor F. J. Hume of New Westminster, Lt-Col. A. W. Sparling and Lt-Col. Macgregor Macintosh, were political appointments who adhered to the policies of the provincial government on Asian matters.[22]

In addition to Mackenzie, two other important members of the wartime Cabinet held firm, if private, anti-Asian opinions: Louis St. Laurent, the Minister of Justice, and Humphrey Mitchell, the Minister of Labour. Neither Mitchell, a union organizer from Hamilton, Ontario, nor St. Laurent, a Quebec judge who functioned as Quebec Lieutenant after the death of Ernest LaPointe, had any direct contact with Asians. Both, however, appear to have accepted the common Asian stereotypes. As late as 1946, Mitchell still referred to Japanese Canadians in derogatory terms,[23] while St. Laurent "fought strongly and bravely" for the deportation of Japanese Canadians, citing the common arguments of inassimilability and the undesirability that they should receive the same rights as white Canadians.[24]

Anti-Asian attitudes also prevailed within the senior civil service. The importance of these sentiments increased as the power of these civil servants, like that of the Cabinet, expanded dramatically in the emergencies of the Depression and the Second World War. Faced with highly technical and complex problems, the Cabinet, its own power bolstered by the War Measures Act after September 1939, became increasingly dependent on the experts within the bureaucracy for guidance on policy, guidance which in turn was coloured by the attitudes of the senior civil servants.

As with the majority of Canada's Caucasian population, the attitudes of Ottawa's mandarins were based on Asian stereotypes and in the identification of Asian Canadians with their racial homelands. The acceptance of the Asian stereotype was probably strongest in the Fisheries Department. There, as early as 1919, senior bureaucrats had urged that Asian Canadian fishing licences be reduced to "gradually eliminate Oriental fisherman from the industry."[25] The reduction in licences, they maintained as late as 1939, was intended to encourage the displaced fishermen to leave the province or return to Japan.[26] In promoting these policies, the senior fisheries officials had accepted the Japanese Canadian stereotype as promoted by the United Fishermen's Federal Union of B.C., and continued to accept that stereotype as late as 1947. That year Stewart Bates, the Deputy Minister of Fisheries, advised against granting licences to ten relocated Japanese Canadians at Great Slave Lake in the Northwest Territories. The reason which he gave was as follows:[27]

> On account of their frugal means of living and their acceptance of long hours of work, together with their fishing ability, fishermen of Japanese origin would likely make it impossible for white fishermen to compete with them if licencing privileges are granted.

Like King, the senior civil servants felt that the role of government was to protect Caucasian labour by excluding Asians.

The habit of thinking of the Asian minorities in terms of their racial homelands is evident in an October 1941 External Affairs memorandum. Discussing possible retaliations against Japan for the arrest of Canadian missionaries, an External Affairs officer concluded as follows:[28]

> While retaliatory arrests of Japanese nationals in Canada might result in the release of Canadian missionaries now in custody, I am inclined to think that no action of this sort should be initiated, *at least at the present time.*

The identification of a racially discernible minority with its potentially belligerent homeland, it appears, followed as easily in Ottawa as it did in Vancouver. In addition, it appears that in both locales Asian minorities were not considered to possess any civil rights.

Ottawa's mandarins were also sensitive to the political implications of Asian Canadian policy. Norman Robertson and other King advisors consistently analyzed the political implications that Asian Canadian policy would have in British Columbia. In 1946, sensitized by a pro-Japanese Canadian public relations campaign,[29] Robertson summarized this situation as follows:[30]

> We do discriminate against the Japanese, against the Chinese, and
> against the British Indians, in our immigration laws and indirectly in
> our electoral laws, but until my native province of British Columbia
> achieves some change of heart, I do not see what we can do about it
> except to strive to limit and lessen the discriminations every time an
> opportunity offers.

There was little concern in 1939, however, with attempts "to limit
and lessen the discriminations every time an opportunity offers."
Preparing for a possible war, a committee of senior civil servants
considered the position of the Japanese minority should Japan become
belligerent. Their conclusions clearly demonstrate both the traditional
position of B.C. attitudes in Asian Canadian policy and the lengths to
which the senior civil servants were already prepared to support those
attitudes. Reporting in February 1939, the committee concluded as
follows:[31]

> [I]f the enemy should be an Asiatic power, ... [i]t might become
> necessary in that contingency, to recommend the internment of nearly
> all enemy nationals, since it is recognized that public feeling in that
> section of Canada [B.C.] on the part of Canadian citizens and other
> Asiatics might render this course necessary, not alone to avoid the
> danger of espionage and sabotage, but also for the protection of the
> person and property of enemy aliens.

Conditioned through the 1920s and 1930s to determining Asian
Canadian policy by the "public feeling" of British Columbia as
expressed by the B.C. caucus and Ian Mackenzie, Canada's senior civil
servants had concluded, almost three years before the attack on Pearl
Harbor and Hong Kong, that they should intern the alien portion of
the Japanese minority if that "public feeling" so dictated.

By 1941 the stage was set. In a political climate which still regarded
equal rights for non-whites as a radical and politically dangerous
proposition, a small, politically impotent and friendless minority,
racially the same as a potential enemy, faced a government whose
sympathy with British Columbia's traditional anti-Asian lobby predisposed it to conform to the dictates of that lobby. Guided by principles which held that the role of government on racial matters was
to follow, not lead, elements of that government were already prepared
by 1939 to intern the alien portion of that minority should the B.C.
caucus so decide. With the outbreak of the Pacific War on December 7,
1941, these traditional attitudes and methods of deciding Asian Canadian policy would combine with two further considerations, the parallel
American experience and an evolving conscription crisis, to produce a
policy far more extreme than any yet contemplated.

The initial response of both Ottawa and British Columbia to the Japanese offensive in the Pacific was calm action. Defense decisions, taken in conjunction with the Americans as early as 1938, were activated. Within days the R.C.M.P. had rounded up the thirty or so Japanese Canadians considered suspicious; the Royal Canadian Navy had begun the impoundment of Japanese Canadian fishing vessels; the Japanese Language Schools had been closed; the minority press, with the exception of the English language section of the *New Canadian,* had been suppressed and Japanese nationals had been ordered to register with the R.C.M.P.[32] By December 10th the American Ambassador, Pierrepont Moffat, had been consulted on the issue of synchronizing policy on the Japanese minority of both countries, and the Chiefs of General Staff in Ottawa had prepared an analysis of the Pacific military situation which concluded that a major land operation or invasion by the Japanese was not considered practical.[33]

The calm of the capital was initially matched by a relative calm on the Pacific Coast as the press and the federal Cabinet affirmed their belief in the loyalty of Canada's Japanese minority.[34] This mood, however, soon began to dissipate over two issues: the fate of the idle Japanese Canadian fishermen and their 1200 vessels, and the question of potential saboteurs among the Japanese minority on the Coast and in Hawaii. The first issue was an extention of the traditional antipathy between the Japanese Fishermen's Association and the United Fishermen's Federal Union of B.C. While relations between these groups had improved considerably in recent years,[35] the Union rapidly reverted to its traditional stance that Japanese Canadians were unfair competition, were responsible for any and all difficulties within the industry, and were not necessary for the continued production of the industry. The impounding of the Japanese Canadian vessels gave the Union an opportunity to squeeze the Japanese Canadians from the industry as they had been trying to do since 1918.[36] Using the patriotic argument that the vessels were required to maintain production to supply the needs of Great Britain and the domestic market, the Union, with the backing of the Canadian Legion and provincial politicians, began to demand that Japanese Canadian licences be suspended and their vessels made available to non-Japanese operators.[37]

The impounding of the vessels as a "defensive measure"[38] also reinforced rumours of sabotage by resident Japanese Americans at Pearl Harbor which were freely circulating along the coast. Such rumours added to the insecurities induced by the almost daily warnings of impending Japanese attacks emanating from the panic-ridden and amateurish Western Defense Command Headquarters in San Francisco.[39] On December 15, the confusion over West Coast security was deepened by the hurried and ill-considered remarks of the American Secretary of the Navy, Frank Knox, on his return from a quick inspection of the damages at Pearl Harbor. Knox, without considering the implication of his words, described the attack there as "treachery" and "the most effective fifth column work that's come out of this war except in Norway."[40] These remarks generated editorials on both sides of the border. Typical of the ensuing articles was the *Vancouver Sun's* December 16th editorial which warned that the fate of Japanese Canadians would depend on their own conduct and that, at the slightest evidence of sabotage or lack of cooperation, British Columbian Japanese should be interned.[41]

Rumours of Japanese American treachery also provided grist for the mills of political race-baiters. In a province where an anti-Asian stance was a traditional requirement of Establishment politicians, politicians at all levels sought public attention on the issue. Alderman Halford Wilson, a viciously anti-Asian[42] member of the Vancouver City Council, not only personally demanded harsh measures against Japanese Canadians, — including evacuation — but also organized the Pacific Coast Security League with friends of similar sympathies.[43] By the end of December, members of the federal B.C. Caucus, the B.C. Premier, John Hart, and his Attorney General, R. W. Maitland, were urging Ottawa "to take action to remove the menace of Fifth Column activity from B.C."[44] The Pacific War, one B.C. politician acknowledged privately, was a "heaven-sent opportunity" to rid the province of the Japanese and the economic threat they were presumed to pose[45] — sentiments which were reiterated, along with the usual racist myths, in the largely unsigned letters appearing in the press.[46]

By the end of December, the advisory Standing Committee on Orientals and Major-General R. O. Alexander, the Commander-in-Chief, Pacific Command, had both begun to advocate the "internment of Japanese males between the ages of 18 and 45,"[47] the former publically, the latter privately. No longer restrained by the liberalizing influence of Professor H. F. Angus, who had gone to Ottawa as a special assistant in the External Affairs Department, the three political appointees on the Standing Committee aligned themselves with Premier John Hart of B.C. Pledging to urge that all male Japanese of military age be interned and that the fishing vessels be sold back into the industry; Mayor Hume, Lt.-Col. Macintosh, Lt.-Col. Sparling and an unenthusiastic Assistant Commissioner Mead set out for a conference on the "Japanese Question" in Ottawa in early January, 1942.[48]

Preceding them to Ottawa was a private letter to the Chiefs of General Staff in which Major General Alexander gave his support to the position of the B.C. politicians. Following private discussions with

Premier Hart and Lt.-Col. Sparling, Alexander wrote his superiors about the difficulty of protecting the widely dispersed Japanese Canadian population should scheduled anti-Japanese demonstrations turn into riots. Such riots would be prevented, he argued, if Japanese males of military age were interned. Without acknowledging that nothing worse than minor vandalism had as yet occurred in Canada, Alexander ominously concluded that his recommendations "might well prevent inter-racial riots and bloodshed and will undoubtedly do a great deal to calm the local population."[49] The Chiefs of General Staff, however, while aware of a certain potential for violence by the white population, were completely satisfied that the R.C.M.P. had the situation under control.[50] Their view of the reaction on the West Coast is evident from the comments of the then Vice-Chief of General Staff, Major-General Maurice A. Pope:

> At times I almost hoped that the Japanese would attempt a raid of some kind, for this would have been repulsed and, most assuredly, our people would have recovered their balance.[51]

In order to decide policy on this issue, Prime Minister King had called a conference in Ottawa. Accompanying the Standing Committee on Orientals to it were the Honourable George Pearson, Minister of Labour and Provincial Secretary of British Columbia, and T. W. S. Parsons, Commissioner of the British Columbia Provincial Police. Joining them in Ottawa were three Cabinet Ministers, J. E. Michaud of Fisheries, J. T. Thorson of National War Service, and Ian Mackenzie of Pensions and Health. The Department of External Affairs was represented by its Under-Secretary, Norman Robertson, and three subordinates, while Brigadier S. T. Wood represented the R.C.M.P., Major-General Maurice A. Pope represented the General Staff and Commodore H. E. Reid was authorized to speak for the Naval Staff.

Opening on January 8, 1942 under Mackenzie's chairmanship, the Conference initially proceeded smoothly. The participants quickly reached consensus on the principles behind Japanese Canadian policy, on the formation of a civilian service corps which would employ male citizen Japanese Canadians on public works projects, and on the formation of a committee to arrange the "sale, lease, requisition or charter" of the impounded vessels. They further agreed to recommend the suspension of fishing licences for the duration of the war, and the prohibition of shortwave radios and transmitters to Japanese nationals. In a divided decision they also recommended that Japanese Canadians be encouraged to join the armed forces.[52]

Consensus vanished, however, over a proposal to intern all male Japanese nationals between 18 and 45 years of age. Introduced by the delegation from British Columbia, this proposal was consistent with the stance of the Canadian Legion and the politicians of that province. The position of the Ottawa experts was very different. Speaking consecutively on the issue, Brigadier Wood, Commodore Reid and Major-General Pope all expressed opinions that the situation was under control, that they were not concerned about the presence of Japanese Canadians on the West Coast, and that they had no further recommendations to make. The reaction of the B.C. delegation was predictably violent, causing the meeting to be adjourned for the day.[53] When the conference reconvened the next day, External Affairs spokesmen backed the position of the R.C.M.P. and the military arguing that the proposal contradicted the American policy and Allied professions of justice and humanity, and, most importantly, would result "in cruel retaliations by Japanese authorities against Canadians now in their power."[54] Confronted with an impasse, Ian Mackenzie, in his role as chairman, proposed that both views be presented to the Cabinet in the conference report.[55]

When presenting that report to Cabinet, Ian Mackenzie dropped all pretext of neutrality and threw the full force of his considerable influence behind the minority British Columbian position. His position, he explained in a letter to King, was based in his fear that "our white people may resort to unwise tactics in Vancouver."[56] Under a "wise and prudent policy of consideration," Mackenzie argued, the Japanese nationals could be "transferred" to work camps and kept under surveillance "without necessarily being interned." Such a plan, he urged, would remove from the West Coast the 1,700 male Japanese nationals of military age, while Canadian nationals could be controlled through the proposed civilian service corps. Included with this letter were selected excerpts from Alexander's letter to the Chiefs of General Staff, excerpts which supported the B.C. arguments. As a close personal friend of the Prime Minister and as a former Minister of National Defence, Mackenzie was undoubtedly aware that King was suspicious of the Ottawa military establishment.[57] Through Alexander's letter Mackenzie deftly implied that while the brass in Ottawa opposed B.C.'s requests, the soldier on the ground supported them.

In accordance with twenty years of tradition the Cabinet agreed to the B.C. requests in their entirety. Rejecting the counsel of Canada's senior police and military officers, the Cabinet amended the Defence of Canada regulations to grant the Minister of Justice the power to remove "all or any enemy aliens" from any "protected area" in Canada and to detain those enemy aliens "as he may . . . direct."[58] The Order also allowed the Minister of Justice to order the arrest of anyone residing in a "protected area" "in order to prevent such persons from acting in any manner prejudicial to the public safety or to the safety of the state."[59] The two clauses, "an officer of the Department of External Affairs"[60] explained to the American Ambassador, Pierrepont Moffat, would be used to remove the male Japanese nationals of military age and "between 800 and 1,000 Canadian citizens" of Japanese ancestry.[61] Other citizen Japanese Canadians of military age would be enlisted into the proposed service corps.

While tradition predisposed the Cabinet to grant B.C.'s request in full, other political and diplomatic considerations reinforced that tradition. The Cabinet was preoccupied in this period with a question it considered far more serious than the rights of enemy aliens — the conscription crisis of 1942. The rising manpower needs of the Second World War had again raised the issue of conscription for overseas service. The Liberal Cabinet, and indeed the whole party, was divided on the issue. Within those divisions, Mackenzie King and Ian Mackenzie were both opposed to overseas conscription, while J. L. Ralston the Minister of National Defence, with the support of the Chiefs of Staff, supported it.[62] In the period preceding the attack on Pearl Harbor, King had decided to defuse the situation by means of a plebiscite in which the voters would be asked to release the government from its commitment against overseas conscription. King's intent in proposing this plebiscite, however, was not to impose conscription, but to lay the question to rest, at least temporarily.[63]

A threat to the Pacific Coast could only reinforce King's position on overseas conscription. A Pacific War, King is said to have commented in November 1941, would mean mobilizing and equipping men for service on the coast, necessitating a cut in aid to Britain, while the realization of peril on the Coast would put an end to talk of conscription for overseas service.[64] Accordingly, as pressure for overseas conscription from Ralston and the military increased, King began to emphasize the "possible if not probable" danger of invasion by Japan.[65] True to King's November assessment, with the outbreak of the Pacific War, British Columbians appeared to be revising their earlier sentiments favouring conscription in line with King's views.[66] Because this support rested tenuously on British Columbia's concern for an adequate defence against an expected Japanese attack, King was loath to discourage such support by making known to the public how little danger they actually faced. Consequently, a frank declaration of the actual dangers, which might have done much to calm the public of British Columbia, became politically impossible in the midst of a conscription crisis considered far more important than the civil rights of an unpopular minority.

Second, contrary to the January 9th statements of the Department of External Affairs, the evacuation of enemy aliens from designated coastal areas had become American policy. This policy had evolved from the dangerous mixing of traditional West Coast racism with the tactics of a military clique centered on the office of the Provost Marshal General, Major Allen W. Gullion. This clique, with the support of senior War department officials, was attempting to transfer control over enemy aliens from the Justice to the War Department. In Lt. General John L. DeWitt, the Commander of the Western Defence Command in San Francisco, Gullion and his subordinate Karl R. Bendetsen, found a very confused and rabidly anti-Japanese commander who could be persuaded that enemy aliens should not be left under civilian control. Importantly, they also found a West Coast populace with well developed racist traditions which was suspicious of aliens, especially Japanese aliens, and which willingly believed and supported DeWitt's racist views. To effect the transfer of jurisdiction over enemy aliens, Gullion and Bendetsen had been using DeWitt and West Coast politicians to put pressure on the Justice Department for stronger measures against enemy aliens. Aware that the Justice Department opposed the creation of a massive internal bureaucracy, Bendetsen and DeWitt met on January 4, 1942 with federal and local officials to demand the initiation of measures against enemy aliens which included their exclusion from the Pacific Coast through a pass and permit system. To their surprise, the Justice Department officials agreed to most of their demands.[67]

The American decision is important in view of the extent to which Canadian officials were actively attempting to insure continental uniformity in the handling of their respective Japanese minorities. To ensure such uniformity, liaison with the American government existed at two levels. At the diplomatic level, the Under Secretary of State for External Affairs, Norman Robertson, and the American Ambassador, Pierrepont Moffat, had already agreed to "the importance of our pursuing parallel policies as nearly as possible," and of keeping each other informed of any intentions "to enlarge the numbers now interned on the Pacific Coast."[68] At the military level, extensive liaison existed between DeWitt's Western Defense Command and Alexander's Pacific Command.[69] With the Canadian liaison officer in Seattle "in a position to be acquainted with the information and views of Generals Joyce and DeWitt,"[70] there can be little doubt that the Joint Services Committee of the Pacific Command at Victoria B.C. knew of the American development when recommending to Ottawa on January 9, 1942 that "steps be taken to remove all male Japanese and other enemy aliens between 16 and 50 from the Coastal areas of British Columbia."[71] Given also that General Alexander's previous recommendation to his superiors had been leaked to the Cabinet through Lt. Col. Sparling of the Standing Committee on Orientals, and Ian Mackenzie,[72] it is probable that the Cabinet was aware of this recommendation and the American development when deciding on January 13 to evacuate male enemy nationals of military age from the Pacific Coast.[73] The parallel American experience by mid-January had served not only to fuel the fears and prejudices of the anti-Asian lobby in B.C., but also to reinforce both the 1939 conclusions of the Committee on Aliens and Alien Property, cited earlier, and the immediate needs and inclinations of a Cabinet faced with conscription crisis.

The Cabinet's promise to remove Japanese enemy aliens from the Pacific Coast calmed the press and politicians of British Columbia, but only temporarily. In the face of continuing military losses in the Pacific, false or erroneous reports of sabotage and impending attacks, and the lack of any concrete action by the federal government, agitation for the removal of Canada's Japanese minority — agitation still confined almost entirely to politicians, the Canadian Legion and anti-Asian interest groups — soon re-escalated.[74]

Government inaction was the primary target. In both Canada and the United States the respective authorities were discovering that the definition of defence areas and the removal of aliens from them was no simple matter. Before the aliens could be removed, employment had to be found and road camps constructed; both difficult tasks when those being removed were assumed, by that action, to be dangerous, and when winter hindered the construction of facilities. Consequently, it was not until February 13 that a date for the removal of Japanese aliens was set.[75] At the same time the formation of the proposed Civilian Service Corps for citizen Japanese Canadians languished. Citizen male Japanese Canadians of military age, it was assumed in both Ottawa and British Columbia, would seek to prove their loyalty by readily joining this corps. This assumption was based on the conforming stereotype of Japanese Canadians and on the pledges of *nisei* organizations made following the attack on Pearl Harbor.[76] When young Japanese Canadians chose instead to wait and see the final form of the Corps before signing up, the press and politicians began to talk of forcing citizen Japanese Canadians from the West Coast.[77] Ottawa's apparent inaction — contrasted unfavourably in the press with the well publicized, if inaccurately reported efforts of the American authorities to ferret out Japanese agents[78] — served to compound insecurities induced by fresh rumours of impending attack or sabotage.

While many of these rumours were home grown,[79] many had their origins in false or erroneous reports originating in the United States. There, DeWitt's Western Defense Command Headquarters was continuing to disseminate reports of non-existent Japanese craft and of radio signals emanating from the mainland. These reports have since been demonstrated patently false, but were used by DeWitt, Gullion and Bendetsen to convince civilian officials in Washington of the "military necessity" of the emergency measures they were proposing, measures which now included a complete evacuation of all Japanese Americans, both citizens and aliens.[80] By the end of January, DeWitt also expressed the opinion that the lack of sabotage by Japanese Americans was proof that control was being exercised over them by Japan in preparation for future coordinated sabotage.[81] Fears of sabotage were also fanned by the publication of Owen J. Roberts's investigation of the attack on Pearl Harbor which erroneously concluded that spies and saboteurs, "not directly connected with the Japanese foreign service," had increased the effectiveness of the attack.[82]

The demands of British Columbia's politicians and traditionally anti-Asian groups continued to be opposed by the Department of External Affairs and the R.C.M.P. In late January, Hugh Keenleyside, the Assistant Under-Secretary of State for External Affairs, warned the Prime Minister that the compulsory movement of citizens, because they were of the Japanese race, could have severe repercussions on the two thousand Canadian prisoners of war in Japanese hands. Such a policy, he contended, was unnecessary and would only provide grist for Facist propaganda.[83] The R.C.M.P. position also remained unchanged as Commissioner Wood continued to reject demands for the removal of citizens, on the grounds that the R.C.M.P. lacked the authority to do so.[84]

Despite this opposition, however, there was considerable sympathy within the Cabinet for the removal of all male Japanese Canadians from the Coast. Such sympathies were especially strong in the Special Cabinet Committee on Japanese Canadians set up in mid-January. Responsible for advising the Cabinet on Japanese Canadian policy, none of the members of this committee — Ian Mackenzie of Pensions and Health, Humphrey Mitchell of Labour and J. G. Gardiner of Agriculture — held pro-Japanese attitudes. Indeed, Mackenzie and Mitchell were among the more strongly anti-Japanese within the Cabinet. On January 27, at Mackenzie's insistence, this committee resolved to recommend to Cabinet "that if in the event it developed that the [Japanese] Canadian nationals did not enlist in large numbers, the whole situation would have to be reviewed and the question of compulsion considered."[85] The issue was not, nor had it ever been, whether to evacuate citizen males of military age, but whether that evacuation should be voluntary or compulsory.

The B.C. Caucus declared its position on the issue the next day. Resolving to insist "on the compulsory evacuation of Canadian nationals if they do not volunteer," that caucus initiated a concerted campaign of pressure and influence intended to implement that resolution.[86] While the more virulent anti-Japanese members continued their demands for the evacuation, and even the deportation of the entire minority, the more subtle members began urging for the more feasible removal of all Japanese Canadians from around strategic installations, while intimating that the families of the evacuated males would likely prefer to join their men east of the Rocky Mountains.[87]

The fall of a presumed impregnable Singapore on February 15 brought matters to a head. From the Japanese Canadian point of view, defeat could not have come at a worse time. In B.C. the press, politicians and the Canadian Legion were all seething over Ottawa's rejection of Vancouver's Air Raid Protection budget. The fall of Singapore, they speculated, would free Japanese forces to attack the Pacific Coast, a coast which Ottawa, in its continuing neglect of British Columbia, had left woefully unprotected from attack from without, and sabotage from within.[88] "[T]here is a growing impatience," the editors of the *Vancouver Daily Province* warned, "with the seeming inability of Ottawa to tell the people of this coast what has been done and what it is proposed to do."[89]

Amid Ottawa's continuing silence and the growing fears of an inadequate defence, the agitation against Japanese Canadians began to change. The seeds of a complete evacuation, planted in the earlier demands for the removal of all Japanese from near defence installations, matured. While the early agitation had centered in groups with economic motivations or extremist attitudes, the issue now began to be taken up privately and publicly by the more respectable elements of British Columbia's political community. The Hon. George Pearson, B.C.'s Minister of Labour and Provincial Secretary, began to talk of the progressive removal of Japanese Canadians from British Columbia.[90] On the 20th, a group of British Columbia's most respectable citizens, most of whom had extensive connections with provincial politics, formed the Citizens Defence Committee as a "responsible voice of public opinion".[91] Supported by Vancouver service clubs and labour organizations, the Action Committee of the C.D.C. took it upon itself to consult with the local authorities on the matter. Concluding that some immediate action was needed, twenty-three members of that committee, including the leader of the provincial C.C.F., Harold Winch, petitioned Ottawa on the 24th for a protective evacuation of the Japanese minority, without knowing that the evacuation decision had been made earlier the same day.[92] The past and present Attorney Generals of B.C. had earlier written Ottawa, urging the removal of the Japanese minority, as had the Commissioner of Provincial Police,

T. W. S. Parsons.[93] Despite the obvious racism of comments like Parsons's "With these people neither Canadian birth nor naturalization guarantees good faith,"[94] the prestige and respectability of their authors, and the apparent genuineness of their fears, made their suggestions hard for a sympathetic Cabinet to ignore.

The fall of Singapore and the lack of any denial by Ottawa of the dangers paraded in the B.C. press, also generated a sudden upsurge in the number of petitions and resolutions reaching Ottawa, but contrary to the claims of supporters of the evacuation, they remained small in number. Between the January 14th decision to evacuate enemy aliens and the February 24th decision for complete evacuation, the Department of External Affairs collected 37 resolutions and 19 letters demanding the internment of all Japanese Canadians. The bulk of these letters and resolutions — 26 resolutions and 10 letters — were sent after the fall of Singapore.[95] Ian Mackenzie's files show a similar, though again small, number of letters and resolutions.[96] The paucity of such concrete evidence of public sentiment, however, did not restrain the B.C. Minister from writing his colleagues on the morning of February 24 that he was "beseiged with telegrams and letters from some of my closest friends and strongest supporters, the contents of which are not much less drastic than the Victoria City Council resolution,"[97] which called for Mackenzie's resignation in protest to government inaction. Such exaggeration by a politician seeking support for his position may well be the source of the myth that "thousands of west-coast whites petitioned Ottawa for the immediate evacuation of all Japanese."[98]

Ottawa's silence, which only served to aggravate B.C.'s claims of neglect, had its source in the continuing conscription crisis, as the bill authorizing the plebiscite on that issue was due before the Commons for its final reading. As noted earlier, peril on the Pacific Coast, whether real or imagined, internal or external, would serve to reinforce King's position on that issue. King's appreciation of this situation is evident in his lecture to the Cabinet and the Chiefs of Staff on February 20. Summarizing that lecture in his diary, he wrote:[99]

> I was glad to see the Defense Ministers come round to the point of view that we would have to take increasing account of the possibility, though not the probability of invasion.
>   I pointed out the possibility of the Burma Road being closed; China dropping out if the Japanese continue to win; uprisings in India; strategic centers of the world in the hands of the enemy cutting off routes of supply, and the possibility of something more than raids on the coasts, resulting therefrom. Stressed the need of now regarding Japan as a potential aggressor in this continent; especially with Alaska a part of it. . . . Stressed from now on giving more attention to the purely Canadian defenses and to considering possible dangers from

coastal air raids, all of which would necessitate increased numbers of soldiers in Canada. . . . The Japanese problem in B.C. itself might become a very difficult one to handle requiring more in the way of troops.

As his lecture indicates, the "Japanese problem in B.C." very nicely gave substance to his argument that more attention be given to the existing and potential needs of home defence. In addition, this argument held, whether the "problem" was considered from the point of view of defending Japanese Canadians from rioters, or of defending British Columbia from raids and sabotage.

Just how much of this assessment was based on political considerations, and how much was based on a genuine fear of the power of Japan will never be known. C. P. Stacey has commented on "that wishful exaggeration of the direct threats to Canada which was characteristic of King and his civilian advisors," and which led them to order unnecessary reinforcements for the Pacific Coast for political reasons.[100] From King's diary it is evident that the successes of the Japanese forces had both surprised and shocked him, but not to the degree of frightening him.[101] In addition, becoming obsessed with a "possible but not probable" course of enemy action was inconsistent with King's political behavior which was always soundly based in the probable realities of a problem. King was not a man given to panic unless that panic served his purposes.

He had, however, accepted Mackenzie's evaluation of the temper of British Columbia and of the difficulty of the problem. "I fear it is going to be a very great problem to move the Japanese," he wrote on February 19,[102]

> and particularly to deal with the ones who are naturalized Canadians or Canadian born. There is every possibility of riots. Once that occurs, there will be repercussions in the Far East against our prisoners. Public prejudice is so strong in B.C. that it is going to be difficult to control the situation, also moving men to camps at this time of year is very difficult indeed.

Policy by this date was "complete removal of adult males from the protected area."[103] In accordance with past Asian Canadian policy, the deterrents restricting the immediate implementation of that policy did not include any moral, ethical or legal questions arising from concern with the civil rights of the minority. Rather, implementation was held up only by the administrative difficulty in moving those involved, and the diplomatic problem of accomplishing that move without repercussions on Canadian prisoners of war in Japanese hands.

On the day that King made this assessment, two events reinforced the arguments of the B.C. Caucus. Exposed to the influences of the press and politicians of British Columbia, and to the opinions of DeWitt through their liaison officer, the Joint Services Committee of the Pacific Command elected on February 19 to recommend the removal of Japanese Canadian citizens from five strategic areas. Those areas, defined with the assistance of Commissioner Parsons, included Ucluelet, Prince Rupert, the Skeena River to Terrace, B.C., the Queen Charlotte Islands, and the Quatsino Sound area, and contained approximately 1,500 Japanese Canadians.[104] Their views, however, were still not shared by the senior officers of the Armed Forces. The Chiefs of General Staff, in possession of the overall picture of the Pacific War, concurred with their American counterparts, that an invasion by Japanese forces was impractical, and that the resident Japanese minority did not represent a risk to internal security.[105]

On the same day, President Franklin D. Roosevelt signed Executive Order 9066. That Order granted any American military commander authorized by the Secretary of War, the power to designate areas from which "any and all persons" could be excluded. This document, drawn up by Major General Gullion, was intended primarily to provide a legal basis for a mass evacuation of Japanese Americans. While this intention was still not specific on February 19, rumours of a complete evacuation, and West Coast support for such a policy, had been building for some time. Given also the personal views of the West Coast Commander, General DeWitt, there could be little doubt as to his policy, once granted authority by the Secretary of War.

Within four days, the issue was settled. On the morning of February 24, 1942, the Cabinet passed an Order-in-Council almost identical in powers to the American Order.[106] By Order-in-Council, P.C. 1486, the Cabinet amended the Defence of Canada Regulations to empower the Minister of Justice, with the authority to remove and detain "any and all persons" from any designated "protected area" in Canada. As in the American case, the Order was broad enough to be used against any resident of Canada and was intended, King announced the next day, to be used to effect "all necessary security measures to safeguard the defenses of the Pacific Coast."[107] In five short days the Japanese minority had changed, in the opinion of the Cabinet, from a "problem" in need of protection from rioters to a threat to the safety of Pacific Coast defences as charged by the anti-Asian lobby of B.C.

When and why the policy of complete evacuation materialized remains obscure. On the 22nd, the Cabinet had been unable to reach consensus on the matter, while on the 24th, the Order was passed on the understanding that it would be used "to evacuate all persons of Japanese race in the protected area on the Pacific Coast and to make provision for them elsewhere."[108] The developments in the intervening forty-eight hours apparently are not recorded, although two strong considerations suggest themselves, one or both of which could have cinched the question. First, the diplomatic consideration of synchronizing policy with the United States may have tipped the scales. The evidence for this position is patchy. The Canadian government understood on the 26th that the Americans not only intended a complete evacuation of their Japanese minority but that evacuation would be carried out by the Army.[109] Just when and from whom they received this impression is unclear, but such intelligence would undoubtedly have gone a long way toward convincing reluctant Cabinet members of the desirability of a total evacuation.[110]

A second consideration might simply have been administrative ease. Evacuating the adult males to road camps, where they could only earn twenty-five cents an hour, created the problem of assuring that their families and properties were maintained and protected in their absence. Many of the administrative difficulties involved could be overcome more readily if the families of these men were concentrated in camps where they could be kept cheaply, and the earnings of the men would cover much of their necessary support. Reinforcing such a scheme were the demands of the B.C. Caucus for a complete evacuation and the reluctance of the Japanese Canadian males to leave before measures for the care of their families and property had been announced.[111] A policy of complete evacuation, therefore, would not only satisfy political and diplomatic considerations, but showed every sign of easing the problems of administering the program.

The evacuation of Canada's Japanese minority from the Pacific Coast was not based on "military necessity" as suggested at the time. Indeed, the program was opposed by Canada's senior police and military officers. Rather, it evolved from a variety of factors, including the existence of a traditional anti-Asian lobby in British Columbia, and importantly, a Cabinet and civil service predisposed to deciding policy by the whims of that lobby. Such traditions meant that the expanding demands of the B.C. Caucus — demands which reinforced the Prime Minister's position in the intervening conscription crisis — found sympathy in a government traditionally unconcerned with the rights of non-white minorities. Reinforced by political, diplomatic and administrative considerations, the federal government successively expanded its Japanese Canadian policies through the month of February, 1942, until those policies were far in excess of anything contemplated in the prewar period.

NOTES

1. Order in Council, P.C. 1486, February 24, 1942.

2. See Forrest E. La Violette, *Canadian Japanese in World War II,* (Toronto: University of Toronto Press, 1948); and W. Peter Ward, "British Columbia and the Japanese Evacuation," *Canadian Historical Review,* Vol. 57, No. 3, September 1976, pp. 289-308.

3. See J. L. Granatstein, *Conscription in the Second World War, 1939-1945.* (Toronto: The Ryerson Press, 1969)

4. See Roger Daniels, *Concentration Camps U.S.A.: Japanese Americans in World War II.* (New York: Holt, Rinehart and Winston, 1972); and his *The Decision to Relocate the Japanese Americans.* (Philadelphia: Lippincott, 1975) For the Latin American cases see Michi Weglyn, *Years of Infamy: The Untold Story of America's Concentration Camps* (New York: Wm. Morrow, 1976).

5. As early as February 1944, a Gallup Poll indicated that 59% of Canadians favoured allowing citizen Japanese Canadians to remain in Canada. By September 1945, submissions to the federal government were 85 to 19 in favour of a moderate policy. Memorandum, R. G. Robertson to W. L. Mackenzie King, King Papers, MG26J4, Vol. 361, F3850, C249600-C248606. Unless otherwise specified, all documents are from the Provincial Archives of Canada.

6. See Richard Hofstadter, *Social Darwinism in American Thought* (Boston: Beacon Press, 1972), and Roger Daniels, *Politics of Prejudice* (Gloucester, Mass: Peter Smith, 1966).

7. See Patricia E. Roy, "Educating the East: British Columbia and the Oriental Question in the Interwar Years," *B.C. Studies,* No. 18, Summer 1973.

8. See C. J. Woodsworth, *Canada and the Orient* (Toronto: Macmillan, 1941), pp. 49, 108-114.

9. In 1923 the "Gentlemen's Agreement" of 1908 was revised so that only 150 labourers and agricultural workers could enter Canada from Japan annually in addition to the families of Japanese immigrants already in Canada. In 1928 that agreement was further revised to permit the immigration of only 150 Japanese persons annually. *Ibid.*

10. See Canada, House of Commons, Special Committee on the Elections and Franchise Act, *Minutes of Proceedings and Evidence,* May 22, 1936, pp. 190-210.

11. H. S. Ferns and B. Ostry, *The Age of Mackenzie King: The Rise of the Leader* (London: William Heinemann, 1955), p. 80.

12. W. L. Mackenzie King to R. Lemieux, December 30, 1907, Lemieux Papers, as quoted by *Ibid.,* pp. 83-84.

13. *Ibid.*

14. *Ibid.,* p. 81.

15. A split labour market is one in which a readily definable group systematically receives a lower wage for the same work than another definable group.

16. Memo, W. L. Mackenzie King, May 2, 1908, Lemieux Papers, as quoted in H. S. Fern and B. Ostry, *op. cit.*, pp. 86-87.

17. W. L. Mackenzie King to Wilfrid Laurier, January 31, 1909, Laurier Papers, as quoted in H. S. Fern and B. Ostry, *op. cit.*, p. 88.

18. *Ibid.*, p. 91.

19. Patricia E. Roy, *op. cit.*, and "The Oriental 'Menace' in British Columbia," from S. M. Trofimenkoff (ed.), *The Twenties in Western Canada* (Ottawa: Museum of Man, 1972).

20. King Diary, MG26J13, January 19, 1946: Bruce Hutchison, *The Incredible Canadian* (Toronto: Longman, Green and Co., 1952), p. 216. Blair Neatby, *William Lyon Mackenzie King, 1924-1932* (Toronto: University of Toronto Press, 1963), pp. 332, 358. Ian Mackenzie Papers, MG 27IIIB5, Vols. 24, 25 and 32. His belief that his anti-Asian stance played an important part in maintaining his seat and inhibiting the C.C.F. was expressed in the Commons in 1945. See Canada, House of Commons, *Debates,* December 17, 1945, p. 3704.

21. P. E. Michaud to Ian Mackenzie, January 17, 1940, Ian Mackenzie Papers, MG27IIIB5, Vol. 19, 29-7.

22. Macintosh was particularly anti-Asian and had advocated the deportation of all Asians as early as 1938. His reputation was so bad that Norman Robertson, the Under Secretary of State, refused Mackenzie's recommendation of him for the Commander of a proposed civilian service corps for Japanese Canadians on the grounds that no Japanese Canadian would serve under him because of his views.

23. Interview with Andrew Brewin, M.P., September 14, 1976.

24. King Diary, January 22, 1947, King Papers, MG26J13.

25. H. F. Angus, "The Legal Status in British Columbia of Residents of Oriental Race and Their Descendants," in Norman Mackenzie, ed., *The Legal Status of Aliens in Pacific Countries* (Toronto: Oxford University Press, 1937), p. 34.

26. Memo re Licencing, A. J. Whitmore, Deputy Minister of Fisheries, November 24, 1939, Fisheries Records, 716-14-19, Vol. 1, Department of Fisheries Archives.

27. Memorandum, Stewart Bates, September 24, 1947, British Columbia Security Commission Papers, RG36/27, Vol. 34.

28. Emphasis mine. C. M. J. to Norman Robertson, October 21, 1941, King Papers, MG26J4, C194865.

29. See F. E. La Violette, *op. cit.*, pp. 226-274.

30. Memo, N. A. Robertson to W. L. Mackenzie King, January 5, 1946, King Papers, MG26J4, Vol. 283, F2965, C194932.

31. Canada, Committee and the Treatment of Aliens and Alien Property, *First Interim Report,* February 9, 1939, Ian Mackenzie Papers, MG27IIIB5, Vol. 32.

32. King Diary, December 7 to 10, 1941, King Papers, MG26J13; *The New Canadian,* December 12, 1941.

33. Canada, War Cabinet Committee, *Documents,* Privy Council Office Records, Vol. VII, 126,3; and N. A. Robertson to W. L. Mackenzie King, December 10, 1941, King Papers, MG26J4, Vol. 361, F3849, C249381.

34. King Diary, December 7, 1941, *op. cit., Vancouver Sun,* December 8, 1941, p. 1.

35. Rolf Knight and Maya Koizumi, *A Man of Our Times: The Life-History of a Japanese Canadian Fisherman* (Vancouver, New Star Books, 1976), pp. 67-69: *The New Canadian,* April 11, 1941, p. 5.

36. C. H. Young, H. R. Reid and W. A. Carrothers, *The Japanese Canadians* (Toronto: University of Toronto Press, 1939), pp. 38-39.

37. See *Vancouver Sun,* December 22, 1941, p. 9; Ian Mackenzie Papers MG27IIIB5, Vol. 19, 29-7.

38. Canada, War Cabinet Committee, *Documents, op. cit.*

39. Roger Daniels, *Concentration Camps U.S.A., op. cit.,* pp. 36-38.

40. *Ibid.,* p. 35.

41. *Vancouver Sun,* December 16, 1941, p. 17.

42. Wilson had urged the establishment of legal ghettos in Vancouver in which Asians would be required to reside. *The New Canadian,* February 14, 1941, p. 1.

43. *Vancouver Sun,* January 3, 1942, p. 17; F. E. Laviolette, *op. cit.,* p. 39.

44. *Vancouver Sun,* December 29, 1941, p. 1., January 5, 1942, p. 13.

45. Maurice A. Pope, *Soldiers and Politicians: The Memoires of Lt-Gen. Maurice A. Pope* (Toronto: University of Toronto Press, 1962), p. 177.

46. Prior to Christmas the *Vancouver Sun* printed 19 anti-Japanese letters and one letter deploring such letters.

47. Major-General R. O. Alexander to the Chiefs of General Staff, December 30, 1941, Pacific Command Records, 322.009 (D358), Directorate of History, Department of National Defense.

48. *The New Canadian,* January 5, 1942, p. 1.

49. Major-General R. O. Alexander to the Chiefs of General Staff, December 30, 1941, *op. cit.*

50. Canada, War Cabinet Committee, *Minutes,* December 29, 1941, Privy Council Office Records, Vol. VII, 132,5.

51. Maurice A. Pope, *op. cit.,* p. 179. General Alexander was not considered a strong commander. His views on the internment of Japanese males were made from political, not military, considerations.

52. Conference on the Japanese Problem in British Columbia, *Report;* and Ian Mackenzie to W. L. Mackenzie King, January 10, 1942, Ian Mackenzie Papers, MG27IIIB5, Vol. 32, X-81.

53. Maurice A. Pope, *op. cit.,* p. 177. Pope described the reaction of the B.C. delegation as follows:
    All hell broke loose. I thought for a moment that my former friends [from B.C.] might charge across the table to manhandle me. Their rage was a sight to behold.

54. Conference on the Japanese Problem in British Columbia, *Report, op. cit.,* pp. 6-7.

55. Ian Mackenzie to W. L. Mackenzie King, January 10, 1942, *op. cit.*

56. *Ibid.*

57. C. P. Stacey, *Arms Men and Governments: The War Policies of Canada, 1939-1945* (Ottawa: The Queens Printer, 1962), p. 48.

58. Order-in-Council, P.C. 365, January 16, 1942.

59. *Ibid.* One American evacuation study concludes that this Order-in-Council served as a model for Executive Order 9066 which authorized the American evacuation. The Canadian Order did not entail an elaborate pass system which the American authorities had previously thought would be necessary for legal reasons. See Michi Weglyn, *op. cit.,* pp. 69, 290.

60. Presumably Norman Robertson.

61. Pierrepont Moffat to Cordell Hull, Secretary of State, February 3, 1942, Department of State Papers, RG59, 740.00115 PW/147. National Archives, Washington.

62. King Diary, December 9, 1941, King Papers, MG26J13.

63. C. P. Stacey, *op. cit.,* pp. 399-400.

64. *Ibid.,* p. 47.

65. King Diary, February 20, 1942, King Papers MG26J13.

66. J. L. Granatstein, *op. cit.,* p. 43.

67. Roger Daniels, *op. cit.,* pp. 44-46. If Justice had refused, Gullion and Bendetsen had planned that the War Department would, by that action, be "forced" to take over responsibility for aliens.

68. N. A. Robertson to W. L. Mackenzie King, December 10, 1941, *op. cit.*

69. Joint Services Committee, Pacific Command, *Minutes,* December 5, 1941, Pacific Command Records, 193.009 (D3), D.H., D.N.D.

70. *Ibid.,* December 19, 1941.

71. *Ibid.,* January 9, 1942.

72. A. W. Sparling to A. Dixon (Mackenzie's secretary), Ian Mackenzie Papers, MG27IIIB5, Vol. 32, X-81.

73. Order-in-Council P.C. 251, January 13, 1942. The Press Release accompanying the announcement of this Order stressed that "Canada will continue to collaborate with Great Britain and the United States with a view to the substantial coordination of their policies in relation to persons of Japanese racial origin." Moffat's report on this Order makes no mention of any plans to remove anyone other than Japanese enemy aliens or citizen Japanese Canadians under this Order. P. Moffat to Cordell Hull, February 3, 1942, *op. cit.*

74. F. E. La Violette, *op. cit.,* pp. 40, 48.

75. Joint Services Committee, Pacific Command, *Minutes,* February 13, 1942, Pacific Command Records, 193.009 (D4) D.H., D.N.D.

76. Ian Mackenzie to W. L. Mackenzie King, January 10, 1942, *op. cit.*

77. See Ian Mackenzie Papers, Vol. 32, X-81 and X-81-2.

78. F. E. La Violette, *op. cit.,* p. 50.

79. See Gwen Cash, *A Million Miles From Ottawa* (Toronto: Macmillan, 1942). How typical Cash's opinions are is open to question. As a journalist who had very little positive to say about anything Ottawa did with respect to B.C., her biases are obvious. Her concern is not supported by other measures of public opinion. Between the January 14th announcement and the fall of Singapore on February 15th the Department of External Affairs, which was largely handling this issue, collected only 11 resolutions and 9 private letters on the subject.

80. Roger Daniels, *The Decision, op. cit.,* p. 24.

81. *Ibid.,* p. 25.

82. *Ibid.*

83. Hugh Keenleyside to W. L. Mackenzie King, January 26, 1942, Ian Mackenzie Papers, MG27IIIB5, Vol. 32, X-81-2.

84. Ian Mackenzie to J. L. Ralston, February 12, 1942, Ian Mackenzie Papers, MG27IIIB5, Vol. 32, X-81-2.

85. Hugh Keenleyside to N. A. Robertson, January 27, 1942, Ian Mackenzie Papers, MG27IIIB5, Vol. 32, X-81-2.

86. Ian Mackenzie to N. A. Robertson, January 28, 1942, Ian Mackenzie Papers, MG27IIIB5, Vol. 32, X-81-2. In all discussions of the B.C. Caucus the members are the 4 Conservative, 10 Liberal and 1 Independent M.P.'s from B.C. The 16th M.P. from B.C., Angus MacInnes,

a C.C.F. member consistently opposed the above on their Asian Canadian policies.

87. *Vancouver Sun,* January 15, 1942; Ian Mackenzie to J. L. Ralston, February 12, 1942, *op. cit.*

88. *Vancouver Sun,* February 16, 1942 and subsequent editions in that week.

89. *Vancouver Daily Province,* February 17, 1942.

90. F. E. La Violette, *op. cit.,* p. 49.

91. See "Citizens Defense Committee," British Columbia Security Commission Papers, RG36/27, Vol. 2/50.

92. *Ibid.;* and F. E. La Violette, *op. cit.,* p. 42.

93. G. S. Wismer to Ian Mackenzie, February 16, 1942; R. W. Maitland to Ian Mackenzie, T. W. S. Parsons to Louis St. Laurent, February 17, 1942, Ian Mackenzie Papers, MG27IIIB5, Vol. 32, X-81.

94. T. W. S. Parsons to Louis St. Laurent, *op. cit.*

95. Of the 70 resolutions collected between December 7, 1941 and February 24, 1942, 30 were from locals of larger organizations and 4 were repeats. All data are courtesy of the External Affairs Records, file 773-B-1-40, parts I and II as summarized by officials of the Directorate of History, Department of External Affairs.

96. The Mackenzie Papers Vol. 25, 70-25-1, -2, and -3 contain 18 anti-Japanese resolutions and 7 letters received before February 24, 1942, most of which were copies of resolutions sent to the Prime Minister and hence collected by the External Affairs Department. There are in addition 3 pro-Japanese Canadian letters and, contrary to the standard evacuation accounts, (See La Violette, p. 41), an 11 to 6 split *in favour* of accepting Japanese Canadian labour in the Okanagan Valley.

97. Ian Mackenzie to W. L. Mackenzie King, February 24, 1942, Ian Mackenzie Papers, MG27IIIB5, Vol. 25, 70-25-2.

98. Peter Ward, *op. cit.,* p. 302. In support of this statement Ward cites the Exernal Affairs and Mackenzie files cited above and a King file which this researcher found contained letters and resolutions written after the February 24th decision. The bulk of resolutions from other than traditional anti-Asian groups were sent after the announcement of evacuation and urged that the evacuation should be as rapid as possible.

99. King Diary, February 20, 1942, King Diary, MG26J13.

100. C. P. Stacey, *op. cit.,* p. 48.

101. King Diary, February 2, 1942, December 9, 1941, King Papers, MG26J13.

102. *Ibid.,* February 19, 1942.

103. Ian Mackenzie to Reeve Musselman, Haney B.C., February 22, 1942, Mackenzie Papers, MG27IIIB5, Vol. 32, X-81-3.

104. Joint Services Committee, Pacific Command, *Minutes,* February 13, 15, 19, 1942, *op. cit., Census of Canada 1941.*

105. Maurice A. Pope, *op. cit.,* p. 179.

106. King Diary, February 24, 1942, King Papers, MG26J13.

107. Canada, House of Commons, *Debates,* February 25, 1942, P. 810, as quoted in Patricia E. Roy, "The Evacuation of the Japanese, 1942," in J. M. Bumsted, ed., *Documentary Problems in Canadian History: Post Confederation* (Georgetown: Irwin Dorsey Ltd., 1969), p. 240.

108. Canada, War Cabinet Committee, *Minutes, op. cit.,* February 26, 1942.

109. *Ibid.*

110. If such intelligence had been received on the 23rd it would provide an explanation for the entry in King's Diary for that day which read: "I feel too we have been too slow in getting the Japanese population moved in B.C.," which otherwise does not fit the context in which it appears.

111. F. E. La Violette, *op. cit.,* p. 55.

9

Accommodation, Adaptation, and Policy: Dimensions of the South Asian Experience in Canada

Norman L. Buchignani
University of Alberta

Over the past twenty years, individuals of South Asian origin have become an important factor in Canadian immigration and presently constitute one of the fastest growing segments of the Canadian population. The purpose of this paper is to evaluate the present situation of South Asians in Canada and to suggest what implications these findings have for a range of governmental policies.[1] In doing so, I would like to deal with two basic questions. Section I addresses the first of these in temporal perspective: how and to what degree have other Canadians *accommodated* to South Asians? Framed differently, what progress has been made over the years in South Asians being accorded the rights, privileges, and responsibilities of other Canadians? The second question (Section II) concerns the nature of South Asian *adaptations* to this changing context: in what ways have South Asian individuals adapted to life in Canada?[2] In what areas have these adaptations been notably successful and why? Correspondingly, have there been any notable failures in adaptive strategies which have had detrimental effects on South Asian individuals? The third section considers how governmental *policies* in the areas of immigration, social participation, economic planning, and multiculturalism could be modified in the light of these interacting processes of accommodation and adaptation.

I. ACCOMMODATION: FROM DOMINATION TO TOLERANCE

A. The Early Years (1904-20)

The first South Asians to land in Canada were Sikhs, who arrived in British Columbia around 1900. These enterprising individuals came predominantly from the Far East looking for work. They quickly found jobs, wrote home to their relatives and friends of their good fortune, and thereby prompted an increasing number of others to sail for British Columbia. This new immigrant population could not have arrived at a time less likely to guarantee the fulfillment of their goals. Rising animosity to continued Chinese and Japanese immigration had recently resulted in the establishment of a $500 head tax on each Chinese immigrant (1903), and political moves were in progress to negotiate a restrictive immigration treaty with Japan. Worse still, not only were those South Asians identified as part of the "Asian Menace;" they were unfortunate enough to arrive in this hostile environment in the midst of a severe depression (1907-8) which left thousands out of work.[3]

Without home government support, these pioneers had few political resources with which to protect their situation, and soon found themselves formally and informally subordinated to a caste-like position in Canadian society. The federal government unilaterally banned the subsequent immigration of South Asians in 1909, including the wives and children of those legally here. The provincial government passed a series of laws which effectively barred South Asians from full social, political, and economic participation in the larger society. The severity of these restrictions is indicated in Table I.

The pattern of accommodation towards South Asians which predominated in that day was characterized by a wish for total exclusion. The physical removal of those South Asians then resident in British Columbia was politically impossible, even though an unsuccessful attempt was made in 1908-9 to convince South Asians to move to British Honduras (Harkin 1909). Failing in this ideal objective, the

European population settled for the next best solution: isolate those South Asians who were here in every way possible from the interests and activities of the dominant population.[4]

TABLE I

Accommodation to South Asians (1900-1920)[5]

	Barred or restricted from	Allowed
I. Formal-legal Rights		
A. Political Participation		
1. franchise	X	
2. citizenship	X	
3. office	X	
4. jury duty	X	
5. legal equality	X	
6. military duty	X	
7. legal redress	X	
8. immigration	X	
B. Social Participation		
1. cultural practices	X	
2. public facilities and services	X	
3. residential choice	X	
4. education facilities	X	
C. Economic Participation		
1. public occupations	X	
2. private occupations	X	
3. equal wages	X	
4. equal workplace rights	X	
5. purchase of property	X	
6. equality of taxation		X
7. business opportunities	X	
II. Additional Informal Rights of Social Participation		
1. freedom from arbitrary violence and abuse	X	
2. exogamy	X	
3. social group membership	X	
4. free association with others	X	
	22	1

B. The Quiet Years (1921-47)

Despite numerous court battles, the ban on further South Asian immigration established in 1909 was to remain in effect until 1947. The wives and dependent children of legal South Asian residents were allowed to immigrate after 1920, but by that time most of the 5,000 individuals who had originally come to Canada had returned home or moved on to California. The population stabilized at about 1,100 and was not to reach its earlier peak of 5,000 well into the 1950s. During these years, virtually all of the legal restrictions placed on South Asians prior to World War I continued in effect. Nevertheless, while South Asians were still seen as being an intrinsically different and inferior type of person and continued to be socially segregated, the economic depression of the 1930s was of such intensity as to mitigate some of the anti-South Asian practices of shopkeepers, real estate agents, and other businessmen. Consequently, resident South Asians were allowed to participate in an ever-increasing range of economic activities, even though they were still kept socially and ideologically separate.

During this same era, Chinese and Japanese immigration was almost completely terminated, with the result that British Columbian anti-Asian hostility subsided considerably. To an increasing extent, all three local Asian groups benefited from what, in essence, constituted an ideology of carefully delimited tolerance; as long as Asians remained "in their place" and did not agitate for change they were allowed a measure of freedom and decision-making in the private spheres of family and community. Table II approximates the pattern of accommodation characteristic of that era.

The end of the War found South Asian Canadians still socially, economically, and ideologically subordinate to most European Canadians. In 1946, South Asians in British Columbia continued to be denied the vote and therefore could not become Canadian citizens.[6] The immigration of their countrymen was completely barred by federal statute, and resident South Asians remained formally excluded from the professions and from political office. Occupationally, a caste line still constrained the vast majority of South Asian workers to unskilled jobs in the woods industries.

C. The Postwar Era (1947 - present)

The past three decades have seen a fundamental shift in the range of rights and privileges which have been accorded to South Asians in

TABLE II

Accommodation to South Asians (1920-1947)

	Barred or restricted from	Allowed
I. Formal-legal Rights		
A. Political Participation		
1. franchise	X	
2. citizenship	X	
3. office	X	
4. jury duty	X	
5. legal equality	X	
6. military duty	X	
7. legal redress	X	
8. immigration	X	
B. Social Participation		
1. cultural practices		X
2. public facilities and services		X
3. residential choice		X
4. educational facilities		X
C. Economic Participation		
1. public occupations	X	
2. private occupations	X	
3. equal wages		X
4. equal workplace rights		X
5. purchase of property		X
6. equality of taxation		X
7. business opportunities		X
II. Additional Informal Rights of Social Participation		
1. freedom from arbitrary violence and abuse		X
2. exogamy	X	
3. social group membership	X	
4. free association with others	X	
	13	10

Canada. Concurrently, there have been marked ideological shifts in how other Canadians view South Asians, and modes of social interaction have altered as well. These changes in accommodative patterns have nevertheless not occurred in a uniform manner, and in order to reflect this variation, it is useful to divide accommodation into three basic aspects and to discuss each in turn. These are:

1. formal legal allocation of rights and privileges
2. practical access to rights and privileges
3. social and ideological responses to South Asians

1. *Formal Allocation of Rights and Privileges*

Of these three, South Asians have seen accommodative responses move the furthest towards a situation of equality in their being granted legal rights similar to those of other Canadians. The British Columbian statutes, which barred South Asians from citizenship and the vote, were removed in 1947-8 as a result of the combined efforts of local South Asians and concerned provincial politicians. At the federal level, the postwar government found it increasingly difficult to hold a racially biased immigration policy in the face of increasing world criticism. Moreover, Canadian manpower demands argued for greater emphasis on economic, rather than racial or cultural criteria for immigrant selection. These two trends combined in an increasing liberalization of the immigration regulations regarding South Asians, from 1947 to 1964. In 1967, the immigration process was reorganized to formally disregard race, ethnicity, and nationality in the selection of immigrants. Today there exist no legal limitations which differentially affect South Asian Canadians.[7]

2. *Practical Access to Rights and Privileges*

It is obvious that the formal equality of South Asians does not constitute evidence that South Asians have been accorded practical access to the rights and privileges suggested by the law. This is not to imply that legal equality has not been without direct consequences. In most instances, it is now difficult for either individuals or institutions to overtly discriminate against South Asians without incurring liabilities incommensurate with gains. Formal, institutionalized discrimination of the pre-World War II variety no longer exists.

This is not to say that discrimination has been totally eliminated, for it has not. Rather, it has been severely restricted and no longer commands social or political approval. While data on the degree to which discrimination affects the life chances of individuals is very sparse, a considerable number of South Asians believe that they have been the victims of discrimination, and such evidence as exists confirms their opinions.[8] The most frequently mentioned types of discrimination seem to concentrate in two areas: hiring procedures and freedom from abuse and violence.

Analysis of the degree to which South Asian Canadians are the victims of discriminatory hiring practices is severely hampered by lack of data and by practical and methodological problems; these problems make it difficult to isolate discrimination from other processes. Certainly, job discrimination today is insufficient to produce the occupational castes of yesterday. In fact, there are indications that immigrant South Asians tend to find jobs quickly and are seldom unemployed for any length of time; neither of these could be possible if discrimination was a fundamental factor in hiring practices.[9]

At the same time, it has been my experience that South Asian immigrants have difficulty in acquiring jobs in their prior line of work, especially at the equivalent level they had before coming to Canada. Although downward occupational mobility has become a fact of life in a country with one million unemployed, I do not believe that this alone accounts for the number of South Asians working at jobs below their skills and abilities. Many South Asians moved into jobs for which they were overqualified in the late 1960s, when the unemployment rate was far lower than it is now; furthermore, the life histories of individuals clearly show the effect of other processes. Of these, I would consider the most important to be the inflexibility of employers in interpreting the occupational skills and work histories of prospective South Asian employees. Employers rarely make the effort to translate South Asian occupational qualifications into Canadian terms, thus placing the burden to do so on the applicant. South Asians do not enter the Canadian occupational spectrum at the bottom unless required to by economic considerations, yet they lack Canadian experience; consequently, any difficulties which arise in recertification, retraining, or establishing one's work record can be fundamental liabilities. This points out an important trend in the nature of present day accommodation:

> While South Asians have increasingly been accorded the right to participate in Canadian society in ways similar to other Canadians, in no fundamental way has the social and economic structure of Canadian society been modified in order to accommodate the particular backgrounds, skills, and objectives of South Asian immigrants.

Occasionally, this results in South Asians not achieving access to rights and privileges which are identical to those suggested by their equal status under the law.

3. *Social and Ideological Responses to South Asians*

Full social and ideological acceptance of South Asians by other Canadians has been very slow to arrive, and is a goal far from reach. In particular, a number of studies suggest that ideological acceptance of South Asians is at present far from being achieved.[10] Canadians still show a great sensitivity towards the display of divergent cultural practices. In this regard, critiques of presumed South Asian cultural and social practice abound, notably that they:

1. use deviant dress, food and language
2. live in overcrowded and unsanitary conditions
3. are violent and think themselves above the law
4. drain social services
5. immigrate illegally
6. exploit each other

These are all elements of a stereotypic Canadian view of South Asians which is over three-quarters of a century old.

While today this ideology is no longer realized in law and custom in such a way as to constitute a significant element in determining social stratification, it does have other negative consequences. For some individuals, these beliefs provide the rationale for name-calling, vandalism, and other expressions of prejudice, which in turn make South Asians question their place in Canadian society. These beliefs also signify that ideologically South Asians are *not* equal, even though they may enjoy a style of life which seems to indicate it.

Social responses to South Asians seem to be moving in two directions at the same time. Perhaps because of the failure of the legal system to impress upon individuals the belief that abuse and violence against South Asians will be met with certain punishment, both continue to be prevalent enough to warrant deep concern. With the exception of Native Canadians, I believe it would be difficult to argue that individuals of any other ethnic or national status are more likely to become victims of this sort of discrimination than South Asians. At the same time, the depth and frequency of interpersonal relationships between South Asians and others have increased, and South Asians are in no way as socially isolated as they once were. It would seem that this dualistic pattern of accommodation accurately reflects South Asian perceptions on this point: that responsible citizens at least minimally accept their presence, while abuse and violence are largely the work of a small number of irresponsible law breakers.

Summary

There can be no doubt that Canadian patterns of accommodation have shifted markedly over the past thirty years. Before World War II, South Asian Canadians constituted an almost ideal type subordinate racial caste. Today, limitations faced by South Asians are comparatively minimal. It is ironic that most of these changes have *not* been direct responses to a South Asian presence in Canada. Even today, South Asians constitute considerably less than 1% of the Canadian population and are widely dispersed across the country. Rather, the transformation of Canadian responses to South Asians which has occurred must be ascribed to more general factors. These must minimally include the following:

1. Changes in the structure of Canadian social stratification away from ethnic and towards class criteria for access.
2. Increasing urbanization, with a consequent diminution of ethnic-based communities and occupations.
3. Consequent changes in the ideology of what constitutes a Canadian, away from a specifically British definition towards one which devalues ethnicity and emphasizes "right action."

II. ADAPTATION

To go further in this analysis, one must consider the various adaptations that South Asians have made to life in Canada. Adaptation is of particular importance, for in it South Asians possess the only significant means other than political action by which they themselves can modify the overall process. In the following discussion, I would like to take a theoretical approach to adaptation which is based on the guiding principle that:

> people will hold to past ways of doing only in the absence of evidence that doing so has direct negative consequences. If alternative patterns of behaviour are seen by the *individual* to possess clear advantages over past practices those new patterns will be quickly accepted.

In this respect one can see cultural background as a variable — as a resource which individual immigrants strategically *use* and *modify* in the furtherance of their individual goals. By doing so, the action element of adaptation becomes individual decision-making. Taking such an orientation, each immigrant becomes a cultural entrepreneur, a person with a delimited set of cultural and economic *resources* looking for an adaptive *niche* which allows him to develop his resources towards the achievement of personal *objectives*. Consequently, the following questions about South Asian adaptive responses are relevant:

1. Does the immigrant's cultural, economic, and intellectual background provide sufficient resources to facilitate the achievement of his or her goals in Canada?
2. To what degree have immigrants seen it necessary to modify their cultural practices in an attempt to develop successful strategies for the fulfilment of goals, and what has been the measure of their success?
3. In what ways have new alternatives modified individual goals?
4. Have there been areas in which immigrants have not easily developed successful goal-directed strategies and if so, what have been the consequences of these adaptive failures?

A. Basic Goals and Fundamental Values

It has been frequently suggested that South Asian immigrants suffer, in particular, from being culturally different from other Canadians. In this regard it has become an orthodoxy that their set of basic life goals and orienting values are at variance with those of other Canadians, and consequently, that they are ill-prepared to contend with Canadian society. These presumed differences are said to have the consequences of limiting their economic prospects, minimizing their interaction with others, and generating numerous psychological problems of adjustment.

Are there fundamental cultural differences between South Asians and other Canadians? At a surface level, it might seem that cultural differences outweigh the similarities. Most certainly, South Asian values are not identical with those of native Canadians, as has been illustrated in selective areas, such as familial relations (Ames and Ingles 1973; Filteau 1978).

But consider those values and beliefs which underlie important social action and which are important to the immigrant's life chances — those concerning notions of economic success, basic rights and freedom, philosophies of society, and right and wrong behaviour; are things so different there? Consider the cultural, class, and national origins of the great majority of South Asian immigrants. Though they come from around the world, virtually all possess a common cultural denominator: the lasting effects of colonial British legal, economic, educational, and social institutions.

While I make no claim for the evaluative worth of these British derived institutions or the uses to which they have been placed in the post-colonial era, their prevalence has assured that South Asian immigrants have already been inculcated with the basic values of the industrialized nation state towards economics, politics, and society. In colonial India, one sees this process of value conversion well established by the late 1800s among those Indians who participated in the bureaucracy, the military, and the wage labour market (Mason 1971: 156). By the 1890s, overseas Indians in such diverse places as Fiji, South Africa, and the Far East were proving the thoroughness of their training by offering stiff economic competition to their British mentors (Gupta 1971). The rationalization of colonial rule during the early 1900s saw the establishment of modified forms of Western industrial, bureaucratic, and social organization in virtually all of the many places that South Asians then lived. With these institutions, there developed a neo-British style of life for the middle classes which duly revered cricket, tea, and the club. This process continues today, to the point where the organization of a factory, university, or governmental bureaucracy in Calcutta or Suva is now fundamentally no different than one in London; even the language spoken in these various contexts may be the same.

Thus, one can go further than affirming that the basic philosophical values of South Asians are similar to Canadian ones. South Asians are also in control of extensive practical knowledge about industrial social organization long before they ever came to Canada. Moreover, stiff immigrant selection criteria serve to amplify these ideological and practical parallels between South Asians and other Canadians by preferentially selecting individuals from among the skilled, educated, resourceful, and heavily anglicized middle classes. Furthermore, concurrent trends of modernization, urbanization, and economic rationalization in North America and the various source countries of South Asian immigrants, have also been factors in guaranteeing this ideological congruence.

This congruence is of great significance to the question of adaptive change. If an immigrant will modify his beliefs and practices only when he sees a concrete yield in doing so, maladaptive differences in fundamental values might persist for long periods of time, simply because basic philosophical stances are not easily refuted by experiential data.

These beliefs range in importance, individual commitment, and temporal persistence, from the philosophical and value-laden to practical, value-free knowledge about the everyday world. Clearly, any maladaptive beliefs held by the individual which lie at deeper levels are less

TABLE III
Levels of Belief

Consider the following interdependent levels of belief:

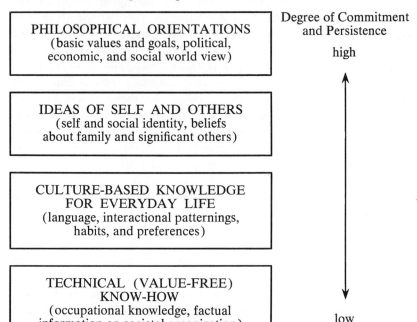

| PHILOSOPHICAL ORIENTATIONS (basic values and goals, political, economic, and social world view) | Degree of Commitment and Persistence
high |

IDEAS OF SELF AND OTHERS
(self and social identity, beliefs
about family and significant others)

CULTURE-BASED KNOWLEDGE
FOR EVERYDAY LIFE
(language, interactional patternings,
habits, and preferences)

TECHNICAL (VALUE-FREE)
KNOW-HOW
(occupational knowledge, factual
information on societal organization)   low

amenable to change than those which do not directly involve self and world view. In this light, the claim of essential value and goal similarity between South Asians and other Canadians radically diffuses possible critiques of maladaptive cultural difference, by relegating such differences to those areas of belief and practice which are either amenable to rapid modification or irrelevant to successful adaptation.

B. Institution Adaptation

Strong supporting evidence to this claim of South Asian cultural preadaptation comes from their quick and successful adjustment to the institutional order of Canadian society. Take employment, for example. Despite their initial unfamiliarity with the Canadian job market, most South Asian immigrants quickly find jobs and soon secure ones which are at least minimally satisfactory. By way of example, I have found that over one-third of South Asian Fijians in the metropolitan Vancouver area secured their first job within two weeks of arriving here; the majority were employed within a month, and virtually all found jobs within the first two months.[11] Moreover, their institutional adaptation to the economic structure here has been such that presently over 60% of wives work.[12] Nowhere does one find evidence of "otherworldly" work habits (Weber 1958). Rather, South Asian Canadians are paradigm "work ethnics."[13]

Further, these new immigrants rapidly adapt to the material preferences of other Canadians and to the means by which such goods and services are procured. Immigrants commonly buy their own homes within five years of arriving in Canada, by which time they have unreservedly accepted Canadian patterns of material consumption, save for a very limited range of consumer items, such as food. In fact, they typically hold to a "protestant ethic" of work and expenditure much more firmly than their Protestant neighbours.[14] Rarely do cultural considerations impede the buying of bargains or trying new things.

South Asians tend to come from countries with legal and political institutions which are at least formally similar to their counterparts in Canada. Thus, in this sphere, there is very little need for adaptation. South Asian Canadians rather scrupulously respect the law, and there is no evidence that their criminal participation rates are in any way unusual. Moreover, they already know basically how the legal and informational system operates and how to gain access to it. This same rapidity of institutional adjustment has been enthusiastically pursued in the areas of education and social services.

C. Cultural Difference as an Adaptive Resource

In a very concrete sense, each immigrant, South Asian or otherwise, must constantly decide where to activate, suppress, or modify behavioural practices learned elsewhere. In the context of such decision-making, cultural difference cannot be regarded only as a liability. Rather, it often constitutes an important individual *resource*. Thus immigrants tend to continue to use whatever there is in their cultural inventories that they perceive furthers their goals.

Many instances of this active calculus of decision-making exist. In the public realm, one must more or less acquiesce to the institutional order as it stands. While working, shopping, or driving down the street, divergent cultural practice is largely irrelevant, constrained as such activities are by their setting; it is not possible to drive a car in a "South Asian manner."

With the exception of a few small businessmen and community spokespersons, the adaptive advantages of a different background in the public sphere are minimal. Predictably, in public South Asians have almost instantaneously adjusted to Canadian practice. In the world of family, friends, and kin the potential advantages of using cultural difference as a resource are far greater. In particular, a considerable number use forms of community-based social organization to their concrete advantage. As an instance, take the process of immigration itself. An immigrant who goes it alone from the point of application to establishment here pays a very heavy penalty for his independence, and gains no compensating positive benefits; the development of an informational, financial, and social basis for the transition rests entirely on one person's limited abilities and resources. Relatively few South Asian immigrants follow this route. Instead, they selectively activate their relationships with kin and friends in such a way as to make the transition easier, less costly, and of lower risk.

It is well known that South Asian immigration has always been characterized by extensive chain migration. This is hardly a "genetic" tendency, but rather has persisted because of its tangible yields. Very often, the only substantial information about Canada that a prospective immigrant will receive comes from his Canadian kin and close friends. Immigration itself is an extremely expensive proposition, especially in respect to source country incomes, and Canadian relatives very often carry a portion of this burden until the family has established a Canadian income and can repay the loan.

Upon arrival in Canada, most South Asians are able to continue to benefit from this sort of support while they establish themselves. At the very least, they are met at the airport by kin and friends, brought home, introduced to others, and informationally assisted in finding a job and a place of their own. Many stay temporarily with relatives while they get their bearings; it is from this psychologically safe spot that they make their first forays into, what is at that point, an alien and anonymous country, unassisted by the Canadian establishment. By doing so, new immigrants benefit considerably over individuals who cannot exercise these culturally-based options; they are with people who understand their needs, they are freed from a heavy expenditure of funds when they can least afford it, and they get quick (though not necessarily accurate) answers to their numerous questions.

Different social conventions also aid the longer term prospects of many immigrant South Asians, especially where South Asian practice allows them to operate in association with each other to achieve goals which other Canadians normally aim for individually. A considerable number, for instance, continue to live with kin for varying lengths of time subsequent to arriving in Canada, and in so doing, derive numerous advantages. Their *per capita* expenses are cut because residence with relatives (even if in separate suite) usually leads to lower economic costs. In extended households there are also the benefits of scale: lower capital furnishings costs, lower levels of per capita household work (such as baby-sitting), the sharing of utility and food costs, and the like.

Most South Asian Canadians participate in extensive social networks of kin and friends which provide the basis for the re-establishment of a measure of community within an urban setting — something that most of us have lost as an indirect consequence of industrialization. Such social networks clearly serve to mitigate the necessarily alienating aspects of immigration, which among other immigrant groups has led to high levels of anxiety and depression. To a certain extent, these relations also serve to support individual self identity by providing a social framework wherein individuals can interact with others with the knowledge that they will be understood in their own terms and judged by their own criteria. In this manner, the community serves as a beneficial bridge between two social orders.

At the community level, adaptive advantages conferred by prior practice and belief are largely limited to the private sphere. This is especially so in economic terms. Nowhere in Canada have South Asians been able to build up an ethnically-based economic infrastructure sufficient to confer economic benefit on more than a handful of resourceful entrepreneurs. Economic entrepreneurship for most is of small scale and is relegated to the provision of goods and services not duplicated by larger and more capital-intensive firms. Few South Asian Canadians are presently in a position to hire their kin and countrymen.

Nevertheless, community networks provide several important benefits, notably in the areas of the provision of information and in mutual aid. For instance, dense community networks are extremely sensitive to job openings, and often serve as informational routes to jobs that would otherwise go to others. Community also ties South Asian Canadians to the concerns of those overseas; most immigrants neither choose to nor are able to completely detach themselves from concerns and responsibilities in their source countries, and a steady flow of visitors in both directions is an important link between these two spheres. Community based mutual aid can also be quite important. Loans often pass from one relative to another, enabling individuals to buy houses sooner than they would be able to if they were to depend entirely on their own resources. Tragedies, like a death in the family, are usually met with extremely solid support.

Finally, close kin and friendship networks also provide a sort of interpersonal common ground which transcends the very marked individual differences between one South Asian individual and another. Although other Canadians tend to see South Asians as one homogenous group composed of individuals with similar backgrounds and present circumstances, this is manifestly not so. Even within one ethnic or national group there exists a measure of heterogeneity which may be greater than exists in most Western nations; nevertheless, techniques of social interaction based on kinship and common origin are of such effectiveness that individuals of very divergent backgrounds can be molded into a common social network.

D. Key Problems in Adaptation

The establishment of South Asians in Canada has not come without some adaptive problems, but these are relatively minor in the light of what must be judged an overall success. At the level of the individual, adaptive failures rarely seem to be fundamental, and virtually all difficulties which exist seem to arise in the areas of secondary cultural practices, technical knowledge, or in response to what is perceived as their incomplete acceptance by others.

Let us consider culture-based practice first. Let an unsuccessful adaptive strategy be defined as one which less profitably leads to the attainment of valued goals than another strategy which might reasonably be utilized in the same situation by the same individual. By these criteria, the only way in which the expression of culturally different behaviour leads to maladaptive results seems to be through such behaviour providing other Canadians with ethnic diacritica which serve to support preconceived negative stereotypes of South Asians. These diacritica are of a fairly restricted nature, and include the public display of what are presumed by others to be South Asian:

1. *Food, Dress, and Personal Appearance*
   (curried food and associated smells, use of saris, turbans, and different footware, different colour sense, beards, long hair, etc.)

2. *Linguistic Etiquette*
   (use of South Asian language, different accent, speaking loudly, etc.)

3. *Interactional Strategies*
   (high social distance, argumentativeness, aggressiveness, attempted negotiation of the non-negotiable, etc.)

4. *Domestic Practices*
    (extended residential groups, care of the house, noise, constant
    coming and going)

The immediate negative consequences *for the individual* experiencing
these things seems to be minimal; occasionally they provoke prejudicial
responses like name calling and vandalism, but rarely are these responses such that they significantly limit the goal achievement of
individuals. That the first three of these might negatively affect ethnic
relations has been concluded by many South Asian Canadians, and
they have become bicultural in a true sense, switching behaviour
patterns depending on circumstance.

By far, the most significant impediments to a smooth individual
adjustment to Canada do *not* spring from cultural differences and are,
for the most part, problems shared by all immigrants from non-Western
countries. They are problems which arise from a simple lack of
information. By this, I do not mean to suggest that South Asian immigrants are uneducated or that they could use more formal training.
Rather, I would claim that it is very common that immigrant South
Asians lack access to specific types of practical knowledge which in
turn limits their social and economic mobility in ways not dictated by
their skills or personal ambitions. In particular, this selective disadvan-
tage seems to affect occupational prospects and access to social services.

Occupational skills and related job demand are two of the most
important criteria for immigrant selection, and unless one calls the
whole selection mechanism into question, it must be presumed that
immigrants are capable of doing the jobs for which they have been
selected. Nevertheless many South Asian immigrants experience considerable downward occupational mobility. It would seem that a
number of South Asian immigrants have become trapped between two
somewhat opposed objectives: the immediate need for a secure financial
base for their families and the achievement of a job commensurate
with their qualifications. Often necessity determines that the former
route be taken at the expense of the latter; after an unsuccessful initial
attempt at finding work in their field, immigrants rationally accept work
for which they are overqualified. In turn, the subsequent achievement
of an adequate standard of living, combined with the constraints which
working puts on searching for a more rewarding job, results in many
never returning to their original line of work.

Informationally, South Asians and other non-Western immigrants, are
selectively disadvantaged in finding appropriate employment in the
following areas:

1. In finding job openings: trained South Asians normally must rely on formal advertisements rather than informal information.

2. In making an application: recent immigrants frequently have problems in documenting and presenting their training and work experience.

3. In becoming recertified: often South Asians find that their overseas union or professional statuses do not have precise equivalents here or that the route to recertification is not clear.

4. In upgrading their qualifications: rarely do immigrants know the range of available specific educational options or the benefits of occupational upgrading.

5. In entering the work force for the first time: women in particular find it difficult, lacking both overseas and Canadian experience.

6. In knowing their rights on the job: once employed, South Asians are often unaware of occupational mobility rights in the workplace.

Similar sorts of informational limitations occasionally affect the life chances of South Asians in other areas. The extensive Canadian availability of credit can lead to problems of financial overextension; individuals are occasionally taken in by salesmen because of a similar lack of experience. Additionally, lack of a clear understanding of the nuances of the immigration regulations sometimes has the effect of individuals not maximizing their access to that process.

D. Self and Social Identities

The view of South Asian Canadians developed thus far has been largely a sociological one, which has attempted to evaluate whether the adaptive strategies and goals of these individuals are commensurate with their present situation. But the question of adaptation is also a *social* question of obvious importance to the individuals involved. How do South Asian Canadians view their situation? If not happy with their new environment and their place in it, do they see these as adequate? Moreover, what effects have immigration had on their ideas of self and others? These are very complex questions for which only tentative answers can now be put forward; definitive answers are likely to be highly dependent upon individual situation, class, and ethnicity.

Let us first consider whether South Asians in Canada seem satisfied with their achievements and with the response of other Canadians to them. Satisfaction is clearly a relative measure: satisfied as compared to what? Relative to the past, most seem pleased by their material success and by their future material prospects. Save for a few, immigration has brought a marked advance in material standards of living — especially in housing, consumer goods, wages, and access to social services.

In comparing their present *social* circumstances with those of the past, many individuals are less certain that they have benefited from coming to Canada. South Asians often see themselves as being more socially isolated than ever before in their lives, and those who do not find structural replacements for community often feel severely disadvantaged. Women, especially, seem to suffer from this loss of community, for unlike men, their relative lack of jobs and easy transportation often prevent them from developing alternative self definitions. This is a phenomenon which is hardly restricted to South Asians.

Also, the fact that criteria for social status are not the same in pre- and post-immigration contexts usually leads to the experience of status inconsistency. One finds that immigration results in a rapid conversion of status indicators, from the multiplicity of factors (power, authority, ascribed honorific status, privilege, etc.) active in the source context, to essentially one — privilege — as expressed by a good home, secure job, and established family. This change in the calculus of status results in a measure of uncertainty of how one's own social worth is being evaluated; it also results in the continual renegotiation of status within the arena of conflicting measures. Many of those whose prior statuses were based on criteria such as honour, or elite occupation, find that immigration results in a considerable status demotion.

In measuring satisfaction against the perceived successes and failures of other Canadians, many South Asians express feelings of extreme relative deprivation. They believe that they are not doing as well as other Canadians and that they are not accorded social honour commensurate with what they have achieved. While it is evident that these ideas are not altogether realistic, they are nonetheless of extreme importance, for they are likely to have direct and long-term effects on the immigrant's perception of his place in Canadian society.

It would seem that one of the most important sources for these feelings of relative deprivation stem from an intellectually consistent but empirically false comparison between immigrant material success and the relative situations of other Canadians. South Asian immigrants know the nature of the severe social and economic constraints of their source countries; access to power, privilege, and prestige was extremely limited and highly dependent on birth. In contrast, immigrant South Asians often tend to uncritically accept idealistic Canadian immigrant lore on how access to these same scarce resources is determined here: they believe that hard work leads to success (at least for other Canadians) in this "open" society of unlimited resources. They are convinced that nothing but a lack of effort will keep them from the certain path, from the "log cabin to Whitehorse."[15] South Asian immigrants are also convinced that the rights and privileges formally granted to Canadians are, in fact, generally available.

It is obvious that *anyone* measuring his situation by axioms such as these must experience considerable relative deprivation, for he is, in effect, comparing his own experience with an ideal measure. Worse yet, it is only consistent that individual South Asian limitations often tend to be explained in terms of (visible, individualized) discrimination rather than in terms of (invisible, impersonal) social constraints, and thus is generated a considerable measure of unwarranted paranoia. No one can see a "social force" or an unemployment rate, and it is not inconsistent to think that one did not get a job because of discrimination, despite there being over one million other Canadians also out of work. The prevalence of poverty among native Canadians, for instance, is quite invisible to their eyes. It is therefore not uncommon that South Asians see far more social problems surrounding their establishment in Canada than are warranted by the facts. These problems are often voiced as abstract concerns over such things as discrimination and prejudice (re: jobs, housing, immigration, personal attacks), and the decay of societal morals.

These ideas are reinforced by the limited nature of individual informational access and by the place of community spokespersons in these communication channels. Of structural necessity, spokespersons are gatekeepers who interface between two quite different constituencies — the ethnic group and the "public" (read government and the media). As such, spokespersons increase the saliency of social problems, even if they do not intentionally wish to do so. The government and the media take spokespersons to be representative of ethnic group members, and both the government and media tend to emphasize the problematic; they expect spokespersons to be speaking in a problem mode. On the other hand, individual ethnic group members think that spokespersons can accomplish far more than they can. Of necessity, the problems fed through spokespersons must be relatively abstract and generalized if they are to have a wide ranging impact on government and media. Unfortunately, abstract statements on discrimination and prejudice (for instance, on police racism) made by spokespersons must simultaneously give support to feelings of relative deprivation on the part of ethnic group members.

Because of the limited and sometimes contradictory sources of information they receive, many South Asians are unsure of how they are perceived by other Canadians. Frequently, South Asian social relations with other Canadians are warm and friendly, but are these exceptions to the rule or do they prove it? South Asians in Canada must acknowledge the depths of Canadian ignorance of their cultural background, and must realize that others do not fundamentally understand who they are. Moreover, these friendships are commonly constrained from the overt discussion of ethnicity and ethnic worth. At the same time, contrary opinions suggesting that other Canadians dislike or discriminate against them is readily available via the press and community. Thus, South Asians psychologically operate under a dual burden of having to reformulate their self identity in a context where they are also unsure of their social identity. Often this leads to individuals turning inward to the protection of their ethnic-based social networks and to a consequent minimization of social contacts with other Canadians — especially in the realm of (non-ethnic) community organization and politics.

E. Future Prospects

Prospects for the future development of South Asian adaptive strategies presently appear positive. Certainly, they are better than is generally imagined. First generation South Asian Canadians have to date rapidly adjusted to the Canadian context in ways that benefit both the individual and society. Ineffective or incomplete adaptations are such that they only partially limit access or satisfaction; positive aspects of adaptation so predominate that virtually all South Asian immigrants soon enjoy a standard of living well above the lowest quartile of the Canadian born population.

One obvious change that the future will see is increasing acculturation among South Asians to Canadian values and behaviour. Fundamental acculturation is almost certain to occur in the second generation, who are today rapidly adjusting to the acculturative forces of school, television, day care centres, and their peers. To the degree to which accommodative patterns allow it, the Canadian born will in most respects be culturally identical with their age mates. There is no evidence that cultural differences persist longer among second generation South Asians than among many other types of immigrants.

III. POLICY IMPLICATIONS

These interrelated processes of accommodation and adaptation have direct implications for public policy, notably in regard to individual access to rights under the law and the maximization of societal human resources.

A. Accommodation

Let us first consider ways in which governmental action can affect accommodation. Broadly speaking, I believe that there are two basic areas in which policy changes might realistically hope to affect the accommodation of Canadians to others: education and the law.

In considering the possible re-education of Canadians about South Asians and others, it must be kept in mind that there is no hard evidence that prior policy decisions of any sort have significantly contributed to the positive changes in Canadian attitudes towards South Asians. Canadians have, in a sense, re-educated themselves on this question. Nevertheless, I do believe that selective and well planned governmental entry into this area would generate useful results.

I believe that it would be extremely difficult and inefficient to attempt to change adult attitudes towards those of other cultural backgrounds. There exist no institutionalized settings where this might efficiently be done. Moreover, what other Canadians lack, particularly, is realistic, personalized information about South Asians, yet I see no ready vehicle for conveying such information through governmental programs; cultural events or problem-solving meetings are likely to attract only the committed, and their effects are likely to be diffuse.

There are, however, areas of adult information communication where I believe that governmental action might effectively be taken. One of these concerns media coverage. Regardless of the contrary claims of media spokespersons, coverage of South Asians in the media is heavy and stigmatic (Indra 1978a, 1978b). The media must stand as a source of information about those things one cannot experience directly, such as the ethnicity of others. A reasonable governmental response would be to suggest to newspapers and other media that they generate human rights press codes (as has been done in the U.K.), regulated by boards made up of both media personnel and citizens from the community.

Another informational realm open to possible governmental intervention is in publicizing immigration. Immigration constitutes a governmental policy, one supposedly based on a clear charter of objectives. Nevertheless, I believe that the government has been extremely lax in not actively defending and explaining its immigration policy to the public and outlining what effects immigration has on Canadian society and economy. Many Canadians hold a number of misapprehensions about immigration which might be mitigated by aggressive governmental public relations. It is commonly believed that immigration is a form of foreign aid to source countries or that it serves to reduce their populations. Immigrants are suspected of draining social services and causing unemployment. There can be no doubt that governmental silence on this issue contributes to the *de facto* scapegoating of immigrants.

Finally, the CBC and the National Film Board should be sensitized to the almost total English and French domination of their respective products which currently exists; both could provide effective vehicles for the presentation of ethnicity and ethnic relations in Canada by simply incorporating individuals of various ethnic backgrounds into programs and films in such a way as to reflect the Canadian population.

Educational programs directed at children would seem to be the most effective means by which government might affect patterns of accommodation. Such programs need not be of high cost, seem to be effective where they are presently being attempted, and constitute a general learning experience beyond their "applied" intent. There presently exists a general ignorance of the place of those who are of neither English nor French heritage in Canada — a selective ignorance of the lives of over one-third of the population. Considering this situation, programs aimed at informing children of the variety of cultures represented by present day Canadians would also educate them about the place of their forefathers in Canadian history.

Beyond attempting to change societal values in the above ways, government could positively affect the direction of accommodation by changing the present treatment of discrimination by the law. Present human rights legislation has not demonstrated its effectiveness in convincing potential discriminators that there is much of a likelihood that their illegal acts will be dealt with severely. Racially motivated abuse and violence are often treated by the legal system as acts of ignorance rather than as what they are — criminal assault and crimes against property. At present, the defense of "not knowing the other fellow's culture" is often seriously considered by the courts (Saram and Hirabayashi 1978). Government should make it clear that those who violate the human rights of others are very likely to be jailed.

B. Adaptation

On the whole, I believe that there are good reasons for believing that governmental programs addressing adaptations would be far more effective and beneficial to South Asian Canadians than those dealing with accommodation. For one thing, the per capita resources that government can bring to bear on problems of adaptation are far greater. Moreover, immigrants are already in a mode of change, and ought therefore to be more susceptible to policy programs than other Canadians. Perhaps most importantly, it is evident that there exist specific areas where governmental programs are almost certain to have immediate and positive results.

Let us begin with the process of immigration itself. While the Canadian government has no responsibility to advertise or advocate immigration in source countries, it is in the government's interest to give potential immigrants a realistic assessment of their Canadian prospects. In areas where immigration has traditionally been high, it might be possible to arrange meetings of prospective immigrants, where government staff address the question of one's first few years in Canada; such sessions should *not* be made with intentions of propagandizing an ideal view of Canada, but rather should be specifically problem-related. It would not be inappropriate to change the immigration regulations in order to require that all those granted immigrant visas take a short pre-immigration course in how to facilitate themselves in Canada. Such a course could be offered in Canada or abroad or both. Subjects dealt with might include:

1. how to apply for and secure jobs
2. how everyday social services work and how they are funded
3. where to go for specific types of problems
4. a factual analysis of the things to which some other Canadians are sensitive
5. a realistic assessment of the expected range of situations an immigrant is likely to face
6. an assessment of the tradeoffs of immigration, and what strategies help to mitigate them

Any such program would have to be interactional to be effective, and I would suggest that the use of earlier immigrants as resource personnel might be especially productive.

Subsequent to immigration, it remains in the government's self interest to assure that these new Canadians establish themselves in a fashion commensurate with their skills and abilities. At present, immigrants walk off the plane into a new societal world completely unassisted. Even though South Asian immigrants will likely have relatives and friends waiting at the airport, the lack of information services at that point usually begins a more or less permanent separation of the immigrant from governmental agencies, which in turn may lead to exploitation and unnecessary difficulties.

Government could also participate more vigorously in guaranteeing that the skills which allow immigrants entry into Canada are used once they are here. Again, it would be extremely productive if government would attempt to develop mechanisms to match immigrants to jobs. This is now done by the Department of Employment, but I believe that the development of a set of separate mechanisms specifically translating overseas qualifications into Canadian terms, educating new immigrants on application techniques, and informing them of routes towards further skill development would be beneficial. These activities might be taken on by local immigrant aid centers, whose primary function is now one of directing immigrants to other agencies.

As it stands, South Asians are severely underrepresented in community affairs, politics, sports, the police, the armed forces, and entertainment — areas where participation would help to further their acceptance by other Canadians. There are three obvious approaches to this problem: make these organizations aware of the need to solicit South Asian recruits, inform South Asians of the advantage of participating, or create bridging institutions to connect these organizations with their South Asian equivalents. Untapped potential exists in each of these directions.

In certain specific ways, government needs to interface with South Asians as immigrants or as members of various ethnic groups, in order to address immigrant problems and to gain South Asian input into multicultural programs. This sort of communication between South Asian individuals and government is at present weakly established, largely because of the heavy dependence of both government and people on spokespersons to provide the connecting links. While spokespersons can be valuable political assets to an ethnic group when acting as advocates for general group objectives, they cannot be expected to be able to effectively communicate the everyday concerns of individuals to government. Because of their duty to reflect a constituency which often has a specific ethnic, national, or class background, spokespersons also find it difficult to foster intergroup South Asian harmony and collective action.

As a means of mitigating these communication difficulties, I believe that government should move in two directions. First, government should attempt to represent itself more aggressively at the grassroots level to identify the ways South Asian Canadians might be assisted by government. Direct mail advertisement of government services would be useful. The development of ongoing informational programs aimed at immigrant (rather than specifically South Asian) problems would also be beneficial if modeled after the successful English language classes now found across the country. I believe that similar programs dealing with such topics as entering the workforce, routes to job re-training, women as new Canadians, and day care leader training would be likewise supported if they were more commonly available. Second, government should create more organizations which crosscut specifically ethnic considerations or which minimally unite the multitude of South Asian organizations in terms of common goals. South Asians are likely to remain less effective politically than they might be in representing themselves, until they join together organizationally and develop support from others who share their interests and problems.

Because of the breadth and increasing diversity of today's federal multicultural program, I would like to address it at the level of philosophy and policy. Multicultural policy has clearly become more flexible over the past few years, and I believe that it has performed creditably, especially in consideration of the wide range of group and individual interests which it addresses. Nevertheless, I believe that the following qualifications remain relevant, especially with respect to South Asian Canadians:

1. Multiculturalism should not foster social isolation, rivalry, or mutual suspicion, yet it often does by requiring small ethnic groups (often of the same nationality) to organize and compete against each other for funding. Save for exceptional circumstances, funding for cultural programs and events should be directed through pan-ethnic organizations with heavy governmental input.

2. It is not at this point clear what is to be preserved by multiculturalism: is it ethnic identity or material culture?

3. Too much funding for cultural happenings presently goes into activities in which most individuals can participate only as viewers.

4. What officially is recognized to be ethnic culture often bears no relationship to what today's people do. Rather, it often centers around activities which always were elitist, and which represent arts and crafts of another era. In this sense, (High) Culture is being confused with (everyday) culture, and only the former receive significant governmental support.

5. An important aspect of multiculturalism is to foster a *Canadian* awareness of the diversity of cultures in Canada, and to redefine what constitutes a Canadian. In furthering this objective, more funding should be directed to Canadian ethnic history and to ethnic culture which has developed in the Canadain context.

Finally, I believe that government should fund more social science research on South Asians. Such funding should not be given uncritically; ignorance on this general subject is considerable, but not all research would be equally useful at this point. The following topics seem to have greater priority than others:

1. ethnographies accentuating adaptation and establishment
2. ethnic relations research based on actual, observed behaviour
3. empirical assessments of the degree to which discrimination (not prejudice) affects individual life chances
4. studies of the immigration process from source country perspectives
5. analyses of social service use
6. concurrent research on the implementation of new governmental programs dealing with South Asians

NOTES

1. Because of the general level of this paper, I have chosen to deal with individuals of South Asian origin as a whole, recognizing that considerable variation exists among the individuals and groups subsumed under such a broad category. I would like to thank Doreen Indra and P. A. Saram for their editorial suggestions during the development of this paper. This paper was presented in the Asian Canadian Symposium held at the Annual Meeting of the Canadian Society for Asian Studies and funded by the Secretary of State (multiculturalism).

2. By adaptation, I refer to the patterns of response which individuals make to their social and intellectual environment. I therefore do not mean to infer that adaptation is synonymous with assimilation, accultration, or absorption.

3. An extensive bibliography of South Asians in Canada can be found in Buchignani (1977a).

4. These limitations very closely paralleled those which were developed to subordinate the Chinese and Japanese (Angus 1937).

5. Where formal restrictions existed, often so did informal ones of a similar nature. In order to avoid redundancy, I have listed under "informal restrictions" only those which did not overlap with formal

restrictions. For more detail on historical restrictions against South Asians in British Columbia, see Lai (1976) or Buchignani (1977b: 1-76).

6. In order to avoid being overruled on constitutional questions by the federal government, virtually all the restrictions which the British Columbia government placed on South Asians were ultimately dependent on them being barred from the provincial voting list.

7. The one exception to this statement would be those South Asian Canadians who remain landed immigrants: landed immigrants do not enjoy the same rights and privileges as do Canadian citizens.

8. There are a number of studies which indicate that some Canadians harbour prejudicial attitudes towards South Asians; see note 10. On discrimination, see Chandra (1973) and Pitman (1977). Indra and Buchignani (1978) have shown through survey techniques that both Sikh (n = 100) and Fijian (n = 120) South Asians consider discrimination and prejudice to be significant social problems. We found, however, that Sikhs on the whole ascribed more importance to these questions than did Fijians and that there was extreme individual variability of response to questions in this area among both groups.

9. By this statement I do not mean to minimize the importance of dealing with discrimination in employment. Because employment is so crucial to the establishment of immigrants, I believe that even relatively low levels of discrimination are intolerable and should be aggressively dealt with under the law.

10. See Richmond (1974), Berry (1977), Frideres (1978), and Naidoo (1978).

11. This data derives from Buchignani (1977b) and from the survey mentioned in note 8.

12. See note 11.

13. The term "work ethnics" was suggested by P. A. Saram. On Sikh work habits in rural British Columbia, see Joy (1978). On the weaknesses of applying the Weberian thesis to Indians, see Buchignani (1977c).

14. This sort of economic resourcefulness was shown by pioneer Sikh immigrants as well. Although the majority came during and immediately prior to the severe depression of 1907-8, by the end of 1909 they were able to commence construction of an expensive and substantial Sikh *gudwara*.

15. This phrase suggesting the Canadian version of the American dream is also from P. A. Saram.

BIBLIOGRAPHY

Ames, Michael M., and Joy Inglis.
1973. Conflict and Change in British Columbia Sikh Family Life. *B.C. Studies* 20 (Winter): 15-49.

Angus, H. F.
1937. The Legal Status in British Columbia of Residents of Oriental Races and their Descendants. In *The Legal Status of Aliens in Pacific Countries.* N. A. M. Mackenzie, ed. pp. 77-87. London: Oxford University Press.

Berry, John, et. al.
1977. *Multiculturalism and Ethnic Attitudes in Canada.* Ottawa.

Buchignani, N. L.
1977a. A Review of the Historical and Sociological Literature on East Indians in Canada. *Canadian Ethnic Studies,* IX(1):86-108.

Buchignani, N. L.
1977b. Immigration, Adaptation, and the Management of Ethnic Identity: An Examination of Fijian East Indians in British Columbia. Ph.D. Dissertation, Department of Sociology and Anthropology, Simon Fraser University.

Buchignani, N. L.
1977c. Weber, Work, and Religion: A Reconsideration of the Protestant Ethic thesis as applied to India. *Archives de Sciences Sociales des Religions.* 42:10-25.

Chandra, K. U.
1973. *Racial Discrimination in Canada.* San Francisco: R & E Research Associates.

Filteau, L.
1978. "Family among East Indian Immigrants." Canadian Society for Asian Studies annual meeting, Guelph. presentation.

Frideres, J.
1978. British Canadian Attitudes Toward Minority Ethnic Groups in Canada. *Ethnicity* 5:20-32.

Gupta, A., ed.
1971. *Indians Abroad: Africa and Asia.* New Delhi: Orient Longman.

Harkin, J. B.
1909. *The East Indians of British Columbia.* A Report regarding the Proposal to provide Work in British Honduras for the Indigent Unemployed among Them. Ottawa: Minister of the Interior.

Indra, D.
1978a. "The Production and Legitimation of South Asian Stereotypes by the Vancouver Press." mimeo.

Indra, D.
1978b. The Portrayal of Ethnicity in the Vancouver Press, 1901-1976.

Ph.D. Dissertation, Department of Sociology and Anthropology, Simon Fraser University. in progress.

Indra D. and N. L. Buchignani
1978. A Comparison of Sikh and Fijian Attitudes about their Place in Canada. in progress.

Joy, A.
1978. "Portuguese and East Indians of the Okanagan Valley," CSAS annual meeting, Guelph. presentation.

Lal, Brij
1976. East Indians in British Columbia, 1904-1914: A Historical Study in Growth and Integration. M.A. Dissertation, History Department, University of British Columbia.

Mason, Philip
1971. *Patterns of Dominance*. London: Oxford University Press.

Naidoo, J.
1978. "Canadian Perspectives on East Indians." CSAS annual meeting, Guelph, presentation.

Pitman, W.
1977. *Now is Not Too Late*. Toronto: Metro Toronto.

Richmond, A.
1974. *Aspects of the Absorption and Adaptation of Immigrants*. *Ottawa:* Department of Manpower and Immigration.

Saram, P. A. and G. Hirabayashi
1978. "Some Issues Regarding Ethnic Relations Research." CSAS annual meeting, Guelph, mimeo.

Weber, M.
1958. *The Religion of India*. New York: Free Press.

10

The Foreign Student Experience in Canada Today

Ruth Groberman
Director Student Affairs
University of Alberta, Edmonton, Alberta

International Students in Canada have become a topic guaranteed to arouse the emotions of the Canadian public. There are those who feel they are an imposition on our institutions and a drain on our economy — there are others who feel that they make an important social, cultural and educational contribution to our society, and shudder at the provincialism that would prevail without their presence in our institutions. Whatever the attitude, pro or con, it appears that it has been formulated on the basis of gross generalizations and relatively little factual information. This is partially due to the fact that until 1972, International Students were a rather "ill-defined" group who could change their status from Student Visa to Landed Immigrant from within Canada. This is no longer possible. Information on the numbers of International Students, their countries of origin, programs of study and provincial distribution was not readily available and, as a result, people speculated about International Students in Canada.

We know that the distinction between Landed Immigrants and Student Visas was not always clearly drawn, therefore, many people with Landed Immigrant status were identified as Foreign Students. We know that many people did, and still continue to, react to visible minorities, identifying all those students who "look" foreign as Foreign Students, regardless of the possibility that they may be fifth generation Canadians, and that Canada is, in fact, a multi-racial society. The common complaint that Foreign Students were taking up limited spaces in faculties such as Medicine, Dentistry, Law, etc., was unfounded once enrollment figures were analyzed; people were assuming that the "foreign looking" students in those faculties were Foreign Students. Furthermore, the tendency to react to visible minorities often made people overlook the second largest group of Foreign Students in Canada — the American students who "looked Canadian." Rumours spread fast about the thousands of students receiving Federal support through programs such as CIDA and Canada Commonwealth Scholars, when, in fact, less than 10% of all Foreign Students in Canada receive Federal support. We also tend to forget the thousands of Canadians who did and still are studying abroad, and that approximately 57% of the Ph.D. population in Canada obtained their doctorates in other

TABLE I

Origin of Earned Doctorates by
Country and Selected Disciplines*

Country	Economics	Sociology	English	Chemistry	Engineering
Canada	200	105	350	1,630	1,230
	(21.6)**	(22.6)	(36.6)	(53.7)	(49.1)
United States	485	280	390	435	520
	(52.4)	(60.2)	(40.8)	(14.3)	(20.8)
France	65	30	5	30	25
	(7.0)	(6.4)	(0.5)	(1.0)	(1.0)
Other Countries	95	20	50	275	210
	(10.3)	(4.3)	(5.2)	(9.0)	(8.4)
Sub-Total					
Foreign Countries	725	360	605	1,405	1,275
	(78.4)	(77.4)	(63.4)	(46.3)	(50.9)
Total	925	465	955	3,035	2,505

Source: Highly Qualified Manpower Survey of 1973. Unpublished data, "The Foreign Student Issues in 1976-77" by Max von Zur-Muehlen.

* Data refers to both Canadian citizens and landed immigrants in Canada in 1973.

** Percentage distribution by country in brackets.

countries. Table I illustrates where doctorates were obtained for the various disciplines. The data refers to Ph.D. holders in Canada in 1973 and includes both Canadian citizens and landed immigrants. We know that all of these misconceptions contributed to the negative public reaction we are told exists regarding Foreign Students in Canada.

This paper will deal with three aspects of the International Student issue: the statistical background of Foreign Students in Canada; the external forces such as immigration regulations and institutional policies (or the lack of them) and the internal forces which influence the Foreign Student's experience; and finally, the implications of both these factors in terms of the future of Foreign Students in Canada.

A Foreign Student is a person in Canada on a temporary visa (Section 7(1)(f) of the Immigration Act) enrolled in an educational institution for the purposes of pursuing a course of studies. His presence in Canada is on a temporary basis only; upon completion of his program, he is expected to leave the country. During the time the student is in Canada, his visa must be renewed at regular intervals through the Department of Immigration, and renewal of the visa is contingent upon the student fulfilling the requirements specified by the Department of Immigration. (These requirements include proof of financial support and continued enrollment in an educational institution.) Students with Landed Immigrant status are not Foreign Students. A person in Canada with Landed Immigrant status is eligible for the same benefits, with the exception of voting privileges, that all Canadians receive. They are not subject to the same regulations and restrictions that apply to Foreign Students. The tendency to confuse the two categories of students is responsible for the frequent distortion of enrollment figures for Foreign Students.

Manpower and Immigration statistics on the number of Foreign Students in Canada do not distinguish between the students entering the country each year and the visas being renewed by students already here. Manpower and Immigration also does not keep track of the student's actual attendance at an institution, therefore, the student may enter Canada with a letter of acceptance from an institution but may not necessarily enroll there. Institutions, on the other hand, do not usually verify the Foreign Student's Immigration status. (These factors explain, to some extent, the discrepancies in figures between statistics issued by various institutions and those of Manpower and Immigration.)

According to Immigration statistics, there were approximately 56,000 Foreign Students in Canada in 1976, representing an increase of 26,000 students since 1973. Of this number, 1.9% were in primary schools, 16.6% in secondary schools, 12.4% in the category termed "other," which refers to religious institutions, private trade schools, etc., 16.4%

in community colleges, trade and technical institutions, and 52.7% in universities (Max von Zur-Muehlen, 1977, 26). The number of Foreign Students in the universities has increased over the last four years, whereas, those attending secondary and non-university post-secondary institutions has declined.

In 1976, 3.6% of these students came from the "Least Developed" countries,[1] 4.1% from Guyana, 8.8% from the West Indies and other islands,[2] 12.2% from the "Developing" countries,[3] 9.6% from the semi-industrialized countries,[4] 31.9% from Hong Kong, 4.2% from the oil-rich countries,[5] 8.2% from the industrialized countries,[6] and 17.4% from the United States (von Zur-Muehlen, 1977, 38).

In 1976, there were 29,436, or 52.7% of the total Foreign Student population in Canada registered in universities.[7] This group represented 1.6% of the total full and part-time university student enrollment in Newfoundland, 2.4% in Prince Edward Island, 6.2% in Nova Scotia, 2.9% in New Brunswick, 6.0% in Quebec, 5.1% in Ontario, 4.8% in Manitoba, 7.5% in Saskatchewan, 5.8% in Alberta, and 4.1% in British Columbia. Altogether, this group constituted 5.3% of the total full and part-time university student enrollment in Canada. (As compared to approximately 2% of the fulltime university student enrollment in the USA, 10% in the U.K., 9% in France, 8% in West Germany, 22% in Switzerland, 10% in Scandinavia, 8% in Australia and 10% in Belgium (The London Times, 10/2/76) (von Zur-Muehlen, 1977, 31).)

In 1976-77, numerically the largest group of Foreign Students was found in Ontario (11,631 — 40.4%) and Quebec (8,164 — 28.4%). These two provinces accounted for 68.8% of all the Foreign Students in Canadian universities. The next largest group was in Alberta, which had 8% of all Foreign Students in Canadian universities. Next came British Columbia with 5.8%, Saskatchewan with 5.7%, Manitoba with 4.9%, Nova Scotia with 4.5%, New Brunswick with 1.4%, Newfoundland with 0.6% and Prince Edward Island with 0.2%. The Prairie provinces have seen the greatest growth rate, with Saskatchewan having the largest increase of Foreign Students of any province in Canada (von Zur-Muehlen, 1977, 31).

Foreign Students in universities across the country tend to be most prevalent in the faculties of Graduate Studies. In 1975-76, 17.3% of all full-time doctoral students in Canada were Foreign Students, 15.7% of all full-time masters students were Foreign Students, and 4.9% of all full-time undergraduates were Foreign Students. Grouping all three categories together, the greatest number of Foreign Students in Canada were studying in the fields of Engineering and Applied Sciences. Next came Mathematics and Physical Sciences, Social Sciences, Agriculture and Biological Sciences, Humanities, Fine and Applied Arts, and Health professions, with the smallest number found in the field of Education (von Zur-Muehlen, 1977, 61).

There is an increase in the number of Foreign Graduate Students throughout Canada. In 1972-73, approximately 12.8% of all graduate students were Foreign Students. The overall increase in enrollment in faculties is due to the larger Foreign Student enrollment (von Zur-Muehlen, 1977, 63).

Any discussion on Foreign Students in Canada must include information on CIDA trainees, as this group represents many of the students coming from Developing Countries. The first five CIDA students arrived in Canada in 1950; they came from Cambodia, Haiti, India, Iraq, and Mexico. This number grew to 1,655 students by 1975. Students from 141 Developing Countries have been trained through the CIDA trainee program. Altogether, 21,306 students had been sponsored by CIDA in 1975. India had the largest single group of trainees over those 25 years (1969-75), with the next largest group coming from Pakistan, followed numerically by Nigeria, Malaysia, Ghana, Tanzania, Thailand, Indonesia, Vietnam, Kenya, Jamaica, Guyana, Singapore, Algeria, Sri Lanka, Trinidad & Tobago, and Uganda. Trainees from these 17 countries account for 10,881 or half of all the CIDA students trained in Canada. In 1975, the largest groups of students came from Algeria, Cameroon, Dahomey, Ghana, Malaysia, Mauritania, Nigeria, St. Lucia, Tanzania, Togo, Uganda, Upper Volta, Zaire and Zambia. There appears to be an increase in the numbers of Francophone trainees coming to Canada, but the overall CIDA trainee program seems to be slowly declining, as more and more students are trained in Third World Country institutions. There also appears to be more emphasis placed on training in technical institutions and specialized practical training programs and less being placed on university programs (Foreign Students Administered by CIDA, 8/12/75).

Canada is not a haven for International Students — as a country, we do very little to encourage their presence here or to welcome them to our society. There is no policy at either the federal, provincial, or institutional level that defines objectives, expectations and commitment to International Education. The Department of Manpower and Immigration controls the entry of Foreign Students into Canada and determines the regulations to which they must adhere during the time they reside here. The Department of External Affairs is concerned with the ramifications of International Education in the context of Canada's international relations. The individual institutions control the numbers of Foreign Students entering Canada in the sense that they determine which students and how many they care to admit. The Provincial Governments are intricately involved on an economic level. It is unfortunate that very little communication and cooperation exists between the interested agencies, especially in view of the fact that the policies of one so crucially affect the interests of the other.

The external pressures on Foreign Students in Canada are great. The greatest restrictions lie in the area of finance. For undergraduates there are few, if any, financial resources available to assist Foreign Students (with the exception of CIDA students and a limited Emergency Fund administered through the CBIE). Graduate students are eligible for assistantships if they qualify and funds are available. Neither group is permitted to work without a work permit, issued through the Department of Manpower and Immigration only after they have determined that there are no Canadians or Landed Immigrants available to do the job the Foreign Student has applied for, in essence, a work permit is almost impossible to obtain. If a student is married, the spouse is also not permitted to work. In fact, Foreign Students have no means of supplementing their income despite constant increases in the cost of living. If a student works illegally, as many are forced to do, they suffer severe consequences if and when they are caught; their visa may not be renewed, they may be fined, or they may be deported — work becomes a crime for Foreign Students. Foreign Students are also not eligible for Government Student Loans and can rarely qualify for bank loans, regardless of the situation they may find themselves in. In countries such as the U.S. and the U.K., although differential fees exist, there are opportunities for financial assistance. Many institutions have some system of fee remission; there are scholarships, grants and bursaries at both the undergraduate and the graduate levels that Foreign Students may qualify for, and there are some limited opportunities for employment. In countries such as West Germany, Australia, Sweden, and Norway, university education is free; in France, tuition and lodging are heavily subsidized. In Canada, we welcome only those students who can totally pay their own way — our policies dictate that only students from certain socio/economic brackets can afford to study here.

Few institutions offer special programs for Foreign Students. In most cases, students adapt to our educational programs with little thought given to the relevance of this study for their own countrys' needs. The exception to this is the special programs often negotiated on a bilateral basis between CIDA and a particular country, or between certain institutions and governments where special programs are designed for particular groups of students. Services for Foreign Students are sporadic at best; some institutions employ Foreign Student Advisers and provide

Foreign Student Offices, others delegate the responsibility for International Students to various people on campus. Some institutions provide reception and orientation services for incoming Foreign Students, others do not. Generally speaking, there is an ad hoc attitude towards International Education and International Students. There appear tc be few guidelines or policies which state official attitudes, rather the student sinks or swims on the basis of his own adaptability.

Foreign Students are marginal members of our society — their status in Canada restricts them from participating fully in the economy or in policy-making processes. They are aware that their residency here is on a temporary basis and this influences both their attitudes and their experiences. There are tremendous variations within the Foreign Student population — in fact, their only common denominator is their status in Canada as defined by immigration policy. The foreign exchange difficulties that exist for a student from India do not present problems for the student from the U.S.A.; the TOEFL test that confronts a student from Hong Kong is not a problem for the student from Australia; the discrimination that an African student may experience in his search for housing is rarely a factor for the student from the U.K.; therefore, it is not possible to generalize about the adjustment of Foreign Students. Unquestionably, the most important variable in adjustment is the unique personality of a student.

Probably the most important single factor is the motivation of the student in coming to study in Canada. Why is he here? There are several reasons, each with their own implications. Some students come because it is considered prestigious to study abroad and obtain a foreign degree, others come because their chosen field of study is not available in their own country. Many desire the experience of living in a new culture, while others see education as a passport to upward mobility. The reasons for studying in Canada are related to the expectations of the student upon his arrival in Canada, and his attitude towards Canada upon his return to his country will ultimately be based on the realization of his goals. Many students have to contend, not only with their own expectations, but with those of their families who may have invested heavily in the student's education. The pressure to succeed, not only for personal reasons, but for the sake of the family back home, creates additional strain for many students.

Much has been written on culture shock and its effect on Foreign Students, often based on the findings of studies done on Foreign Students in North America and on North Americans living abroad as CUSO volunteers, CIDA or AID consultants, etc. Both these groups share the experience of adjusting to life in a new environment, but the similarity ends there. Most North Americans abroad find themselves with elevated status within the new society, often they have more prestige than they would have at home in a similar position. On the other hand, Foreign Students coming to Canada usually find themselves with reduced status. They may come from respected families, have had responsible jobs and a secure position in their communities, only to find themselves in the role of student which normally carries little prestige. They are a nonentity within this society, often a minority, racially and culturally and, as a result, they may not receive the respect they feel they deserve. In an effort to protect his self-image, the Foreign Student is often described as arrogant by his Canadian counterparts. His effort to maintain his view of his home status, despite the fact that his status has changed in Canada, is often misinterpreted.

Homer Higbee defines culture shock as, "the shock of having to learn and cope with a vast array of new cultural cues and expectations."

Dr. Kalvero Oberg describes the various stages of culture shock in the following way. The "honeymoon" stage which occurs in the first few weeks or months where people, fascinated by the "new" are in a state of excitement upon their arrival in a new environment. This euphoric state ends and is replaced with a hostile and aggressive attitude towards the host country, as a result of the genuine difficulties that occur in the process of adjusting to a new system. The members of the host society are often blamed for creating problems which are, in fact, unavoidable. Slowly, as the visitor learns about the system, he enters a third stage, characterized by a growing interest in the people of the host society and an increasing involvement in the community. The final stage occurs when the visitor finally accepts the customs of the host society and adopts a "c'est la vie" attitude. This same process is described in the U Curve phenomenon, which is characterized by a state of euphoria, a period of anomie and finally, a new understanding of the society, coupled with the emotional readiness to accept it.

Most people would agree that some period of adjustment is inevitable, but the degree varies with the individual. Some believe the period of adjustment is closely related to the degree of differentness of the new society, with people coming from very different cultures facing the greatest problems. Others relate the period of adjustment to the country the student comes from, with students coming from countries of great international prestige experiencing less difficulties than students coming from countries of low prestige.

In discussing adjustment, one must take into consideration the readiness of the host society to adjust to foreign students. A foreign student can make countless efforts to be accepted within the host society, but if his overtures are rejected, his efforts are in vain. The willingness of the Canadian society to accept foreigners is questionable.

A study done at the University of Alberta by a graduate student, Ralph Schuh, on *Canadian Student Attitudes Towards Foreign Students,* suggests that Canadian students are not very enthusiastic over the presence of Foreign Students. The U. of A. has a Foreign Student population that comprises 5.6% of the total student enrollment; most Canadian students felt this was adequate, some felt there should be less, few wanted more. They also indicated that their level of interaction with Foreign Students was superficial in terms of developing lasting friendships or having regular contact. Most associated with Foreign Students within the classroom environment, some had contact in residences or organizations, but few reported intimate friendships with Foreign Students. Older graduate students developed the closest friendships with Foreign Students. It appeared that the more interaction Canadian students had with Foreign Students, the more meaningful their relationships became, and the less threatened they were by competition for jobs, grades, and spaces in limited enrollment faculties.

One of the arguments for the presence of International Students in Canada has always been the opportunities that are derived for increased crosscultural communication — the sharing of ideas and lifestyles and the learning process that takes place for both groups of students about each other's cultures; however, the exchange appears to me to be overestimated. The quality of interaction is related to the opportunities provided for intercultural activities and the positive attitude of the institution towards the presence of Foreign Students.

Several recent developments will have a great effect on the future of International Students in Canada. The new Immigration Bill, which is presently under discussion in Parliament, appears to be even more restrictive where Foreign Students are concerned. Foreign Students will have to have Student Visas before coming to Canada. They will not be able to change their status from visitor to student from within the country. Students will not be able to change institutions or their programs of study without authorization from Immigration officials, and there is no indication that employment regulations will be eased.

Two provinces, Ontario and Alberta, have already introduced a differential fee system whereby Foreign Students entering institutions for the first time, as of September 1977, will pay higher fees than Canadians or Landed Immigrant students. These two provinces account for nearly 50% of all Foreign Students in Canada. It is possible that other provinces, if faced with an onslaught of Foreign Students from Alberta and Ontario, will be forced to implement a differential fee structure too. Many institutions are introducing quota systems in some or all faculties. There may also be efforts at some institutions to control the numbers of students from any one country; such quotas will directly affect the number of students from Hong Kong who represent 31.9% of all Foreign Students in Canada and at many institutions constitute approximately 50% of the total Foreign Student population.

Over the last four years there has been a slight decline of students from the "Least Developed" countries; this is also true for students from Guyana and the West Indies. The percentage of students from the "Developing" countries has remained stable, while the students from the "Semi-Industrialized" countries have increased from 7% to approximately 10% of the total number of Foreign Students in Canada. Students from Hong Kong comprise 31.9% of the Foreign Student population as compared to 20.6% four years ago. In the same four-year period, the number of students from the U.S. dropped from 30% to 17%; they are still the second largest group of Foreign Students in Canada. Students from the industrialized countries have shown a slight increase over the past four years, while the number of students from the oil-rich countries has doubled over the period, although they only represent 4.2% of the total Foreign Student population in Canada (von Zur-Muehlen, 1977, 37-40).

Many of the oil-rich countries are negotiating with Canadian institutions to train groups of their students. It would seem safe to predict that this particular group of students will continue to increase in the coming years. The OPEC countries are requesting special programs designed to meet their students' needs and, as they appear to be willing to pay full cost, it seems likely that many institutions will comply with their request.

These trends seem to indicate a new composition of Foreign Students for the future. There is no reason to suggest that the overall numbers of Foreign Students in Canada will decrease, but their composition will change. We will probably see more students from the oil-rich countries in Canada on specially designed programs, and less of the private, non-sponsored students from the "Least Developed" countries. Canada will undoubtedly continue to open its doors to Foreign Students if they can pay our price.

Unless the presence of Foreign Students in Canada is encouraged — at all levels of government, and unless we make it possible for them to exist once they get here, either by providing them with opportunities for employment or establishing a system of grants, scholarships and/or fee remissions, it seems safe to predict that we will soon be catering to a very elite group of International Students. Unless Canadians view the presence of Foreign Students as a positive contribution to Canadian society, see them as "givers" not only as "takers", there is no reason to believe that the quality of intercultural communication will improve.

International Students are sensitive to the climate of the country; they know when they are welcome, they know when they are not. Their experience in Canada will be reflected in their attitudes once they return to their countries. The impact of their impression should not be underestimated.

NOTES

1. Countries considered as "Least Developed Countries" are as follows: Afghanistan, Bangladesh, Brunei, Laos, Equatorial Guinea, Haiti, Botswana, Burundi, Central African Republic, Chad, Dahomey, Ethiopia, Gambia, Guinea (Portuguese), Lesotho, Malawi, Yemen Arab Republic, Mali, Niger, Rwanda, Somali Republic, Sudan, Swaziland, Tanzania, Uganda, Upper Volta. GNP less than $100, literacy rate under 20% and less than 10% of their GNP produced by the manufacturing sector.

2. Countries considered as "West Indies and Other Islands" are: Antigua, Bahamas Islands, Barbados, Belize, Bermuda, Cayman Islands, Dominica, Dominican Republic, Grenada, Guadeloupe, Jamaica, St. Vincent, Trinidad-Tobago, others.

3. Countries classified as "Developing Countries" are: Angola, Congo, Egypt, El Salvador, Gabon, Ghana, Ivory Coast, Kenya, Liberia, Malagasy Republic, Mauritania, Mozambique, Nigeria, Senegal, Sierra Leone, Togo Land, Zaire, Zambia, Burma, China, India, Indonesia, Jordan, Khmer Republic, Lebanon, Mongolia, Macao, Nepal, Pakistan, Sri Lanka, Timor (Portuguese), Vietnam North, Vietnam South, Honduras, Namibia.

4. Countries considered as "Semi-Industrialized Countries" are: Argentina, Bolivia, Brazil, Chile, Columbia, Dutch Guiana, Ecuador, French Guiana, Paraguay, Peru, Uruguay, Algeria, Morocco, Rhodesia, Tunisia, Cyprus, Korea North, Korea South, Malaysia, Philippines, Singapore, Syria, Taiwan, Thailand, Costa Rica, Cuba, Mexico, Nicaragua, Guatemala, Panama, Panama Canal Zone, Puerto Rico.

5. The countries listed as "Oil-Rich Countries" are as follows: Bahrain, Iran, Iraq, Kuwait, Libya, Saudi Arabia, United Arab Emirates, Venezuela.

6. Total Europe, South Africa, Israel, Japan, Australia, New Zealand.
   In some instances, an arbitrary distinction was made between "Developing" countries (India and Ghana) and "semi-industrialized" countries (Morocco and most of Latin America). "Oil-rich countries" include Saudi Arabia and Venezuela, but exclude Indonesia and Nigeria, which were classified as "Developing" (von Zur-Muehlen, 1977, 39).

7. This discussion will concentrate on Foreign university students, but it should be pointed out that a large number of these students enter universities after taking secondary school or community college courses in Canada.

162   *Visible Minorities and Multiculturalism*

BIBLIOGRAPHY

Cussler, Margaret.
"The Foreign Student — Innovator of the Future," in Sociology of Underdevelopment, Copp Clark Publishing Co., 1970.

Higbee, Homer.
"Role Shock — A New Concept," reprinted from the Spring 1969 issue of *International Educational and Cultural Exchange,* a publication of the U.S. Advisory Commission on International Educational and Cultural Affairs (Department of State, Washington, D.C.)

Klineberg, Otto.
"Psychological Aspects of Student Exchange"

Oberg, Dr. Kalvero.
"Culture Shock and the Problem of Adjustment to New Cultural Environments," a publication of the Canadian Bureau for International Education, 1958.

von Zur-Muehlen, Dr. Max.
"The Foreign Student Issues in 1976-77," a publication of Canadian Bureau for International Education, 1977.

"The London Times," 10/2/76.

11

Changes in Canadian Immigration Patterns Over the Past Decade With Special Reference to Asia[1]

Doreen M. Indra
Department of Anthropology
University of Alberta

Canadian immigration policy has always been closely tied to economic development and nation building. Throughout the last century, its intent has been to select immigrants increasingly on the bases of national economic development and especially upon occupational requirements. Nevertheless, cultural and class preferences were also important criteria of immigrant selection, paralleling, yet sometimes in conflict with economic considerations. Until 1962, the Canadian immigration regulations were constructed in such a way as to assure easier access to potential immigrants from Britain, Northern Europe, and the United States.

Since the Second World War, Canadian immigration regulations have moved through a series of changes reflecting the evolving pattern of world political development and Canada's new position in world affairs. It became increasingly difficult for the Canadian government to assume a role as mediator in world affairs when its own immigration policy was one based upon discriminatory selection, and the decolonizing Third World was fast becoming a source of criticism of that policy. At the same time, demands for an increasingly close fit between immigrant selection and Canadian manpower requirements argued for a far greater weighting of economic rather than cultural factors.

These pressures resulted in constant changes in the regulations, and culminated in the Immigration Act of 1967. Through this new legislation the Canadian government removed all formal criteria of preference based upon race, nationality, or ethnicity, and established a formally non-discriminatory basis for the selection of immigrants. This legislation was aimed at closely relating immigrant flow to Canadian manpower needs. Subsequent to its enactment, selection was based upon a point system, whereby an individual applicant was assessed according to the requirements of the labour market, his or her occupational skills, education, age, and language ability. By law, applicants were not to be evaluated in terms of their country of origin or any other cultural factor, with the exception of French or English language capability.

Ten years later, this immigration act has been supplanted by new legislation, ending another era in Canadian immigration, and this makes it an appropriate time to assess the actual changes in immigration which resulted from the 1967 Act. This paper investigates the empirical changes in the Canadian immigrant flow over the past decade (1964-1975) in the light of an expressed government policy of non-discrimination. By comparing immigration before (1964-66) and after (1973-75) these fundamental modifications of the immigration regulations, it attempts to answer two basic questions. First, did changes in the distribution of immigrants actually reflect the intent of the 1967 regulations? Second, did Canadian immigration practice actually become divorced from this country's increasing economic, political and social involvement with the rest of the world, as the latter immigration policy's formal program suggested? The variables which are used to gauge these changes are the population of source countries, their degree of economic development, and the amount of trade which those countries have with Canada. Because Canada's involvement with Asia and with Asian immigration have increased greatly over the past ten years, this paper will concentrate particularly upon this relationship.

I. CANADIAN IMMIGRATION PATTERNS, 1964-1966

Cartogram I diagrams the average Canadian immigrant flows from their source countries for 1964-1966. The width of the arrows is proportional to the flow of immigrants. As is graphically illustrated by this cartogram, immigration to Canada in the mid-1960s was over-whelmingly European, and Great Britain still provided the largest number of immigrants of any country.[2] Together with the United States, European countries accounted for about 85% of all immigrants. In contrast, Asian countries contributed less than 7% of the total.

Moreover, immigrants came from very few source countries. Only fifteen countries contributed more than 1,500 immigrants per year to the total. Most of the world's population and most of the countries of the world were not represented at all. During this period, strong preferences for certain source countries were exhibited, even among those countries which did contribute immigrants. British, Western Europeans, and Americans clearly made up the lion's share. These cultural and national preferences are well illustrated by the fact that among immigrant source countries one finds that there was no correla-tion between these countries' population and the number of immigrants which they sent to Canada.[3] This lack of correlation can be seen clearly on Cartogram I, where the size of countries is proportional to their populations. Indeed, Canada's immigrants came primarily from the rich, developed countries of the world. This is illustrated by the fact that in the mid-1960s there was a quite high correlation between the immigrant flow and source country gross domestic product ($r = .354, s = .027$).[4] Since most countries with low GDPs sent no immi-grants at all to Canada, this correlation remains about the same even when the whole world is considered.

Asian immigration to Canada in the mid-1960s was from very few sources, notably Hong Kong (3,706), India (1,876), Pakistan (424), Japan (285), and Sri Lanka (117). Each of these Asian countries was either a "traditional source country" or was covered by a specific immigration treaty. As with the total sample, there was only a weak correlation between the number of Asian immigrants and their national populations ($r = .329, s = .231$). There existed no correlation at all between immigrant flows and source country GDP ($r = .019, s = .940$).

By far the strongest correlations between immigrant flows and any of these measured variables are those with Canadian trade. I hope to show that for both periods in question, immigration follows Canadian trade with very high certainty, despite the rhetoric of Canadian immi-gration policy.

To begin with, although the Canadian immigration policy of the early 1960s was overtly biased towards Europeans, immigrant flows were nevertheless closely related to Canadian world trade. Canadian exports, in particular, were highly correlated with immigrant flows ($r = .459, s = .001$).[5] Inversely, if there was very little trade with a

Cartogram I

WORLD POPULATION DISTRIBUTION AND CANADIAN IMMIGRATION AVERAGES FOR 1964-66

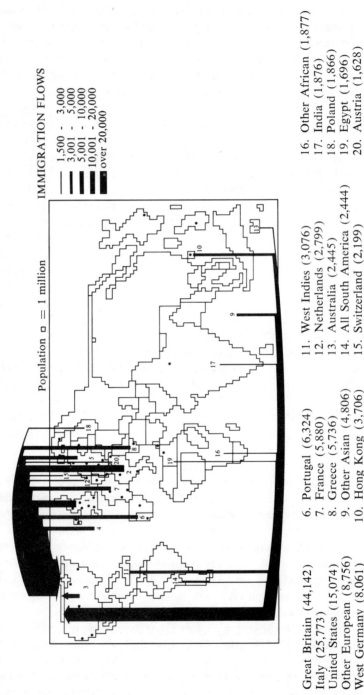

Population □ = 1 million

IMMIGRATION FLOWS

1,500 - 3,000
3,001 - 5,000
5,001 - 10,000
10,001 - 20,000
over 20,000

1. Great Britain (44,142)
2. Italy (25,773)
3. United States (15,074)
4. Other European (8,756)
5. West Germany (8,061)

6. Portugal (6,324)
7. France (5,880)
8. Greece (5,736)
9. Other Asian (4,806)
10. Hong Kong (3,706)

11. West Indies (3,076)
12. Netherlands (2,799)
13. Australia (2,445)
14. All South America (2,444)
15. Switzerland (2,199)

16. Other African (1,877)
17. India (1,876)
18. Poland (1,866)
19. Egypt (1,696)
20. Austria (1,628)

given country, very few immigrants would likely come from it. The exceptions were the United States and Japan, both of which have very large trade with Canada but send *relatively few* immigrants to this country. If they are excluded from this calculation, the correlations between immigant flow and Canadian trade go far higher. For instance, Canadian exports and immigration for this period then show a correlation coefficient of .873 (s = .001). This pattern was strongly evident among European source countries — even though it is a common assertion in the literature that cultural preferences and immigration 'push' factors were largely responsible for the patterns of that day. Clearly, the connection between these two cannot be altogether arbitrary. It is interesting that one does not see such strong correlations for the rest of the world, with the marked exception of Asia.[6] During this period, Canada's Asian trade constituted about the same percentage of Canada's world trade (6%) as did Asian immigration (7%).

Why might there be such correlations between Canadian trade and immigrant flows in this earlier period? This is an almost impossible question to answer without a detailed analysis of the actual process of immigration from specific source countries. While I suggest a few plausible reasons for the strength of this relationship in both time periods, one factor seems to be evident in the mid-1960s data. This is the distribution of Canadian immigration centres shown as black dots on all Cartograms.[7] The immigration centres on Cartogram I correspond to those countries with high trade with Canada. There were seven centres in the U.K. alone; only one in Sub-Saharan Africa and none in Latin and Central America. The four which had been established in Asia (Tokyo, New Delhi, Hong Kong, Manila) were located in the capitals of what were then Canada's first, second, fourth and fifth Asian trading partners, respectively.

One can gain additional insight into this relationship if one compares the distribution of Canadian Immigration Centres with the locations of Canada's Trade Commissioner Service Posts, as shown in Table 1. Even at this early date, 29 out of 40 immigration centres were located in the same cities as were Canadian Trade Commissioner Service Posts. Only *one* of these 40 immigration centres was in a country without such a trade centre.

II. TEN YEARS LATER: CANADIAN IMMIGRATION PATTERNS, 1973-75

In 1967, the government brought into existence the most economically rationalized act in Canada's immigration history. As mentioned,

TABLE 1

Canadian Trade and Immigration Centres, 1965

Area	Trade Centres	Immigration Centres	Both in the same cities	Immigration centres without trade centres
West Europe	21	29	19	10
East Europe	0	0	0	0
Asia	7	4	4	0
Africa	4	0	0	0
Near East	4	2	2	0
Caribbean	4	0	0	0
Latin & Central Am.	9	0	0	0
United States	11	5	4	1
Totals	60	40	29	11

Source: Annual Report of the Department of Industry, Trade and Commerce, 1965.

through this legislation the Canadian government removed the notion of preferential or favoured immigrant source countries and specified that questions of national, racial, or ethnic origin were not to be considered as factors for admission to Canada. The new regulations established that Canadian immigration would no longer discriminate among applicants on bases other than those of individual merit and Canadian manpower needs.

If this policy was actually implemented, one would expect that:

1. The number of non-European immigrants would have increased.
2. The number of immigrants from source countries with high populations would have increased.
3. More immigrants would have come from the developing world.
4. The correlations between Canadian trade and the immigrant flow from source countries would have decreased.

These predictions are four ways of saying the same thing — that the structure of immigration would have changed towards the selection of immigrants on the basis of individual skills and abilities rather than national, cultural, or international economic factors.

The answers to these questions are not simple. The number of immigrants coming to Canada from other than the United States and

Cartogram II

WORLD POPULATION DISTRIBUTION AND CANADIAN IMMIGRATION AVERAGES FOR 1973-75

Population □ = 1 million

IMMIGRATION FLOWS

1,500 - 3,000
3,001 - 5,000
5,001 - 10,000
10,001 - 20,000
over 20,000

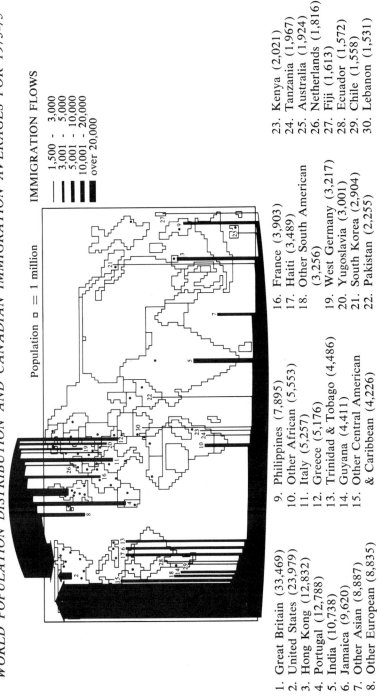

1. Great Britain (33,469)
2. United States (23,979)
3. Hong Kong (12,832)
4. Portugal (12,788)
5. India (10,738)
6. Jamaica (9,620)
7. Other Asian (8,887)
8. Other European (8,835)

9. Philippines (7,895)
10. Other African (5,553)
11. Italy (5,257)
12. Greece (5,176)
13. Trinidad & Tobago (4,486)
14. Guyana (4,411)
15. Other Central American & Caribbean (4,226)

16. France (3,903)
17. Haiti (3,489)
18. Other South American (3,256)
19. West Germany (3,217)
20. Yugoslavia (3,001)
21. South Korea (2,904)
22. Pakistan (2,255)

23. Kenya (2,021)
24. Tanzania (1,967)
25. Australia (1,924)
26. Netherlands (1,816)
27. Fiji (1,613)
28. Ecuador (1,572)
29. Chile (1,558)
30. Lebanon (1,531)

Europe have increased dramatically in the last ten years, as can be seen on Cartogram II. Whereas European and American immigrants once constituted 85% of immigrants, they now make up 47% of the total. Both the number of countries supplying immigrants and the number of non-European immigrants have increased greatly.

Canadian immigration has clearly shifted towards a more equitable distribution with respect to the population of source countries, as can be seen on Cartogram II. The correlations between source country populations and the number of immigrants coming from these countries is now quite strong (r = .409, s = .001), whereas it was very low in the mid-1960s. Nevertheless, increases in non-European immigration have not derived from a random increase in the numbers of immigrants who have come from the rest of the world. Rather, non-European immigrants of this era tended to come from specific areas, notably Asia, the West Indies, and South America. Black Africa remains almost totally unrepresented.

Asians have more than shared in this increase, for they have moved from 7% of all immigrants in the mid-1960s to over 25% in the mid-1970s, as both Cartogram II and Table 2 illustrate.[8] The correlation between Asian source country population and immigrant flow is now much higher (r = .473, s = .088) than it was ten years before.

At first inspection, immigrants would seem to still come from the wealthier countries of the world, as measured by a high gross domestic product per capita. Gross *national* products are mapped against immigration on Cartogram III. This tendency for immigrants to come from wealthier countries has weakened considerably over ten years, so much so that if one removes Japan and the United States from the calculations, the relationship between GDP and immigration disappears completely.

The most significant correlations of that era are still those between immigrant flow and trade — which one would *not* expect if Canadian immigration policy were taken at its face value. In fact, for all potential sources of 1973-75 immigration, these correlations have actually *increased*.

Having two sets of figures from different time periods, one can learn something about the dynamics of these relations. First of all, it can be stated with some certainty that immigration follows trade, and not vice versa. As evidence of this relationship, Canadian world trade figures for the mid-1960s predict mid-1970s' immigration flows *better* than do the Canadian trade figures for the 1970s.[9] This relationship implies that there is a lag between increases in level of trade and subsequent increases in immigration from those countries. These correlations reach wondrous proportions when European source countries

TABLE 2

Canadian Immigration From Asia and Asian Trade

Country	Canadian Trade Imports (millions)	(1974) Exports (millions)	Number of Immigrants (1973-75 averages)
Hong Kong	135	40	12,832
India	59	121	10,738
Phillippines	16	50	7,895
South Korea	135	71	2,904
Pakistan	16	71	2,392
Taiwan	194	42	1,295
South Vietnam	—	7	1,020
Japan	1,430	2,220	866
Malasia	62	29	571
Sri Lanka	19	4	434
Singapore	52	29	360
Indonesia	5	54	220
Burma	—	1	103
Thailand	7	25	81
Afghanistan	—	2	12
	2,135	2,767	43,336
Asian Total Trade	2,197	3,302	
World Total Trade	31,692	31,293	
Total Asian Immigration			43,336

are considered, and earlier European trade figures will almost completely predict present-day European immigration from those same countries.[10]

Similar patterns are developing in other parts of the world, although clearly the lead remains with the European source countries. This is especially so with Asia, considering the earlier Canadian commercial involvement with Asia as compared to other parts of the developing world.[11]

This trend is evident in the West Indies, where Canadian trade has also developed early. Export trade to the West Indies is the strongest predictor of immigration from the Caribbean. For Latin and Central America, and Africa, there remains no significant indicators.

Considering that Canada is both an industrialized country as well as a supplier of raw materials to other industrialized countries, one might have expected that imports from poorer countries would have a predominant influence upon immigration, but this is not the case. For

Cartogram III

GROSS NATIONAL PRODUCTS AND CANADIAN IMMIGRATION AVERAGES FOR 1973-75

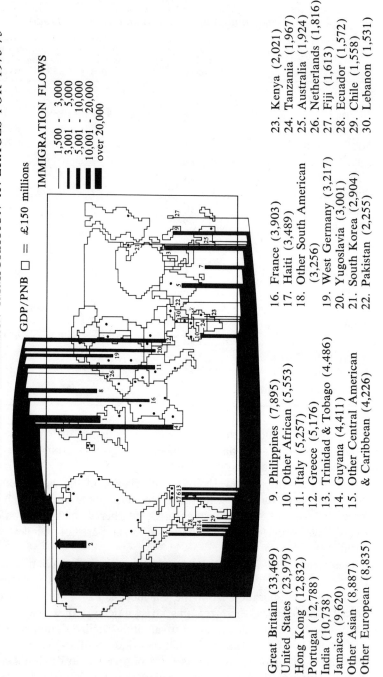

GDP/PNB □ = £150 millions

IMMIGRATION FLOWS

1,500 - 3,000	
3,001 - 5,000	
5,001 - 10,000	
10,001 - 20,000	
over 20,000	

1. Great Britain (33,469)
2. United States (23,979)
3. Hong Kong (12,832)
4. Portugal (12,788)
5. India (10,738)
6. Jamaica (9,620)
7. Other Asian (8,887)
8. Other European (8,835)

9. Philippines (7,895)
10. Other African (5,553)
11. Italy (5,257)
12. Greece (5,176)
13. Trinidad & Tobago (4,486)
14. Guyana (4,411)
15. Other Central American
    & Caribbean (4,226)

16. France (3,903)
17. Haiti (3,489)
18. Other South American
    (3,256)
19. West Germany (3,217)
20. Yugoslavia (3,001)
21. South Korea (2,904)
22. Pakistan (2,255)

23. Kenya (2,021)
24. Tanzania (1,967)
25. Australia (1,924)
26. Netherlands (1,816)
27. Fiji (1,613)
28. Ecuador (1,572)
29. Chile (1,558)
30. Lebanon (1,531)

countries with a gross domestic product per capita below $1,500, Canadian exports remain a far more significant indicator than imports.

The locations of Canadian immigration centres presently almost completely overlap with trade centres. This may help to explain why Canadian trade from ten years ago seems to have a direct connection with present day immigration. Forty-six out of the sixty immigration centres which were in operation in 1975 were located in cities which had Canadian Trade centres in 1966, *ten years earlier.* This is shown in Table 3.

TABLE 3

Canadian Trade Centres (1965) and Immigration Centres (1975)[12]

Area	Trade Centres (1966)	Immigration Centres (1975)	Both in the Same Cities	Immigration centres without Trade Centres
West Europe	21	24	17	7
East Europe	3	3	2	1
Asia	7	7	5	2
Africa	4	1	1	0
Australiasia	4	1	1	0
Near East	4	5	4	1
Caribbean	4	3	2	1
Latin & Central Am.	9	4	3	1
United States	11	12	11	1
Totals	67	60	46	14

Source: United Nations (1965, 1974).

All but four of these centres (1975) were in countries which had Canadian trade centres a decade before. This trend towards immigration centres corresponding with trade centres continues today. Port au Prince, Haiti is the only permanent Canadian immigration centre which is not located in a country with a Canadian trade centre.

III. CANADA AND THE PACIFIC RIM

The data suggest that while immigration to Canada now originates from a wider area of the globe, in some respects it remains highly selective. Analysis of this data suggests that the principles established in earlier immigration periods are continuing to operate today. This is especially so of trade and immigration, for they correlate very highly, both before and after these changes in the immigration regulations.

Asian trade and immigration clearly show the development of this pattern which has already been well established in Europe. Canadian trade with Asia has risen to almost twice the proportion of total trade it had in 1965, as indicated in Table 4.

TABLE 4

Canadian Trade With Asia, 1965 and 1974

	Percentages of Total Trade	Percentages excluding the U.S.A.
% Canadian exports to Asia, 1965	6.8	16.1
% Canadian imports to Asia, 1965	4.3	13.7
% Canadian exports to Asia, 1974	10.5	30.8
% Canadian imports to Asia, 1974	6.9	20.9

This importance of Asian trade is a new phenomenon, for throughout its history, Canada has been tied into the Atlantic community. Indeed, early Canadian economic and social development rested upon large amounts of British capital, trade and immigrants. Raw materials, fish and wheat were shipped to Europe and in return Canada provided a market for British manufactured goods. While British investment developed the basis for Canadian industry and trade, British immigrants provided the labour, skills, and resources to exploit the minerals and markets of Canada. As parts of the colonial process, Britain provided the legal, economic and political foundations for Canada. By providing a continuous flow of immigrants, social and psychological ties to Britain were maintained and continually reinforced.

In order to develop its hinterland, Canada required larger numbers of specialized agricultural immigrants than were available from Britain. As a consequence, Canadian government (and industry) began to recruit over a wider range of countries for skilled agricultural immigrants. Thus in the latter part of the nineteenth century and in the early part of the twentieth, various Western and Eastern Europeans were solicited to settle the "empty" Canadian prairies. Influx from the United States was also high. These settlers developed the prairie agricultural base and became a market themselves for manufactured goods, as did their countries of origin.

At the end of World War II, Canada had become a world class industrial nation. Stimulated by World War II, this growth in industry created large demands for industrial workers, and immigration once again provided the people to fill jobs that an expanding economy required. Moreover, industry required new markets, and these were to be sought overseas.

At the same time, massive American investment in Canada increased the dependency of Canada on American trade and trading patterns. By 1965, over 60% of Canada's foreign trade was with its southern neighbour and this dependency upon United States trade has increased in the last ten years.

The strong connection between the economics of the United States and Canada has had the effect of weakening Canadian economic ties with Western Europe, particularly with Britain. Moreover, the development of the European Economic Community itself has had a deleterious effect on Canadian-European trade and has thrown Canada even more into the American economic orbit.

Today, a high proportion of Canadian industry is dependent upon United States parent corporations. Moreover, the Canadian and U.S. modes and standards of living are closely comparable. Both of these factors must have a direct influence on the direction of Canadian overseas trade; Canadian trade is increasingly following patterns developed by the United States. As illustrated by Table 5, today's Canadian trade closely parallels American trade of the mid-1960s.

George Grant has noted that the orientation of Anglo Canada towards England and Western Europe prior to World War II ". . . was simply a loyalty based on the flow of trade, and therefore destined to change when that flow changed" (1965: 69). Indeed, reflecting this change in new international economic structures, Canada has moved from the British to the American Empire psychologically as well as economically. While both American and Canadian interests and economic activity remain high in Europe, Canada and the United States are active in the Pacific Basin regions. Both countries have increased financial aid to the developing Asian countries. At the same time, trade has increased between these developing Asian nations and North America.

Social relations between Canada and its trading partners are changing to reflect these developing economic relations, and clearly changes in immigration flows are one result of this new economic order.

Although the official policy dealing with immigration would have one believe that its determinants are purely domestic or individual, I cannot believe that what was once so vital an aspect of this country's foreign policy could in fact be divorced from it now. I do not believe that the

TABLE 5

Canadian and American Trade Figures (Not including to each other)

Area	American		Canadian	
	Imports (1965)	Exports (1965)	Imports (1974)	Exports (1974)
Western Europe	39.5%	42.8%	36.3%	43.5%
Eastern Europe	1.7	1.1	3.0	2.9
Middle East	2.1	4.4	12.4	2.9
Asia	26.6	26.3	20.9	30.8
Africa	2.5	3.0	4.2	3.5
Oceania	2.8	4.6	3.0	3.5
South America	12.4	9.0	15.0	7.9
Central America	12.5	11.0	3.9	5.8

relations between Canadian trade and immigration, illustrated in this article, can be the simple result of the location of immigration centres. Bureaucratic and political decision making must also be important factors, although one is not likely to ever substantiate this.

It is, however, obvious that the Canadian government is playing a key role in promoting Asian markets for Canadian business. For instance, Canada is a founding member of the Pacific Basin Economic Co-operation Committee, which was organized in 1968 to promote trade among the member nations — Canada, New Zealand, Australia, Japan and the United States. One year later, the Private Investment Corporation of Asia was formed. This organization was established to underwrite private loans to developing Asian nations in order for them to buy from the developed Pacific nations. The management of the Export Development Corporation Act is also heavily involved in Asia. Under this organization, the Canadian government guarantees loans made by Canadian companies with the stipulation that 80% of the products involved are Canadian. The Economic Council of Canada (1975: 55) has clearly identified the newly emerging Asian nations to be of major future significance to Canadian trade.

Other links to Asia are also being established. Some of these are cultural and informational. For instance, the Canadian Society for Asian Studies was begun in 1969, and is funded by the Canadian government. Asian studies programs have been initiated in the last decade at the University of British Columbia, the University of Toronto and McGill University.

IV. IMPLICATIONS FOR ASIAN IMMIGRATION

The data suggest several implications for Asian immigration. First of all, it is highly likely that immigration trends established in the 1960s will continue in the future. Immigrants will likely continue to come from those Asian countries whose GNP is increasing rapidly — Taiwan, Hong Kong, South Korea, Singapore and the Phillipines. The two exceptions to this trend will be Japan and India. Japan will not likely be a source of immigrants to Canada because the incentives for Japanese people to emigrate are low. India will probably continue to send out as many immigrants as Canada will accept because of the large number of skilled people who cannot be absorbed into the Indian work force. Immigration from those Asian countries with weak trade relations with Canada will probably remain low.

Most Asian immigrants will therefore be coming from urban industrialized contexts and the point system will further select individuals who have been shaped by industrialization, and by Western ideas and practices. Table 6 shows the intended occupations of immigrants from the top three immigrant source countries of Asia indicative of this trend (Department of Manpower and Immigration 1971). Already, a majority of Asian immigrants to Canada belong to the highly skilled and qualified work force, and the future will likely see an increase in this trend.

TABLE 6

Intended Occupations of Immigrants, 1971

	Managerial	Professional & Technical	Clerical	Commerce & Finance	Other
Hong Kong	6.2%	35.2%	20.8%	2.5%	34.8%
India	3.3%	34.5%	10.1%	4.9%	47.0%
Philippines	2.9%	22.1%	37.8%	5.6%	31.3%

Moreover, Asian immigrants will continue to be from cultural backgrounds which reflect many Western ideas, institutions, and ways of doing. In particular, they will continue to come from those countries which are heavily influenced by British or American contact. Hong Kong, India, Singapore, Taiwan, South Korea and the Philippines have at one time been part of either the British or American spheres of influence. In a sense, this experience has preformed these new immigrants for Canadian society.

Finally, Asian Canadians will almost certainly play an increasing role in the network of economic and social relations linking Asia and Canada. Most Asian Canadians already are part of dense social networks which connect Canada with their home countries, and through these networks information, values, and economic relations from these two areas are continuously brought together. As trade between Canada and Asia develops, Asian Canadians will, in all likelihood, increasingly mediate Canadian and Asian economic, cultural and political systems, and in this way will almost certainly become a major factor in determining the future direction of Canadian-Asian relations.

NOTES

1. I am indebted to P. A. S. Saram, Norman L. Buchignani and Michael Eliot-Hurst for their assistance in the formulation of this paper.

2. In this paper "European" is used to refer to either immigrants who are literally in Europe, or are from Australia, New Zealand, South Africa, or Rhodesia.

3. Throughout this paper, reference to a "world sample" includes all those sources listed in the 1973-1975 immigration figures, plus all other countries in the First or Third Worlds. Eastern European countries are not included in the sample, with the exception of Poland and Yugoslavia, nor is China or those other countries where emigration is severely restricted. Inclusion of these countries would severely distort the reality of immigrant flow. The total world sample was of 169 political or geographical entities. For both 1964-1966 and 1973-1975 analyses, United Nations population figures for 1970 were used (United Nations 1976a). Immigration figures by country were derived from Department of Citizenship and Immigration Annual Reports (1964-6) and the Annual Reports of the Department of Manpower and Immigration (1967-75).

4. Because of the inaccuracy of world population figures, this and other statistics in this paper must be considered approximate. Figures for national per capita GNP are also derived from United Nations information for 1970 (United Nations 1976b).

5. Canadian trade figures are for the year 1965 (United Nations 1965). In the discussion of 1973-75 immigrations, trade figures for 1974 were used (United Nations 1974).

6. Japan is not included in these Asian calculations for reasons discussed in the text. The only significant deviation from this pattern is Japan, and it could plausibly be argued that the Japanese, like Americans, express high degrees of ethnocentrism and nationalism, which in conjunction with the high standard of living they enjoy, reduces the number of immigrants. Canadian exports compared with Asian immigration give $r = .557$ ($s = .058$). For example it is $r = .621$ ($s = .018$).

7. Details on the location of Canadian immigration centres overseas were provided by the Department of Manpower and Immigration.

8. For these 1973-5 averages, the percentages of all immigrants coming from Asia, combined with the predominantly Asian flows from Uganda, Tanzania, and Fiji is about 27%, or over 50,000 immigrants in a total of approximately 197,000.

9.
		r	s
1970's immigration and 1960's imports:		.553	.001
1970's immigration and 1970's imports:		.517	.001
1970's immigration and 1960's exports:		.638	.001
1970's immigration and 1970's exports:		.543	.001
Cross correlations are much lower:			
1960's immigration and 1970's imports:		.315	.001
1960's immigration and 1970's exports:		.346	.001

10.
1970's Asian immigration and 1960's imports:	.577	.031
1970's Asian immigration and 1960's exports:	.751	.002

11. For instance, comparison of 1960's exports to Europe and 1970's immigration from Europe gives an $r = .901$ $(s = .001)$.

12. The locations of Canadian Trade Commissioner Service Posts in 1975 were derived from an in-house Department of Industry, Trade and Commerce mimeo.

BIBLIOGRAPHY

Canada. Department of Citizenship & Immigration
1964-6. *Annual Report*. Ottawa: Queen's Printer.

Canada. Department of Industry, Trade, and Commerce
1965. *Annual Report*. Ottawa.

Canada. Department of Manpower & Immigration
1967-75. *Annual Report*. Ottawa: Information Canada.

Canada. Economic Council of Canada
1975. *Looking Outward: A New Trade Strategy for Canada*. Ottawa: Information Canada.

Grant, George
1965. *Lament for a Nation: The Defeat of Canadian Nationalism*. Princeton, N.J.: Van Nostrand.

United Nations
1965. *Yearbook of International Trade Statistics*. New York: United Nations.

1974. *Yearbook of International Trade Statistics*. New York: United Nations.
1976a. *Statistical Yearbook: 1975*. New York: United Nations.

1976b. *Yearbook of National Accounts Statistics: 1975. vol. III,* New York: United Nations.

12

East Indians in Alberta: A Human Rights Viewpoint

Jennifer K. Bowerman
Department of Sociology
University of Alberta, Edmonton, Alberta

The exact number of East Indians living in Alberta is not known, although estimates range from twelve to fifteen thousand. They originate from a variety of countries, from India, Pakistan, Fiji, Tanzania, Kenya, Uganda, Singapore, and the West Indies. They form a variety of cultural and religious groups. Thus, there are Sikhs, Hindus, Christians, Muslims, but within these groups there may well be vast differences between people in their linguistic and cultural background, as well as their country of origin.

For Albertans, particularly those in Edmonton and Calgary where the majority of these immigrants live in this province, this is a relatively new influx. An East Indian who came to Canada in 1965, gives the following account:

> Until 1965 there were hardly any Indians in Calgary. There was one Indian family that was farming in a community south of Calgary and they had been there since 1928. Another Sikh family also farmed nearby, and they had been there since 1908.

> In 1965 when I moved to Calgary, there were only a few Indian students at the University of Calgary. In 1967 there were five families, three doctors, one coach at a sports club, and another family related to me. Since then, the Indian population has increased tremendously and the people have come from Fiji, Kenya, Uganda, Trinidad, and the Indian subcontinent itself.

Given this somewhat sudden influx of East Indians into the province, it is perhaps not surprising that there has developed a racial problem. Furthermore, the racial situations in British Columbia and Ontario where East Indians are bearing the brunt of hostilities, were bound to be repeated, at least to some degree, in Alberta. The purpose of this paper is not to explain the problem, but rather to examine it from the point of view of an official agency whose mandate is to investigate complaints of discrimination, and to educate people against racism.

The particular problem that this paper attempts to reveal is that many people have a subjective and emotional awareness that a serious racial situation is brewing in this province, yet there is a lack of objective or hard evidence to prove this. Very few racial incidents against East Indians are officially reported, either to the Human Rights Commission, the police, or the media. Thus, while everybody knows somebody who has been discriminated against in some way, the authorities have no way of proving it.

Alberta Human Rights Commission Reports Since 1966

An agency to deal with human rights has been in this province since 1966. While the Act concerning discrimination has changed considerably since that time, and particularly since 1973 when the Human Rights Act became The Individual's Rights Protection Act and the Human Rights Commission came into being, nevertheless, complaints have been registered by East Indians on a fairly regular basis. It should be kept in mind however, that early agency statistics are somewhat less refined than later ones.

In 1969, out of a total of 80 complaints registered, one was from an East Indian. The largest number of complaints were received from Native Indians. Indeed, in the race category, Native Indians have formed the largest category of complaints since the agency began, with Blacks second, and East Indians third.

In 1970, 101 complaints were received; 28 were from Native Indians and Metis, 9 from East Indians, and 9 from Blacks. In 1971, 291 complaints were received, and of those in the race category, 80 were from Native Indians, 31 from Blacks, and 11 from East Indians. In that particular year, most of the complaints were in the employment area.

In 1972, 311 complaints were received, with 28 from East Indians. Of these, 19 were formal and fell under the direct sphere of the Act. The other 9 complaints were investigated informally because they did not fall within the legislation directly.

In 1973, the new Individual's Rights Protection Act became law. An independent Commission was set up to carry out the mandate of the Act, and a new office was established in Calgary. As part of the new Act, the Commission was charged with a very specific education mandate in the field of human rights. At this time, reporting procedures were changed, and the subsequent annual reports provide more detailed specific information. In 1973, then, 17 complaints were received from East Indians, 5 in the area of public accommodation and services, 2 in tenancy, and 10 in employment. In the same year, 4 informal complaints were received.

It should be noted that still the largest number of complaints in the race category for that year came from Native Indians, with Blacks as the second highest category. By far, however, the largest number of complaints that year were lodged by females. In 1975, after a fifteen month period, the pattern remained similar, with females, Natives, and Blacks forming relatively large categories. In this period, the number of complaints from East Indians declined to 11; 7 in employment, 2 in tenancy, and 2 in services. In the final annual report of the Commission, for the twelve month period from April to March of 1976, 31 complaints were received from East Indians. Of these, 15 were in employment, 10 in tenancy, and 4 in services.

The common theme of these statistics is that East Indians have complained mostly in the field of employment. They have usually formed the third largest category of complainants in the area of race, and while there has been a steady increase in the overall number of complaints from this group, it has not been a significant increase.

Formal Complaints Since 1974

The statistics in the annual report, while interesting in that they demonstrate the actual number of complainants, fail to provide any information about the number of complaints investigated by the agency and found to be valid. Some statistics since 1974 are available that provide this kind of information.

Formal complaints are those brought to the Commission by individuals acting on their own behalf, or initiated by the Commission itself, which fit the criteria as outlined in The Individual's Rights Protection Act. These cases can be in the areas of signs and notices, employment and employment ads, tenancy, services customarily available to the public, membership in trade unions or other professional organizations, and equal pay. It should be noted that the Human Rights Commission is not advocacy oriented; it does not act as an advocate on behalf of complainants. Its mandate is to investigate claims of discrimination in the most objective way possible, and to conciliate settlements where such claims are found to be warranted. Since 1974, 59 complaints have been filed by East Indian persons claiming that they were discriminated against on the basis of colour, race, ancestry, or place of origin. Of these complaints, 38 concerned employment, 13 concerned tenancy, 6 concerned services, and 2 were received referring to membership in a trade union, employers' organization, or occupational association. Only 3 were found to be valid, and these were in the tenancy category. Of the rest, 3 were withdrawn; in a few others, settlements were reached whether or not the complaints were substantiated, and 40 were found to be invalid. Most of those 40 were in the employment category. Indeed, in most of the employment cases, there were persons of the same race (in this case East Indians) and persons from other racial minority groups, who received the benefit about which the complainant was claiming denial or discrimination.

The employment area is perhaps the most important for new immigrants. With a secure good "job," other benefits follow. Accompanying such a job is status and earning power, and with earning power comes additional status. However, in times when employment is relatively scarce for everyone, and when new immigrants have special difficulties, not only because of their newness but also because of cultural differences, it is hardly surprising that this is the area where most strains are felt. One of the major factors operating against East Indians in their search for employment in this country is the devaluation of their educational degrees and diplomas obtained in their mother countries. Although there may be legitimate reasons for this devaluation in some cases, such devaluation, whether reasonable or not, is often perceived as discriminatory by the individual person. A number of such cases have come to the Human Rights Commission. For example, a group of people complained to the Commission that an Alberta professional certificate application contained a discriminatory reference to persons from the Philippines and India. Graduates from these countries had to undergo additional training, regardless of the standing of the individual institution from which they graduated. After intervention by the Human Rights Commission, the offending sections from the form were deleted.

But the policy of treating these students differently, simply because they have graduated in these particular countries, remains.

Another profession in Alberta has a similar policy whereby graduates are divided into two groups. One group consists of those graduates from the U.K., South Africa, Australia, New Zealand, Canada, and the U.S. The other group consists of graduates from the rest of the world. These graduates have to undergo intensive additional training in their profession in order to practice in Alberta. Such a distinction between countries is obviously very arbitrary. It reflects a white colonial view of the world. Surely, a rating of institutions from all countries would be more appropriate. Until such a change is made, East Indians, and many other immigrants, will continue to feel that their education has been devalued, and perhaps with some justification.

At this point, it should be asked whether the Human Rights Commission is the agency to deal with these kinds of problems. Indeed, there is a jurisdictional problem. Alberta legislation specifies place of origin as grounds for complaint, not place of education which is the implication in the above kind of complaint. This question has to be determined at the Board of Inquiry level, and ultimately, will probably be decided by the courts. This may appear to be a slow process for those new immigrants who are impatient for change, but it should always be remembered that the Human Rights Commission cannot exceed its mandate, no matter how urgent or pressing or in violation with the spirit of the Act, a case may be.

Many of the employment complaints received by South Asians reflect a tight job market, a problem of placing over-qualified persons, and a problem of too many persons qualified in areas such as the social sciences. Thus, there have been a number of complaints from East Indian school teachers who have taught in their home countries for many years, who are well qualified, and who have taken additional qualifications here. They apply to numerous school boards for jobs with no success. Without ruling out the possibility that some such refusals may be motivated by race, many of these decisions reflect the state of the market as much as anything else. White graduates face the same problem. At other times, individuals just do not measure up to the standards required for a particular position. In one case for example, a person who came to the Alberta Human Rights Commission had been refused jobs, along with many others who were not East Indian, because his standards were not high enough. He had been rejected for jobs several times, had constantly badgered his professors for referrals, and finally, out of frustration, had complained to the Commission. In another case, a person hired on a contract basis continued to demand another job even though the contract had expired. Another complained to the Premier about discrimination even though she had been unable to pass the test for persons in her field. Another recent complainant was terribly upset when he was casually asked to take out some garbage as part of his job. He felt that this was a distinct reflection upon his race, and considered such duties too degrading. Yet another person, when fired, totally refused to admit that his job performance had not been satisfactory. These types of cases seem to be sufficiently reported to form a pattern. They may reflect a difficulty in adjusting to the Canadian work scene. Perhaps for such individuals, a settlement services programme of the type in Vancouver, with experienced multilingual counsellors, would be more helpful than a Human Rights Commission whose real purpose is to look for evidence of discrimination.

It should be pointed out that for every one such case of the kind described above, there are many East Indians who do adjust very well to Canadian life, and who excel in their chosen occupation. Indeed, one of the paradoxes facing East Indians is that they are the victims of double stereotyping. On the one hand, they are stereotyped as being lazy, superior, unwilling to work, but on the other hand, they are stereotyped as being too successful, too pushy, too work oriented and too wealthy. Thus they are placed in a losing situation. In fact, evidence from B.C. suggests that the number of immigrants of East Indian origin turning to social assistance to survive is remarkably low.[1]

That East Indians are sometimes resented, whatever their socio-economic position, was demonstrated in a case investigated by the Human Rights Commission recently. The case involved a complaint of discrimination from a white tenant. In the course of the investigation, it was discovered that the owners of the apartment building were East Indian; neither they nor their agents discriminated, but they, themselves, were the victims. Their tenants had, in fact, scrawled racist slogans about them in the elevators and on the walls of the apartment building. The owners did not want to complain about these things, considering them a part of the business.

Employment is the category in which the Commission receives most of its complaints. This is true not only for East Indians, but also for other minority groups. Since so few complaints are found to be justified for East Indian cases, multi-headed approach might be more useful. Certainly a professional counselling service, working hand in hand with the Human Rights Commission where complaints regarding employment are made, would be of more service for both complainants and respondents, at least on a short term basis.

Informal Complaints

Informal complaints are those complaints which do not fall within the specific sphere of the legislation. When the Commission accepts these kinds of complaints it is recognized that they have no legal backing, but are operating on a suasion basis only. Complaints of name calling, violence to persons and property, and general attacks of racism are accepted by the Commission as grounds for informal investigation. Here it is argued that an increase in these kinds of informal complaints would reflect the increase in the apparent racial incidents that are occurring in this province — the figures, however, do not substantiate this. There has been no increase in the number of informal complaints made by East Indians in the past two or three years. Indeed, in an absolute sense there has been a decrease. Between 1975 and 1977, there were only 8 informal complaints from East Indians. Between 1971 and 1974, there were 19 informal complaints received. The high number of 19 between 1971 and 1974, possibly reflects that Commission policy on informal complaints was not clearly formulated at that time. Thus, for example, referrals to Manpower and Immigration were marked as informals, whereas now they would be referrals.

Out of the 19 complaints that were informal, 10 related to employment and very generally concerned the problem of the individual versus the institution. Thus, some people complained of their inability to find work in their areas of expertise, but were unable to lay complaints against specific institutions. Other people were unable to obtain their qualifying papers from their mother country, and thus faced the threat to be retrained. In such cases, intervention by the Alberta Human Rights Commission served to clarify the issues. Only one of the 19 complaints referred to racial harassment on the job, and that was never followed up by the complainant.

Of the more recent informals, only 2 refer to complaints of racism and racial incidents. In one case, a boy complained that he had his face painted with lipstick at a junior high school by other boys. In the investigation of that complaint, the principal of the school refused to co-operate with human rights officials. Since The Individual's Rights Protection Act conveys no mandate in such cases, this was perfectly his right. A number of other similar incidents were rumored to have occurred in other schools in that area, but no one would come forward to specify any complaints. When school authorities were approached about the possible introduction of programmes to counter the problem, they refused. They denied a problem and stated that any programme, instead of countering a possible problem, might serve to create one.

The other informal case, concerned a family from Fiji, of East Indian origin, who complained of being harassed and taunted; oil had been poured over their car, and rocks thrown through their windows. Since such offences are criminal, they were also reported to the police. In this case, two Human Rights officers knocked on every door within a four block radius of the family's home, explaining what was happening to them. It was emphasized that this family was not Pakistani, as the name Paki implies, and which they had been taunted with, but that they were Fijian. Interestingly enough, some people appeared to feel better that the family was from Fiji, rather than from Pakistan.

As a result of the Human Rights community work, or possibly as a result of other factors, the incidents against this family appear to have stopped. But it should be noted that the family in question had only recently moved to this house in this area. In the house was a basement suite, formerly unused because of zoning laws. The Fijian family had brought in a family of their relatives to live in this suite. Such an arrangement is understandable, given the emphasis on extended family among many immigrant groups, and also given the high costs and shortage of suitable housing. Nevertheless, zoning, and a sense of space are important values to middle-class Canadians, and recognition of this might at least enable such families to recognize why they are resented.

Racial Incidents in the Community

In the past year, there have been several racial incidents reported in Alberta, some of which have been fairly serious. Perhaps the most notorious is the Daysland incident which occurred in October, 1976. It involved a railway crew consisting of whites and East Indians who started attacking each other with bottles and axes. No official inquiry was ever conducted into that incident, apart from the police investigation at the scene. No report of that incident nor official complaint arising therefrom was made to The Alberta Human Rights Commission.

Another racial incident concerned East Indian school children who had their turbans removed and were physically attacked by other children. They were taunted as being "Pakis." According to one press report, a young Lebanese girl was attacked and beaten by other girls, and called "Paki." None of these incidents nor similar ones have been reported to the Commission. In another case, one man was physically attacked in downtown Calgary, and had his turban removed. This is a serious incident to happen to a Sikh. Indeed, for some very orthodox Sikhs, such an assault could lead to an outbreak of sectarian violence. In this case, the offender was prosecuted by the police.

Several incidents have been telephoned in to the office, but in every case, the complainants have failed to come forward to document and substantiate their cases. One man complained of harassment and having a dead mouse placed in his sandwich by white workers. Another complained of being taunted and jeered every time he took his child for a walk. An incident was reported concerning an East Indian woman with a child in her arms who had asked a bus driver to let her off outside a medical clinic, but was let off outside a veterinary clinic about a mile further down the road. These kinds of reports are relatively numerous, but unless the victims come forward to back up their stories, they amount to little more than rumors.

Summary and Conclusions

This author believes that there is a climate of racism in Alberta, and that East Indians are bearing the brunt of it at this time. This belief is based partly on the above examples, and partly on conversation with both prejudiced whites, and those who are sympathetic to the particular ethnic group. Some of the comments from prejudiced whites are "Punjabs are not even people", and "They don't live like us."

However, officially, if we look at the facts as contained in the official records, the author's belief cannot be substantiated to any great degree. Therefore the question must be asked, if incidents of the kind described previously are happening, then why are they not being reported to the relevant officials? There are many reasons given for this reporting failure, for example:

"You people can't do anything anyway;"
"You emphasize women more than minority groups;"
"You are a government agency, and we are afraid of government;"
"If we report these incidents, then people will only retaliate, and they will become even worse;"
"Of course we must face some discrimination, it is natural;"
"By reporting these incidents, we are merely advertising the problem, and so will make it even worse."

These kinds of rationalizations are given as reasons for people's failure to come to the official agencies.

These reasons may be valid from the immigrants' viewpoint. It is perhaps interesting to note that the situation is somewhat different in British Columbia and Ontario, where more and more East Indians are coming forward to complain of discriminatory and directly racial incidents. But in Alberta, where the Commission has a twofold mandate to investigate complaints of discrimination, and to develop programmes aimed at countering prejudice, it is a frustrating situation. The solution to the impasse probably lies both with the East Indian organization in the community, and with the Human Rights Commission. On the one hand, the leaders themselves must emphasize the importance of reporting such incidents. On the other, agencies such as the Human Rights Commission must make themselves more visible to the organizations and their membership. For an agency with limited resources and time, the natural direction is to move in those areas where the problem seems greatest. The old argument of "you show me a problem, and I'll do something about it," is not after all totally unreasonable. I believe that there is a problem. Others must be convinced. In order to be convinced, every incident, no matter how apparently minor, should be reported to the official agencies. Only then will agencies such as the Human Rights Commission be able to mobilize others, including those in the education system and the community organizations, and work together to counter it.

Some Relevant Case Summaries

1) An engineer who graduated from a university in India believed he was discriminated against because of his place of origin, when a professional association he was obliged to join required him to write a confirmatory examination first. It was found that the association was following regulations in requesting candidates who graduated from non-accredited universities to write examinations. The association recognized several institutions in India, but the man did not take his training in one of them.

2) A Sikh claimed religious discrimination when he was fired from his job as a draftsman for refusing to shave his beard in accordance with safety regulations enforced by his employer. Investigation showed that these safety regulations were in accordance with government requirements, and did constitute a spurious means of forcing the Sikh to leave his job. When the employer realized that it was against the employee's religion to shave his beard, he was offered an alternative job where the mandatory rule of "clean shaven" did not apply. The man refused the job. An offer of two weeks' pay plus airfare to his

home ground was made and also refused. Under the circumstances, it was the Commission's view that religion was not a factor in the man's termination. In sympathy, however, with his economic plight, the employer was urged to repeat its offer of two weeks' pay and airfare.

3)   A medical doctor who had graduated from a medical school in India and interned in a Uganda hospital, filed a complaint against an Edmonton hospital when she found it used an intern matching service which gave preference to graduates from medical schools in Canada, U.S.A., Britain, New Zealand, Australia, Ireland, and South Africa. The cases were subsequently closed when the service amended its policy to treat medical graduates from all World Health Organization recognized schools similarly.

NOTES

1.   *Vancouver Province,* March 30, 1977.

13

East Indian Women in the Canadian Context: A Study in Social Psychology*

Josephine C. Naidoo
Psychology Department
Wilfrid Laurier University, Waterloo, Ontario

1. INTRODUCTION

Empirical research on peoples of non-western origin living on the North American Continent has emerged only in recent years. A survey of the literature reveals that research on the East Indian culture is generally meagre. Comparative studies of this culture and the dominant North American culture are scattered. No coherent body of theory basic to an understanding of value and ideological differences between the two cultures exists. The present study contributes to this understanding. It provides data about the influence of cultural habits on concepts of male-female roles and functions. This data is useful for the assess-

---

* Generalizations about East Indians in Canada on the basis of this research should be made cautiously until further studies have been conducted to indicate that such generalizations are warranted.

ment of attitudes towards women based on concepts of biological determinism which tend to undermine the potential achievement-orientation of North American women. Finally, the study gives insight into the dynamics of acculturation in a non-western sub-group within the context of cultural *pluralism* which characterizes Canadian society.

At this critical point in the history of Canadian unity, the fullest participation and active commitment of all segments of the population to Canada, Canadian institutions, Canadian society and culture, is an issue of urgent dimensions. Such commitment poses complex questions for new Canadians. These questions revolve around the *dual demand* of identification, communication and social acceptance within the host culture, and the retention of those facets of the original culture perceived as critical for cultural identity and integrity of the inner self-concept.

This paper has several objectives. First, it examines the role perceptions, sense of accomplishment, and achievement aspirations of a large sample of women (N=105) of East Indian origin who reside in two adjacent cities in Ontario, Canada. Second, it makes a comparative analysis of similar dimensions for a sample of women (N=105) of Anglo-Saxon origins, matched by residential location. Third, it reports on the gross corollary data pertaining to the intercultural image of Indian and Anglo-Saxon women by a random sampling of respondents in each subcultural group. Finally, the paper poses certain questions and reflections about the Indian woman in the Canadian context, her potential contributions to Canadian society, and the realization of this potential.

II. CHARACTERISTICS OF THE SAMPLES

For the study, 210 volunteer respondents of East Indian and Anglo-Saxon origins were interviewed by trained senior Canadian women students in two detailed sessions conducted in the women's homes. An in-depth interview schedule probing the variables of interest to this study, drawn from the literature and modified for research pertinent to the Indian culture, in particular, was utilized. The study was viewed as exploratory; its basic objectives were to identify and refine variables yielding insightful knowledge, again in particular, about the Indian culture.

Since official population records by ethnic background are not available in Canada, the population estimates for the Indian group resident in the twin cities were based on listings provided through the courtesy of local cultural and religious organizations and well-informed individuals within the Indian community. A randomly selected sample of 10% from each sub-group within the Indian community was set as a target sample. Tables 1 and 2 indicate that this "target" sample requirement was largely met. Women from India, Pakistan, Bangladesh, Sri Lanka, East Africa, Guyana, and Trinidad were, therefore, included in the "target" sample. Respondents of Anglo-Saxon origins were randomly selected from the City Directory (Vernon, 1976) on the basis of residential "match" with the Indian women.

TABLE 1

Composition of Survey Sample by Country of Origin

Country	Families	10% Sample	Obtained Sample	% Frequency
India	250	25	55	52.4
Pakistan	80	8	12	11.4
Bangladesh	10	1	3	2.9
Sri Lanka	10	1	4	3.8
East Africa	150	15	10*	9.5
Guyana	110	11	12	11.4
Trinidad	75	8	9	8.6
Totals	685	69	105	100.0

* under represented

Note: The local Indian population is approximately 3,000.

Detailed biographical data were obtained from the respondents. Selected data are presented in Table 3. They reveal a good "match" between participants in the two groups on demographic variables which investigators, employing the survey technique, generally attempt to control. Thus, both Indian and Anglo-Saxon women had spent most of their childhood and adolescence within their respective home countries, primarily in cities and towns (rather than metropoles or rural areas). Most women in both groups were relatively young, in the 20-34 age bracket. The husbands were older than their wives, and most women in both groups had been married 1-5 years. The Anglo-Saxon group peaked at one other age level, 50 years +, married 20 years +.

Primary and high school education were most frequently received by women in both groups. There was a nucleus of women with higher

TABLE 2

Survey Sample by Religion

Home Country	Religion	Frequency	Total N = 105
India	Hindu	41	
	Sikh	6	
	Muslim	4	
	Christian	3	
	Jain	1	55
Pakistan	Christian	7	
	Muslim	5*	12
Bangladesh	Muslim	3	3
Sri Lanka	Christian	4	4
East Africa	Ismaili (Uganda)	5*	
	Ithna-Asheri (Uganda)	3	
	Hindu (Kenya)	1	
	Muslim	1	10
Guyana	Hindu	6	
	Muslim	3	
	Christian	3	12
Trinidad	Hindu	2	
	Christian	7	9

* under represented

degrees (Bachelor's degree, in particular) among Indians and Anglo-Saxons. There were more respondents with clerical-professional training among the Anglo-Saxon women. Husbands in both groups tended to have more formal education than the women, with a nucleus of men possessing higher degrees for both groups. Respondents' parents had roughly the same educational background. Mothers and fathers generally had attended primary and high schools; a small number of fathers in both groups had obtained Bachelor's degrees. There were more cases of skilled labourers among the fathers of the Anglo-Saxon group.

Respondents in both groups were, in general, "non-students," and the salary bracket of $15,000-$20,000 was most frequently indicated by both groups where a response had been given. There were, however, twice as many Anglo-Saxon couples in the $30,000 + bracket.

TABLE 3

Salient Demographic Data (N = 105 Indians, 105 Anglo-Saxon Canadians)

Variables	Indians Frequency	Anglo-Saxons Frequency
Women's Age:		
20-24	24	17
25-29	23	15
30-34	24	23
35-39	20	11
40-44	7	11
45-49	6	8
50+	1	17
Length of Marriage (years)		
1-5	33	25
6-10	22	18
11-15	25	16
16-20	9	11
20+	10	30
Number of Children:		
1	18	14
2	31	20
3	16	32
4	5	10
5+	4	3
Length of Stay in Canada (years)		
1	10	
2	13	
3	16	
4	7	
6	14	
10-16	14	
>16	—	103

Variables	Indians Frequency	Anglo-Saxons Frequency
Family Salary:		
Under $4,999	0	6
$5,000- 9,999	16	12
$10,000-14,999	13	11
$15,000-19,999	20	20
$20,000-24,999	6	12
$25,000-29,999	9	6
$30,000+	7	15
Women's Education:		
Primary School	87	92
High School	85	90
Clerical	18	16
Secretarial	24	18
Teaching Diploma	17	18
Nursing Diploma	2	14
B.A. Degree	38	8
M.A. Degree	18	31
Medical Degree	1	3
Ph.D.	1	0
Women's Religion:		
Hindu	46	Roman Catholic 10
Muslim	20	Protestant 74
Christian	22	Jewish 1
Other	12	Other 19
Immigration Status:		
Citizen	27	105
Landed	73	
Visitor	5	

Note: Data was missing on several items.

Husbands were main wage earners in both groups, and women who worked contributed just a small percentage of the total income. There was, however, a small group of women (5.7% for Indians; 5.8% for Anglo-Saxons) who, seemingly, were the sole wage earners in both groups.

Indians most frequently had a two-child family; Anglo-Saxons three. Indians were primarily Hindu by religion; Anglo-Saxons were primarily Protestant. Women in both groups considered themselves "somewhat religious." Anglo-Saxons said their religious beliefs had changed "somewhat" since leaving the parental home; Indians said that their religious beliefs had not changed at all since living in Canada or other western countries. For the Indians, their length of stay in Canada varied, ranging from one to sixteen years. Most Indians were landed immigrants, and most planned to become Canadian citizens.

III. THE PRIVACY FACTOR IN THE INTERVIEW PROCESS

A characteristic aspect of East Indian culture, manifested during our interview that warrants attention, is the extreme *privacy* with which Indians regard their attitudes, values, and relationships. Questions, which in the North American culture, investigators would not hesitate to ask and anticipate frank responses, seemingly are considered extremely private in the Indian culture. Thus, for example, questions about family relationships, perceptions about the self, parental treatment of boys and girls, inter-ethnic marriage, and the perception of Canadians in the larger society were more difficult to probe with Indian respondents than with Anglo-Saxon respondents. Contrary to the general results concerning the interview process with ethnic samples, Indian participants did not necessarily respond more receptively to their own in-group interviewers. Presumably, they preferred talking with "strangers" because this allayed their anxieties regarding possible "leaks"* in data they viewed as very private.

Enlisting the co-operation of the community entailed more than the usual steps researchers take in the initial soliciting stages of a project. Although most people responded with interest and even enthusiasm to the project, there were individuals, albeit a minority, who expressed fears that such research was "premature," possibly "damaging"* to the community. In some instances, it was extremely im-

---

* Exact words used by potential respondents

portant to convince the husband of the importance and confidentiality of the wife's participation in the project.

Personal contact, allowing respondents to verbalize their fears, moving from an indirect to a more direct approach in eliciting responses, and talking about individual anxieties regarding the effects of empirical research for the larger community, were approaches that contributed to establish rapport and co-operation. Mailed questionnaires yielded negligible responses. Telephone discussions, obtaining entry to speak about the project at religious and cultural gatherings, and explanatory meetings with leaders of sub-groups within the community, served as excellent "step-in-the-door" techniques. Television and radio presentations on Indian programs, and flyers placed in Indian grocery stores and cinemas alerted some people.

No single set of interviewer characteristics can be labelled as the more appropriate or "successful" set for entry into the homes of this particular minority group. Mature, trained, attractive, and courteous interviewers were employed throughout the project. Patience, and a "waiting it out" approach helped. Interviewer-respondent relationships that "clicked" yielded productive, enjoyable, and even memorable experiences for both participants in the interview process.

IV. COMPARATIVE FEATURES OF THE SAMPLES

A. Women's Role Perceptions

The advent of the women's liberation movement in the western world triggered off a series of studies which focussed on the age-old question of what kinds of behaviours are socially appropriate for men and women. An extensive survey of how ideology shapes women's lives, conducted by American sociologist, Jean Lipman-Blumen, and published in *Scientific American* in January 1972, attracted my attention. Perhaps, not surprisingly, she reported that the sex-role ideology, i.e., the system of beliefs regarding the appropriate behaviour of women with respect to men, acquired during childhood and adolescence, guided the adult woman's perceptions, life goals, educational, and occupational aspirations. The Lipman-Blumen study was conducted on the wives of graduate students in the Boston area. In her study, 27% of the women adhered to a category she labelled "traditional" ideology and 73% held a "contemporary" ideology. According to the traditional view, the female role revolves about the belief that a woman's responsibilities are home-making and child rearing; men are responsible for financial support of the family, and women with children should not expect to have a career. The contemporary view is based on the belief that women should be as free as men to pursue educational and occupational goals, and that men and women should share equally in responsibilities inside and outside the home.

Similar questions have rarely been asked to immigrant women of non-western origin currently living on the North American continent. The present study posed the following questions: How does the contemporary Indian woman view herself? What are her beliefs about role division in the home, male dominance, responsibility for children and household chores, women's education and work outside the home? What would she like to accomplish in her life, and how do these aspirations differ from those of women in her family in the home country?

The picture of the Indian woman's role perceptions emerging from this study is more complex than findings reported by Lipman-Blumen for the American sample. Specifically, the women's beliefs about their role in life show a *complementary interaction* between *traditonal* and *contemporary* expectations for women. Thus the data reveal a slight belief in role division and male protection, but a strong belief that the responsibilty for household chores should be shared even where a woman works outside the home primarily for her own fulfillment, rather than to supplement the family income (79.0%). The resistance to sole responsibility for household chores may be understood in the context that 72.2% of the respondents report that their mothers had domestic help, and 50.5% had full-time help. Respondents, therefore, came from homes in which women were largely freed from the heavier domestic role that characterizes the woman's role in North American culture. Further, the data show quite conclusively that many women believe in their own ability, and in the opportunity for education and careers for married women, even when they have children (82.0%). Many respondents felt that women were capable of assuming positions over men, making their own decisions about voting, and sharing equally in decision-making in the family. But, the respondents show a decided traditonal trend with regard to children. There is considerable feeling that the natural mother is best for the child, that a mother with young children should not work outside the home, and a strong belief that even good day-care centres cannot take the place of a mother in caring for the child (77.1%).

Table 4 compares the trends in the data for Indians and Anglo-Saxons on two dimensions, viz., beliefs about responsibility for children (most traditional category for Indians) and beliefs about women's education and work outside the home (most contemporary category for

TABLE 4

Women's Role Perceptions

A. Beliefs about responsibilty for children.

Items:	Indians		Anglo-Saxons	
	% A-T*	% D-C*	% A-T	% D-C
1. Discipline of children is mother's task	39.1	54.3	15.3	80.9
2. Physical care of children is mother's job	53.4	40.0	30.5	67.6
3. Natural mother is best for the child	68.6	24.8	15.3	79.0
4. Even warm affectionate others cannot raise child	54.3	38.1	11.5	84.8
5. Even good day-care centres cannot replace mother	77.1	12.4	54.3	38.0
6. Husband's remarriage where wife childless	9.6	87.6	1.9	94.4

B. Beliefs about women's education and work outside the home.

Items:	Indians		Anglo-Saxons	
	% A-T*	% D-C	% A-T	% D-C
7. Women's function is that of wife-mother, not of development of talents outside of home	33.3	60.0	17.2	80.1
8. Mothers with preschool children should not work outside	69.5	26.7	56.1	38.1
9. More necessary for men rather than women to attend college/university	16.2	79.1	14.3	80.0
10. Mothers with children should not expect a career	17.2	82.0	3.9	95.3
11. Professions should be more available to men than to women	27.6	71.4	15.3	81.9
12. Women's career ambitions must be curtailed if they interfere with the family	53.4	39.0	45.8	49.5

* A-T = Agree or Traditional response
  D-C = Disagree or Contemporary response
  Note: Missing data where figures do not sum to 100%

Indians). Anglo-Saxon women are clearly extremely "contemporary," more so than Indian women; items on which they take a "traditonal" stance, they are less traditional than Indian women. Overall (all categories), the Anglo-Saxon data is very "contemporary," inclusive of beliefs about household chores and related responsibilities. Unlike the Indian families, 68.6% of the Anglo-Saxon homes had no domestic help, and hence mothers of respondents engaged in heavy household work (71.4%) and grocery shopping (86.7%) in additon to child care, cooking, and light household duties. Anglo-Saxon respondents in this study, therefore, have not modelled their behaviour in this respect on that of their mothers.

As Table 4 shows, Anglo-Saxon women, too, are conservative on items such as day-care centres for children, and work outside the home where children are involved, but this tendency is less marked than in the case of Indian women.

B. Self-Identity of Indian Woman

In traditional Indian thinking, the ideal woman is selfless, gentle, devoted, retiring, loyal, and obedient. These were characteristics symbolized in the figure of Sita, devoted wife of Rama, and acted out in extreme acts of loyalty as embodied in the ancient practice of "suttee." Naturalistic observations, however, indicate that the contemporary Indian woman has experienced change and acculturation due to forces within India and in the western world.

Insight into the woman's self-concept and self-identity was gleaned from a series of measures which probed responses to questions such as: Who am I? How do I view my real self? What would I like to be ideally? What attitudes do I have toward myself? (Naidoo, 1977).

Pertinent data from the "Who am I?" measure is reported in this paper and presented in Table 5. When confronted with the question, "Who am I," the respondents' initial reactions were those of uncertainty, reticence, and a feeling of "being at a loss" to verbalize their insights about the inner self. It appears that most respondents seldom reflected on this question, possibly because of other more immediate environmental demands on them, or because they are culturally not "tuned" to probing the self for the meaning of their lives. Seemingly, Indian women incorporate life events as they occur, adjust, and "flow" with these events. However, once respondents felt at ease, they responded more readily, and even with enthusiasm. Overall, descriptions were simple, concrete, and straightforward. A content analysis of a

TABLE 5

*Qualitative Analysis of Indian "Who Am I" Responses**

Cue Phrase	Most Frequent Responses	Categorization
1. "I have"	small children good husband	family-centred
2. "I am"	a wife, mother a Woman nice, happy, impatient a teacher, typist	family-centred female identity personality traits occupation
3. "I want"	good education for children realize own potential happy family	family education self-achievement family-centred
4. "My goals are"	further own education happy family life share Indian culture	self-improvement family centred inter-group relationship N = 25

* further data analyses in progress

random sampling of responses (N = 25; Total N = 105) reveals the pattern described below:

> To the cue phrase, *"I have,"* primary focus centred on the family (I have small children, good children, a good understanding husband, a happy life in the family). There was little focus on material possessions.

> To the cue phrase, *"I am,"* responses revolved about the home and family (I am a wife, mother, good wife and mother), on the self as "woman," on personality traits possessed, balanced between desirable and undesirable traits (I am kind, nice, sincere, unselfish, intelligent, happy, *versus* I am impatient, get annoyed, like to gossip, have a bad memory) and frequent mention was made of skills, training, education, professions (I am a teacher, artist, nurse, doctor, typist, etc.).

> To the cue phrase, *"I want,"* three major emphases emerged: (i) a good education, success, high achievement for children, (ii) realization of a woman's potential, more knowledge, education, (iii) a happy life, peace, contentment for family and self, and (iv) making a good impact on Canadians, embodied in statements such as: prove I'm a Canadian, remove discrimination, share old civilization of India, show Indians are not underdeveloped, understand ethnic groups in Canada.

To the cue phrase, *"My goals are,"* the following responses were elicited: (i) further education, learning English, careers, e.g., teaching, social work, (ii) a happy life, being a good wife and mother, (iii) helping others, serving the community, doing volunteer work, doing something for the world and the poor.

Several respondents mentioned religious values and the importance of these values for children ("I have devotion to God," "show Canadians that because of *Karma* we are all here"). Some others mentioned their desire of wanting to return to India.

Analysis and Reflections

The data indicate that the Indian woman in this study portrays a complementary interaction between traditional and contemporary roles in life. She is strongly traditional with regard to motherhood and children, but is quite contemporary with regard to education and careers outside the home, pursuits viewed in the past as the prerogatives of men. Nevertheless she is both more traditional on motherhood-children issues, and less contemporary on education-careers issues, than her Anglo-Saxon counterpart. Her strong family-orientedness emerges again on the self-identity sentence completion test, as does her concern about education for herself and her family.

C. Sense of Accomplishment

Lipman-Blumen (1972) defines three categories of mode of achievement adopted by women in her study: direct, balanced, and vicarious. Women who prefer the *direct mode* tend to satisfy their achievement needs predominantly through their own efforts; those who choose the *balanced mode* place an equal weight on their husband's accomplishments and on their own; and those who choose the *vicarious mode* fulfill their achievement needs predominantly through the accomplishments of their husbands.

Lipman-Blumen, on the basis of her study on graduate student wives, presents data which indicate that the direct mode of achievement was preferred by one-third of the women who shared a contemporary view of life, whereas it was preferred by only one-sixth of the women with the traditional viewpoint of life. As might be expected, 76% of those women with the traditional ideology, compared to 54% of those with the contemporary viewpoint, adhered to the vicarious mode of achievement. It is interesting to note with reference to this study, that relatively few women seemed to prefer the balanced mode of achievement in which the accomplishments of both husband and wife carry equal weight (16% contemporary, and 7% traditional).

As already discussed, in terms of role perceptions, the nature of the Indian sample tested appears to be complementary, reflecting a combination of traditional and contemporary characteristics. Following the Lipman-Blumen procedure, questions pertaining to the respondents' sense of accomplishment *outside* the home were posed, and an attempt was made to trace the development of their sense of achievement aspiration from home to host country.

Most Indian women chose the vicarious mode of achievement (52.4%), i.e., their sense of accomplishment outside their home is mostly fulfilled by the husband's achievements, but they do express a need to accomplish something on their own. Some (26.7%) chose the balanced mode of achievement, i.e., their sense of accomplishment is fulfilled only when both husband and wife accomplish equally, and a minority (10.5%) chose the direct mode, i.e., they feel fulfilled mostly by their own accomplishments, though they also need to feel that the husband is accomplishing something. Only a few respondents chose the extremely contemporaneous position, i.e., fulfillment completely on the basis of one's own outside activities (2.9%) (see Table 6).

Inspection of Table 6 reveals that the trend for a sense of accomplishment outside the home for Anglo-Saxon women is almost a reversal of the trend for the Indian data. These women chose the direct mode of achievement, i.e., for a sizable percentage of this group (46.7%), achievement needs are satisfied largely through the woman's own efforts. About one-third of the sample (30.5%) chose the vicarious mode, which is considerably lower than the figure for Indians. Interestingly, a higher percentage of the Indian, rather than the Anglo-Saxon group, chose the balanced mode of accomplishment (26.7%; 18.1% respectively).

D. Changes in Achievement Aspirations

An attempt was made to examine evolution and changes in the women's sense of achievement. In response to appropriate questions, respondents maintained that the sense of achievement generally shown by women in the family circle in India was *traditional* — related to roles as mother, wife, involvement in home arts, and some outside activities. However, the sense of achievement encouraged in respondents by their parents moved from traditional to *balanced-contemporary,* with

TABLE 6

Sense of Accomplishment

My sense of accomplishment *outside my home* can be:

	Mode	Indians % Frequency	Anglo-Saxons % Frequency
1. Completely fulfilled by my husband's work	Vicarious Traditional	3.8	1.0
2. Mostly fulfilled by my husband's work but I need to accomplish something of my own		48.7	30.5
3. Fulfilled when each accomplishes equally	Balanced	26.7	18.1
4. Mostly fulfilled by my own accomplishments but I need to feel my husband is accomplishing something	Direct Contemporary	10.5	34.3
5. Completely fulfilled by my own accomplishments		2.9	12.4
		N = 97	N = 101

a clear component related to seeking higher education, a career or stable occupation, earning money, and status. This pattern is endorsed by the Indian women as the sense of achievement they experienced most of their lives.

By contrast, Anglo-Saxon women, raised within a traditional family circle in most cases, were also largely encouraged by their parents to continue to pursue the traditional role.

A further change is reported by Indian women on coming to Canada. The women find that their present sense of achievement is traditional.

They are homebound and have few activities outside the home. They feel this experience is common to other Indian women acquaintances in Canada. Dissatisfaction with this situation is revealed in questions probing the sense of achievement the women *want* for themselves. The data shows clearly that the women want a more balanced sense of achievement for themselves in activities of equal weight inside and outside the home. They view the balanced mode as ideal for a woman and as something most Indian women in Canada would like for themselves. Moreover, they encourage this balanced sense of achievement in their daughters.

Much of the same life experience and aspirations are endorsed by the Anglo-Saxon women. They too are homebound and traditional in their present lives, but more of them report on achieving activities of equal weight inside and outside the home. Like the Indians, they think the balanced mode of life is ideal and encourage this ideal in their daughters.

To appropriate inquiries, 70.4% of the Indian women say they day-dream about playing another role in life or of achieving something more. For 28.6% of the women, their present role is the major cause of their frustration because they cannot pursue creative activity outside their home. But, in spite of their aspirations and feelings of discontent at not attaining these aspirations, most respondents fulfill their sense of accomplishment in the traditional vicarious mode through the accomplishments of their husbands. Further, most respondents (78.1%) claim they are satisfied with their roles — ranging from mostly being in the home (one-third of the sample), part-time work/outside activities (one-third of the sample) or full-time work outside the home (one-third sample).

It would seem, then, that Indian women would really like a fuller sense of achievement for themselves, but most settle for less and slip into a vicarious mode of fulfillment through their husbands' accomplishments. About one-third of the Anglo-Saxon sample share the Indian experience, two-thirds of that sample, however, experience a more satisfying degree of fulfillment. These individuals fulfill themselves in a more balanced or direct fashion largely through their own achievements. Thus, 84.4% indicate satisfaction with their roles in life.

Another point of difference between Indians and Anglo-Saxons relates to their perception of women's liberation movements. Although both groups were largely unaware of these movements during adolescence, their present views differ. Indian women tend to view women's movements in the West, and events such as International Women's Year, favorably; Anglo-Saxon women were more uncertain about their attitudes towards these movements and events.

Analysis and Reflections

The traditional orientation of Indian women, already observed in the foregoing, reappears more pointedly in the sense of accomplishment measure — Indian women choose the *vicarious mode* of fulfilling their achievement needs. They satisfy these needs largely through the accomplishments of their husbands. They do, however, reveal some underlying dissatisfaction with this experience, though on the surface, they claim satisfaction with their role in life. Ideally, they would prefer a more *balanced mode* of achievement in which equal weight can be placed on their own and their husbands' achievements. This level of achievement is attained by only 26.7% of the Indian sample.

In contrast, Anglo-Saxon women accomplish more through their own efforts, i.e., the *direct mode* of achievement although they are exposed to a much more traditional socialization process than the Indian women. The Anglo-Saxon women also feel that the *balanced mode* of achievement is ideal, though most have surpassed this level.

Achievement Aspirations

As is commonly recognized in Protestant societies, hard work and the pursuit of success became moral ideals, and many analysts contend that it was this factor which led to the economic accomplishments of Protestant societies. Given this hard work-success oriented climate, why is it that the female sector of North American society is besieged by a condition described and documented by American psychologist, Matina Horner, as "fear of success?" In other words, why is it that girls in North American society experience anxiety about achieving, and they expect unfavourable consequences arising from success, such as the fear of losing friends, of not finding a marriage partner, fear of becoming lonely, isolated, and unhappy?

Horner used a storytelling imagery technique to elicit achievement responses from American female college students. Her content analysis of these data revealed that even girls who were competing successfully at college displayed fear of social rejection, concern about their femininity/normality, and denial of success.

In general, coverage of achievement motivation in women is limited; even less research has been conducted on cross-cultural samples. To my knowledge, no empirical research has been conducted on achievement aspirations in cultures, such as the East Indian, where there is no dating system, where every girl's marriage is almost assured because part of her father's duty is to find a spouse for her, where romantic love is not a major component of marital expectation, and where marriage is often by parental arrangement (present Indian sample: marriage by arrangement 46.7%; by own choice 41.0%), i.e., where many experiences likely to generate anxiety and fear, as identified by Horner, are not a significant aspect of the culture.

The present study utilized Horner's storytelling method to probe the nature of achievement motivation in Indian and Anglo-Saxon women. Participants were asked to tell a story about an imaginary figure, Anne, who finds herself at the top of her medical school class after her first term final examinations. The themes in the stories were analyzed using Horner's categories.

Table 7 reveals that for Indian respondents there was negligible occurrence of anxiety connected with the expectation of success. Respondent story imagery did not reflect feelings that success would result in social rejection or loss of femininity/normality. Rather, success was viewed as bringing happiness to the individual involved, as well as to her family. A bright and continued career was predicted, and potential contributions to the society were envisioned. Indeed, many Indian stories had a "fairytale" tone to them: "Anne will become a doctor, and everyone will be happy ever after."

Stories by Anglo-Saxon women were more complex, especially with regard to analyses of the anxieties likely to be experienced by Anne. Table 7 shows clearly that while the "happiness-success-continued career" theme of the Indian stories did emerge in their stories as well, there was a well defined anxiety component based on fear of social rejection of various descriptions.

The storytelling analysis of achievement was augmented with tests of achievement attitudes, aspirations for the women themselves, and for their daughters. In the achievement attitudes' test (Mehrabian, 1968), the respondents were asked to indicate their preference for one of two settings or experiences. A higher level of achievement orientation is inherent in one of the two choices. Thus, for example, agreement with the following statement indicates high achievement: At school/ college I would think more about getting a good grade, than worry about getting a bad grade. Agreement with the statement, i.e., focussing on getting a good grade indicates higher achievement orientation than disagreement with the statement, which focusses on worrying about getting a bad grade. Only the data for the Indian respondents is reported in this paper. Data analysis for the Anglo-Saxon participants is in progress.

Overall, the Indian respondents exhibit a high achievement orientation. Thus, for example, at school they would focus more on getting a good grade, than worry about getting bad grades. They think of the

TABLE 7

Analysis of Story Themes* (Naidoo-Dybka, 1977)

Theme	Indian Stories (N = 90) Frequency	Anglo-Saxon Stories (N = 89) Frequency
1. Anne's happiness	32	23
2. Happiness, pride and/or influence of Anne's parents	41	17
3. Continuation of career only	57	37
4. Combination of career and marriage	18	20
5. Career ends after marriage	1	3
6. Poverty in Anne's background	6	0
7. Anne's contribution to society	18	4

Analysis of Story Themes (Horner's Categories, 1975)

Theme		Indian Stories Frequency	Anglo-Saxon Stories Frequency
Social Rejection Loss Femininity	General social rejection	6	28
	Sacrifice, no dating	0	39
	Conflict female-marriage, career	0	12
	Parental fears re: social rejection	0	2
	Anxiety about future	0	17
	Surprise at results, chance	3	6
	Parental pressure into career	0	4
	Changes career (reality, imagery)	0	2

* Data analysis in progress

future rather than the past or present; they would rather take total responsibility for a group's activities than share in the decision-making progress; they think it very important to do a job well, even if this means not getting along with co-workers, etc. Further, the respondents claimed that they would take advantage of opportunities for higher education and careers for themselves, should openings in the community be made available, and that they would be willing to help in the promotional work entailed. Finally, they indicated that they think "very often or occasionally" about education and careers for their daughters for whom they have high aspirations; most people indicated a doctoral level (31.4% of 50.5% responding), in particular, a medical career (26.7% of 54.3%) for their daughters.

Analysis and Reflections

Seemingly, the Indian woman at the present time has negligible anxiety about success and achievement. She has wants both for herself and her children, and she possesses the achievement motivation attitudes and values for bringing high achievement and high aspirations to realization. This picture may change as marriage patterns change, as Indian women experience more aggressive competition, and as achievement attitudes for women within the larger culture infiltrate her domain.

Inter-cultural Perceptions of Women*

Courtesy of my students and contacts in various settings in the community, East Indian and Canadian student and non-student respondents of both sexes were asked about their inter-cultural perceptions of *women*. The following three broad questions were asked: How do women of East Indian origin (Canadian) "come across" to you? What do you *like* about them, and what do you *dislike* about them? To date, 79 Canadians have responded; 34 Indians. Hand-distributed questionnaires yielded less response from Indians than from Canadians. Telephone inquiries tended to yield more insightful data from Indians. Non-student Canadians were mainly white-collar workers, a few professionals, and housewives. Non-student Indians had similar occupational backgrounds, including a few blue-collar workers.

---

* Study in progress. Findings should not be generalized to other settings or populations until further data have been collected.

Table 8

Canadian Perceptions of Indian Women* (N = 79)

Trait Description	Most Frequent Responses
Like, positive	beauty grace intelligence femininity
Disliked, negative	dirty abrupt customs (dress, "tikka") home languages (public use)
Combined, positive — negative	quietness, politeness — aloof, unfriendly commitment family — subservience to men

* Study in progress—findings should not be generalized until further data are collected

Canadian perceptions of Indian women ranged from statements that were clearly favourable or unfavourable, to combined favourable and unfavourable impressions, to non-judgmental, non-committal type statements. The most frequent responses are shown in Table 8. Examples of positive, liked characteristics pertained to the Indian woman's beauty, grace, intelligence, femininity, mystique and self-control. Negative adjectives used to describe disliked characteristics were: dirty, greasy, smelly. Only a minority of the respondents liked Indian women wearing their traditional dress (the correct label for the Indian dress, "sari" was not used at all) and then only on special occasions. The "tikka" (dot) on the Hindu woman's forehead was not liked. One respondent wrote: "we are all equal here." Others wrote: "if in Canada dress as Canadians." (Incidentally, I may add, these negative reactions to the sari are experienced by Indian women in other parts of the world. I recall that in South Africa, where I was born and raised, Indian women in sari were often rudely addressed as "Mary" by white South Africans, rather than by their correct names, because of the resemblance of the sari to the dress worn by Mary, the Mother of Christ!) There was strong dislike too, of Indians speaking their home languages. Again, the feeling expressed was that Indians should speak English if they live in Canada. Several respondents experienced Indian women as pushy, rude, abrupt, out of touch with Canadian culture, ignorant of Canadian customs, and unwilling to change.

Table 9

Indian Impressions of Canadian Women* (N = 34)

Trait Description	Most Frequent Responses
Liked, positive	friendly frank
Disliked, negative	drinking smoking negative generalizations (re-Indians) racism
General impressions	helpful outspoken nice reserved

* Study in progress—findings should not be generalized until further data are collected

Examples of combined favourable-unfavourable impressions are as follows: Canadians tended to like the Indian woman's quiet, shy, polite manner, but this liking moved to perceiving her as cold, aloof, and unfriendly. A small percentage of the respondents commented thus: "they think they are better than anyone else, snobbish, arrogant." Further, while they tended to like the Indian woman's commitment to her husband and children, they disliked what they described as her submission to her husband, her place behind a man, her subservience. Several Canadians said there was nothing they liked or disliked about Indian women; Canadian males had almost no contact with them. A few people said they had no basis for making judgments about Indian women because of lack of contact; a few refused to generalize from limited contact, and a few said, "they are human like us; when you get to know them, they have a hidden warmth, commitment to friends, and hospitality."

Table 9 summarizes Indian impressions of Canadian women. These data are not elaborated in this paper as the present focus centres on the Indian woman in the Canadian context. Some discussion of these impressions are given elsewhere (Naidoo, 1976). It suffices to mention at this point that Indian impressions of Canadian women are extremely varied. The most common liked adjective listed is "friendly"; the most common disliked descriptions pertain to racism. Thus, statements such as the following were made: "look down on immigrants," "brag only they are Canadians," "belittle us."

Analysis and Reflections

Negative impressions of Indian women emerging from the data should be viewed in the perspective of well-known socio-psychological theory. Data should not be generalized to other settings and populations without reflection. Positive inter-cultural experiences by women who retain traditional dress, customs, and home language on occasion, within educated, cosmopolitan work settings are not questioned by this study. Rather, the perceptions of a random sampling of people — a few professionals, students, and the ordinary man on the street — are presented. In the dynamics of social perception, the *visibility factor* — whether physical (i.e., different skin colour, eye or hair type, etc.) or behavioural (i.e., different dress, social customs, etiquette, etc.) tends to create *social contrast effects*; i.e., the differences are exaggerated, and socially distant relationships may arise. This is experienced more intensely by people who cannot identify with others beyond certain limits. Other influencing factors are education, their culture, and individual life experiences. Thus, it is not the experience of people with wider education, cultural and life experiences. The latter category, commonly defined as "liberal," comprises some 20% of the population in social-psychological estimates, some 60% fall in the middle range in terms of tolerance of minority groups persons, with 20% falling into the clear "non-liberal" category (Campbell, 1963).

Since one basis for good inter-cultural relationships lies in the *identification* process, there is an onus on people in a *multi-cultural* and pluralistic society to take steps likely to promote the process. As is widely recognized, one way to achieve this is through increased *communication* and *interaction* between people preferably on an informal basis. Unfortunately, the data in this study indicate a general lack of such communication. Of the Anglo-Saxon respondents, 67.6% say they enjoy informal activities with other Canadian (white) men and women in general, and 77.1% state that they interact socially most frequently with other white Canadians. Of the Indian women respondents, 63.8% indicate that they enjoy informal activities most with "East Indian women speaking my home language," 42.9% say that they interact socially most frequently with other Indians, and 46.7% state that they interact equally with Indians and white Canadians.

Strong in-group feelings within ethnic groups are understandable. In a pluralistic society which is still searching for a common identity while simultaneously respecting the cultural identity of its multi-ethnic groups, it is disturbing to note that such a high level of exclusiveness within groups exists.

EAST INDIAN WOMEN IN THE CANADIAN CONTEXT

There emerges a complex duality in self-identity, commitment, and in behavioural expressions of the East Indian women studied in depth in this survey.

The study reveals that the Indian woman is entrenched in the traditional values of her cultural heritage *but* she also exhibits contemporary, future oriented aspirations. She is deeply committed to her family and home *but* at the same time, she exhibits the potential for high achievement. She also possesses high aspirations for herself and her children. The Indian woman adapts to many forms of behavioural expression in the larger society *but* there are forms of expression which she feels are an integral part of her cultural identity and these she adamantly retains. As stated elsewhere, (Naidoo, 1976), my readings, study, observation and experience lead me to believe that it is important to retain selected aspects of both old and new values and traditions for the wholesome evolution and integration of one's personality. Those values which are perceived by individuals as critical to the inner self, to the sense of identity, and to personal worth, should be nurtured and preserved to develop a healthy "new" self within the host culture. People cannot be expected to, nor should they, simply abandon values and philosophies basic to their sense of "being" in too short a period of time, as it has occurred in the case of Canadian Indians. I have been a member of a minority group all my life and my perception of the gradual evolution in adapting and reconstructing the inner self as one moves from home to host culture is a psychologically sounder process than the rapid change and abandonment of values that are profoundly meaningful to the inner self. The latter process may well produce disintegration of the inner self with resultant negative features for the minority group itself and the whole culture.

Further, there is an urgent need for more contact and communication between ethnic "newcomers" and the larger Canadian Society at a deeper, more meaningful level, rather than at the level of ethnic food and folk dancing. The diversity of values, philosophies, and interpretations of life that immigrant peoples bring with them implies a potentially rich contribution to the host culture.

People of non-western origin have made impressive adaptations to western culture; the reverse cannot be said of people of western origin. Except for a minority, western people remain relatively uninformed about non-western cultures, philosophies, languages, and religions adhered to by millions around the world. In a pluralistic society some compromises, some degree of tolerance, and enlightenment on the part of established Canadians can surely be expected by new Canadians.

Finally, there is a great deal of talent, intelligence, and energy among the East Indian women which this research has barely addressed. The Canadian interviewers employed in this study were impressed with the respondents they met. It remains for those of us who are concerned about ethnic groups and their contribution to Canadian society to assist in mobilizing and channelling these attributes towards promoting the creative genius of this great country and "the just" society.

REFERENCES

Bardwick, Judith M.
    1972. *Readings on the Psychology of Women.* New York: Row Publishers.

Beny, R. & Menen, A.
    1969. *India.* Toronto: The Canadian Publishers, McClelland and Stewart Ltd.

Bhatnagar, J.
    1976. "Education of Immigrant Children," *Canadian Ethnic Studies,* 8, #1, 52-70.

Callahan, S.
    1971. "Feminine Response to Function," *Humanitas,* Vol. 6(3), 295-310.

Campbell, D. T.
    1963. "Social Attitudes and Other Acquired Behavioural Dispositions." In S. Koch (ed.) *Psychology: A Study of a Science, Vol. 6. Investigations of Man as Socius: Their Place in Psychology and the Social Sciences.* New York: McGraw-Hill.

Cormack, Margaret L.
    1974. *The Hindu Woman.* Connecticut: Greenwood Publishing Company.
    _____,
    1961. *She Who Rides a Peacock: Indian Students and Social Change.* London: Asia Publishing House.

Dybka, Donna
1977. "A Cross-Cultural Comparison of the 'Fear of Success' Motive." Unpublished paper, Wilfrid Laurier University.

Green, Helen B.
1971. "Socialization Values in West African, Negro, and East Indian Cultures: A Cross-Cultural Comparison," *Journal of Cross-Cultural Psychology*. Vol. 2(3), 309-312.

Horner, Matina
1975. "Femininity and Successful Achievement: A Basic Inconsistency." In Krupat, E. (ed.) *Psychology is Social*. Glenview, Illinois: Scott, Foresman and Company.

Kapur, R.
1969. "Role Conflict Among Employed Housewives," *Indian Journal of Industrial Relations*. Vol. 5(1), 39-67, July.

Lipman-Blumen, Jean
1972. "How Ideology Shapes Women's Lives," *Scientific American*, (January), 34-42.

Mehrabian, A.
1968. "Male and Female Scales of the Tendency to Achieve," *Educational and Psychological Measurement*, Vol. 28, 493-502.

Naidoo, J. C.
1977. "The East Indian Woman: Her Potential Contribution to Canadian Society: Recommendations." Paper presented at the conference on *Indians in Toronto*. Toronto, Canada. (May)

——————,
1976. "The East Indian Woman," *Proceedings of an Inter-Cultural Seminar on East Indians*. Toronto.

——————, & Fiedler, F. E.
1962. "Perceptions of Self and Significant Others by Indian and American Students," *Indian Journal of Psychology*, Vol. 37, 115-126.

Osgood, C. E., Suci, G. J. & Tannebaum, P. H.
1957. *The Measurement of Meaning*. Urbana, Illinois: University of Illinois Press.

Price-Williams, D. R. (ed.)
1969. *Cross-Cultural Studies: Selected Readings*. Penguin Modern Psychology Series. Don Mills, Ontario: Longman, Canada Ltd.

Queen, S. A. & Habenstein, R. W.
1967. *The Family In Various Cultures* (3rd ed.), Toronto: J. B. Lippincott Co.

Rapoport, Rhona & Rapoport, R. N.
1971. "Early and Later Experiences as Determinants of Adult Behavior: Married Women's Family and Career Patterns," *British Journal of Sociology*, Vol. 22(1), 16-30.

Report of the Royal Commission on the Status of Women in Canada. Ottawa: 1970. Information Canada.

Robinson, J. P. & Shaver, P. R.
1969. *Measures of Social Psychological Attitudes.* Ann Arbor, Michigan: Publications Division, Institute for Social Research. The University of Michigan.

Thiagarajan, K. M. & Lukas, R. A.
1971. "Personal Values Across Cultures: A Study of Managers and Students in India and the U.S.," *Journal of Social Psychology,* Vol. 85 (1), 139-140.

Vernon Directories Ltd., City Directories Publishers, 17th edition, 1976. 1975-76. Ontario: Griffin & Richmond Co., Ltd.

Warner, W. L., Meeker, M & Eels, K.
1949. *Social Class in America.* Chicago: Science Research.

Whiting, J. W. M.
1968. "Methods and Problems in Cross-Cultural Research." In Lindzey, G. & Aronson, E. (eds.) *Handbook of Social Psychology,* Vol. 2. Reading, Mass.: Addison-Wesley, 2nd ed., 1968.

14

Attitudes, Parental Identification, and Locus of Control of Korean, New Korean-Canadian, And Canadian Adolescents

Bo Kyung Kim
Department of Psychology
Huronia Regional Centre, Orillia, Ontario

It has been well established that immigrant children assimilate more quickly than their parents and that the differences in speed of assimilation between the children and parents may become a source of the parent-child conflict (Taft and Johnstone, 1967: Danziger, 1972), diffuse and uncertain identity (Taft and Johnstone, 1967), or feelings of powerlessness or alienation on the part of children (Okano and Spilka, 1971: Wolfgang, 1973). Little is known about the differential determinants for immigrant children and their parents regarding the speed and patterns of assimilation, the factors influencing the parent-child relationship and its consequence on the children.

In the present study, Rotter's (1954) Social Learning Theory of Personality is applied to analyze the situation. The simplest formulation of Social Learning Theory's principal tenet is that behavior is a function of (1) the expectancy or probability held by the individual that a particular behavior will, in a given situation, have a successful outcome and (2) the value the individual places on the outcome (Rotter, Chance, and Phares, 1972). In the viewpoint of Social Learning Theory, the individual's behaviour in familiar situations will be guided mainly by his previous reinforcement history in those situations. In novel settings, he must rely on generalized expectations gained from situations perceived as similar to the one at hand. In such a view, the new society will be perceived by the immigrant as a broad unfamiliar situation in which he must rely on expectations gained from the situations in his own society. This seems to suggest that the immigrants will experience a great deal of failure in the new society if the cultural diversity between the two societies where the immigration occurred is great.

The immigrant assimilation may be conceived in the Social Learning Theory framework as the process whereby the immigrants learn that expectancies developed in their own society result in the failure of reinforcement in the new society, and adopt alternative behaviours which have a relatively higher expectancy in the new society. In this sense, the younger immigrants, who have a relatively shorter reinforcement history in the society of origin, are expected to experience a smaller degree of discrepancy in their expectancies than the older immigrants. Thus, it is expected that children would show a lesser degree of frustration and a faster expectancy change resulting in speedier assimilation into the new society. In addition, children would show fast reinforcement or need value change. Rotter et al. (1972) indicated that adults have more difficulties in reinforcement value change than children. Thus, immigrant children find it easier to change their preference for the set of functionally related reinforcements arranged by one culture over the set arranged by the other. This seems to suggest that the adult immigrants mainly adopt those alternative behaviours necessary to obtain the goals which they had learned to value in their society of origin, while the children learn new behaviours that lead them to the goals they have learned to value in the new society. If the assumption that the adults' assimilation patterns will be characterized by the expectancy change, while those of the immigrant children's will be characterized by the reinforcement value change, the parent-child value conflict observed among the immigrant families may be well explained in terms of the expectancy-reinforcement discrepancy the parents and children experience in their interaction. Thus, the children who changed their reinforcement value would reject their parents who no longer served as primary sources of social skills or models of behavior for them in the new society. As a result, especially in the families which immigrated from a society where loyalty to the parents is stressed, a great deal of frustration will be experienced by the children.

The aim of the present study was to investigate whether Korean attitudes, perception of parental attitudes and the feelings of powerlessness of new Korean-Canadian adolescents differ from the non-immigrant children and to investigate the relationship between these variables. The following hypotheses were tested:

1. New Korean-Canadian adolescents will show lower scores on the Korean Attitudes Scale than Korean adolescents.
2. New Korean-Canadian adolescents will show lower correlations between their own attitude scores and those of their perceived parental attitudes on the Korean Attitude scale than Korean adolescents.
3. New Korean-Canadian adolescents will show lower parental identification than Korean adolescents.
4. New Korean-Canadian adolescents will show significantly higher external scores on the Internal-External Control Scale than the non-immigrant adolescents, Korean and Canadian.

The hypotheses were tested by: (1) a 2×2 analysis of variance, male and female, Korean, New Korean-Canadian and Canadian groups and (2) by obtaining intercorrelations of the following three variables: (a) demographic (age, ages of parents, educational levels of parents and occupational level of father) and (b) psychological (self attitudes, perceived parental attitudes, parental identification and locus of control) and (c) immigration related variables (length of residence, father's previous occupational level in Korea and parents' acculturation index). These variables were compared by sex and group. A two-factor analysis of variance was performed to examine the effects of sex and length of residence on the Korean attitudes, parental identification, and locus of control in New Korean-Canadian adolescents.

METHOD

Subjects

The subjects of the present study were three groups: Korean, New Korean-Canadian and Canadian students totalling 275 subjects. The Korean group included 117 subjects (58 boys and 59 girls) attending high schools in Taegu, Korea. Taegu is the third largest city in South Korea and the population is approximately one million. The Korean students were from two, sex segregated schools (in Korea, most second- ary schools are sex-segregated). The Korean subjects were all selected from the four classes of grades eleven and twelve from the two schools. The reason for choosing these particular two schools in Taegu was to get comparable subjects with other groups of subjects, the Canadian and New Korean-Canadian groups in terms of an urban environment, socio-economic status and the nature of school. The New Korean- Canadian group included 67 subjects (30 boys and 37 girls) attending high schools in the Metropolitan Toronto area. To obtain the New Korean-Canadian subjects, the ministers and the youth club leaders of the five Korean ethnic churches located in Toronto were contacted, and the purpose of the study and the necessary arrangements for the testing were explained. All of them agreed to help and provide subjects. The New Korean-Canadian subjects were selected totally from the students' activity clubs in the Korean churches. The Canadian group included 91 subjects (49 boys and 42 girls) attending schools located in the north-east part of Toronto, where the immigrant population was known to be small. The criteria for the selection of the Canadian sample were: (1) must be Canadian-born Caucasian, and (2) mother tongue must be English. Also excluded from the Korean, New Korean- Canadian and Canadian sample were those students for whom data was incomplete and those students from single parent families.

The mean ages of the subjects in the Korean, New Korean-Canadian and Canadian groups were 16.97 (SD = .65), 16.70 (SD = 1.95) and 15.97 (SD = .84) respectively. The mean length of residence in months for the New Korean-Canadian male group was 29.53 (SD = 22.87) and for the female group, 38.03 (SD = 28.83).

The three groups did not differ to a statistically significant degree in either the subjects' ages or the ages of their parents. The groups were, however, different in respect to the socio-economic status measured by the Blishen Occupational Class Scale (1958). The fathers' Blishen standard scores as determined by income and education of the Canadian group (Mean = 59.45, SD = 7.99) were significantly higher than both Korean (Mean = 51.81, SD = 6.50) and New Korean-Canadian (Mean = 50.30, SD = 7.91) groups. A direct comparison of the socio-economic status of the immigrant subjects with those of the Canadian or Korean subjects may not be appropriate because it was found that the correlations of the years of schooling and the occupa- tional level for the New Korean-Canadian fathers was .20 (n.s.), while the Canadian fathers showed .49 (p < .001) and the Korean fathers .59 (p < .001). The correlation for the immigrant fathers was significantly lower than those of the Canadian and Korean fathers on the Fisher's Z-transformation test. It seems to suggest that the socio-economic status of the recently arrived immigrant families may not be the same in nature as that of natives to the society. It is also true that an occupational class scale constructed on the basis of the social structure of a certain country in a certain period is not appropriate for cross-cultural study.

Since the main objective of the present study was to investigate the relationships among the variables and to utilize a factorial design, it was possible to control the effects of socio-economic variables among the groups.

The Instruments

1. *The Korean Attitude Scale*

The scale was a twenty-six item, five point scale. The fifteen items were adopted from various sources; five items from Taft's (1965) Australianism, four items from Lai's (1971) Chinese attitude measurement, three items from the Parental Attitude Research Instrument (PARI, Schaefer and Bell, 1958), two items from Kohn's (1972) Authoritarianism-Rebellion Scale, and one item from the Chinese Tradition-Modern (T-M) Attitude Scale, Dawson, Law, Leung and Whitney (1971). The rest of the items were constructed by the senior author. In adopting and constructing the items, it was asked if the items could discriminate the attitude of Koreans from Canadians in the areas of family relations, sex and marriage, education, attitudes toward authority, friendship and so on (e.g.: it is important for a girl to remain a virgin until she is married. Education is more important than money). The discriminative capacity of the individual items and the total scale between the Korean and Canadian group adolescents was statistically acceptable.

The perceived parental attitudes were measured on the same scale. The subjects were asked to respond to the statement if they agreed or disagreed and were immediately asked to react as their mother and father would react to the same statement on the scale.

2. *The Measurement for Parental Identification*

Bowerman and Bahr's (1973) Parental Identification Scale was adopted in this study. In the original study, parental identification was defined as the value orientation that adolescents have toward their parents. It seemed to be adequate to use the same definition in the parent study since it was an attempt to investigate value change of the immigrant adolescents toward their parents attributable to the cultural shift. The scale was an eight-item, five point scale. Two identical sets were used to measure father and mother identification separately by simply interchanging the words father and mother. (e.g.: do you trust your father's (mother's) judgment about important decisions you must make?).

The Hoyt estimate of reliabilities of the father identification scale were as follows: Korean sample, .75; New Korean-Canadian sample, .87; Canadian sample, .90; entire sample, .85. The reliabilities of the mother identification scale were as follows: Korean sample, .81; New Korean-Canadian sample, .87; Canadian sample, .90; entire sample, .86.

3. *The Internal-External (I-E) Locus of Control Scale*

The scale was a twenty-nine item, forced choice test with six buffer items. A thorough discussion of the test is presented by Rotter (1966). According to Rotter, an internal person feels that he controls his reinforcement contingencies. By contrast, the external person feels that his reinforcements occur on a chance basis, or are due to fate or luck. Seeman (1959) has defined the sense of powerlessness as the expectancy or probability held by the individual that his own behavior cannot determine the occurrence of the outcomes, or reinforcement, he seeks. He indicates that the sense of powerlessness is very closely related to the notion of internal-external control of reinforcement. He then refers to the externally oriented person on the I-E scale as being in a state of "powerlessness" or as being "alienated." The cross-cultural differentiation of the scale has been proven in recent studies (Wolfgang, 1973: Tin-Yse et al., 1969: Schneider and Parsons, 1970).

The Hoyt estimate of reliabilities of the scale were as follows: Korean sample, .93; New Korean-Canadian sample, .93; Canadian sample, .57; entire sample, .89. The reliabilities of the scale for both the Korean and New Korean-Canadian samples are significantly high, while the reliability for the Canadian group is relatively low. This distinctively different pattern in the reliability between the two different ethnic group samples seems to suggest that the internal consistency of the I-E scale would be different between ethnic group memberships.

4. *The Acculturation Index*

To examine the relationship between the parents' acculturation level (the ability in English) and other variables; Danziger's (1971) Acculturation Index was adopted in the present study. The Acculturation Index was an eight-item index to measure the level of acquisition and use of English in the immigrant parents. In the Danziger original study, the first five items demonstrated a slow and gradual acquisition of the rudiments of English by the Italian mothers. In the present study, only these five items were used to measure the ability of the New Korean-Canadian parents in English. This index ranged from the level to read street and direction signs in English to the ability to read English newspapers.

The Korean Versions of the Instruments

The above instruments were translated into Korean by the senior author. The Korean versions of the I-E scale was re-translated into English by the two Koreans who had experience working as official translators for the Canadian government. This re-translated English version of the I-E scale was administered to 10 Korean students attending the University of Toronto. One month later, the 10 students were again tested with the original English version. The correlation obtained between the re-translated English version and the original I-E scale was .96 which indicates a high level of agreement in the score obtained on the two versions of the scale.

Procedure

Korean subjects were tested with the Korean versions of the instruments in the classroom situation. The tests were administered by the guidance-counsellors in the school. New Korean-Canadian subjects were tested in various locations. With the help of the ministers and the youth club leaders, many of the subjects were tested in the church. Other students who did not come to the church were tested at their homes or other places, individually or in small groups. New Korean-Canadian subjects were tested by the English or Korean versions of the instruments according to their preference. Twenty-one boys (70%) and 28 girls (76%) chose the Korean version of the questionnaire. Only Canadian students who obtained their parents' permission to participate in the present study were tested in the classroom setting.

To help guard against students giving socially desirable responses, the students were not told that their data would be compared with other ethnic groups and they were not asked to put their names on the sheet.

THE RESULTS

A. Group Differences in Self Attitudes and Perception of Parental Attitudes on the Korean Attitude Scale and the Inter-correlation with Other Variables.

Table 1 presents the means and standard deviations of self attitudes, perceived parental attitudes, parental identification and locus of control. Tables 2, 3, 4, 5, 6 and 7 present the inter-correlations of all variables by group and sex.

The summary of analysis of variance and Scheffe test indicated that the Canadian group differed from both the Korean and New Korean-Canadian groups in their self attitudes and in their perception of parental attitudes. The New Korean-Canadian group did not differ from the Korean group in their attitudes or in their perception of parental attitudes. However, the standard deviations of New Korean-Canadian adolescents on the Korean attitude scores when compared with those of Korean adolescents, showed that the attitudes of the individual immigrant adolescents are more varied ($F_{(116-66)} = 1.87$, $p < .05$), which seems to indicate that the Korean attitudes in the immigrant group are affected by immigration.

As may be seen from the tables of inter-correlations of all variables, in the New Korean-Canadian female group, the scores on the Korean attitude scale were significantly negatively correlated with length of residence in Canada ($-.33$, $p < .05$). In the New Korean-Canadian male group, no significant correlation was shown between the two variables. The tables indicate that all groups show significant positive correlations between their own self attitude scores and those of their perceived parental attitudes, except the New Korean-Canadian female group. The results of Fisher's Z-transformation of r indicated that the New Korean-Canadian female group had a significantly lower correlation between the self attitudes and their perceived father attitudes than any other group. This same female immigrant group had a significantly lower correlation between the self attitudes and their perceived mother attitudes than any other group except the New Korean-Canadian male group ($Z = 1.24$, n.s.) and Canadian female group ($Z = .007$, n.s.). The correlation between the self attitudes and perceived father or mother attitudes in the New Korean-Canadian male group was not significantly different from any other group.

The hypothesis concerned with the low correlations between self and perceived parental attitudes in the New Korean-Canadian group was supported with the female group.

TABLE 1

Means and Standard Deviations of Self and Perceived Parental Attitudes, Parental Identification and Locus of Control

Group	N	Self Attitudes M (SD)	Perceived Father Attitudes M (SD)	Perceived Mother Attitudes M (SD)	Father Identification M (SD)	Mother Identification M (SD)	Locus of Control M (SD)
Korean							
Male	58	81.88(8.54)	95.07(9.11)	93.71(7.08)	29.72(4.88)	28.38(4.88)	9.25(2.87)
Female	59	82.03(7.58)	92.95(8.86)	92.81(8.49)	29.41(3.55)	29.98(4.08)	9.95(3.23)
Combined	117	81.96(8.03)	94.00(9.01)	93.26(7.80)	29.56(4.96)	29.19(4.55)	9.59(3.06)
Kor-Can.							
Male	30	81.50(10.69)	91.20(7.81)	91.27(7.26)	30.17(4.67)	28.70(4.86)	8.97(2.39)
Female	37	78.50(11.21)	78.50(11.21)	93.92(6.76)	27.95(4.90)	28.73(5.02)	9.14(3.23)
Combined	67	79.96(10.99)	94.10(8.82)	92.73(7.06)	28.94(4.88)	28.75(4.91)	9.06(2.87)
Canadian							
Male	49	65.37(10.02)	76.41(9.17)	76.76(8.78)	28.57(6.23)	26.63(5.51)	10.84(3.48)
Female	42	59.00(7.61)	73.81(10.51)	70.76(9.81)	26.64(6.67)	29.19(6.03)	11.05(3.98)
Combined	91	62.43(9.50)	75.21(9.84)	74.00(9.69)	27.68(6.46)	27.81(5.86)	10.93(3.70)

TABLE 2

Intercorrelations of all Variables in Korean Male Subjects (N = 58)

Variables	2	3	4	5	6	7	8	9	10	11	12
1. Age	-.04	-.09	.21	.08	.16	-.29*	-.13	-.21	-.17	-.02	.02
2. F-Age	—	.89***	-.37***	-.17	-.11	.16	.00	.05	.18	.15	.07
3. M-Age		—	-.29*	-.19	-.10	.20	.09	.04	.12	.14	-.04
4. F.-Ed.			—	.69***	.47***	-.04	-.06	-.15	-.34***	.05	.00
5. M-Ed.				—	.34***	.08	-.05	.06	-.12	.13	.12
6. F-Occ.					—	-.05	-.09	-.01	-.10	.20	.09
7. L-C						—	.00	.16	.08	.17	.25*
8. Self-Att.							—	.51***	.44***	.07	.25*
9. F-Att.								—	.81***	-.02	.07
10. M-Att.									—	.04	.31
11. F-Id.										—	.47***
12. M-Id.											—

Note: F = Father; M = Mother; Ed = Years of Schooling; Occ. = Occupational Level; L-C = Locus of Control; Att. = Attitudes; Id. = Identification.

*$p < .05$
**$p < .01$
***$p < .001$

TABLE 3

Intercorrelations of all Variables in Korean Female Subjects (N = 59)

Variables	2	3	4	5	6	7	8	9	10	11	12
1. Age	-.20	-.20	.06	.05	.22	-.15	-.35*	-.34*	-.33*	-.07	-.10
2. F-Age	—	-.88***	-.16	-.07	-.22*	.02	-.16	-.30*	-.23*	-.28*	.05
3. M-Age		—	-.02	-.11	-.15	-.08	-.06	.30*	.30*	-.18	.15
4. F-Ed.			—	.56**	.70***	-.24*	.12	.00	.13	.18	.01
5. M-Ed.				—	.32	-.16	-.14	-.21*	-.19	-.06	.00
6. F-Occ.					—	-.11	.02	.04	.05	.10	.01
7. L-C						—	.06	.14	.29	-.17	-.13
8. Self-Att.							—	.57***	.63***	.15	.14
9. F-Att.								—	.89***	-.16	.19
10. M-Att.									—	-.11	.12
11. F-Id.										—	.53***
12. M-Id.											—

Note: F = Father; M = Mother; Ed = Years of Schooling; Occ. = Occupational Level; L-C = Locus of Control; Att. = Attitudes; Id. = Identification.

*p < .05
**p < .01
***p < .001

TABLE 4

Intercorrelations of all Variables in Korean-Canadian Male Subjects (N = 30)

Variables	2	3	4	5	6	7	8	9	10	11	12	13	14	15	16
1. Age	.60***	.62***	-.37**	-.55***	-.33	-.13	-.38*	-.36*	.16	.16	.08	.19	.31*	.12	-.17
2. F-Age		.95***	-.46***	-.62***	-.01	.02	-.38*	-.42**	.38*	.38*	.13	.20	.39*	-.03	-.29
3. M-Age			-.42***	-.59***	-.10	-.01	-.33*	-.42**	.43*	.40*	.19	.29	.52***	.00	-.28***
4. F-Ed.				.77***	.39**	.21	.59***	.56***	.17*	.05	-.33*	-.21	-.31*	.01	.06
5. M-Ed.					.49***	.27	.63***	.59***	-.16	.01	-.18	-.24	-.29	-.08	-.06
6. F-Pre. Occ.						.64***	.48***	.50***	.30*	-.11	-.21	-.04	-.11	-.13	-.27
7. F-Occ.							.44***	.53***	.29*	-.30*	-.34*	-.38*	-.32*	.04	-.06
8. F-Acc.								.58***	.30*	.12*	-.27	-.21	-.12	-.18	-.11
9. M-Acc.									.23	-.13	-.42**	-.39*	-.35*	.11	.07
10. L. of Res.										.21	-.23	.25	.34*	.12	-.10
11. L-C											.10	.10	.31*	-.22	-.43***
12. Self-Att.												.60***	.48***	.02	.03
13. F-Att.													.86***	.01	-.12
14. M-Att.														.05	-.23
15. F-Id.															.70***
16. M-Id.															

Note: F = Father; M = Mother; Ed = Years of Schooling; Pre. Occ. = Previous Occupational Level in Korea; Occ. = Occupational Level; Acc. = Acculturation; L. of Res. = Length of Residence in Canada; L-C = Locus of Control; Att. = Attitudes; Id. = Identification.

*p < .05
**p < .01
***p < .001

TABLE 5

Intercorrelations of all Variables in Korean-Canadian Female Subjects (N = 37)

Variables	2	3	4	5	6	7	8	9	10	11	12	13	14	15	16
1. Age	.53***	.55***	-.11	-.11	.00	.06	-.23	-.26	-.28*	-.18	-.19	.19	.28*	.03	.07
2. F-Age		.92***	-.33*	-.26	-.16	-.15	-.43***	-.56***	-.23	-.23	-.15	.02	.17	.07	.19
3. M-Age			-.39**	-.31*	-.07	-.02	-.36*	-.49***	-.25	-.23	-.13	.13	.19	.14	.33*
4. F-Ed.				.73***	.41**	.20	.64***	.58***	.31*	.22	.13	.05	.09	.01	.08
5. M-Ed.					.38**	.43***	.64***	.71***	.33*	.10	.03	.11	.19	-.09	-.10
6. F-Pre. Occ.						.63***	.20	.32*	.28*	.00	-.02	.12	.25	.02	-.09
7. F-Occ.							.37*	.31*	.24	-.16	.03	.17	.34*	.12	.08
8. F-Acc.								.70***	.22	.37*	.00	.20	.19	-.11	.03
9. M-Acc.									.18	.15	.03	.21	.13	-.24	-.17
10. L. of Res.										.44***	-.33*	.08	.11	.33*	-.45***
11. L-C											.35*	.01	.06	-.21	-.37*
12. Self-Att.												.10	.20	.55***	.48***
13. F-Att.													.77***	-.09	.06
14. M-Att.														.05	.06
15. F-Id.															.69***
16. M-Id.															

Note: F = Father; M = Mother; Ed = Years of Schooling; Pre. Occ. = Previous Occupational Level in Korea; Occ. = Occupational Level; Acc. = Acculturation; L. of Res. = Length of Residence in Canada; L-C. = Locus of Control; Att. = Attitudes; Id. = Identification

*p < .05
**p < .01
***p < .001

TABLE 6

Intercorrelations of all Variables in Canadian Male Subjects (N-49)

Variables	2	3	4	5	6	7	8	9	10	11	12
1. Age	.23	.19	-.01	.00	-.08	-.13	-.27	-.10	-.01	-.19	-.09
2. F-Age	—	.80***	.16	-.13	.01	.03	.05	.03	-.11	.00	-.04
3. M-Age		—	.22	-.07	.22	.09	-.17	-.17	-.22	.18	-.05
4. F-Ed.			—	.64***	.31*	.07	-.18	-.33**	-.28*	.33**	.11
5. M-Ed.				—	.32*	.04	-.22	-.30*	-.28*	.02	.09
6. F-Occ.					—	.30*	.16	-.11***	-.18	.08	-.10
7. L-C						—	-.22	-.06	-.10	-.11	-.31*
8. Self-Att.							—	.72***	.63***	.18	.18
9. F-Att.								—	.82***	-.19	-.07
10. M-Att.									—	-.20	-.20
11. F-Id.										—	.53***
12. M-Id.											—

Note: F = Father; M = Mother; Ed = Years of Schooling; Occ. = Occupational Level; L-C = Locus of Control; Att. = Attitudes; Id. = Identification.

*p < .05
**p < .01
***p < .001

TABLE 7

Intercorrelations of all Variables in Canadian Female Subjects (N = 42)

Variables	2	3	4	5	6	7	8	9	10	11	12
1. Age	.04	.08	.08	-.10	.21	.06	-.04	.00	.11	.00	.09
2. F-Age		.78***	.00	.21	.02	.20	-.17	.21	.19	-.13	-.39**
3. M-Age			-.12	.19	-.11	.23	-.20	.09	.11	-.15	-.34*
4. F-Ed.				.27*	.64***	-.01	.03	.04	.05	.03	.12
5. M-Ed.					.23	-.22	-.09	-.06	-.05	-.20	-.15
6. F-Occ.						.01	.04	-.04	.12	.09	.08
7. L-C							-.45***	-.10	-.17	-.22	-.06
8. Self-Att.								.37***	.36**	.48***	.41***
9. F-Att.									.76***	-.15	-.08
10. M-Att.										-.05	-.27*
11. F-Id.											.64***
12. M-Id.											—

Note: F = Father; M = Mother; Ed = Years of Schooling; Occ. = Occupational Level; L-C = Locus of Control; Att. = Attitudes; Id. = Identification.

*p < .05
**p < .01
***p < .001

B. Group Difference in Parental Identification and the Inter-correlations With Other Variables

The analysis of variance of father and mother identification indicated that there were no significant mean differences between groups. It was constantly found that the Korean total group showed the highest scores in father and mother identification, the Canadian group showed the lowest scores in father and mother identification, and the New Korean-Canadian group stood in the middle. New Korean-Canadian male adolescents showed the highest in father and mother identification than any other male group, while New Korean-Canadian female adolescents showed the second lowest (Canadian female group was the lowest) scores in father identification and the lowest scores in mother identification of any other female group. These phenomena were comparable with the compatibility shown between their own Korean attitudes and those of their perceived parental attitudes in the New Korean-Canadian male adolescents (the father-self mean difference, 9.70; the mother self difference, 9.77) and with the incompatibility shown between self and perceived parental attitudes in the New Korean-Canadian female adolescents (the father-self mean difference, 19.96; the mother-self difference, 15.42). In the New Korean-Canadian female group, there was a significant negative correlation between length of residence and father identification ($-.31$, $p < .05$), and the length of residence and mother identification ($-.45$, $p < .001$). In the New Korean-Canadian female group, the Korean attitudes were positively correlated with father identification (.55, $p < .001$) and with mother identification (.46, $p < .001$). In the New Korean-Canadian male group, the Korean attitudes were not significantly correlated with parental identification. In the Canadian group, only the female group showed a significant positive correlation between the Korean attitudes and father identification (.48, $p < .001$), and the Korean attitudes and mother identification (.41, $p < .001$).

The hypothesis concerned with the mean differences in parental identification between the immigrant group and the non-immigrant group was not supported. The results indicated, however, that in the New Korean-Canadian female group, variations in Korean attitudes were inversely related to parental identification.

C. Group Differences on the Internal-External Locus of Control Scale

The summary of analysis of the three groups indicated group differences in the mean scores on the I-E scale. The Scheffe test showed that Canadian adolescents were more external than New Korean-Canadian adolescents. The New Korean-Canadian group showed lower external scores than the Korean group, but the difference was not significant. The results did not support the hypothesis that the immigrant group would show higher external scores on the I-E scale than the non-immigrant groups, Korean and Canadian. To analyze the contribution of the demographic, psychological and immigration related variables to the development of external locus of control of the Korean, New Korean-Canadian and Canadian group, the technique of stepwise regression was adopted. The data is shown in Table 8. For Korean adolescents, age contributed significantly to the prediction of external locus of control. For New Korean-Canadian adolescents, mother identification, length of residence, father's present occupation, father's acculturation level, father identification and father's age, were important predictors of external locus of control. For Canadian adolescents, mother identification, father's occupation and father's education were important predictors. In contrast to New Korean-Canadian adolescents, father's occupation and father's education were positively related with external scores in Canadian adolescents. Thus the Canadian adolescents who had fathers with higher occupation and education felt more powerless than those who had fathers with lower occupation and education. The results indicated that, in the immigrant adolescents, the sense of powerlessness was positively related with length of residence, father's acculturation level and father's age. It was negatively related with mother identification, father identification and father's present occupation level in the new society. The results of the stepwise regression analysis also indicated that the sense of powerlessness was predictable with the different variables between male and female adolescents. For New Korean-Canadian and Canadian male adolescents, mother identification and father's occupation level were the two most important predictors while for New Korean-Canadian and Canadian female adolescents, self attitude was the most important psychological variable related to the sense of powerlessness. For Korean female adolescents, father's educational level, mother attitudes and father attitudes were the predictors of the sense of powerlessness. For Korean male adolescents, self age and mother's age seemed to be related with the sense of powerlessness, but they were not statistically significant.

As Schneider and Parsons (1970) and Parsons and Schneider (1974) suggested, the I-E scale was sub-categorized into Luck-Fate (Rotter scale items, 2, 9, 15, 18, 21, 25 and 28), Personal Respect (items, 4, 7, 20, and 26), Politics (items, 3, 12, 17, 22 and 29), Leadership-Success (items 6, 11, 13 and 16) and Academics (items

TABLE 8

Stepwise Regression Analysis with the External Locus of Control as Criteria and all Other Variables* as Predictors, Korean, new Korean-Canadian and Canadian Group

Korean

STEP	Variable	R	R^2	F	Variable	R	R^2	F	Variable	R	R^2	F
	Male (N = 58)				Female (N = 59)				Combined (N = 117)			
1	Age	.29	.08	5.06	F-Ed.	.24	.06	3.45	Age	.22	.05	5.98**
2	M-Age	.33	.11	3.47	M-Att.	.34	.12	3.65*				
3					F-Att.	.38	.15	3.17*				

New Korean-Canadian

STEP	Variable	R	R^2	F	Variable	R	R^2	F	Variable	R	R^2	F
	Male (N = 30)				Female (N = 37)				Combined (N = 67)			
1	M-Id.	.43	.18	6.33*	Length	.44	.20	3.56**	M-Id.	.39	.15	11.58**
2	F-Occ.	.54	.29	5.52**	F-Acc.	.52	.27	6.37**	Length	.47	.22	9.05**
3	Length	.61	.37	5.02**	F-Occ.	.65	.42	7.99**	F-Occ.	.55	.30	9.02**
4	F-Att.	.64	.41	4.39**	S-Att.	.68	.46	6.87**	F-Acc.	.62	.39	9.82**
5	M-Att.	.69	.47	4.34**					F-Id.	.64	.41	8.48**
6	S-Att.	.72	.52	4.15**					F-Age	.65	.43	7.46**
7	F-Ed.	.75	.56	4.08**								
8	F-Age	.77	.59	3.92**								

Canadian

STEP	Variable	R	R^2	F	Variable	R	R^2	F	Variable	R	R^2	F
	Male (N = 49)				Female (N = 42)				Combined (N = 91)			
1	M-Id.	.31	.10	5.16*	S-Att.	.45	.21	10.33**	M-Id.	.39	.15	7.59***
2	F-Occ.	.42	.17	4.83*	M-Ed.	.52	.27	7.41**	F-Occ.	.44	.19	6.09****
3					M-Age	.56	.31	5.75**	F-Ed.	.47	.23	6.09****

*p < .05
**p < .01
***p < .001

* Variables: Age, Father's (F-) and Mother's (M-) Age, Father's and Mother's Education, Father's Occupation, Self (S-) Attitudes, Perceived Father and Mother Attitudes, Father and Mother identification. For the New Korean-Canadian group, Father's Occupation in Korea (Pre. Occ.), Father and Mother Acculturation (Acc.) and Length of Residence in Canada (Length) were added.

5, 10, and 23). The summary of analysis of variance performed over the five subscales of the I-E scale indicated significant mean differences within the "Respect," "Luck-Fate," "Politics," and "Academics" subscales. However, the Scheffe test with alpha level of .05 only differentiated the Canadian group from the other groups within the "Respect" subscales. Thus both Canadian male and female groups had significantly higher external scores than any other group on this subscale (Canadian, Mean = 2.55; SD = 1.09; Korean, Mean = 1.57; SD = 1.11; New Korean-Canadian, Mean = 1.60, SD = 1.16).

To examine the effects of sex and lengths of residence on the Korean attitudes, parental identification and locus of control, a 2 × 4 analysis of variance (2 way), male and female, Group 1 (0-12), Group 2 (13-24), Group 3 (25-26) and Group 4 (37 months or more) was performed. It was found that the effects of sex and length of residence on the Korean attitudes and parental identification were not significant, but the effects of length of residence on the external locus of control were significant (F = 4.57, df − 3, p < .01). There was no significant sex by length of residence interaction on the external control. Figure 1 shows the effects of length of residence on the external scores on the I-E scale of the New Korean-Canadian group.

DISCUSSION

The results of this study suggest that New Korean-Canadian adolescents' perceived relationships with their parents are affected by immigration. They also suggest that the effects of immigration on self attitudes, perceived parental attitudes, parental identification and locus of control are different between male and female adolescents. The different effects of immigration on the male and female adolescents can be explained in terms of the expectancy-reinforcement discrepancy experienced in the new society.

In Korea, parents are more permissive with their sons and there is no strict interference with their behavior. In contrast, the daughters are closely supervised by their parents. This may mean that the same amount of assimilation between New Korean-Canadian male and female adolescents will have quite different effects on their relationship with their parents. Thus a small amount of behavioral change, as a result of assimilation, in the female immigrant adolescents may create a great amount of expectancy-reinforcement discrepancy between the parents and daughters. A similar amount of change may not create such frustration in the male adolescents' relations with their parents.

Figure 1
The I-E Scores By Length of Residence in Canada

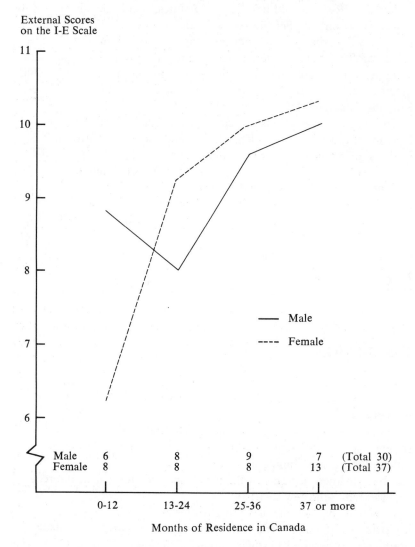

External Scores
on the I-E Scale

Male	6	8	9	7	(Total 30)
Female	8	8	8	13	(Total 37)

0-12   13-24   25-36   37 or more

Months of Residence in Canada

Second, New Korean-Canadian female adolescents, who have experienced more restrictions than their male adolescents in their own
country, may find the new culture to be more favourable towards their
needs for individual rights and freedom. Consequently, the female
adolescents may quickly come to prefer the values and attitudes
emphasized in the new culture. This reinforcement value change on

the part of New Korean-Canadian female adolescents may create more intensive value conflicts with their parents.

The results of the data analysis on the I-E scores of Korean, New Korean-Canadian and Canadian groups showed that Canadian adolescents had the highest external scores, New Korean-Canadian adolescents the lowest, and Korean adolescents had the intermediate scores. These findings did not support the hypothesis that immigrant adolescents would show the highest external scores. The findings of the present study also did not support the cross-cultural hypothesis generated by Tin-Yee Hsieh, Shybut and Lotsof (1969), that "an individual raised in a culture that values self-reliant individualism, pragmatic ingenuity, and personal output of energy" (p. 124) would be more internally oriented than individuals from a culture (such as the Chinese) that emphasizes a different set of values. When Canadian and Korean cultures were compared in this respect, Canadian adolescents were expected to show a lower externality than Korean adolescents. With regard to this cross-cultural hypothesis, the results of the present study suggest that the locus of control of the adolescents is determined by their individual expectations in a given situation rather than by the culture itself. In other words, one of the necessary factors in the determination of locus of control may well be the consistency in terms of expectancy of reinforcement which the individual experiences in his behavior within the society rather than by the culture. The results of the present study seem to suggest that the attitudes reflected on the Korean Attitude Scale are also valued to a certain degree in the Canadian culture. When it is considered that the Canadian culture has a Judeo-Christian tradition, the values stressed in the Korean culture such as educational achievement, respect for parents, sex-discrimination, sex-morality and so on, also seem to be emphasized in the Canadian society.

Since the two societies are traditionally male oriented and provide more freedom and support for men than for women, the current liberation movement in these two societies may not affect the male members of the society as much as the female members. In the Canadian society where the traditional roles of the female are more likely challenged than in Korea, the traditional attitudes of women are more likely changed. But at the same time, the females in the Canadian society, with less traditional attitudes, would experience much greater frustration in their social interaction.

This assumption seems to be supported by the results of the present study. Both New Korean-Canadian and Canadian female adolescents showed a significant negative correlation between the self Korean attitudes and the external locus of control. This relationship between the two variables was not found in any other group, Korean, New

Korean-Canadian, Canadian male, or Korean female adolescents. The cross-cultural hypothesis concerning the relationship between the ethnic membership and locus of control seems to need further verification.

The reason why New Korean-Canadian adolescents showed the lowest external scores on the I-E scale is not clear. It is assumed that the Korean immigrants are more internally oriented persons when compared with the average Koreans who remained in the original country. Not only are immigrants required to pass the selection criteria set by the Canadian immigration policy such as the educational qualification, vocational skills, a certain ability in English, personality, and general health conditions, immigrant families must make the decision to leave their positions, relatives and country to start their lives all over again in a strange country. It may be also added that, since the average length of residence is relatively short (the mean years of residence in Canada of the immigrant subjects was three), the initial aspiration of the immigrant families believing that they could determine their own destiny in a new country may have contributed to the immigrant adolescents showing the lowest external locus of control. The results of this study did not support the hypothesis generated by Wolfgang (1973) or the hypothesis established by the present authors that the immigrant students would have higher external scores on the I-E scale than the non-immigrant students. Nevertheless, the significant positive correlation found between the length of residence and external locus of control in the present study seems to suggest that the difference between the mean years of residence in Canada of the sample group in Wolfgang's study (in the study, the mean years of residence of the Italian group was nine) and the present study should be taken into account for this comparison. Thus the results of the present study are not necessarily in contradiction to Wolfgang's findings.

The present study shows that, in New Korean-Canadian male adolescents, those who had mothers with a high acculturation level (their ability in English) perceived their fathers' and mothers' attitudes to be less traditional. These adolescents, however, did not perceive a similar negative relationship between their fathers' acculturation and their parents' Korean attitudes. The results also show that their own Korean attitudes were negatively related to their mothers' not to their fathers', acculturation level. Danziger (1971) reported that the mothers with high acculturation level had less father-son value conflict in Italian immigrant families. The study did not indicate if the same relationship existed between father's acculturation level and the parent-child value conflict. The different effects of acculturation of the two parents on their sons found in the present study, may indicate that mothers with high acculturation levels have less Korean attitudes and they in turn influence a change in the attitudes of their sons and husband. As a consequence, the parent-child value conflict is reduced by mother's acculturation, not by father's. The results of the study indicate that the Korean female immigrant adolescents perceive a difference between their own attitudes and their parental attitudes, but their Korean attitudes are perceived as being not independent from their parental identification. The relationship shown by the New Korean-Canadian female group between the self attitude and the perception of parental attitudes, parental identification and locus of control were distinctively different from the rest of the groups. The postulation that the more assimilated the children become the less they would tend to identify with their parents and therefore would create a sense of powerlessness in the children is supported by the female immigrant adolescents.

BIBLIOGRAPHY

Blishen, B. R. "The Construction and Use of An Occupational Class Scale." *Canadian Journal of Economics and Political Science,* XXIV, 1958, 591-531.

Bowerman, C. E., and Bahr, S. J. "Conjugal Power and Adolescent Identification with Parents." *Sociometry,* 1973, 36, 366-377.

Danziger, K. *Socialization of Italian Immigrant Children Part I.* Toronto: Ethnic Research Program, Institute for Behavioral Research, York University, 1971.

Dawson, J. L. B., Law, H., Leung, A., & Whitney, R. E. "Scaling Chinese Traditional-Modern Attitudes and the GSR measurement of 'Important' versus 'unimportant' Chinese Concepts." *Journal of Cross-Cultural Psychology,* 1971, 2, 1-27.

Kohn, P. M. "The Authoritarianism-Scale: A Balanced F Scale with Left-Wing Reversals." *Sociometry,* 1972, 35, 176-189.

Lai, V. The New Chinese Immigrants in Toronto. In J. L. Elliot (ed.), *Immigrant Groups,* Prentice-Hall of Canada, 1971.

Parsons, O. A., and Schneider, J. M. "Locus of Control in University Students from Eastern and Western Societies." *Journal of Consulting and Clinical Psychology,* 1974, 42, 456-461.

Rotter, J. B. *Social Learning and Clinical Psychology,* Englewood Cliffs: Prentice-Hall, 1954.

Rotter, J. B. "Generalized Expectancies for Internal Versus External Control of Reinforcements." *Psychological Monographs,* 1966, 80, (Whole No. 609).

Rotter, J. B., Chance, J. E., & Phares, E. J. *Applications of a Social Learning Theory of Personality.* Holt, Rinehart & Winston, 1972.

Schaefer, E. S., and Bell, R. Q. "Development of a Parental Attitude Research Instrument", *Child Development* 1958, 29, 339-359.

Schneider, J. M., and Parsons, O. A. "Categories on the Locus of Control Scale and Cross-Cultural Comparisons in Denmark and the United States." *Journal of Cross-Cultural Psychology,* 1970, 1, 131-138.

Seeman, M. "On the Meaning of Alienation." *American Sociological Review,* 1959, 24, 783-791.

Taft, R. *From Stranger to Citizen.* Tavistock Publications, Australia, 1965.

Taft, R., and Johnston, R. "The Assimilation of Adolescent Polish Immigrants and Parent-Child Interaction." *Merril Palmer Quarterly,* 1967, 13, 111-120.

Tin-Yee Hsieh, Shybut, J., & Lotsof, E. J. "Internal versus External Control and Ethnic Membership: A Cross-Cultural Comparison." *Journal of Consulting and Clinical Psychology,* 1969, 33, 122-124.

Wolfgang, A. "Cross-Cultural Comparison of Locus of Control, Optimism Toward the Future, and Time Horizon Among Italian, Italo-Canadian, and New Canadian Youth." *Proceedings* 81st Annual Convention, APA, 1973.

15

The People of Pakistani Origin in Canada, Their First Twenty-Five Years[1]

Sadiq N. Awan
Ottawa Board of Education

Over the last twenty-five years there has been a rising tendency for Pakistanis to emigrate to Canada. Those who come tend to be young, married and well educated. The largest percentage settled in Ontario, with Quebec being the second most popular province, although the larger population centres have been popular areas for settlement, regardless of the province. Unlike other immigrant groups, Pakistani immigrants have resisted the pattern of organizing a clearly defined community for themselves within the larger community. Rather, they have spread themselves throughout the city areas, renting or owning private dwellings, and this has helped them to facilitate their assimilation into the Canadian life-style. Their command of the English language has also been a significant key to their successful integration.

Pakistani immigrants have come to Canada for numerous reasons: to search for better educational facilities for their children, to obtain better housing, and to better themselves economically. They have come because of war scares, the population explosion, the rising cost of living, the lack of assurance about their future, and the high poverty levels in their home country.

Most have come with the clear intention of taking up permanent residence in Canada. A significant proportion of the immigrants have taken out Canadian citizenship. Many of the immigrants have been successful in achieving a high standard of living, high salary scales and a high standard of education. As far as professional status is concerned, there have been no significant occupational changes for Pakistani immigrants in their transition from Pakistan to Canada. Executive class immigrants have tended, however, to suffer a sharp decline in status, a situation which many feel confident will be remedied after they have been here for a few years and have accumulated experience.

The main points of contention for the immigrants have been the lack of strong family ties in Canada, the feeling of strangeness regarding Canadian life-styles, and the lack of support for their own customs and religion. This latter factor is particularly important to immigrant parents who are concerned that their children receive training in these areas. A small number of immigrants have responded to these disadvantages by returning to Pakistan. For a large number of immigrants, however, the overall satisfaction with Canadian life has led them to seek solutions to these problems by establishing and supporting Islamic centres and by providing instruction in their own homes.

Some characteristics of Pakistani immigrants are as follows:

— they are mostly men;
— the majority of them are university graduates and hold degrees in physics, economics, engineering, medicine, law, journalism, mathematics, accounting and pure and applied sciences;
— many have come as single immigrants;
— subsequently some have married Canadian girls and some have gone back to marry girls chosen by their relatives or parents;
— almost all have settled in large Canadian cities;
— approximately two thirds have settled in Ontario and Quebec in that order;
— approximately 81.4% profess the Islamic faith, 17.6% are Christian and the remaining 1.0% have not stated their religion.

The Religious Education of Muslim Children

Pakistani-Canadian parents are making every effort within their power to keep with progress. The overall picture of the Islamic centres in Canada remains unsatisfactory according to a significant number of their members. Nevertheless, it is worthwhile to recognize the merits of their determined efforts in the cause of Islamic education for Muslim children in Canada. The greater influx of Pakistani immigrants to Canada has revealed the merits and deficiencies of the Islamic centres, and has demonstrated the need for reform within these institutions. Canadian society is so basically different from Pakistani Islamic society that the necessity for the Islamic centres to make fundamental changes suited to a new environment is an accepted fact by most Muslim immigrants. Islamic centres are expected to supply dynamic leadership in providing diversity in thought, and flexibility in attitudes, while maintaining the basic teaching of Islam.

Pakistani immigrants have a very positive attitude towards the Canadian cultural and educational lifestyle. They have come to Canada not only in reaction against certain elements in Pakistan, but also in anticipation of certain advantages to be offered here.[2] For the most part, they have found these anticipated advantages to be a reality. Their children are receiving adequate education which will prepare them for the task of providing for themselves. Many families have been able to buy their own homes, and some have established residence in the better districts of their chosen areas. The parents attempt to take full advantage of the cultural, social and educational opportunities available in Canada and encourage their children to do the same.

The sincerity of Pakistani-Canadians in establishing permanent homes in Canada is shown in their efforts to adapt themselves to the Canadian lifestyle. The tendency is, especially for the young people, to wear Canadian clothes, participate in Canadian sports, clubs, and other activities, and to accept the values of their Canadian peers. It is with respect to this latter point that Pakistani immigrant parents register some disillusionment and discontent with their new homeland. Most of these parents are of the Muslim faith, and it is their desire that their children maintain the moral values and customs of the Islamic faith, rather than to adopt the more relaxed Canadian values. Pakistani parents have taken a number of positive steps to achieve this goal. They have provided religious and moral teaching for their children in the home, and they have aided in the establishment and support of Islamic centres. The Islamic centres have had a slow development, and most parents have not been happy with their achievements. Their ineffectiveness has been due to numerous factors: lack of economic backing, lack of volunteer qualified teachers, lack of space, and lack of population density in any one area. As the number of immigrants increases, however, and as these immigrants become more secure and more established in the Canadian lifestyle, it is anticipated that a concentrated effort will be made to improve the quality of services offered by the Islamic centres. Furthermore, this effort will be supported by the educated and professional Pakistani parents who have a genuine concern for the economic, social, religious, moral and educational well-being of their children. Rather than complain about the drawbacks of Canadian life, they attempt to improve these drawbacks by exerting an extra amount of time, energy and money on their own part. Pakistani parents expect much of their children, but they also offer much in return in material and psychological support.

It is perhaps the closeness of the immediate family which has helped the Pakistani immigrants to adapt so well to Canadian life. When a problem arises, as in the question of dating and courting habits, the tendency has been for families to try to solve the problem within their own framework, rather than make it a cause of family rift.

The Pakistani immigrants have also been confronted by the usual problems faced by new immigrants: the problems of language, of adjusting to new cultural values, of finding employment, of having their qualifications recognized, of finding a place for themselves in the educational system, of having their rights protected by law, and of establishing a part of their own culture within the framework of a new country. Available evidence seems to indicate that because the Pakistani immigrants are willing to take advantage of the positive aspects of Canadian lifestyles, are willing to work towards goals which are lacking in this lifestyle, and are willing to make whatever contributions they can to the Canadian lifestyle, they have, therefore, succeeded in making Canada their new and permanent home.

NOTES

1. This paper covers the period 1947 to 1972. Prior to 1956 the data on Pakistani immigrants to Canada are included with that of India. The controversy vis-a-vis the Immigration Policy emerged subsequent to this paper.

2. *A History of People of Pakistani Origin in Canada* was published in 1976. The proceedings of the National Multicultural Symposium of Pakistanis in Canada held in 1976 is now being printed. These publications are available ($4.00 each) by writing to the Canada Pakistan Association of Ottawa-Hull, P.O. Box 558, Station B, Ottawa, Ontario, K1P 5P6.

16

The Vietnamese in Canada: Some Settlement Problems

Nguyen Quy Bong
International Development Research Centre

In April 1975 the Republic of (South) Vietnam fell to the Democratic Republic of Vietnam. Approximately 150,000 Vietnamese exiles suddenly landed in North America, some 144,000 in the U.S.A., and 6,000 in Canada.

Resettlement in a new land has brought a host of problems, especially for this group of refugees who hurriedly left their homeland under extremely difficult circumstances. Without any plan or preparation, they were totally disoriented. Moreover, unlike other refugees, such as the Hungarians or the Cubans, the Vietnamese had no established community here for support which made their settlement problems even more critical.

While there has been a number of studies about the Vietnamese *newcomers in the U.S.A.*[1], similar studies have not been made in Canada. This short paper will attempt to explain the Vietnamese way of coping with the culture shock and their daily "struggle for survival" in this new world. A brief outline of the Vietnamese socio-cultural background will be provided to facilitate our understanding of the adjustment situation.

To the people of the Western world, Vietnam may be a new country but to the Vietnamese people, Vietnam has an old culture rooted in a very long past. Indeed, Vietnamese history extends back almost three thousand years before Christ. From that period until 1975, the history of Vietnam may be divided into five eras: the early establishment of the Vietnamese nation until a hundred years B.C., the Chinese domination until the tenth century, the great national dynasties of one hundred years ago, the French domination to the end of the Second World War, and lastly the post-World War II period characterized by thirty years of war (1945-1975).

The history of Vietnam is that of a small nation which resisted assimilation by China for two thousand years, and which has thus far overcome colonialism. Unfortunately, its escape from foreign domination of one kind was often followed by the domination of a different kind. Nevertheless, the Vietnamese people's endurance has become proverbial and their propensity for survival throughout history is a documented fact. In the words of a French historian, the late Bernard Fall,[2] in 1960:

> Vietnam has often been invaded in her history, occupied by foreigners, subjugated even in the latters' customs and language. She was occupied by the Chinese for a thousand years, subjected to Chinese customs, writing, religion, and yet freed herself at the end of a thousand years.
>
> She was occupied by the French for eighty years; she learnt their language, romanized her writing, westernized her cities, but she remained Vietnamese.
>
> Today two other great powers, each of them dynamic in its own way, each believing in the superiority of its philosophy and techniques, are fighting each other once more for the Vietnamese mind. Let us bet that Vietnam will observe, learn, even imitate, and that she will remain Vietnamese in spite of all.

Situated at the crossroads of Asia, Vietnam served, in ancient days, as a meeting place for the two Asian cultures of India and China. By land and sea routes, they converged on this territory during the early centuries of the Christian era.

The main religion in Vietnam is a pluralistic Indo-Chinese combination of Buddhism, Taoism, Confucianism, and the worship of ancestors — the predominant element being *ancestor worship*. Vietnamese religion leads to strong family ties, veneration for older people, respect for teachers, and has a great gift for blending all faiths.

The "continuity of incense and fire" also meant the maintenance of ancestor worship originally aimed at the perpetuation of a great complex binding together the living and the dead of the same clan. It became the foundation of the Vietnamese family and provided strength and stability to the individual, as well as continuity to the family at large, composed of all those descending from the same male ancestor.

The cult of the ancestors holds an important place in Vietnamese family and social life. It was set up as a sort of religious dogma and, in a certain sense, as a national religion. It is in reality the continuance of pious duties toward one's parents after their death, the expression of veneration for those to whom one owes his life. Filial piety, in the politico-moral system of Confucius, is the base of all virtues, the foundation of family morals, and consequently of society and of the nation.

The cult of the dead is also a demonstration of the relation which exists between the world of the living and that of the dead. The traditional belief is that death does not mean the annihilation of man, but rather, that the dead may always participate in the life of their family and their descendants. One calls on them on all solemn occasions, such as births and marriages, as well as in family crises. Moreover, death is the return to Eternity and precedes a further reincarnation, the form of which depends upon the way the earthly sojourn is spent.

In short, it is a philosophical religion, a religion of memory and gratitude, which the Vietnamese have practiced for centuries. Interestingly enough, most Vietnamese find no difficulty in assimilating elements of each of these doctrines and paying their reverence to all. In the words of Virginia Thompson, "The Vietnamese work on the principle that if one religion is good, three are better."[3] So, in the same day a man may go to a Taoist temple and a Buddhist pagoda while not neglecting the various rites and practices ordained by Confucius. Only Christianity, a late arrival and the most rigid, has remained unaltered and apart and has established a fairly compact religious community.

A thousand years of Vietnamese history were enacted in the area stretching from the over-populated, dike-crossed plains of the Red River Delta, the ancient home of the nation in the north, to the generously abundant Mekong River Delta in the south. In their long "march to the south," wherever the Vietnamese settled, they brought with them two institutions — the *family* and the *village,* which formed the centre of Vietnamese life. For countless generations these two institutions remained unchanged, regardless of regional differences.

Of these two basic social institutions, only the family survives, although in many cases, adversely affected. As to the traditional village which went through thirty years of political changes and destructive war, first between Vietnam and France, then later between North and South Vietnam, little is left.

Handicapped by the loss of the village community, the Vietnamese hold tighter to the only institution left, their family, which remains the basic source of security and meaning to their existence. This was observed among the one million Northern Vietnamese who migrated to the South in 1954, when the country was partitioned at the end of the first Indochinese war. The 1975 exodus, at the end of the second Indochinese war, found a number of them again as refugees, yet this time with even more loss and uncertainty.

As mentioned earlier, some six thousand Vietnamese exiles have come to Canada since the fall of South Vietnam in April 1975.[4] They came via Hong Kong, Guam and different refugee camps in the continental U.S.A. None of them went directly from their country to Canada. Thus the difference between them and their many fellow-countrymen, who found themselves in the U.S., was that they chose Canada to go to and Canada in turn chose to welcome them. The mutually complementary desires benefitted both Canada and the selected Vietnamese. The criteria used by the Canadian immigration officers to grant the refugees interviews and entry visas were: (1) in addition to good health, the applicants had to have some relatives in Canada, or (2) they had to possess some skills in demand in Canada. They were offered a loan for their cost of transportation rather than the free trip offered to those bound for the U.S. In turn they became landed immigrants rather than refugees on parole, as their compatriots in the U.S. were.

The reasoning by which the Vietnamese chose Canada was deliberate and interesting, considering the confusing context of mid-1975 and the fresh memories of the aftermath of the Vietnam war. At that time, a feeling of being deserted ran high among every South Vietnamese. In the refugee camps, many — especially the intellectuals — cautiously weighed the pros and cons of venturing to Canada. They were aware of the lengthy and severe winters, the lack of Vietnamese communities, the absence of acquaintances and professional connections, and the non-existence of large-scale federal assistance to the Indochinese refugee program. They, however, would be admitted as landed immigrants who could obtain Canadian citizenship after three years instead of the five years required previously. This issue was of utmost importance, considering their "statelessness." Politically, Canada was not involved in the Vietnam war, so she was not an enemy of the regime now in power in Vietnam. For the Vietnamese exiles that meant there would be total rupture with their homeland and their past. For those whose immediate families were left behind in Vietnam, communications were soon restored, letters and even money could be sent home, for there was no Canadian trade embargo imposed on Vietnam. The most important factor was Canada's policy of family reunification and her 1973 success in dealing with China on this humanitarian issue.

Out of six thousand Vietnamese newcomers, four thousand settled in Montreal, Quebec. Belanger, Edouard Montpetit and Barclay streets, the area around the University of Montreal, were soon known as "the Vietnamese village". The Vietnamese were fairly well accepted in Quebec, which preferred Francophone immigrants, however, not all Vietnamese in Montreal were French-speaking. Everywhere in North America there were many Vietnamese without either French or English. In addition to the French language, Quebec had deep cultural similarities with the Vietnamese: its strong family ties, its relatively slower pace of life, and interestingly, its minority feelings. The Vietnamese community in Montreal established its own Buddhist association, its Vietnamese shops and restaurants.

Other Vietnamese immigrants scattered throughout Canada. About five hundred chose to settle in Toronto, another four hundred in Ottawa. Some smaller groups were found in Sherbrooke, Trois-Rivières, Moncton, Vancouver, Edmonton, and Calgary. There were more young males than females among the Vietnamese in Canada. Consequently, some Vietnamese young men in the Prairies married Fillipinos while others in Eastern Canada travelled as far as Maryland and Virginia to look for Vietnamese brides. Seldom were there inter-marriages between newly-arrived Vietnamese and Canadians, unlike the cases of approximately one thousand Vietnamese who studied in Canada well before the 1975 political changes in Vietnam. Most of them were in Montreal and Quebec City, with a few in Ottawa, Toronto, and London. Consequently, their parents and families were allowed by the Canadian authorities to enter Canada in 1975. Only a few of those relatives, however, were successful in getting out of Vietnam when the Southern regime collapsed.

Since the 1975 Vietnamese exodus to "the free world", some Vietnamese have prospered, but the majority in Canada and in the U.S. still face enormous problems. These problems may be classified broadly into two areas: employment and cultural adjustment.

As a group, the Vietnamese seem to be doing well economically, given the wrenching dislocations they have survived. Most are working and self-supporting. For many of them, their living standards in the material sense are better now than before. Their employers may have trouble communicating with them, but praise them for their energy and skills.

It is regrettable that no survey concerning employment for the Vietnamese in Canada has been carried out; yet the ones conducted in the U.S. may give some insight into the job problem, given the similarity of the economic situation of the two North American societies:

> There was a marked increase in the employment rates over a period of one year, from 62.7% at the time of Survey I (October 1975) to 78.4% at Survey II (January 1976) and to 87.5% at Survey III (September 1976).
>
> For all three surveys, language proficiency tended to be associated with chances for employment.
>
> People in Survey III, both males and females, in general seemed to be somewhat lower in educational attainment compared to those in Survey I and Survey II. However, they appeared to be doing better in terms of employment.
>
> The majority of employed persons (79.7%) were working 40 hours or more per week. With regard to job satisfaction, 45% said they were very satisfied, 42.0% somewhat satisfied, and 12.0% dissatisfied. Females in general were more satisfied with their job situation than males. The increase in employment was also greater among females than among males.[5]
>
> Of those working full time, 23.6% were making less than $500 a month, 68.2% were making between $500 and $995, and 8.2% were making $1,000 or more.
>
> Two thirds of the heads of households surveyed had held white-collar jobs in Vietnam. However, of those employed in this country, only 33.0% held white collar jobs with the remainder doing blue-collar work. Moreover, of the 33.0% white-collar jobs, only 11.2% were in professional and managerial positions, while the rest were in clerical and sales positions.[6]

In general, as far as employment for Vietnamese immigrants is concerned, three primary problem areas may be cited: (1) the language barrier; (2) the lack of job skills applicable in the current labour market; and (3) the tightness of the job market as a whole. As a consequence, the majority of Vietnamese are doing manual work, typically factory work.

As mentioned earlier, it is as true in the U.S. as in Canada that professional people — especially the ones in the humanities — are having difficulties in finding proper employment. Some lawyers and teachers become house-painters, bakers, security guards, hospital aides, parking lot attendants, or restaurant and hotel workers. However the professionals in the engineering fields found good fortunes in Canada, particularly the ones who ventured to Alberta. Among the eighty Vietnamese physicians, four have already practiced medicine, sixty have been admitted as interns — all in Quebec. Only the remaining group of sixteen are preparing themselves for both the American ECFMG and Quebec qualifying examinations.

Generally speaking, the Vietnamese immigrants are coping satisfactorily with their economic survival in Canada. They might not be satisfied with, nor secure in, their present employment; yet no one is starving. On the contrary they have already begun to send their meager savings home to help their stranded families. The picture is not as somber as it might have appeared during the first year, and so far there has been no doomsday for the Vietnamese newcomers as some propaganda predicted.

While the employment problem may eventually be solved, the cultural adjustment will remain far from complete. By nature the Vietnamese are strongly attached and identified with their families and their homeland. Under normal circumstances very few would choose to migrate to other countries. Despite decades of war, the brain drain problem for Vietnam was no more serious than that of other peaceful Third World countries.

To the people stranded in former South Vietnam, this tiny group of 150,000 escapees may be considered the most fortunate, the "first prize lottery winners," as they are called. Since very few complete families could escape, those who did became a sign of hope, a resource to their families left behind.

To be fair, one should recognize that the agony is immense for both. On this side of the Pacific, few Vietnamese — except the children — are being assimilated into the North American mainstream. The new habits and customs challenge Vietnamese traditions in painful ways, beginning at the basis of Vietnamese life, the family. The Vietnamese took it for granted that the elderly would be venerated, that youth would know its place, and that the entire extended family would live (and multiply) under one roof. All that is different here. The old people have the most confused position now. They have become more of a burden, relegated to being baby-sitters, completely isolated during the long winter, and without the comfort of their families or their contemporaries. Their wisdom is no longer applicable, their English is often non-existent, and their ability to adapt is negligible.

As a result of changing attitudes toward the elderly, ancestor worship is becoming outdated. "You cannot send your father to an old-age home and then worship him after he dies," observed an elderly Vietnamese.

Children, being the quickest to learn new languages and new ways of life, sometimes become the crucial members of the family: their elders often rely on them as guides and interpreters. In Vietnam, parents liked to show off their children, then dismiss them. Here the dismissing is often impossible. The children's ability to move into the new life is simultaneously a source of pride and concern — pride at their accomplishments (some Vietnamese children are doing excellent work in Montreal schools), and concern that they will lose their ties with Vietnam. And inevitably they will, in this huge kaleidoscope of peoples. At first the parents worried about their new schooling; now they worry about their children's inability to use Vietnamese correctly. They also worry that their children will pass beyond parental control and leave home in their teens. In fact, some young Vietnamese adults have discovered that the extended family under one roof is not necessarily the ideal living arrangement. They have discovered that the privacy and independence of having their own apartment, as soon as they can afford it, can be more enjoyable. This is another source of alarm for their elders.[7]

In a paper presented at the recent AAS (Association for Asian Studies) meeting in New York, Walter Slote, a psychoanalyst at Columbia University, who has spent years studying the Vietnamese, observed:[8]

> The Vietnamese here fear most that the children will lose their sense of Vietnamese-ness, their sense of personal and national identity and that they will be lost to the family. "In 5 years, 10 years, will our children be the same? Will they still speak the language? How shall we deal with them? We have a sense of history (referring to both the generational sequence — ancestor worship and filial piety, and the nation's history). How can we pass this along? Can we endow our children with our sense of history or will they have a new one that comes from the schools and from life here and that is very different from ours." A very touching statement made by a 56 year old, well educated man who brings his 14-year-old up in the traditional, authoritarian way.

"What is most important now is the children." That is the hope and comfort for Vietnamese parents toiling in their exile. Canada is certainly a land for the young who will embark on a new future. To the Vietnamese adults, the past might be dearest and golden, but it is so only for those who cling to it, have to deal with it, and who continue to be tortured by not being able to replicate it. It is certainly not so for the children who come here, regardless where they come from.

In conclusion, one may recognize that migration has never been easy. Most Canadians are in a sense migrants. Looking back into their own pasts, not further than perhaps one or two generations, they may discover the sacrifice entailed in establishing a new life in an alien environment. In that way the Vietnamese immigrants are no different from their predecessors. Their situation might be more painful since their departure was totally unprepared and since they had no established community here to join. Moreover, by not being Caucasian, they were "different" from the white majority in this country. Since 1975 they have been fighting five difficult problems: unemployment, weather, loneliness, the language barrier, and adjustment to a new culture.[9] It may take them a generation or even more before they are fully assimilated into this new life. Fortunately, the warmth and generosity that have characterized the Canadian hospitality and welcome serve as reaffirmation of the ideals of Canadian society. Certainly, there is awareness of the contributions former immigrants have made to the character and enrichment of Canadian civilization. Once again Canada has been enriched by a new culture, which will soon be one of her many sub-groups.

The interchange between the Vietnamese immigrants and other Canadians has just begun. There is every reason to hope and expect that as it continues, it will be educational and rewarding to all.

NOTES

1. The President's Advisory Committee on Refugees. Background Papers. Interagency Task Force. May 19, 1975. Washington, D.C.: Department of State.

    Reports to the Congress. Interagency Task Force on Indochinese Refugees. Washington, D.C.: Department of State:
    June 15, 1975
    September 15, 1975
    December 15, 1975

    Reports to the Congress HEW Refugee Task Force. Washington, D.C.: Department of Health, Education, and Welfare:
    March 15, 1976
    June 15, 1976
    September 20, 1976
    December 20, 1976
    March 21, 1977

    Vietnam Resettlement Operational Feedback. Prepared for the HEW Refugee Task Force, by Opportunity Systems, Inc. Washington, D.C.:
    First Wave Report — October 8, 1975
    Second Wave Report — January 1976
    Third Wave Report — September 1976

2. Free translation by the writer from: Bernard B. Fall. *Le Viet Minh: La Republique Democratique du Vietnam*. 1945-1960. Paris: Librairie Armand-Colin, 1960, p. 340.

3. Virginia Thompson. *French Indo-China*, London: George Allen and Unwin Ltd., 1937, p. 54.

4. The Federal Department of Immigration and Manpower estimated a total of 6,600 exiles as of April 1977.

256   *Visible Minorities and Multiculturalism*

5. Vietnam Resettlement Operational Feedback, Third Wave Report, September 1976. Washington, D.C.: HEW Refugee Task Force, pp. 1-3.

6. *Hong Kong Standard,* February 26, 1977, p. 8.

7. "On Parole," *The Washington Post,* May 1, 1977, pp. A-1 10, May 2, 1977, pp. A-1 6, 7.

8. Walter H. Slote, "Adaptation of Recent Vietnamese Immigrants to the American Experience: A Psycho-Cultural Approach", New York: 1977 AAS Annual Meeting, March 1977, pp. 6-7.

9. Vuong G. Thuy *Getting to Know the Vietnamese and their Culture,* New York: Frederick Ungar Publ. Co., 1976, p. 87.

17

Coping With Values in Conflict: Japanese Women in Canada

Yuko Shibata
Department of Anthropology and Sociology
University of British Columbia, Vancouver, B.C.

INTRODUCTION

This is a study of Japanese Canadians, particularly of women and their experiences in Vancouver, B.C., Canada, including aspects of my experience as well. By sharing the experiences of Japanese women and discussing their meanings with them, as persons whose identities are tied to Japanese culture, I plan to provide some understanding of what it means to be Japanese Canadian in Canada. Although Japanese Canadians have been in Canada for over one hundred years, their history is not well documented.

This paper is ethnographic and descriptive in nature, based on my field work during September 1975 to August 1976. It is neither statistically oriented, nor community survey research, nor did I study the political aspects of "Japanese community" organization. Rather, I focused on individual experiences — a research approach which deals with qualitative data. I am interested in the quality of individual experiences of women as they cope with their new environment, various situations, and their daily lives.

Throughout my study I have used the individual as the principle point of reference. I did not assume that Japanese or Canadian cultures were uniform; rather I made an assessment in the light of the individual's status, roles, goals, perceptual habits, and her particular position and situation in relation to the cultural environments she experiences. I did not take it for granted that she behaved like, or identified herself as a "typical Japanese." In fact, the determination of whether or not she did so became one of the most important problems of my research. It enabled me to identify, with some precision, which dimensions of Japanese and Canadian culture the individual perceived, learned, rejected, or reacted against. My objective was not to describe and analyze cultures, but rather to study the experiences of the individual in varying social and cultural reality.

My interest in the individual as a point of reference is given specific form with a method of biographical "life history" analysis. It consists of a study of the personal and unique experience of the individual in the context of actual historical events and cultural patterns, and selections of those experiences that have been of critical importance in the acculturation process. The study consisted of interviews, participant observation and a life history collection over a period of one year in Vancouver, B.C. to examine the experiences of sixty women. I do not regard these cases as a "sample" in the statistical sense. I attempted to study the widest variety of Japanese women I could find in Vancouver.

SAMPLING PROBLEMS

I confined my sample to Japanese-born women residing in the city of Vancouver who were either naturalized Canadian citizens, landed immigrants, or holders of long-term visitor's visas. The selection of the sample population was quite difficult. There was a lack of information in the existing material and many problems arose; the 1971 Census did not have a break-down of the Japanese ethnic group — it included Canadian-born Japanese, and Japanese women who married a non-Japanese were not included in the data since the membership in ethnic groups was determined patrilineally for census purposes.

I spent three months establishing rapport with the Japanese people in Vancouver through various agencies and activities. These included participant observation in social events sponsored by the Japanese Canadian Citizens Association,[1] attending religious services at ethnic churches (United Church, Buddhist Church and others) and bazaars held by social groups, dining and having tea and conversing over lunch with people in general, working as a volunteer at Language Aid,[2] helping pre-war and post-war immigrants, stopping by Tonarigumi[3] (Drop in Center for Japanese Senior Citizens), conducting Japanese Women's Orientation seminars in Vancouver,[4] and working for the Japanese Centennial Project[5] to mount a photographic exhibition of Japanese Canadian history. All these activities allowed me to grasp an invisible structure of the "Japanese community" in Vancouver.

The information I had gathered through secondary sources prior to my field work[6] became relevant and I began to have a deeper understanding of it, as well as adding to it from my own observations. Prior to the fieldwork, I had sought answers to the following questions: Is there a "Japanese community?" Who is involved? How does it operate, by whom? How do the community activities affect the life of Japanese women? These questions were gradually answered.

METHODOLOGY

After three months of work with Japanese community members in Vancouver through participant observation, I began to interview formally. The questions sought to determine the characteristics of the sample population, their social activities and contact with Canadian culture. Japanese was used exclusively through the research.

The interviews were conducted among sixty Japanese women of various backgrounds, both pre-war and post-war immigrants. The questions covered basic information, such as the background information of informants, occupational history in Japan and in Canada, financial condition, purpose of migration, marital status, practice of Japanese customs, usage of English, social network with Japanese and non-Japanese, and family relationships and variations due to cultural change. There were sixty-one questions in closed answer form. The interview also consisted of open ended questions concerning the respondent's impression of Canada, people, custom, social position of women, social difficulties encountered based on one's cross-cultural situations, and language problems which limited self-expression. Most of them expressed frustration caused by the language barrier.

My informants questioned me as much as I questioned them. They were interested in my background, recent status, and the future, question of marriage, parents, career, whether I intend to stay in Canada, etc. Through their questions, I was able to understand their reality and the focus of their interests. They were interested in my project and were very cooperative. Most of them gave me names of friends to contact, although I could not contact all of them because of time limitations.

I had prior contact with all the people I interviewed, either through the activities I had participated in or through friends, thus the interview situation was not the initial encounter. No tape recorder was used. Informants were told that the information provided would be confidential.

CATEGORIES OF THE SAMPLE POPULATION:

I shall provide a brief historical overview of the Japanese in Canada to give a context to my data. At the same time, it can be viewed in a larger historical sense as well.

The history of the Japanese in British Columbia can be divided into six stages, based on the historical events and major policy changes in immigration law. These are:

1) 1877 - 1900: — background to the Japanese community in B.C.
   — development of the fishing, lumbering, mining, and farming industries; Japanese involvement in the primary industries of B.C.
   — immigrants were mostly male and very few women

2) 1901 - 1914: — beginning of the community, arrival of women, e.g. "picture brides"
   — Gentlemen's Agreement in 1907 limited the flow of Japanese immigrants.

3) 1915 - 1935: — development of the Japanese community, birth of second generation (*nisei*), and increasing discrimination against the Japanese.

4) 1936 - 1948: — period of exclusion; mass evacuation, internment years . . . repatriation/deportation . . .
   — total disruption and disintegration of the Japanese community and of individual families

5) 1949 - 1965: — franchise granted in 1949
   — re-establishment of the Japanese community, its growth and conflicts
   — change in immigration law, return of Japanese Canadians to the coastal area of B.C.

6) 1967 - 1977: — expansion and diversification
   — immigration law change allowed many "tech-

nical immigrants" (Gijutsu Imin), and independent immigrants to come to Canada
— increase in foreign trade with Japan allowed
more non-immigrant status, long-term visitors,
and business visa people into Canada
— Centennial Celebration of the Japanese Canadians

The people I interviewed fell into two major categories: a) pre-war
immigrant women and b) post-war immigrant women and the long-
term visitors. World War II was a traumatic experience for the Japanese
in Canada as well as for the Japanese in Japan, so I chose it as a basis
for categorization. The second group was divided into four sub-groups
based on their personal contact with Canadian and Japanese cultural
associations. The pre-war group came to Canada during the 1920s-
1930s and the post-war group came to Canada during the 1950s to
early 1970s.

PORTRAIT OF PRE-WAR IMMIGRANT WOMEN (ISSEI WOMEN)

Most of the women who immigrated prior to World War II came
to Canada in the 1920s or 1930s, at the developmental stage of the
Japanese community in B.C. There were disproportionately few women
in Canada at that time. Women often told me with joy how the men
fought for women. Some of the women came as "picture brides," some
through Prefectural Association matchmakers, and some with their
mothers and siblings to join their father.

Many books on Japanese-Canadian history indicate the importance
of women in the community. Their presence gave stability to the
Japanese-Canadian community.

> . . . the first four or five years I went logging, there were only men in
> the camp. Without women around men got wild. Camps were always
> full of fights — fights and gambling. Men played cards, especially
> Black Jack . . . but when women started to arrive, their life got more
> domesticated . . .
>
> (Knight and Koizumi, 1977:35)

Surprising enough, a great number of my sample population had
university education. Perhaps such women feel most acutely the
conflict between their expected societal role and their own ambitions,
and would be most likely to seek innovative roles. Most (75%) of my

sample population went to *Jogakko* (university for women) at a time when not many women had a university education in Japan. In general, their education exceeded that of their husbands. But they all commented:

> Education did not help much as we thought it would. Physical strength was the most essential then. I worked hard on the farm so nobody would talk about how useless I was.

They all worked; some as cooks at the logging camps and mining camps, some in canneries or as houseworkers, or small corner store keepers. Their social environment forced them to work. They simply could not stay at home as housewives. Their labour was also necessary to maintain their life in Canada. Compared to Japanese women in Japan, they were more open and liberated due to their socio-economic involvement. They did not have mother-in-laws to work under, as is traditional in Japan.

They all have a half-century of Canadian history behind them. They are "pioneer women" who have suffered hardship and discrimination in Canada. And their effort and contribution to the society is not well acknowledged. They often told me that:

> You young people won't believe us, but life upon arrival in America (they all thought they were coming to America, not to Canada) was continuous suffering. For a couple of years, I cried, and wanted to return to Japan. The living in Japan was much better than here. We did not have gas, electricity. You young people are lucky!

Their experience was similar to that of immigrants described by Ito (1973: 256):

> I also came to Canada as a bride when "picture marriages" were common. In Victoria, I asked the owner of the Japanese hotel to send a telegram to my husband. I waited everyday, but he didn't arrive. I felt so helpless I wanted to cry. A week later, he finally appeared. It was in the middle of November and pouring rain. At the Port Hammond train station, his brother-in-law came with a wagon to meet us. Bouncing up and down, we travelled a brush road. At the end of it, I noticed what to me were strange shacks. They looked like the houses of beggars. So even in Canada, I thought, there must be beggars. Then our wagon stopped before the smallest shack of all, and I was told, "this is your house." Was this the land of promise I had anticipated in Japan? Life seems only to consist of backbreaking work that reaps no return.

Many of the immigrants came with the "Dream of Riches." They did not intend to stay. America, they thought, was the land of gold and money, according to the descriptions of the returning Japanese immigrants and the promises of their future husbands. But in reality, they confronted the adverse conditions of the Japanese who were working for primary industries as labourers with a language handicap, lower wages, and discrimination. They were in the lower strata of Canadian society. Instead of mixing in with western culture, they were in a tightly knit Japanese community. There was little contact with other members of Canadian society. Many mentioned that there was no need for English, since everything could be conducted in Japanese. The prewar Japanese community was self-contained and independent from the Canadian main stream. (I can not say whether this was due to the antagonistic attitude of Canadian society toward the Japanese in B.C., or because of other factors.)

The immigrant's attachment to material wealth, such as homes, boats, and cars was quite strong. Money preoccupied their pre-war life. Many women mentioned that the outbreak of the war and subsequent relocation were good for the Japanese community because it brought them back to the basic needs of life.

> We were working too hard to overcome our material discomfort, to reach middle-class Canadian living. We were too conscious of money making. We were too busy trying to make money and were alienating ourselves from our children.

Most of the respondents did not mention the negative aspects of the internment years — some were quite bitter about the war but all of them accepted it as their fate and viewed their experiences positively. The internment experiences differed from one to the other. Some signed the repatriation paper and were deported, some went to the self-support camps, some went to the relocation camps in the B.C. interior. Without going into detail at this stage, it is sufficient to state that the internment or deportation and loss of homes, boats, and roots in the community destroyed Japanese Canadian life to such an extent that it has never reached the same level of integration as the community was prior to 1941.

Today there are many widows living on old-age pension ($286.). Those who own homes live in the East side of Vancouver. Widows seem to concentrate around the old section of Japantown (Vancouver's oldest area, adjacent to Chinatown and Gastown, along the 300 block Powell Street), simply because they cannot cope outside of the Japanese community without speaking English. As Richmond indicates, "Retirement and old age can be more traumatic for an immigrant particularly if he or she lacks the support of a family in Canada" (1970:20). These people tend to gather and live in their past. They do have families, but they prefer living away from their sons and daughters. Their life seems very isolated. Their lack of English allows very little contact with their children and grandchildren. They feel much closer and more comfortable with Japanese-speaking friends. They prefer to live alone, prefer their own food and own lifestyle, use of Japanese, and to be with other Japanese who shared past experiences. They do not want to be dependent on their children or relatives but they do not mind depending on other Japanese in the community. From my viewpoint, their life was not so lonesome, although this opinion was based on my first encounter with them. I was simply imposing my own value judgment.

After their husbands' deaths, some of the women sold their property and returned to Japan to be with their sisters, brothers, and other relatives. However, in most of the cases, they came back to Canada within one or two years. Some of their reasons for returning seem obvious from the following statement which was made by someone who returned to Canada:

> You know in Canada, you don't have to worry about making a living when you are old. The government supports you when you become 65 years of age. There is good medicare. You don't have to be rich to receive this privilege. You don't have to worry much. By the way, what are you going to do after your degree? Stay in Canada? It is a good place. I strongly recommend it. *But* mind you, I am still Japanese and I am fond of Japan. Canada is heaven for a person living alone.

But there are other reasons besides the financial one. Another woman commented:

> Financial reasons are not important for me. But whenever I return to Japan I feel the stiff, or strong social norm or pattern I had forgotten a long time ago. I am not so formal now. It seems to me that I am not a "real Japanese." People in Japan are *too* formal and *too* confined. Here in Canada, I can say 'hello' and the business will be over, but in Japan you bow and bow, comment about the weather that you don't really care about. I don't think I can go back to that formality any more. Also, my relatives overprotect me and I cannot move around by myself. I have even forgotten how to speak polite Japanese. When I came here, people thought I was too snobbish because I talked good Japanese. I had to learn a rough (or crude) immigrant language, but now, I am so used to it I feel uncomfortable being with polite Japanese.

Many of the pre-war women practise religion and attend church services every week. Sixty per cent are Buddhists and forty per cent Christians. Many of them became Christians during the internment years, when "Christians were helpful to us." There was, however, no comment on the internment years as a political issue. They mentioned more experiencial kinds of things when referring to their camp years. One woman mentioned that the relocation levelled the economic differences and destroyed the hierarchy of the pre-war Japanese community. Rouchek's article (1966) also confirms this change.

The social network of the pre-war women is based on the churches and recently established social services around the Japantown area. Direct contact with Canadian culture is almost nil. Some have contact through their children, but even these informants express their preference for the other Japanese generation so that they can chat. At the same time they comment that the Japanese in this community are too nosey. They "talk about other people too much."

Except for a few, most women have very limited knowledge of English and are confined to daily conversation of saying "hi," "hello" and a couple of other words. Many of them told me that it was only after the war that the knowledge of English became important to them.

> I am going to *That World* (Anoyo) soon, so there is no need to learn English now. Well, if one can speak English, there is nothing to worry about in this country. You are lucky!

The pre-war women interviewed had retained their basic Japanese customs such as eating Japanese food, taking Japanese folk medicine, practising gift exchanges, taking their shoes off, etc. One common practise I noticed during my encounter with *issei* women was that all, except for one, served me a Lipton tea bag with evaporated milk and cookies — quite different from that of post-war immigrant people. I am not sure where this custom developed, perhaps from doing housework in English speaking homes . . . or perhaps black tea is considered more modern than the green tea?

Most of the house interiors of my respondents were very traditional Japanese containing a big altar to which they offered fresh food everyday. There were also frames with a picture of Emperor Meiji hanging on the wall — a custom no longer common in Japan.

The pre-war women identify themselves as Japanese, yet whenever they visit Japan, they realize some differences between them and the Japanese in Canada. They complain about the closed network of the Japanese community in Vancouver, of its conformity, tendency to gossip and of the fact that one cannot be unique in it, as they put it, "like Japan." Still, they are attracted to the Japanese community because of its convenience and their dependency upon the older generation Japanese. This latter condition is due to the segregation between the *issei* and *nisei* and *sansei* which is caused by the lack of communication stemming from a language barrier.

PORTRAIT OF POST-WAR IMMIGRANT WOMEN

Because of the heterogenous nature of post-war immigrant women, it is difficult to describe this group as a collectivity. I shall divide them into four sub-groups based on their marital status and social network.

a) Spouses of returning repatriated Japanese Canadians (*nisei*)

These women came to Canada during the 1950s and early 1960s. After World War II, there were a few minor immigration law changes which allowed the Canadian-born Japanese who were deported during the war to return to their home country. The Canadian government granted them citizenship and allowed the entry of their Japanese spouses. Most of the women were high school graduates who had several years of office work experience prior to their marriage. They were familiar with both the pre-war and post-war years in Japan, the transitional stage of Japan from an old to a modern constitution which provided equal rights to women and which also granted a co-educational system of education. They came from the "recovering stages" of Japan. Their marriages were generally "matched marriages" but were slightly different from the pre-war matched marriages. The women were able to speak to their future spouses and to date them before their marriage. Compared to the mating age at that time, their mating age was older than the average. The marriages were based on the idea of coming to Canada. Quite often the marriages were opposed by their parents and relatives.

In contrast to the pre-war women, the post-war immigrant women do not practise religion as much as the *issei* women. They are pre-occupied with their children's education and the future. Most of them are mothers of two to three teenagers and are beginning to consider returning to the job market. Housework and cannery work are common jobs among them. One woman mentioned that somehow one is forced to get into those jobs because everybody is doing it. Among Japanese Canadian housewives, if one does not work, one is labelled lazy.

The main concerns of post-war Japanese immigrant women are: 1) child rearing; 2) language gaps; 3) value differences concerning discipline; and 4) reversed mother-child relationships which affect a loss of self-image. The researcher often encountered situations in which the child teased or talked back to his/her mother in English. The mother would not say anything. (The researcher felt like telling the child to respect his/her mother.) Such circumstances can lead to a negative self-image.

Immigrant women do not have much contact with Canadian culture or society until their oldest child goes to school. Their social network is often based on other *nisei* groups. Most of the mothers mentioned that their initial encounter with the "outside world," as they put it, occurred when the children started to have trouble at school because of the language barrier and problems coping with Canadian culture. Mothers mentioned that they felt helpless to assist their children, since they could not cope with the English speaking world themselves. Thus, their helplessness in such situations could be one contributing factor for the lack of respect evidenced above. The parents' need for English knowledge was acute. Their views of Canada, her people and culture began to form only through their experiences with the school system.

The social network of Japanese immigrant women is closely tied with their relatives (in-laws). One woman mentioned that:

> We spend too much money for gift exchanges among our relatives and Japanese friends in Japan. But at the same time we also follow the Canadian customs. This dual system is not practical but we have to continue it for the sake of *issei* people. I hope that in my daughter's generation they won't have to do it.

The respondents all identified themselves as "Japanese," and encouraged their children to learn Japanese. Most of their children go to the Japanese Language School, an institution which had significant importance in the pre-war Japanese community. During the Montreal Olympics, the question of identification, as Japanese or Canadian, was discussed within the family. Many children asked why their mothers supported Japanese athletes while the children supported Canadians. Many mothers took this issue seriously, and began to question their identity.

b) Women who came as "Technical Immigrants"

Women who came to Canada as technical immigrants in the 1960s can be divided into two groups based on their marital status. Some came as single independent immigrants and married other Japanese immigrants, while others remained single. Some came with their husbands as dependents. Most of them came from large cities such as Tokyo or Osaka, or had moved to the large cities prior to their arrival in Canada. Their residential pattern is in flux; most of them have been moving around for the past few years.

1) *Married Women*:

Most of them are mothers of one or two pre-school children. Two-thirds of the married "immigrant" group own property. These women universally stated their desire to stay in Canada. The rest of the sample population is still debating whether to stay in Canada or not.

Some of their worries and problems are similar to the group I mentioned earlier. The problems are: child rearing, language gaps, value differences, two sets of values and how to discipline their children, fear of a reversed mother-child relationship, and loss of self-image. Most of them are in a state of confusion; they cannot identify themselves, as either Japanese or non-Japanese. Mothers who have a very clear identity do not have many problems with their children's discipline, however, mothers who are not sure about their identity have more problems.

The social contact of married Japanese women are based on the Japanese networks. They all have the desire to become better acquainted with Canadians and Canadian culture, but they feel insecure with their English. Some women who had given birth to a child in Canadian hospitals (it is common for women to return to Japan and have a baby) felt more self-confident and able to cope with life in Canada.

> You know, anybody in that situation is forced to utilize one's knowledge and experiences to communicate with Canadian people. I used to be self-conscious about speaking English but after the birth of my first child I learned that I can converse with people, yes, I can get through what I want to say. They seem to understand what I am trying to communicate. Probably I am used to Canadian culture. And I am getting independent.

Most of the mothers stay at home. They consciously use Japanese at home, but realize that the influence of outside contact is much stronger on their children. These mothers all feel the loss of the Japanese language among them; some have accepted it as being unavoidable. Nevertheless, they would prefer their children to learn Japanese as a second language, rather than French or any other language. Japanese custom, food, and medicine are maintained at home. Sixty percent of the married immigrant women have a university education and their average age is thirty-eight.

ii) *Single Women*:

Women of this group came to Canada in the late 1960s to early 1970s, and were attracted by the idea of an independent immigration policy. They all came from big cities like Tokyo and Osaka, and sixty percent of the sample population had lived abroad prior to their immigration to Canada. Because of their language limitation, more than half of them work for the Japanese community in Vancouver. Most of them (90%) have a university education, however many stated that the language barrier affected their life in Canada more than they had expected and thus found themselves clinging to other Japanese. They realized that they were more "Japanese" than they thought they were and began to re-evaluate "Japanese" culture and people. At the same time they started to re-examine "Canadian" culture. They are still debating whether to live and stay in Canada as their home country or to return to Japan later.

For the single immigrant women, their social contact with Canadian culture is the highest. They are less "sheltered" from the main stream of Canadian culture. Since they must be economically independent, they may have to go through the agony of job hunting in competition with other immigrants and Canadian citizens. Their social network with Japanese and non-Japanese is half and half. They tended to be the most critical toward Japanese men in Canada and Canadian women. The single immigrant women were all post-war educated individuals from modern industrialized Japan, thus, their Japanese customs are similar to those manifested in contemporary Japan. More than half of them are living with companions. Some practice Christianity, but none go to the Buddhist Church. It is difficult to locate their residential pattern. Residential mobility is quite high among them.

The comments by the single post-war immigrant women concerning "Canadian" women in general were: 1) self-assertive and independent (positive aspect), 2) self-centered, no sense of sacrifice, very individualistic (negative aspect). Their comments on Japanese women in general were: 1) too dependent, no individuality (negative aspect), 2) good personal relationships (positive aspect). Single immigrant women were quite talented and independent when compared to contemporary women in Japan. Their incomes, however, indicated low pay because of their language handicaps.

Perhaps because this group is the one where I could place myself, there appeared to be more identification and less envy or "projection" towards me here than with the other groups of women.

c) Women who are married to non-Japanese men

The majority of women in this group came from middle-size cities in Japan and had worked as secretaries for several years in large cities, where they had met their husbands. Most of them (75%) had high school education, and were mothers of one or two children. Their social contact with Canadian culture is the largest; two-thirds Canadian context (with in-laws and association with their husbands) and one-third Japanese. Most of them are anxious to get to know more Japanese in the city since they are recent immigrants — most have lived in Vancouver for less than four years. Their English usage is seventy-five percent but they all feel it is inadequate. Most of them expressed poor communication with their husbands and had no one to talk to about their personal problems. This has in some cases, led to marital problems. Because of their English, they are forced to stay at home. They all commented on their experiences of encountering their in-laws and relatives and their limited knowledge of the proper behaviour.

Resulting from their identification with Canadian husbands, or non-Japanese husbands, their comments on the Japanese were quite direct; too much pride, too much formality, and too much emphasis to keep face. These comments were directed toward the businessmen's wives.

d) Women who came to Canada with husbands working in Japanese companies

Women in this category were the most anxious to absorb Canadian culture and customs, yet their life styles were the most rigidly Japanese. They are wives of Japanese businessmen of researchers who are temporarily residing in Vancouver. Most of them had been here for more than two years.

They are all university graduates from Japan. All of them are housewives with one to three children. Their social contact with the Japanese is the greatest and Canadian contact is minimal. Without exception all of them answered the telephone call in Japanese fashion by saying "moshi-moshi" (hello). They do not have much contact with the Japanese community in Vancouver, but seem to have their own colony here. They reside on the west side of Vancouver. At one expensive townhouse complex, there were six Japanese families.

They all speak Japanese at home and their English usage is almost nil. Their major concern is to retain good Japanese for their children who will be returning later to a Japanese Educational system. Many women try to attend English classes offered by city colleges and private tutors. By practicing Japanese customs, eating habits and ways of social interaction, etc., they create a "Japanese colony" in Vancouver.

Women in this group are anxious to get into the Canadian culture. They mentioned their desire to observe everything about Canada before their return to Japan. Time limitation seems to be the strong factor. They see Canadian women as assertive, having more free time, and independent. They see themselves as overprotected, locked in the house, but at the same time indulging in the situation and becoming lazy.

All of them mention the desire or dream of remaining in Canada. Compared to a very competitive life in Japan, they see Canadian society and culture, and the people's attitude about life as more humane. They see Canada as a better place for their children. Many of them had a very critical view of the Japanese educational system and tight social network where one is forced to conform into a mold.

Summary: Post-War Women:
N = 45, age range from late twenties to mid forties.

Most of the women are from urban areas, or at least have lived or studied and worked in the big cities prior to their migration. They all experienced a language barrier which affected their life in Canada much more than they had expected. Half of them are still debating whether Canada is their place or not. Most of them are anxious to get to know Canadian people and culture, at the same time they find difficulties: language barriers, no means of communication, a lack of self-expression, the unfamiliarity of Canadian customs and norms, are all factors preventing women from doing so. One woman stated:

> I don't know whether I will ever be able to get to know Canadian people. I thought I was doing fine and I thought I *understood* them, but recently, I was confronted with problems, mainly in personal relationships. Their values and interests began to conflict with mine.

Mothers are facing problems of child-rearing and fear of non-communication with their children because of language barriers and value differences — problems which existed and are still unsolved among the *issei* women. They also fear losing their authority by not knowing Canadian culture and language sufficiently to communicate with their children. They cannot protect their children in the English speaking world. They feel quite ambivalent about their children's competency in English and their familiarity with Canadian culture which is foreign to them.

There are many factors which influence the process of acculturation among Japanese women: a) situational influences in Canada which may vary according to time and place, b) the pre-emigration characteristics and circumstances of the immigrants themselves, and c) length of residence in Canada and the effects of interaction with both the host Canadian and Japanese communities. In describing post-war immigrant groups, one realizes the different interests and problems among individuals which tend to reflect one's maturational stages. Thus, it is important to recognize aspects of one's life cycle which may influence the process of acculturation.

DISCUSSION:

At this particular point in my research, the data are not fully analyzed. Nevertheless, I can describe some differences and similarities between the pre-war and post-war Japanese immigrant women.

Differences between pre-war and post-war women

1. The pre-war Japanese immigrant women as a group tend to be more homogeneous because of their shared sense of history, which is based on pre-war events in Canada and also on the social cohesion of the pre-war Japanese community in Vancouver. (Here I define "community" as an entity that is formed by a group of people sharing historical experiences based on their common cultural uniqueness, language, beliefs and values.) The post-war group is more difficult to study because there is no distinct Japanese community as it existed before the war. We cannot rely on the shared historical events among them. Some of them are too new and isolated and they cannot locate themselves in relation to the other Japanese in the city. The nature of post-war independent immigrants was such that they did not need to rely on the Japanese community as much as the pre-war immigrants. Most of their contact with other Japanese occurred at the language classes offered by Manpower and Immigration, various public schools, and the Japanese Language School.

2. The old value of the pre-war era was based on a "you" oriented culture which emphasized self-subordination. In contrast, the post-war value system was based on an "I" oriented culture. In other words, we are seeing one segment of old Japanese values in pre-war women, as G. Yamamoto describes,

> while Japan as a socio-economic source of inspiration for these immigrants kept changing in language, custom and idiom, the image

to which they adhered remained the same as that which the *issei* had carried with them upon leaving. (1974)

The post-war Japanese immigrant women see Canadian women as being very self-centred, or "I" oriented. In turn, the pre-war Japanese women view the post-war women as "I" oriented. The post-war Japanese immigrant women themselves recognize their "I" oriented characteristics when they compare themselves to Japanese women of similar age in Japan.

The impression of Japanese Canadians and the community by recent immigrants is equally revealing in terms of differences with Japan. Recent immigrants have pointed out that the Japanese in the homeland experienced neither discrimination nor the humiliation of alien classification, evacuation and dispersal, as did the Japanese Canadians. Most of the post-war women did not know about the history of the Japanese Canadians except for those who were married to the second generation of Japanese Canadians.

Similarities among pre-war and post-war women

1.   Both pre-war and post-war immigrant women can be viewed as innovators. They were highly educated, intelligent, and had motivation for adventure. They were women who had, even prior to emigration, travelled outside of Japan, attended universities contrary to the customs of their time, married against their parents' wishes, and even encouraged their husbands to leave their security and comfort for greater prospects in Canada. All these things are quite unusual for Japanese women to do, and show that they are independent women.

2.   Language problems were encountered by both pre-war and post-war immigrant women. Their lack of confidence in self-expression created negative self-images, limited their social activities, and resulted in the loss of authority. Language competency relates to cultural competency as well as to a positive self-image which are all part of the process of acculturation. Concerning the importance of language, Lee (1949a: 261) notes that

> language is a cultural measuring device. It incorporates the premises of the culture and codifies reality in such a way that it presents it as absolute to the members of each culture.

3.   Despite the differences in age, background, personality, and length of stay in Canada, there was a definite pattern in the experiences of Japanese women. Given the wide variety of life styles in Canada

and in Japan, and their corresponding cultural and social class variations, it is impossible for all Japanese immigrant women to fit into a single mould during their process of acculturation. Nevertheless, in the life-cycle, in the life process of each individual, we see commonalities. The sample is diverse enough, and spread throughout different levels of the acculturation process as well as the life-cycle so that we can observe segments of immigrant experiences and find commonalities as well as differences. Patterns of experiences can be seen and thus a better understanding of adjustment processes can be obtained.

Through life processes and life experiences, each individual reconstructs realities and redefines his or her situations and identity. By going through the case studies of individuals, the patterns in question could be explored. We can also obtain further information on the differing patterns of personality and experiences that the individual acquires in a cross-cultural situation.

NOTES

1. JCCA (Japanese Canadian Citizens Association), the oldest existing Japanese ethnic organization, was established in 1938.

2. Language Aid was developed in response to the growing awareness of the daily problems of non-English speaking residents in the Greater Vancouver Area. It was established in 1972. The services provided are information referral, counselling, interpretation, translation and house-visits.

3. Tonarigumi (Drop-in-Center for Japanese Senior Citizens) was developed in response to the growing needs of Japanese senior citizens who lived around the Japantown area.

4. Japanese Women's Group: An orientation to Vancouver was sponsored by the Women's Resources Center, and Center for Continuing Education, University of British Columbia. The class provided information on shipping, school system, medical care, social services, and eating habits in Canada. Some other topics were selected as it related to immigrant women's needs. The symposium was held during January 14-March 8, 1976.

5. Japanese Centennial Project; a group of first, second and third generation Japanese Canadians who worked to mount the photographic history of Japanese Canadians to celebrate their centennial year, 1977. The exhibition was shown in various cities in B.C. At present it is in Ottawa. I worked as a research co-ordinator.

6. "Japanese-Canadians: An Annotated Bibliography," Yuko Shibata, 1975.

BIBLIOGRAPHY

Barth, Fredrik, ed.
1969. *Ethnic Groups and Boundaries*. London: George Allen and Unwin.

Berger, Michael.
1975. "Japanese Women — Old Images and New Realities." *The Japan Interpreter*.

Berger, P. L. and T. Luckmann
1966. *The Social Construction of Reality*. New York: Doubleday and Co., Inc.

Bernsterin, B.
1971. *Class, Codes and Control. Vol. I Theoretical Studies Towards a Sociology of Language*. London: Routledge and Kegan Paul.

Brim, O. and S. Wheeler.
1966. *Socialization After Childhood: Two Essays*. New York: John Wiley and Sons, Inc.

Hawkins, Freda.
1972. *Canada and Immigration, Public Policy and Public Concern*. Montreal: McGill-Queen's University Press.

Ito, Kazuo.
1973. *Issei: A History of Japanese Immigrants in North America*. Tokyo: Nichibo-sha.

Lee, Dorothy.
1949. "Being and Value in a Primitive Culture," *The Journal of Philosophy*, 46.

Manpower and Immigration.
1974. *Three Years in Canada: First Report of the Longitudinal Survey on the Economic and Social Adaptation of Immigrants*. Ottawa: Information Canada.

Ministry of Labour, the Dept. of Women and Youth.
1975. *Fujin-no-Ayumi Sanju-nen*. (Women's progress in the Past Thirty Years) Tokyo: Ministry of Labour.

Nakayama, J.
1929. *Canada-Doho-Hatten Taikan*. (Development of Japanese in Canada) Tokyo: Nakayama.

Petersen, William.
1971. *Japanese Americans*. New York: Random House.

Richmond, Anthony H.
1974. *Aspects of the Absorption and Adaptation of Immigrants*. Ottawa: Canadian Immigrant and Population Study.

Roucek, J. S.
1966. "The Japanese in Canada" reprinted from *The Study of Current English*, Vol. 20, #10, Oct. 1965 through Vol. 21, #2, Feb. 1966.

Statistics Canada.
1971. *Census of Canada, Vol. 1, part 3, Bulletin 1.32. Population Ethnic Groups.* Ottawa: Information Canada.

Ujimoto, Victor K.
1976. "Contrasts in the Pre-World War II and Post War Japanese Community in British Columbia: Conflict and Change," *Canadian Review of Sociology and Anthropology,* 13:1, pp. 80-89.

Yamamoto, Grace.
1974. "Nisei: Best of Two Worlds?" *The New Canadian,* Vols. 38, 46, 52, June 18 to July 9, 1974.

Yamauchi and Takeuchi.
1974. *Part One: Need Study.* Vancouver: JCCA.

Young, Charles H., H. R. Y. Reid and W. A. Carrothers.
1938. *The Japanese Canadians.* Toronto: University of Toronto Press.

18

Hinduism in Vancouver: Adjustments in the Home, the Temple, and the Community

Marjorie R. Wood
University of British Columbia

In contrast to Vancouver's Sikh community, the Hindu population has received little attention from social scientists. This may be attributable in part to the belief that Hindus in Vancouver are far less numerous than East Indians of other religions, although this has not been verified. Probably more significant is the fact that the Hindu population of Vancouver does not behave as a community even to the extent that the Sikh population does. Rather, they are dispersed — residentially, linguistically, occupationally — and, until recently, have had no common grounds for communication, let alone concerted action.

In 1974, however, a Hindu temple was founded which has continued to grow in size and complexity. It was from families attending this temple that Professor I. D. Desai of the University of British Columbia chose a sample of children for a study of nutrition patterns among East Indians in Vancouver. One year later, eighteen of the same families were interviewed by a team of anthropologists in a pilot study intended to measure the retention of traditional folklore. It emerged that, to all intents and purposes, folklore is not being retained. But the inquiry revealed that other aspects of Hinduism are being maintained to differing degrees. This paper seeks to describe what form Hinduism appears to be taking in the home, in the temple, and in the larger Vancouver community.

The literature dealing with Hinduism among East Indian immigrant populations elsewhere falls into two broad categories. That concerning the descendants of indentured labourers indicates the maintenance of numerous agricultural and village life rituals and the adoption of local pilgrimage sites, saints, and superstitions (Klass, 1961; Kuper, 1960; Mayer, 1973). The literature on "free" immigrants and their descendants notes a retention of a few domestic rituals, but a lack of any religious roots being put down in the country of immigration (Dotson and Dotson, 1968; Morris, 1968; Pocock, 1957). The Hindus in Vancouver resemble the "free" immigrants more than the ex-indentureds in language, occupation, and class. But whereas the majority of "free" immigrants settled within easy reach of India, the Hindus of Vancouver for the most part cannot travel to India frequently. The question, then, is how Hindus in Vancouver, free immigrants relatively cut off from India, are adjusting their religious practices and beliefs to the realities of their new environment.

In the Home

The focal points of worship in the homes visited range from a single three-inch statue on a bedside table to an entire kitchen cupboard and counter displaying pictures of several dozen deities. In addition, the *Bhagavad Gita* is found in virtually every home and is read frequently by most adults. In some homes, less traditional religious artifacts have been purchased, particularly to help children learn about their heritage. For example, English language comic books depicting episodes from Indian mythology are available from the temple. The *Gayatri Mantra* has also been transliterated on a plaque so that the children can follow the Sanskrit words in the English alphabet. A few families have *pujas* on long-playing records which they import from California, and in one family the children's first request upon getting into the car is to hear *arti* music on the tapedeck!

Religious practices take place on a daily basis in over half of the eighteen homes visited.[1] At least eleven wives perform *puja* or another form of worship every day (It should be noted that one wife is an American Baptist, and that one man's wife has died). Only seven of the eighteen men interviewed indicated that they perform any ritual on a daily basis. It may be that the pattern wherein men appear to be "behind" their wives in attention to ritual also characterizes middle-class urban households in India. Alternatively, men who have chosen to immigrate may be particularly inclined to relegate religion to their women. In his study of East African Indians, H. S. Morris (1968:54) quotes one Hindu as saying:

> The gods are unwilling to cross the sea. Most of them, I think, stayed in India. The women brought over a few that are important to them; but for me, it will be time to pray to God when I go back to India.[2]

In a few cases, a husband and wife stated that they perform their daily ritual together, or that it is their goal to do so. Nuclear family life, whether in Canada, India, or elsewhere, may result in religious couples praying together or the Western concept of the husband-wife relationship may encourage Hindu couples to desire this form of sharing. But I am inclined to believe that these factors combine with a sense of isolation (and perhaps freedom) experienced in the foreign environment to produce the idea of joint worship.

In the home, children sit with their parents during *puja* with varying frequency. Some parents reported that the children participate whenever a ritual is performed, while others indicated that their children rarely take part in or even witness a ritual. Perhaps more so than in India, the attitude of the parents is flexible: it depends on the children's whim whether they participate or not. Certainly one practice occurs that is not common in India: in several households, the children are expected to perform a special ritual of their own. It may be a minor fast, a *mantra,* or a bedtime *bhajan.* This could be an effect of Western values: it is, after all, Western society that has conceived of unique interests and activities for childhood and adolescence. More specifically, as Dotson and Dotson (1968:91) suggest for Indians in Central Africa, the practice may have been picked up from the Christian one of bedtime prayers. In either case, the possibility also exists that parents may be attempting to *counter* Westernization, to offer their children a handle by which to grasp Hinduism on their own.

On special occasions and in times of crisis, men, women and children may participate in rituals even if they do not do so daily. As in India, *Diwali* in particular is a time for household prayers; and in at least a few homes in Vancouver it is the only predictable time. But also during crises, several "*Diwali* Hindus" find themselves acting in a religious manner. One man reported that if he is engaged in a particularly difficult business transaction he will join his wife in *puja* (cf. Morris, 1968:54). Another couple related how their son overcame his fear of dogs when they taught him to face the dog and repeat *"Hari Om"* sternly. Perhaps the most dramatic story of crisis religion came from a refugee from Uganda. This man, who was raised a non-practising Hindu, suffered from severe depression after arriving in Vancouver. He finally cured himself by learning "three good *arthis"* and by starting to pray twice daily (see footnote 2).

A few persons, most of them followers of the *Arya Samaj,* stated that even in times of crisis they do not turn to rituals and the associated gods and goddesses, but to a more abstract entity, God. (Only one man claimed never to pray: "If you break your leg, God won't do anything for you that you can't do for yourself.") Indeed, there was a general tendency on the part of most respondents to stress the oneness of all the various manifestations of God. Dotson and Dotson (1968:92-93), speaking about Hinduism in Central Africa, suggest that a "vague monotheism" emerges because "polytheism is clearly not socially respectable," particularly when the believer is in conversation with a Christian. Certainly, the desire to have his religion understood by outsiders may motivate a Hindu's emphasis on one God to a certain extent. But in Vancouver, the presence of many Arya Samajists and the desire to unite the Hindu community have also favoured the monotheistic aspect of Hinduism.

In the Temple

The *Vishva Hindu Parishad* was reportedly established for social and cultural reasons. According to one of its founders, the temple was intended "to create an East Indian community consciousness" and "to give the kids an idea of their culture." Physically, it gives the impression of a hall rather than of an Indian temple. On the main floor a rich red carpet covers the entire rectangular area, at one end of which is a small stage. Large portraits of Shiva and Vishnu stand garlanded on the left, a life size cardboard figure of Krishna holds centre-stage, and a low table with microphones and a copy of the *Gita* occupies the front right-hand position. Several small images fill spaces in-between these major furnishings. Towards the rear of the room stands an elaborately decorated and canopied wedding *mandap.*

Upstairs are administrative offices and classrooms for Hindi, dance, and music lessons. Although no one in the present temple mentioned taking music lessons, two daughters were studying *Bharat Natyam,* and virtually all respondents' children had either studied Hindi at one time, or were studying it now, or were going to study it when older. Despite the parental concern that their children learn an Indian language, it should be noted that while all but one child could "follow" his parents' non-English conversation, fewer than half spoke the mother tongue, and children from only two families could write in it at all. "As long as we maintain our language, then there won't be any danger of losing our religion," Dotson and Dotson (1968:106) quote a Central African Indian leader as saying. Yet in Central Africa, as in Vancouver, the language is not being maintained.

The temple also serves as a cultural centre in so far as calendrical and life-cycle rituals take place there. Since there are few professional family priests in Vancouver, the temple priest serves the needs of individual families, reading horoscopes, performing wedding ceremonies and occasionally other *sanskaras,* and "giving good advice." One woman remarked that "one way of teaching about marriage is to take daughters to wedding ceremonies." In another case, a couple who fear that their children have lost their religion insist on going to temple at *Diwali* time: "We tell them (the children) we want them to see our Christmas."

A few families also bring their children to hear guest speakers. These are usually men from India, learned members of the Hindu religious community on tour among overseas settlements. As in Central Africa, they frequently "reiterate the ancient past and the great accomplishments of Indian civilization" (Dotson and Dotson, 1968: 108), and strive to relate these achievements to the modern context of their listeners. For the second generation, however, the problem with most of the discourses is the same as that with the wedding rites or *Diwali* hymns: they are not in English.

In the basement of the temple are kitchen facilities and a large room furnished with long tables and folding chairs. It is a room which greatly facilitates the social functions of the temple. About once a month on an irregular basis, a vegetarian meal is served. The meal may be sponsored by a particular individual or family as an extension of the *prasad* offered upstairs, or it may be produced by a group of regular attenders wishing to see a special occasion celebrated. In either case, people of very diverse backgrounds sit down together in what an outsider would have to describe as a relaxed, friendly and happy atmosphere. In a somewhat more restricted vein, the room may also be booked for wedding receptions or other special activities, such as "the Gujarati Ladies' Cooking Competition."

At least one woman who participated in the founding of the temple would not agree that the membership displays a sociable bent. She feels that as a community or social centre, the temple has failed.

According to her, "it is a deep thing in Indian tradition to discriminate a lot." She does not like to listen to discussions about regional origin or religious differences, and she feels that "the people who go to temple are concerned about these things and argue on these grounds." The literature on other overseas communities of free East Indian immigrants lends credence to her view. In East Africa, the description of the Kampala temple resembles that of the Vancouver one, with the addition of a school, rest house, and library (Morris, 1968: 56). But, after an offer of rent-free temple sites, sectarianism split the membership into three factions (pp. 30-32). Eventually, as the East Indian population increased, caste exclusiveness became the organizing social principle, over-shadowing the importance of sect (pp. 61-62). In Central Africa as well, "any attempt to create community-wide support for religious practice immediately runs into sectarianism" (Dotson and Dotson, 1968: 107).

On the other hand, at least two heads of households indicated that their sole reason for attending temple was to see people or to meet people. East Indians new to Vancouver are encouraged to join, both through word of mouth and through the newspaper published by the temple. Official membership has increased to over 700 families, of which an estimated 200 may be represented on an ordinary Sunday morning. The possibility exists that a second temple will be necessary and viable in the not-too-distant future. But whether the present membership would divide, if it does, according to mother tongue, sect, or place of residence in Vancouver, I would hesitate to guess at this point.

Further into the future, what happens to the Hindu temple will depend as much on its second generation as on newly immigrated East Indian membership. As a social centre for youth, however, the temple offers little in the way of organized activity, apart from the Hindi classes. On Sundays, class is dismissed in time for children to hear the reading of the *Gita,* but, in the words of one ten year old, "the priest talks in our language and I don't understand." After worship, groups of adolescent boys stand in small circles chatting and telling jokes, while smaller circles of girls stand more quietly nearby. A committee was organized to study the possibility of a youth group, but it was disbanded when parents objected to the mixing of the sexes. Ironically, the very means by which children could absorb in their own terms the significance of Hindu beliefs and practices was vetoed as too Western.

Despite the apparent lack of religious purpose in the minds of the founders, the temple is thought of as a place of worship by at least some of its members. In addition to Sunday morning prayers and readings, *havan* is offered on Wednesday afternoons and *bhajans* on Thursday evenings. There may be some correlation between the backgrounds of the worshippers and the services they choose to attend. For example, in the present study, the two families going only to *bhajans* are the two lower middle class Gujarati families, one from India and one from Uganda. If further investigation confirms such a correlation, it might provide the answer as to how the membership is divided internally. It would also provide a tentative explanation of how the single institution has accommodated such a diverse population.

Taking all services into account, the present sample of eighteen families divides roughly into thirds: those that go to temple about once a week, those that try to get there once a month, and those who go once or twice a year, on special occasions. Among the middle group are several who would attend more frequently if they could. They complain of lack of transportation, lack of time, and the responsibility of very small children with no live-in babysitters, i.e. relatives, to take care of them. As a rule, older children are not pressed to attend temple; and many of them choose to go far less frequently than their parents. In between babies and adolescents is an age-group very much in evidence during Sunday morning service. They become a bit restless during some hymns, and more so during the interpretation of the *Gita,* but when *arti* is performed no worshipper looks more reverent.

One respondent emphasized that because "everyone comes at 10:30," there is "the appearance of being congregational, but it is just coincidence." On the one hand, the appearance is not completely convincing: services start with a dozen individuals and may finish with hundreds. No one seems to mind, and late-comers make no apology. The only understanding appears to be that even if a person comes forward to the foot of the stage to take *darshan* of the gods, he retreats to the back of the already assembled group before sitting down. Most persons simply *namaste* from a distance and go directly to the left (for men) or right (for women).

On the other hand, even if the membership does not exactly congregate in the Western way, the worship format and functions of the priest do appear congregational, relative to Indian practice. Typically, the priest offers an opening prayer, the congregation sings a couple of familiar hymns in unison or respectively, and one solo is offered in the classical style. Next, the priest reads a passage from the *Gita* and comments on it at length in Hindi. Following the "sermon," worshippers designated by the priest perform *arti* while everyone stands and sings. Finally, there are announcements: the results of a fund-raising drive, the topic of next week's guest speaker, or — on one occasion — brief instruction on the display of the Indian flag (it had been displayed upside down at the temple bazaar).

To some extent, the congregational appearance *is* "just coincidence." The Hindu community supports only one temple, and dispersed as they are residentially, the majority of them can reach it only on Sundays. But it is more than just an "appearance." Members may take turns giving special readings, raising topics of interest, or leading the singing. The priest organizes and leads the service, participates in temple administration, and ministers to the religious needs of member individuals and families. Dotson and Dotson (1968: 107) feel that "any truly integrative effort which would embrace all Hindus in one place could not be by definition traditional Hinduism." They also acknowledge, however, that Hindus take change in their religion for granted (p. 105). A change toward congregational worship may be taking place in Vancouver, not only in the form of worship but also in the religious tenets of the worshippers. At least one young man, in an ongoing debate with his uncle, states that "the mind can go toward God only in temple."

In the Community

From the perspective of the Hindus interviewed, there is no conflict between themselves and European Canadians regarding religion. After all, "all gods are one," "any learning about God is good," and "Hinduism is tolerant" (cf. Dotson and Dotson, 1968: 88). Several respondents went further, explaining the Hindu counterparts to the Ten Commandments, the parallels between Krishna and Christ, and their own appreciation of the Bible. Particularly families with school age children incorporate certain features of Christianity in their lives. Most have a tree and gifts at Christmas time, and some roast a turkey.[3]

Several children attend church or church camps with friends, and one grown niece shares an apartment with Catholic roommates. Parents appear to feel quite comfortable about these arrangements; indeed, they seem proud to be able to prove how flexible and broadminded Hindus are.[4] It is only when the "I found it" campaign sounds *intolerant,* or in one case when two children asked to convert to Catholicism, that the strength of the value placed on having one's own unique religious background shows. The mother of the children hoping to convert told them: "No matter what, we have our religion. You can't change your religion: that it what you are."

Difficulties between Hindus and European Canadians arise, the respondents feel, when the latter mistake them for Sikhs. Several persons suggested that it was the "bad example" of the Sikhs that had "spoiled the reception" for other East Indians. It was said that

Sikh dress, manner, and habits offend Canadians, not Hindu culture generally. (Ironically, the Sikhs with whom the Hindus are categorized are themselves mistakenly called "Hindoos" by Canadians.) With only one exception, the persons interviewed said they experience no racial or religious problems with people they know. But several felt certain that incidents of discrimination did occur when strangers took them for Sikhs.

The relationship between the Sikhs and the Hindus of Vancouver is a complex one. As indicated above, there is a distinct we-they feeling. On the other hand, the Hindu temple has Sikh members (the number 200 was mentioned), and it houses a *Granth Sahib* covered appropriately in pink silk. In some respects, the Hindus have followed the Sikh lead, whether consciously or unconsciously. It is the Sikh temple, for example, which is well-known for offering a hot meal after Sunday worship. (Its large prayer room is also carpeted in rich red.) But in other respects the Hindus explicitly wish not to follow the Sikh example. According to one man, the Sikhs have allowed their temple to become an arena for politics. One woman felt that the Sikh membership was parochial, "not mixing" like that of the Hindu temple.

Conclusion: Realities and Adjustments

Hinduism, as it appears to be developing in Vancouver, reflects a major adjustment to two sets of realities. On the one hand, there are the realities of Western urban life, the features of North American society and religion which impinge on the Hindu immigrant's consciousness. On the other hand, there are the realities of the East Indian Hindu population in Vancouver, its size, diversity, and commonalities. Singly and in combination with one another, these realities may be seen to be either accommodated, ignored at no risk, or ignored at risk by practising Hindus.

Thus, in the home, Hindu children are not obliged to participate in their parents' daily worship, but they may be expected to perform a brief ritual of their own. The parental desire to convey their religion to their children, a reality in itself, must take into consideration the facts that (a) the family lives in a nuclear household, geographically removed from like-minded friends; (b) Canadian friends who interact with them have the tradition of bedtime prayers for children, if they have prayers at all; and (c) Western society tends to age-grade most activities, a fact to which the children may become accustomed before the parents.

In similar fashion, since the Vancouver Hindu community supports just a single temple, several adjustments are required.[5] Given the residential dispersion of its members, temple-going has become a weekly instead of a daily affair (or a monthly instead of a weekly one). Furthermore, since Sunday is the one day when most members can get to the temple, a congregational format has been arranged. And the possibility exists that the single temple manages with diverse linguistic and sectarian groups by offering different types of rituals on weekdays. Perhaps the most noticeable adjustment, due in part to the fact that there is just one temple and one priest, is the agreement to emphasize one God. But this agreement also represents accommodation to the realities that the dominant host community believes in one God, and that the diverse sects agree philosophically that all Gods are One.

Not all realities require adjustment. For example, the Christian church tradition of congregating at a given time (latecomers being seated all together at a specific juncture in the service) has not influenced the Hindu temple tradition of easy coming and going. Nor has the institution of Sunday school and silence during the service changed the custom of having children accompany their parents in most activities. Most significantly, within the single temple and its congregational service, members may continue to engage in individual acts of worship.

But some realities to which the Hindu community has not adjusted are ones which may threaten its very survival: the children of today speak English, and the children of today believe mixed-sex activities are normal and enjoyable. The temple was founded with the second generation in mind, but it does not yet speak to them in their own language. It hopes to attract their interest and participation but it has vetoed the organization of the youth group. Perhaps, but only perhaps, enough young people of today will become adult members in the future that the necessary adjustments can be made.

NOTES

1. Household ritual behaviour is variously referred to as *puja, arti, diwo, agarbati, mantra, bhajan,* and *havan.* Since the significance of these terms changes from place to place and from sect to sect, I do not attempt to distinguish among them here, but consider them all equally as ritual.

2. Among Hindus in Canada, the picture is confused by the fact that a majority of those persons who have come from East Africa, where the importance of religion is supposedly less than in India, are persons who have not emigrated freely but have arrived in Canada as refugees.

In the present sample, all four families from Uganda were forced to leave that country, and all four have husbands who participate daily in household prayers. In contrast, of the three families which immigrated freely from elsewhere in East Africa, none has a husband who performs rituals daily. Whether refugees tend to be religious men who would not have migrated freely, or whether the refugee circumstances produced religious men is a question which could be explored in future. I suspect the answer lies in a combination of both factors.

3. Descriptions of East Indian life in Trinidad and Fiji indicate that Christmas may also be used as a legitimate excuse for alcoholic drinking (Klass, 1961: 163-164; Mayer, 1961: 87).

4. The children of one of the families recited Christian fundamentalist beliefs while the parents smiled. Seven years previously, a woman had knocked on their door and offered to teach the children English and religion. The family accepted her offer and the woman has been coming once a week even since. I asked the fourteen year old daughter whether she believed that everybody went to Heaven, or whether some persons might be reincarnated. She answered: "Oh no, not everybody goes to Heaven, only 144,000."

5. The "realities" of one priest and one temple in turn may be viewed as adjustments, not only to the relatively small size of the Hindu community, but also to its degree of secularization. Vancouver's Hindus could afford family priests and neighbourhood temples if they wished to give them top priority.

BIBLIOGRAPHY

Bristow, Mike, Bert N. Adams, and Cecil Pereira.
   "Ugandan Asians in Britain, Canada, and India: Some Characteristics and Resources," *New Community* 4, 2 (Summer 1975), pp. 155-166.

Dotson, Floyd and Lillian O. Dotson.
   The Indian Minority of Zambia, Rhodesia, and Malawi. New Haven and London: Yale University Press, 1968.

Horowitz, Michael M.
   "The Worship of South Indian Deities in Martinique," *Ethology,* II, 3 (July 1963), pp. 339-346.

Klass, Morton.
   East Indians in Trinidad: A study of Cultural Persistence. New York and London: Columbia University Press, 1961.

Kuper, Hilda.
   Indian People in Natal, Natal, University Press, 1960.

Malik, Yogendra K.
   "Agencies of Political Socialization and East Indian Ethnic Identification in Trinidad," *Sociological Bulletin,* 18 (1967) pp. 101-121.

Mayer, Adrian C.
  Peasants in the Pacific: A Study of Fiji Indian Rural Society. Berkeley
  and Los Angeles: University of California Press, 1973 (second edition).

Morris, H. S.
  The Indians in Uganda. Chicago: The University of Chicago Press,
  1968.

Niehoff, Arthur, and Juanita Niehoff.
  East Indians in the West Indies. Milwaukee: Milwaukee Public
  Museum Publications in Anthropology, Number 6, 1960.

Pocock, David F.
  "Difference in East Africa: A Study of Caste and Religion in Modern
  Indian Society," *Southwestern Journal of Anthropology,* 13, 4 (Winter
  1957) pp. 289-300.

19

The Role of The Concept of Love in The Hindu Family Acculturation Process

Carolyn H. Filteau
University of British Columbia

The intent of this paper is two-fold: one, to describe the findings concerning the family of a two-month pilot study conducted among the Hindu community in Vancouver and two, to provide a theoretical framework within which to place the information acquired. The paper describes the areas of family tradition which are being maintained by the community and focuses on the position of the woman in the family. It further compares the role of family tradition in the acculturation process in Canada with the role of family tradition in modernizing India. The theoretical framework provides a comparative analysis of East Indian ideological concepts with those of the Canadian ideal.

The purpose of the pilot study was to determine to what extent folklore was being retained and used by the East Indian ethnic group in the acculturation process in Vancouver. The study revealed, however, that while the retention of East Indian folklore did not appear to be of major significance to the people concerned, other aspects of East Indian tradition were indeed still important. In fact, the traditions most strongly upheld among all those interviewed were those related to marriage and the family.

Partly because this was a pilot study and partly due to the small number of informants, the methodology adopted in the research was more of an anthropological than a survey approach — probing and discovering rather than testing. We interviewed each family somewhat in depth without the aid of a formal questionnaire. We allowed certain questions to emerge as they suited the interests of the participants themselves.

I would like to commence the description of the data with some background information. First, where do these people actually come from? Of the seventeen families interviewed, half were born in India. The other half were born in Uganda, Fiji, Tanzania or Kenya. Their place of cultural origin was, in all cases, India. As to residency in any other western country, three had resided in England while one had resided in the United States. All others came directly from their country of birth. Finally, the fact that two thirds had arrived within the past 10 years suggests that we are considering a fairly recent immigrant population.

In spite of their fairly recent arrival in Canada, one half of the participants indicated that they had already obtained or were in the process of obtaining Canadian citizenship. Only a small proportion demonstrated hesitancy to obtain citizenship because of a desire to return to India. This information indicated a fairly strong tendency to become legitimate Canadian citizens. In the majority of cases, the participants had returned to India at least once. Most of the others had plans to return in the near future. I think it would be fair to state that only a small number of immigrants in this group expressed either a desire or an intent to return to India permanently, while the majority appeared to have accepted Canada as their permanent place of residence.

On the issue of class status in Canada, our data is somewhat limited. Very generally, I would suggest that the economic circumstances of the participants would tend to place them in a "middle-class" Canadian category. As to their educational background, approximately one-half of the males and one-half of the females had high school education or less. The remaining one-half of the males and females had university training, ranging from one or two years university to the completion of a Ph.D. We therefore are dealing with a fairly well educated group of people; the males and females by and large being equally well educated.

With regard to employment, nine out of sixteen adult females in the study were employed. All males were employed. Six of the males were employed under the authority of someone else; five were self-employed; and four were in professions of one sort or another. Females tended to work part time, for their husbands or in non-professional positions. There were no blaring discrepancies between the type of employment achieved in Canada and the educational background evident. That is, there were no persons with Ph.D.s working as taxi drivers, for example.

In describing the perseverance or non-perseverance of the joint family in the Canadian setting, as well as in India, the usual problem arises in the definition of the term itself. There is, on the one hand, the concrete entity which we call the joint family and, on the other hand, the ideational aspects of the family. Ballard, in his study of Sikhs in England, defines the members of a joint family as a "group of individuals owing a complex network of obligations towards each other," which he says can be described in terms of 'rights and property' (Ballard 1972:2). He reminds us that if the joint family is seen as an institution for the joint exploitation of resources by its members, the fact that one member is living in another country may be no more than a minor rather than a fundamental change. He states that it is the moral and jural values of joint family living that are fundamental to the family's persistence.

It is this ideational realm of family tradition which I believe is still strong in the Canadian setting and acts to preserve the family as a complex network of obligations towards each other. Although the majority of families in the study were nuclear in physical terms, the ideology of 'jointness' remained fundamentally important.

Ames also emphasizes the importance of the 'sacrifice, modification or utilization' of the ideal aspect of family tradition in serving the interests of the individual or family economic welfare. In his view, "some of the continuities and alterations in social life can be explained as rational adjustments to certain economic conditions" (Ames in Singer 1970: 114). He defines the dimensions of the family as five-fold: 1) the commensal dimension (budgeting, cooking and eating); 2) the residential or household dimension; 3) property or coparcenary dimension (joint property rights); 4) idea or sentiment dimension; 5) people's idealized concepts or 'models' of their own social structure. (Ames in Singer 1970: 108.)

Both Ames' and Ballard's viewpoints are concerned with the *process* of modernization and westernization among South Asian groups. I think it would be fair to state that both these studies, along with Singer's Madras study (Singer 1968, 1971, 1972) demonstrated that

modernizing families and individuals employ certain adaptive strategies of compartmentalizing their activity in industry from their traditional ritual and caste obligations in order to reduce conflict and work
out mutual adjustments in both spheres (Singer 1970:11).

Ames claims that the 'universalistic' standards of the West tend to
make change a total experience influencing both the family and the
factory, often resulting in high emotional as well as financial costs.
People in India, he claims, tend to act more selectively and more gradually in the process of change, making it ultimately less traumatic.

By limiting his new behaviour to circumstances where it is obviously
adaptable, that is, to the context of his industrial employment or in
the presence of like-minded people, the worker avoids direct confronta-
tions with traditional sentiments. This restriction of new habits primarily to these contexts where their intrinsic rationality is clearly evident
facilitates their ready acceptance.
(Ames in Singer 1970:128.)

He concludes by stating that this "adaptability and utility of traditional
family structures may not be restricted to Jamshedpur, or even to India."
It is my intention to show that he is, in fact, correct in his assumptions
and that this process of selection and adaptation is going on among
the Vancouver East Asian community. It is not my intention, however,
to prove the utility of such a selection in economic terms but merely
to demonstrate that such a process of selection is an aspect of adaptation.

The manner in which I hope to demonstrate this is by concentrating,
as Ballard, Ames and Singer as well as others have done, on the
importance of the ideational realm or the realm of 'sentiment' in Indian
traditional family thought. By showing that sentiments (or what are
often referred to as emotions) are ideas, and that ideas are adaptable
and adaptive, I hope to show that the East Indian community is
engaged in the rational and selective pursuit of change.

The argument I have chosen to make is that both rational and
emotional actions are carried out by individuals within a certain set
of socio-cultural rules in such a way as to allow them to either
adhere to, make choices between, or ultimately to alter those particular
sets of rules. In other words, both emotional and rational forms of
behaviour are in some sense, adaptive as opposed to destructive or
disorienting. This is contrary to the traditional view of emotions as
'experienced' phenomena in which the individual, while in a state of
emotions, is presumed to be in some sense passive. In contrast to
reasoned action, in which the agent presumably is aware of and is
able to consciously and wilfully select between alternatives and thus

determine his own fate, in emotional behaviour the causal agent is positioned to be not 'I' of the actor but some unknown, generally involuntary force which overcomes the individual. The only way in which emotions can be brought under control, it is felt, is by the rational 'I' or an external agent of some sort.

If one assumes that emotions contain a cognitive element and in some sense are controlled by the individual, rather than accepting the more common view that the individual is a helpless victim, subject to his emotions, one may, in my opinion, begin to explore the possibility of emotional behaviour as ultimately adaptive. What I am suggesting is a departure from the more traditional view of feeling and emotion as superventions in which the individual is genuinely passive. The individual, in my view, has a similar sort of autonomy when he is selecting rationally between other sorts of givens.

If we accept the first tenet of Lamarck's definition of adaptation as "changes in organic behaviour or structure which are caused by direct environmental influence or are the products of the organism's responses to such influences which must be accepted as more than purely biological determinism," then I think we can justifiably consider an immigrant group's recognition of the choices available to them as a first step in the process (Stocking 1968).

The more common notion of rationality is that it works functionally in the modification of environmental and social givens to the advantage of the species. The only qualification towards the ends of action is that they not be (in the mind of the actor) destructive to his own well-being.

Emotions, on the other hand, have traditionally been seen as destructive and unadaptive in terms of problem-solving situations. My argument is that emotions, while involving certain biological dispositions, are also rule-guided (as is all behaviour, including rational action). These dispositions are as much an aspect of a social being as is rationality or life or death or procreation. Just as there are culturally specific forms of living or dying, so there are culturally specific forms of rationality or emotionality. Emotional actions are thus rule-guided and therefore lend themselves to selection and alteration by members of any society. The emotional dispositions which take on certain shape in one context must be modified in accordance with environmental or social changes when such an occasion occurs.

By examining one emotional concept such as the concept of 'love' in the Indian tradition as it relates to the ideology of the family, one might expect to find the following:

(1) a set of ideas which describe the 'feeling' of love

(2) a set of rules or prescriptions for behaviour associated with the feeling

(3) a way of distinguishing between love and other feelings

(4) a set of institutions associated with love

(5) cultural variability in the above four.[1]

In order to test this hypothesis, let us examine some of the data from the Vancouver study. What emerged from the study which was of particular relevance to the hypothesis was a set of intellectual constructs, which explained for the immigrants their 'emotional' world as it related to the family structure in contrast with our own. The interesting part was how the 'emotional' concept — love — could be seen to relate to a whole network of social and prescriptive rules. By asking what love meant in relation to the Indian family, I accumulated a set of descriptive terms which could lead to quite a different definition of love from the definition they assume we advocate in our culture (our culture could, of course, be defined as narrowly as their particular experience, which in many cases does not extend beyond Greater Vancouver).

Love, for the Indian family, appears to entail a whole set of values which they see as conflicting with the Canadian ones. In other words, the East Indian community seems to be recognizing the existence of two models of 'feeling' (the Canadian and their own) and their social consequences. This recognition suggests, in my opinion, that the individuals concerned appear to be forming a strategy for their survival in the Canadian context. It is this process of 'selection' which aids in their adaptation and acts in some way to modify what otherwise might be overwhelming and traumatic changes in the family.

The analysis revealed that the associated values for the notion of Indian love which emerged from the data were as follows: respect, tolerance, obligation, duty, sacrifice, compromise and marriage. Associated with the notion of Canadian love for the Indian, were the values of individualism, materialism, independence, dating, divorce, selfishness and romance.

The problem with the data is that the question which I asked were not framed in such a way that factors (1)-(5) are easily distinguishable from one another. In other words, it is difficult to determine which words are, in fact, associated with feeling (such as respect and tolerance) and which words are associated with the institutionalization of love (for example, love and marriage). The concepts tended to be

---

[1] All refer to the expression and the assertion (both publicly and privately) of love.

intermingled with one another which, I feel, in one sense is a correct way of seeing the reality. They do work together to form a set of principles which affect the individual's thoughts, feelings and actions in complex ways.

The inter-relationship of these concepts can be demonstrated by presenting examples from the data itself which represent the way in which the concept of love was held in the 'heads' of the Indian people. The following statements were elicited on the Indian concept of love:

"It is a more practical thing, it is a family thing more than a romantic one."
"It entails obligation or duty and married persons must share and do things together."
"Requires respect and tolerance"
"Love and commitment grow through long term association and through living and being raised together in a proper way."
"Attitude of giving prevails in Indian marriage — to be of service"
"A good wife must be efficient."
"No one is perfect."
"Love is respect, knowing, and the sacrifice of something to get something."
"Obedience, surrender, and respect."
"Taking care of one another"
"Divorce might be avoided if more tolerant towards one another."
"Husband and wife dimension of family requires resolving of differences."
"Both must learn to change and compromise."

The following statements were made by the Indian people and relate to the concepts of independence, dating, love and marriage in Canada as they see it:

"No clear obligation towards others grows out of the dating pattern in Canada."
"Canadians have too much liberty and independence."
"Canadian kids think that their sixteenth birthday is their passport to freedom. This attitude on the part of the white Canadians is the biggest factor leading to separated families."

The practice of giving children allowance symbolizes, for the Indian community, the concepts of selfishness, materialism and independence. They regard the practice as a most threatening one. Families prefer to give children what they need and perpetuate a bond of reciprocity and obligation from their sacrifice as opposed to encouraging self-initiated action. Parent/child relations should not, they feel, be monetary ones. They were very concerned that allowance would lead to selfishness and diminish the influence of the parents.

"There is nothing in their brain like mine-thine"
"Too much materialism and not enough spiritualism in Canadian society."

This same sense of obligation and love as duty and sacrifice (I might add, expressed as one of joy and pleasure) was extended towards children and towards parents. People were, in general, quite willing to bring their parents here and support them and expressed a hope that their own children, having been taught the same values, would do the same. They were often not completely secure in this hope. They feared the influence of the Canadian society but indicated in most cases that they were prepared for such a change.

The above is, in my view, sufficient information to support convincingly my general thesis that the Indian population, being aware of a conflicting set of what one might refer to as 'emotional values,' was consciously selecting between the alternatives which they saw as available to them. These alternatives, of course, consisted primarily of their native set of rules for how one ought to feel, i.e. behave, (including such things as selflessness, respectfulness, obedience, etc.) and our set of rules for how a Canadian ought to feel, which included in their view such things as independent, self-centered, free to fall in love, free to divorce, and so on.

In conclusion, love has frequently been contraposed to reason and is one of the strongest arguments presented to support the dichotomy of reason and emotion. It is by reputation irrational or blind. Love, in my view, however, is far from being a mere physiological condition which invades the individual's will from time to time. It is more than a disorganizing experience, though these sorts of feelings may very well accompany the emotion at times. Neither is it a pure calculation of pleasure or a drive to satisfy psychological needs. And, it is far more complex than something someone merely 'falls into or out of.' In the Christian emphasis, for example, though love may be highly particularized, it is not altogether immune in its operation from rational considerations. "People may be loved as individuals in their uniqueness, they may not be loved under any general descriptions, but such love is criticizable if it is based on false beliefs" (Peters 1973:31).

The Indian system of love and marriage itself gives us clues to this. Husbands are selected by parents on the basis of presumed compatibility, i.e., what I would describe as cultural similarity. Indian people, as stated, first marry and then love. Persons interviewed expressed great concern over Indian-western marriage because of the difficulties involved in resolving differences, even when it came to such simple things as the naming of a child. Indian women defended their father's choice of husband for them because they felt that he knew better what constituted a good husband because of his 'experience' (in other words, his knowledge of cultural codes of behaviour specific to his Indian heritage and, even more specifically, to his more narrow world of caste and religious beliefs).

The notions of tolerance, respect, resolving of differences, are all, in my view, ways of saying that one enters into a marriage in India with a set of attitudes which in the long run are principles which work toward the maintenance of the institution of the family. I would suggest that the attitudes of self-sufficiency, freedom, individuality, creativeness, etc. are more conducive to developing other social institutions, but perhaps not that of the family, to the extent that the Indian model does. Their observations of our 'emotional' concepts, as well as 'rational' concepts (both words which describe certain types of behaviour) demonstrate, in my opinion, that they are taking the necessary steps in the adaptive process. This further supports the Ames' thesis that the Indian people act selectively and gradually in the process of change.

The above provides an analytical framework for focussing on some of the traditions associated with and maintained by the family. At a more general level, other 'ideals' of the family network of obligations and reciprocity are also being upheld.

After collecting the data, it became apparent that women, in general, seemed to be more conscientious about preserving the traditions of the household. This is also true of the present day situation in the Indian cities where, according to Srinivas

> women generally take the initiative in arranging the marriage of their offspring, and they either articulate their networks or put pressure on their husbands to find suitable spouses.
>
> (Srinivas 1977:226)

While men in general appeared to be more willing to change their views or accept the middle path, women in general tended to express stronger views towards the preservation of arranged marriages. This related to the preservation of their own marriage as well as future possibilities for their sons or daughters. In the words of one married woman, "God brought us together — it is in our blood."

The most common vehicle for the expression of attitudes towards marriage was in relation to their children. We queried various couples on their feelings towards dating in general, mixed dating, and marriage. While men tended to say that they were not too concerned with whom their children married, and perhaps to qualify such statements with certain anxieties about the increased changes of divorce in a mixed marriage, women, on the whole, seemed to prefer arranged marriages. One woman stated that she would like to be able to pick a husband for her daughter because she believed it would be easier for her in the long run. Another stated that she felt that she and her husband would arrange a Punjabi marriage for their children.

Women's more general concerns with the maintenance of religious rituals in the home could quite readily relate to the traditional role of upper caste Hindu women as custodians of the purity of the house and its members. Srinivas explains this concern by claiming that it gives them

> considerable power as the material and spiritual welfare of the household is believed to depend on the meticulous observance of the purity pollution rules, and the periodical performance of ritual (Srinivas 1977:229).

Finally, I looked at the relationship between women and work. A number of women were employed full time or part time and some worked for their husbands. The general attitude was that children, and the raising of children, was a priority. Interestingly enough, some women experienced what they had regarded as social pressure from Canadian society to work. Some saw this as an advantage while many concluded that sacrificing one's self for one's children was a more meritorious way of life.

At the concrete or 'actual' level, however, there is an indication of certain problems arising. As has been shown, the subjective accounts of the people interviewed reveal a strong adherence to the ideal of the family. There is no way of predicting from the data at this point the practical function of maintaining such ideals nor the direction in which the family will go. Further research on the influence that women's employment is having on the values associated with the family could prove most interesting. Women, for example, complained of the loss of support of the kinship network in Canada and the effect that this had upon their freedom to work, as well as the psychological loss which they suffered. Many experienced loneliness and lack of communication with the world outside their homes. Men in general, seemed to be more integrated through the economic sphere. Again, according to Srinivas,

> the crunch might come when, as is already happening in some cities, servants are not available and a more remote possibility, when kinship networks become smaller, and kinship obligations decrease in intensity (Srinivas 1977:236).

A follow-up study at a later date would be helpful in revealing changes or modifications that might occur at both the level of the ideal and the concrete in the family structure.

BIBLIOGRAPHY

Ames, M.
   "Structural Dimension of Family Life in the Steel City of Jamshedpur, India" in Singer, M. *Entrepreneurship and Modernization of Occupational Cultures in South Asia.* 1970. Program in Comparative Studies on Southern Asia. Monograph Number Twelve.

Ballard, Roger
   1972. "Family Organization Among the Sikhs in Britain." *New Community. Vol. II*

Peters, R. S.
   1972. *Reason and Compassion.* Routledge & Kegan Paul, London and Boston.

Singer, M.
   1970. *Entrepreneurship and Modernization of Occupational Cultures in South Asia.* Program in Comparative Studies on Southern Asia. Monograph Number Twelve.

Srinivas, M. N.
   1977. "The Changing Position of Indian Women". *The Journal of the Royal Anthropological Institute. Vol. 12.* No. 2

Stocking, George W. Jr.
   1968. *Race Culture and Evolution.* Free Press. N.Y.

20

Filipinos in Canada: A Socio-Demographic Profile

Anita Beltran Chen
Department of Sociology
Lakehead University, Thunder Bay, Ontario

INTRODUCTION

In more recent years, the Philippines has been one of the ten leading source countries of immigrants to Canada. This paper focuses on the trend of Filipino migration to Canada. The socio-demographic characteristics and geographic distribution of the immigrants are discussed. Comparisons of these features are made with the Filipinos in the United States. Moreover, the paper provides some suggestions for further study of this immigrant group in Canada.

CANADA'S IMMIGRATION POLICIES

Prior to 1962, Canada's immigration policy was fundamentally characterized by an expressed preference for "white" immigrants.[1] In a statement to Parliament at that time Prime Minister Mackenzie King stressed that:[2]

> ... Canada is perfectly within her right in selecting the persons whom we regard as desirable future citizens. It is not a 'fundamental human right' of any alien to enter Canada. It is a privilege.
> ... the people of Canada do not wish, as a result of mass immigration, to make a fundamental alteration in the character of our population. Large-scale immigration from the orient would change the fundamental composition of the Canadian population ...

Essentially, the selection criterion was based on nationality and country of birth; although, of course, it also emphasized the admission of those who can maintain themselves until they find employment and those with a specified family relationship with a Canadian resident or citizen.[3]

Richmond states that "at that time, it was possible for anyone from Britain without a criminal record and in good health to come to Canada." He further adds that "similar privileges applied to those from the United States, France, Ireland, Australia and South Africa . . . landed immigrants (other than those from Asia unless they were Canadian citizens) could sponsor close relatives."[4] As a result of these selective measures, more than two million immigrants arrived in Canada between 1946 and 1967. Of this number, two-fifths were either British, French or from the United States.[5]

A significant change in immigration policy was introduced in early 1962 which in essence abolished racial discrimination. Emphases were also placed on the admission of skilled immigrants and the reunion of families.[6] In 1967, Canada adopted new immigration regulations. This time, in addition to retaining the non-discriminatory policy, it also delineated three main categories of immigrants: "independent," "sponsored" dependent, and "nominated" relatives. A nine-point system of assessment has to be satisfied before an immigrant is admitted on an "independent" status. Out of 100 assessment points, a prospective "independent" immigrant must obtain at least 50 points to qualify for admission. The scheme is largely selective of those who are well-educated and whose occupational skill is needed in Canada.[7] (An outline of the nine-point system is provided in Appendix A.) "Sponsored" dependents include the spouse, unmarried children under 21 years of age, parents and grandparents 60 years or over. "Nominated" relatives include children 21 years of age or over and married children under 21 years of age. It also includes close relatives such as brothers, sisters, parents or grandparents under 60 years of age, nieces, nephews, uncles, aunts or grandchildren. In addition, "nominated" relatives are also assessed in terms of the first five factors: education, occupational skill, occupational demands, age, and personal assessment. "Sponsored" and "nominated" immigrant categories are selective of those who have kinship ties in Canada.

Several features could be noted in comparing the present regulations with those of the previous ones. A major change is that these new regulations removed the element of racial discrimination which previously existed. This is now replaced by universalistic criteria based on educational and occupational qualifications which render the selection process on a more objective basis. Moreover, qualified immigrants are admitted in terms of a number of criteria. Thus a "low" assessment in one may well be compensated by a "high" assessment in others. It should also be noted that this policy of selection, particularly in terms of occupational demands and skills as well as employment opportunities, could be adjusted to meet the manpower needs of the Canadian economy. Immigration is, then, linked to the manpower requirements and to such changes as may occur over time.

From the available data, some noticeable changes in immigration to Canada occurred as a result of changes made in immigration policy and regulations. As shown in Table 1, the proportion of immigrants from Europe had declined from close to 87 percent in 1951-60 to almost 54 percent in 1967-73. On the other hand, immigration from Asia, Africa, the Middle East and West Indies had increased during the same periods. From Asia, the increase was from 2 percent in 1951-60 to almost 14 percent in 1967-73.

As indicated in Table 1 (see footnote 1, Table 1) the Philippines is one of the major countries in Asia that has contributed to this immigration flow. It should be noted further that the Philippines is not only one of the leading countries in Asia that is a major source area of immigrants to Canada, but it is also one of the top ten source countries on a world-wide basis for 1973 and 1975. This is indicated in Table 2.

FILIPINO IMMIGRATION TO CANADA

It was reported that from 1958-62, there were 243 immigrants from the Philippines entering Canada; from 1963-67 this went up to 7,558; and from 1967-73, it rose to 23,802. The total figure from the period 1946 to 1973 was 31,603.[8] The dramatic rise is best seen in Table 3 where the annual figures are presented.

If we were to analyze the figures with reference to Asia as a whole, immigration from the Philippines ranged from 16 percent to 19 percent per year for the past several years. This distribution is shown in Table 4. Other leading countries in Asia that contributed to immigration to Canada are Hong Kong, India, Pakistan, and China.

TABLE 1

Immigration to Canada by Percentage Distribution among Major Countries of Last Permanent Residence, by Major Periods, 1951-1973

PERCENT

Period	Annual Average	United Kingdom and Ireland	Belgium, France, Germany, Netherlands	Italy	Portugal and Greece	Total Europe	USA	West Indies	Asia[1]	Africa and Middle East[2]	South and Central America	Australia and New Zealand	Other
1951-60	157,484	27.7	26.3	15.2	3.6	86.7	6.4	0.7	1.8	2.0	1.1	1.1	0.2
1961-66	115,567	27.3	12.7	17.2	8.4	73.3	11.5	2.1	4.5	4.5	1.9	2.0	0.2
1967-73	163,457	20.0	8.5	7.4	9.6	53.7	13.9	7.0	13.9	5.0	3.7	2.4	0.4

1. Includes Ceylon, China, Hong Kong, India, Japan, Pakistan, Philippines, Taiwan, Asians.

2. Algeria, Egypt, Iran, Israel, Lebanon, Malta, Morocco, Saudi Arabia, South Africa, Syria, Tunisia, Turkey, Africans.

Source: Adapted from Louis Parai, "Canada's Immigration Policy, 1962-74," *International Migration Review*, IX (Winter 1975) p. 470, Table 3.

TABLE 2

Ten Leading Source Countries of Immigrants, Selected Years

1951 (1)	1960 (2)	1968 (3)	1973 (4)	1975 (5)
Britain	Italy	Britain	Britain	Britain
Germany	Britain	United States	United States	United States
Italy	United States	Italy	Hong Kong	Hong Kong
Netherlands	Germany	Germany	Portugal	India
Poland	Netherlands	Hong Kong	Jamaica	Jamaica
France	Portugal	France	India	Portugal
United States	Greece	Austria	*Philippines*	*Philippines*
Belgium	France	Greece	Greece	Italy
Yugoslavia	Poland	Portugal	Italy	Guyana
Denmark	Austria	Yugoslavia	Trinidad	Vietnam

Sources: For 1, 2, 3, and 4. Canada, Department of Manpower and Immigration. *Highlights From the Green Paper on Immigration. Highlights From the Green Paper on Immigration and Population.* Canadian Immigration and Population Study, Vol. 1, p. 28.

For 5. Canada, Department of Manpower and Immigration. *Canada Manpower and Immigration Review,* Vol. 9, No. 1. First Quarter, 1976, p. 3.

TABLE 3
Philippine Immigration to Canada, 1965-1975

1965	1,502	1971	4,180
1966	2,639	1972	3,946
1967	2,994	1973	6,757
1968	2,678	1974	9,564
1969	3,001	1975	7,364
1970	3,240		

Source: Canada, Department of Manpower and Immigration.
Immigration Statistics, Various Years.

TABLE 4
Total Asian and Philippine Immigration to Canada, 1973-1975

	Total Asian (1)	Total Philippines (2)	$\frac{(1)}{(2)}$ in % (3)
1973	43,193	6,757	15.6
1974	50,566	9,564	18.9
1975	47,382	7,364	15.5

Source: Canada, Department of Manpower and Immigration.
Immigration Statistics, Various Years.

AGE-SEX COMPOSITION

The age and sex composition of the Filipino immigrants in Canada shows a high proportion of those in the 20-29 age range followed by those in the 30-39 age group. Such a heavy concentration within the 20-39 age category illustrates quite succinctly the extent to which the immigrant population is concentrated in the working age group. A detailed distribution of the age-sex composition is shown in Table 5.

As seen in Table 5, immigration among the elderly has been considerably on the increase. For those who are 50 years of age or over, there appears to be a more steady increase among the females rather than among the males. It is the writer's opinion that these elderly immigrants are not actively engaged in the labour market. More likely than not, they are "sponsored" dependents if not "nominated" relatives who came to Canada to join their children and in some instances, grandchildren. Although they are not gainfully employed, these elderly immigrants may fulfill a much needed role of doing household chores and baby-sitting, while their married children (and their spouse) are out at work. The idea of an extended family situation is all too familiar to the Filipinos. The same expectation applies to their sojourn as immigrants in a foreign country. These elderly parents and grandparents are thus welcome additions to the household of their married children and grandchildren.

Turning to the other extreme of the age structure is the category of children. The age range from 0-9 has doubled from 1971 to 1975. This escalating growth practically holds true also for those who are 10-19 years of age. It is noted that the substantial increase among both the young and the old age groups reveals a trend which is characteristic of family migration over time rather than migration of single individuals.

Referring to Table 5 again, it is seen that with the 20-29 age group, there are considerably more females than males. This disproportionate distribution was more striking in 1967 and 1971 but gradually reduced in 1975. One possible explanation of this imbalance could be attributed to the movement of a substantially large number of Filipino

TABLE 5

Age-Sex Distribution of Filipino Immigrants in Canada,
In Percent, Selected Years

Age Group	1967		1971		1975	
	M	F	M	F	M	F
0- 9	17	4	14	10	23	19
10-19	3	1	10	8	13	11
20-29	42	68	45	53	33	38
30-39	31	24	23	19	19	15
40-49	4	1	3	4	4	4
50-59	2	2	2	4	2	5
60-69	1	—	2	2	5	7
70 and over	*	*	*	*	1	1
Total in %	100	100	100	100	100	100
Total (N)	(695)	(2,299)	(1,779)	(2,401)	(3,496)	(3,868)

Source: Canada, Department of Manpower and Immigration, *Immigration Statistics,* various years.
    * Denotes less than one percent.

nurses, much more so than any other occupational group. We shall return to this point in a subsequent section when we discuss the occupational composition of the immigrants.

In comparing the sex composition of the Filipino immigrants in Canada and the United States, one notices a striking similarity between the two groups. Filipino immigrants in both countries are characterized by a peculiarly low sex ratio. The considerably large number of nurses admitted to both countries accounts for such a distribution. A comparison of the sex composition between these two groups of immigrants is given in Table 6.

With a sex ratio of 36 for the period of 1967-1969 and 67 for the period of 1970-72, as observed among the Filipinos in Canada, it sufficiently indicates the extent to which the imbalanced sex ratio exists. The gap is somewhat overcome by 1973-1975 when the sex ratio rose to 86. In spite of this, however, it is still characterized by the preponderance of females over males.

Among the Filipino immigrants in the United States, a rather similar observation is made. From 1961-1965, the sex ratio was 53. This increased to 73 in 1966-68 and 70 in 1969-1972. The immigrant population in the United States, likewise, has a low sex ratio but not to the same extent as the immigrant population in Canada. In other words, whereas there are more females than males among the Filipinos in the United States, the magnitude to which this is observed among the Filipinos in Canada is far more pronounced.

A further analysis of the comparison shows that if we were to hold the time period constant, the difference in sex ratio between these two groups of immigrants is noticeably lessened. For example, in the 1970-1972 period, the sex ratio was 67 among the Filipinos in Canada, and within a roughly comparable period 1969-1972, the sex ratio was 70 among those in the United States. If, however, the analysis is made on the basis of an earlier time period, the same observation is not supported. For example, in 1967-1969, the sex ratio was 36 for those in Canada, while in 1966-1968 it was 73 for those in the United States. This means that within roughly the same period, the ratio of inflow of female to male immigrants to Canada was much higher than that of immigrants who entered the United States. As we attributed earlier excess of female over male immigrants in Canada and the United States to the massive movement of Filipino nurses, and since both countries during this period have adopted immigration policies linked to occupational demands, we can conclude that there was a great demand for nurses in both countries. Moreover, the demand for nursing services was more acute in Canada than in the United States particularly during the late 1960s, and hence the admission of female immigrants who

TABLE 6

Age-Sex Compositions of Filipino Immigrants in Canada and United States, Selected Years

CANADA

	Male	Female
Total Immigration	17,802	25,922
1967-1969	2,293	6,380
1970-1972	4,555	6,811
1973-1975	10,954	12,731
Average Annual Immigration		
1967-1969	764	2,127
1970-1972	1,518	2,270
1973-1975	3,651	4,244
Percent Age ≥ 20 years		
1967-1969	80	93
1970-1972	81	84
1973-1975	68	74
Sex Ratio		
1967-1969	36	
1970-1972	67	
1973-1975	86	

UNITED STATES

	Male	Female
Total Immigration	64,835	94,576
1961-1965	5,510	10,419
1966-1968	14,263	19,426
1969-1972	45,062	64,732
Average Annual Immigration		
1961-1965	1,102	2,084
1966-1968	4,754	6,475
1969-1972	11,266	16,183
Percent Age ≥ 20 years		
1961-1965	56	77
1966-1968	68	76
1969-1972	60	73
Sex Ratio		
1961-1965	53	
1966-1968	73	
1969-1972	70	

Sources: (Canadian) Canada, Department of Manpower and Immigration. *Immigration Statistics*, various years. (U.S.) Adapted and summarized from Monica Boyd, "The Changing Nature of Central and Southeast Asian Immigration to the United States," *International Migration Review*, VIII (Winter 1974), p. 514.

were nurses. This is not because more females *per se* were admitted, but rather because more nurses were admitted who happened to be female. It is evident therefore that occupational selectivity as an antecedent factor is inevitably associated with sex selectivity if and when that particular occupation is sex-role oriented. The above observation is a case in point. However, given an occupation which is not essentially sex-role oriented, sex selectivity in migration will be accordingly obscured.

Returning to Table 6 again, some further observations could be made with reference to the age structure of the immigrants. There is a greater percentage of "older" immigrants in Canada than what is observed among this immigrant group in the United States. In this particular instance, "old" is operationally defined as those who are 20 years of age and over. This, in essence, temporarily eliminates the consideration of immigrants in the children's category. The higher distribution of "older" immigrants in Canada holds true for both females and males. In other words, Filipino immigrants in Canada are represented by a relatively "older" group than those who went to the United States. Furthermore, this is represented by a higher proportion of both "older" females as well as "older" males than the immigrants in the United States.

If a comparison of the age structure is made between females and males, it is observed that the immigrant population in both countries is represented by a higher percentage of "older" females than of "older" males. Even if we were to limit the comparison by holding the time factor constant, the same observation emerges: nowhere in the three time periods stipulated can we find a higher percentage of "older" males than "older" females from among the immigrant population that went to Canada and the United States.

In analyzing the age structure of the immigrants from another dimension, those in Canada tend to follow a consistent pattern where the earlier periods were selective of "older" immigrants than those who migrated at a later stage. With a drop from 80 percent in 1967-1969 to 68 percent in 1973-1975 for those who were 20 years of age and older among males, and a decrease from 93 percent to 74 percent during the same periods among the female immigrants to Canada, we can say that during the earlier stage of migration, age selectivity was for a somewhat "older" group. One can offer several possible explanations from this observation. First, the earlier immigrants might have been composed of more single individuals rather than of married ones. Second, the earlier immigrants who were married might have perhaps migrated without bringing their children along with them but only to be reunited with their children at a later date. Third, the later wave of immigrants might have been represented by more family migration (children included) at the time they migrated. This characterized the age composition of the immigrants in Canada as observed through time. This pattern of age selectivity has not been observed, however, among the immigrants in the United States in such a consistent manner as observed among the immigrants in Canada.

OCCUPATIONAL COMPOSITION

Another important characteristic of the socio-demographic feature of the immigrants is an examination of the occupational skills with which they are equipped. Predictably, it may happen that the occupation one intends to pursue in the new country may not be always attainable upon arrival; or it may take quite sometime before one can possibly find employment in one's intended occupation. In a longitudinal survey done by the Department of Manpower and Immigration, it was found that immigrants from different countries experienced different waiting periods before they began working.[9]

> Immigrants from Britain began working about two and a half weeks after arrival.... Germany and Portugal nearly three weeks; Italy, the Philippines and the West Indies approximately four and a half weeks; Greece and India about five and a half weeks; and China and Yugoslavia six and a half weeks.

The distribution of the intended occupation among the Filipino immigrants in Canada is given in Table 7. In 1967, those who intended to be working in various professional jobs accounted for 77 percent of the total number of Filipino immigrants destined for the labour force in Canada. The other area of major occupational concentration was in the service category. This distribution shifted somewhat in 1969. Those in the professional category dropped to 53 percent while those in the clerical and manufacturing categories each increased to 20 percent. Further decline among those in the professional category was seen in 1971 and 1973 when the decrease was 25 percent and 23 percent respectively. The decline in professional category was balanced by an increase again in the clerical category in 1971 and 1973. This was followed by another upswing in the professional category in 1975 which accounted for 36 percent of the Filipino immigrants who intended to enter the labor force that year. From 1967 to 1975, the immigrants showed a heavy concentration in three major occupational groups, namely, professional, clerical, and manufacturing categories. (See Table 7.)

TABLE 7

Intended Occupations of Filipino Immigrants in Canada, in Percent, Selected Years.

	1967	1969	1971	1973	1975
Managerial, Administration	*	*	3	4	3
Professional	77	53	25	23	36
Clerical	7	20	42	29	20
Commercial, Financial	*	1	3	3	2
Service, Recreation	13	4	6	7	5
Transport, Communication	*	*	*	*	*
Agricultural	*	*	*	*	*
Fishing, Trapping, Logging	—	*	—	*	—
Mining	*	*	*	*	*
Manufacturing, Mechanical					
Construction, Fabrication	2	20	17	17	23
Labourers	*	*	*	2	*
Others	*	*	2	14	9
Total in %	100.0	100.0	100.0	100.0	100.0
Total Workers (N)	(2,632)	(2,520)	(2,782)	(3,925)	(3,518)

Source: Canada, Department of Manpower and Immigration, *Immigration Statistics*, various years.
 * Denotes less than one percent.

If one observes the relationship between the proportion of those who intended to join the labor force and total immigration, the pattern shows a consistent decline of those who wished to participate in the work force and a consistent increase of those who are not destined to work. Spouses, children, parents, grandparents constituted the bulk of non-workers. A larger proportion in this category of non-workers was admitted in more recent migration starting in the decade of the seventies. This observation supports an earlier discussion of the age structure of the immigrants where there was a substantial increase of those in the extreme categories, namely, the young and the old age groups. The admission of this group of non-workers somewhat counterbalanced the overall distribution of the proportion of those destined to work. Graph 1 illustrates the shifting proportion between workers and non-workers from the Philippines admitted to Canada.

For example, in 1967, 88 percent of those admitted were destined to join the labor force. In contrast, only 12 percent constituted the non-workers. By 1970, it was evident that the distribution started to shift in opposite directions. Those who intended to work went down to 75 percent. By 1975, the balance was tipped slightly in favor of more non-workers (52 percent) than workers (48 percent).

It was indicated in a previous section in this paper that a large number of professionals were admitted to Canada. Our next focus is to disclose in more detail which particular professions were highly represented by these immigrants. It was observed that proportionately those in the various health professions accounted for a major share of the admission. This includes physicians, surgeons, dentists, nurses, medical and dental technicians, therapists, and other related health professions. The admission of nurses has been far more striking than any other single group of health professionals. This is particularly true in the late 1960s when approximately one-fourth to almost one-third of those intending to work in Canada were nurses. The massive movement of nurses is responsible for the imbalanced sex ratio in favor of females which was discussed previously. Starting from the decade of the 1970s, immigration among the nurses dropped from 21 percent to 3 percent of the total Filipino immigrants who were admitted to join the labor market. This was followed by a slight and gradual increase in demand for more nurses again in 1973-1975. The above data must have reflected the fluctuating demand for nurses in Canada. Table 8 shows the distribution of nurses in relation to the total intended labor force entrants from the Philippines.

If we were to analyze the admission of Filipino nurses in relation to the total immigrant nurses from all over the world, a remarkably high proportion came from the Philippines. This is illustrated in Table 9.

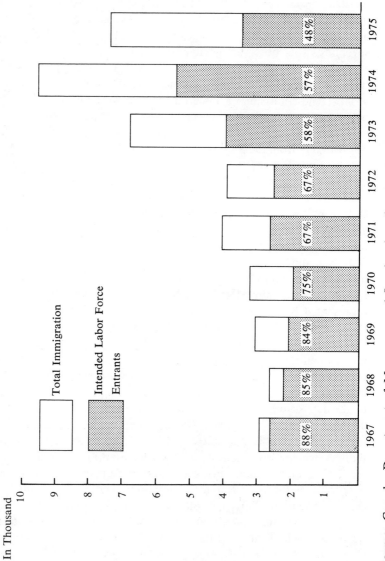

GRAPH 1
Total Philippine Immigration and Immigrants Entering The Labor Market, 1967-1975.

Source: Canada. Department of Manpower and Immigration, *Immigration Statistics,* various years.

TABLE 8

*Total Intended Labor Force Entrants from the Philippines
and Total Nurses, 1967-1975*

	Total Intended Labor Force Entrants (1)	Total Nurses (2)	$\frac{(2)}{(1)}$ in percent (3)
1967	2,632	1,140	43.3
1968	2,288	727	31.7
1969	2,520	757	30.0
1970	2,429	518	21.3
1971	2,782	85	3.0
1972	2,625	89	3.3
1973	3,925	248	6.3
1974	5,471	409	7.4
1975	3,518	389	11.0

Source: Canada, Department of Manpower and Immigration. *Immigration Statistics*, various years.

TABLE 9

*Total Immigrant Nurses and Total Immigrant Nurses from
the Philippines Admitted to Canada, 1967-1975*

	Total Immigrant Nurses (1)	Total Philippine nurses (2)	$\frac{(2)}{(1)}$ in percent (3)
1967	4,262	1,140	26.7
1968	3,375	727	21.5
1969	3,248	757	23.3
1970	2,274	518	22.7
1971	989	85	8.5
1972	892	89	9.9
1973	1,418	248	17.4
1974	1,702	409	24.0
1975	1,713	389	22.7

Source: Canada, Department of Manpower and Immigration. *Immigration Statistics*, various years.

In 1967, one out of every four foreign nurses admitted to Canada came from the Philippines. Proportionately the supply of nurses continued to remain fairly high in 1968 and 1969 where one out of every five came from the Philippines. Although there was a noticeable decline in subsequent admission of Philippine nurses in the early 1970s, this nevertheless started to pick up momentum again in 1974 and 1975 to an extent quite comparable to the high admission during the late 1960s.

In a study of Filipino immigrants in the United States it was observed that there was likewise a substantial flow of those in various professional fields. This was observed starting in the early 1950s and it maintained a fairly consistent pattern of occupational selectivity to the 1970s.[10]

Despite the similarity in occupational selectivity of immigrants from the Philippines to both the United States and Canada, some significant contrast in its relative distribution has been observed. As seen in Table 10, close to 70 percent of those admitted to Canada whose occupational skill was in high demand were those in different health professions. Of this total, almost 45 percent were nurses. If we were to compare this distribution with the Filipinos who went to the United

TABLE 10

Filipinos in Various High-Demand Professions Immigrating to Canada and the United States, 1970

| | Canada | | United States | |
	Number	%	Number	%
Medical Personnel				
Physicians, Surgeons, Dentists	53	4.60	968	10.98
Nurses (Including Students)	518	44.96	954	10.82
Others	232	20.13	640	7.21
Total Medical Personnel	803	69.70	2,562	29.01
Technological Personnel, Engineers	29	2.51	1,163	13.20
Others	117	10.15	1,709	19.39
Total Technological Personnel	146	12.66	2,872	32.59
Teachers	148	12.84	2,285	25.93
Total in High-Demand Occupations	1,097	95.20	7,719	87.53
Total Professional, Technical, and Kindred Workers	1,152	100.00	8,811	100.00

Source: Adapted from Josefina R. Cortes, "Brain Drain and Counter Brain Drain in the Philippines," *The Philippine Economic Journal*, Vol. XII, No. 23, 1973. Table 2, p. 632.

States, only 29 percent of them were in the health professions. Of this, 11 percent were nurses. In a comparable period, 1970, proportionately more nurses from the Philippines were admitted to Canada than to the United States.

On the other hand, more physicians, surgeons and dentists were admitted to the United States than to Canada. There was almost an equal number of nurses and physicians (including surgeons and dentists) admitted to the United States. In Canada, however, eleven times as many nurses were admitted than physicians (including surgeons and dentists). This suggests that although there was a similar demand for doctors and nurses in the United States, the demand in Canada was greater for nurses than for doctors. Of course, this comparison is made only for 1970.

The admission of technical personnel such as engineers and those in related fields is observed to have been greater in the United States than in Canada. Referring to Table 10 again, close to 33 percent of the technical personnel migrated to the United States while only 13 percent came to Canada. Presumably a relatively more advanced industrial economy in the United States is accountable for the admission of such needed skills.

GEOGRAPHIC DISTRIBUTION

Table 11 shows the intended destination by province of Filipino immigrants in Canada. The Atlantic provinces do not seem to have attracted this immigrant group in the same manner as other parts of Canada. Among the Prairie provinces, more immigrants preferred to settle in Manitoba than in either Saskatchewan or Alberta. Quebec was an attractive place in the late 1960s, but gradually less Filipinos were destined to settle in Quebec. The language problem may be an important deterrent factor in settling there. British Columbia continues to attract a remarkably steady proportion of Filipinos. In fact, there is evidence of its growing attraction to the Filipinos if we compare the distribution from 1967 to 1975. A greater percentage of the immigrants, between 49 to 55 percent, however, prefer to settle in Ontario. Although there are no figures available to substantiate this point, it is safe enough to assume that the immigrants are more attracted to Toronto and its metropolitan area than to the whole of Ontario. The same can be said of those who settled in British Columbia and Quebec. Actually it is in the metropolitan areas of Vancouver and Montreal that these immigrants reside rather than throughout the whole province. It is beyond the scope of this paper to trace any discrepancy between

TABLE 11

Destination of Filipino Immigrants, in Percent, 1967-1975

	1967	1968	1969	1970	1971	1972	1973	1974	1975
Newfoundland	2	2	2	1	1	1	1	1	1
Prince Edward Island	*	*	—	*	—	*	*	*	*
Nova Scotia	1	1	1	*	*	*	*	*	*
New Brunswick	1	1	1	*	*	1	1	1	*
Quebec	13	9	9	12	7	6	7	8	7
Ontario	51	52	49	55	55	49	51	51	53
Manitoba	6	9	17	8	13	23	17	16	13
Saskatchewan	3	3	3	1	1	1	1	1	2
Alberta	11	10	6	7	5	4	5	6	7
British Columbia	11	11	11	14	16	14	15	15	16
N.W.T., Yukon	*	*	*	*	*	*	*	*	*
Total in %	100.0	100.0	100.0	100.0	100.0	100.0	100.0	100.0	100.0
Total Immigrants (N)	(2,994)	(2,678)	(3,001)	(3,240)	(4,180)	(3,946)	(6,757)	(9,565)	(7,364)

Source: Canada, Department of Manpower and Immigration. *Immigration Statistics*, various years.
* Denotes less than one percent.

intended destination and actual residence after a period of time. Because of the nature of data available, we can only limit ourselves to the discussion of the intended area of destination.

In the same longitudinal study conducted by the Department of Manpower and Immigration cited earlier, it was found that 54 percent of the immigrant sample signified Ontario to be their intended destination; 16 percent preferred the Prairie provinces; 15 percent Quebec; 12 percent British Columbia and only 3 percent the Atlantic provinces.[11] With the exception of a slightly higher preference for British Columbia, the preferred areas of destination indicated by the Filipino immigrants as shown in Table 11, is seen to be quite similar to the preferences stated by the over-all immigrant population in the survey which was comprised of different nationality groups.

SUMMARY

Prior to 1962, Canada's immigration policy was basically characterized by an expressed preference for "white" immigrants. A subsequent change removed the element of discrimination which brought about a gradual decline of immigrants from Europe on one hand, and a steady increase of those from Asia, Africa, the Middle East, and the West Indies, on the other. In more recent years, the Philippines has been one of the ten leading source countries of immigrants to Canada.

The main focus of this paper was on the socio-demographic characteristics of Filipino immigrants in Canada. Age composition data shows that there is a heavy concentration of population within the 20-39 age bracket. This analysis suggests quite succinctly the extent to which the immigrant population is concentrated in the working age group. Immigration in more recent years, however, shows an increasing number of young and old age groups. There is thus a trend towards family migration rather than migration of single individuals.

The sex composition of the immigrant population has been characterized by an unusually low sex ratio. One obvious explanation of this phenomenon is the movement of a substantially large number of Filipino nurses. A comparison of the sex ratio between the Filipinos in Canada and those in the United States shows a strikingly similar low sex ratio. Such a low sex ratio is observed to be more pronounced in Canada than in the United States. This is again attributed to the migration of a larger number of Filipino nurses to Canada than to the United States.

There is a larger proportion of "older" immigrants in Canada than among the immigrant group in the United States. This holds true for both females and males. Further analysis suggests that immigration to Canada during an earlier period was more selective of "older" immigrants than a later wave of immigrants. The same observation on age selectivity at different stages of migration is not supported by an analysis of the age structure of the immigrants in the United States.

Professional skill constitutes a majority of the occupational qualificaions of the Filipino immigrants in Canada. Two other occupational groups were also fairly highly represented: namely those in the clerical and manufacturing categories. Among the professionals, a majority of them belong to the health professions, such as physicians, surgeons, dentists, medical and dental technicians, and more notably, nurses. In the late 1960s, practically one out of every four foreign nurses admitted to Canada came from the Philippines.

Similarily, there was a large flow of medical personnel from the Philippines to the United States. A distinct contrast exists between the two host countries: while relatively more nurses than physicians migrated to Canada, an even distribution of nurses and physicians went to the United States. This observation is made for 1970.

The admission of technical personnel such as engineers and those in related fields is observed to have been greater in the United States than in Canada. In contrast, the admission of medical personnel, particularly nurses, is greater in Canada than in the United States.

Most Filipino immigrants in Canada preferred to settle in Ontario, notably Toronto, rather than throughout the whole province. A sizable concentration is also found in British Columbia particularly in the metropolitan area of Vancouver. The Prairies and the Atlantic provinces do not seem to be attracting this immigrant group to the same extent as Ontario and British Columbia. Perhaps the economic opportunities in Toronto and Vancouver offer better security to the Filipino immigrants than any other part of Canada.

SUGGESTIONS FOR FURTHER STUDY

This paper mainly relied upon available data from secondary sources such as the immigration statistics. We are thus limited to a descriptive analysis of "who" constitute the Filipino immigrants in Canada. An analysis of the socio-demographic features such as age, sex, and occupational composition answers adequately "who" these immigrants are.

Because of the limitations imposed by secondary sources of data available, it was not possible to analyse responses to such questions as:

(1) "Why" they left the Philippines,

(2) "Why" they chose to come to Canada,

(3) "What" some of the goals and aspirations are which they have set up for themselves and their children, and,

(4) "What" problems, if any, they encountered as they adapted themselves to the mainstream of Canadian society.

The above are some of the salient questions to ask in any future research of this particular immigrant group in Canada.

NOTES

1. Freda Hawkins, "Canadian Immigration Policy and Management," *International Migration Review,* VIII (Summer 1974), p. 144.

2. "Statement of Prime Minister Mackenzie King on Canada's Immigration Policy," Appendix A. The Immigration Program Volume 2 of *A Report of Canadian Immigration and Population Study.* Department of Manpower and Immigration. Ottawa, 1974, pp. 201-207.

3. Louis Parai, "Canada's Immigration Policy, 1962-74," *International Migration Review,* IX (Winter 1975), p. 453.

4. Anthony H. Richmond, *Post-War Immigrants in Canada* (Toronto: University of Toronto Press, 1967), p. 10.

5. Parai, "Canada's," p. 455.

6. Hawkins, "Canadian Immigration," pp. 144-146.

7. Monica Boyd, "Immigration Policies and Trend: A Comparison of Canada and the United States," *Demography,* XIII (February 1976), p. 85.

8. Canada. Department of Manpower and Immigration. Canadian Immigration and Population Study, *Immigration and Population Statistics,* 1974.

9. Canada. Department of Manpower and Immigration. *Three Years in Canada.* First Report of the Longitudinal Survey on the Economic and Social Adaptation of Immigrants. 1974. p. 19.

10. Anita Beltran Chen, "Selectivity in Philippine Migration," in Gordon P. Means (ed.) *Development and Underdevelopment in Southeast Asia* (Ottawa: Canadian Society for Asian Studies, 1977).

11. Canada. Department of Manpower and Immigration. *Three Years in Canada,* pp. 78-79.

APPENDIX A

Units of Assessment, Canadian Immigration Regulations
(P.C. 1967-1616)
October, 1967

	Maximum Assessment Units	
Factors	*Economic*	*Socio-Economic*
1. Education and Training	8	12
2. Personal Assessment by the Immigration Officer		15
3. Occupational Demand	15	
4. Occupational Skill	10	
5. Age		10
6. Arranged employment (designated occupation)	10	
7. Knowledge of English and French		10
8. Relative in Canada		5
9. Employment Opportunities in the Area of Destination	5	
Total	48	52

Source: Adapted from Louis Parai, "Canada's Immigration Policy, 1962-74," *International Migration Review,* IX (Winter 1975), p. 458.

21

Some Random Thoughts From A Novel in Progress

Joy Kogawa

It seems to me that among the most crucial tasks that attends us these days is that of reforming — literally re-forming, re-structuring, re-evaluating, repairing — our imaginations. That is, the task is crucial if the way we perceive affects the reality of what is perceived.

One of the ways we can begin to do this is by opening ourselves to alternative and unfamiliar imaginations that exist around us — to see the ways in which these imaginations serve, for good or for ill, the people who live by them. Another way is to examine the roots and sources of our own imagination — to question our ideas, thoughts, feelings, our intuitions, dreams, memories — all the material that emerges unbidden from our pre-conscious depths.

As a writer I am interested in the relationship of language to our imagination. We commonly understand language to be a tool by which we convey information to one another. But it is not simply a vehicle for our perceptions. Although we use it to understand and recognize reality, we too often do not realize the ways in which our understanding and imagination are themselves formed and informed by the language. There is a two way relationship.

Each language has its own logic and is an expression of a particular civilization's vision of the world and reality. And even when the world in which that civilization lives changes, the language often remains unchanged, reflecting a mode of seeing that is counter to the shifting reality.

Looking at the English language, we know that it is the most nominalizing language in the world; it has the highest capacity to change verbs into nouns. This means we take our dynamic processes and turn them into static entities. For example, the activity we are currently involved in — that is, my communicating with you, my talking with you — is referred to as a 'talk.' Our communicating becomes a communication; our conversing becomes a conversation. A noun, I was taught in school, is the name of a person, place or thing. By turning the talking into a talk, I make a thing of it which I can control and from which I can separate myself. It is as if this communicating could be as independent of us as the walls of this room. What does this do to our consciousness of this activity? Ideally, people communicating are involved in a relational, mutually responsible, inter-penetrating process. But here, now, we could say I am 'delivering' a 'talk.' I can deliver a loaf of bread, but can I deliver a talk? In my imagination, I am objectifying this activity, making a 'thing' out of a process. In fact, by reading it in this manner, I am demonstrating a singular lack of trust in the openness and spontaneity which is essential to relationship. This entire way of conferring together, which we nominalize by calling this activity a conference, is an indication of the way in which we show forth our images of reality. Our communing with one another is limited by this image. All I prove by being subject to this image, is that I lack the confidence and courage to act out of an imagination that is rich in a relational reality. It is the imposition of a fragmented imagination.

There are other ways to be that are more congruent with an alternate, more hopeful, more joyful, and I would say, more accurate imagination. This involves taking the time to question and doubt our perceptions — to begin to uncover the profoundly alienating aspects of our way of imagining. We can, if we choose, begin to reshape the processes that separate us within a faulty imagination.

Another way to begin is by looking at the language of other people. In the simple matter of vocabulary, for example, I am told that in Pali, a dialect of Sanskrit, there are approximately 120 words for different states of consciousness, whereas in English, we have only 4 to 10 words. Our literacy is primarily directed towards material techniques, and our valuing of materiality far exceeds our concern for that which is judged to be 'simply subjective' or 'only personal.' But our very concern with material reality should lead us to venture and penetrate 'what matters' more deeply. If we look at the state of our environmental pollution, for example, and seek to learn from a people, who, par excellence, have not violated and polluted the natural world, we learn that in the language of one native culture, the words for dominance do not exist. The mother does not 'take' the child to the forest. The mother 'goes with' the child.

But in speaking of these matters, I am in no sense an expert. I am here as a writer, a story teller. As Asian Canadians, I believe we are in the unique position of having access to other ways of seeing than those which are dominant in the West. The alternative imaginations which we have to offer are gifts of different and untried windows through which the light can shine when those of the dominant culture in which we live are covered with grime.

Translators and scholars of Asian studies provide a bridge between East and West, opening the way for the traffic of imagination, explaining the thought of one world to another. This is an essential and academic form of work — the detailed labour of bridge building. But the Asian Canadian person bears the bridge within. As writers who are also Asian Canadians, it is our task to ferret out the stuff of our lives, the pre-conscious and silent matter that resides in our limbs. By so doing, we serve to define, to articulate, to lay bare and to make conscious to ourselves, and to the larger community, our individual and collective realities. It is, after all, that which exists in the silences and in the voicelessness, that which is inarticulate and not yet known, that which is victimized, manipulated, trivialized and exploited, that which exists below the tip of the iceberg, that determines the drift of the ice-flow.

All this leads me to present two excerpts from a story about Japanese Canadians that I am currently writing.

The first excerpt deals with the way in which the consciousness of the narrator as a young three year old child began to be formed and molded by the language her parents spoke. The time and place — Marpole, Vancouver, 1939.

"In my memory, my mother rarely speaks, seeming to find most speech an aberration of consciousness. Is it that the word, whether uttered by mouth or pen gives a semblance of solidity, an aura of permanence inconsistent with an inner testimony? If our experience of reality is one of fluctuation, flow and change, the language of words and promise is less accurate, more imprisoning than the fluid language of action.

It is the familiar and safe education of attentiveness that I am given in the home. But outside, even in the backyard, there is an infinitely unpredictable, unknown, and often dangerous world.

One day, I am standing alone in the backyard. Beside the garage is a wire cage placed high above the ground, about the level of a table.

I can barely see the floor of the cage. A white hen struts in here, its head jerking as it scratches at the hay with its claws, jerking as it starts up in alarm, cocking its head sideways, its neck feathers fluffing in and out. Beneath its tiny head, a red tongue shape flaps and jiggles like a rubber flag. It seems constantly alarmed, constantly ready to utter its occasional surprising squawks and gurgles.

My mother and father have bought a dozen cotton batten soft yellow chicks. They are full of cheeps and trembles and their feet are scratchy as twigs. If I stand on a box, I can lift the wire gate. Carefully, I take the babies and put them into the cage.

The chicks are peeping tiny piccolo peeps and standing in a clump where I have placed them in the cage. The white hen stops strutting and cocks her head at them. Two chicks leave the cluster and move randomly away. The others also begin to hop about. One chick is right by the hen's feet. Then to my puzzlement, the hen jabs at the chick. The chick utters a high trilling squeal of distress, spreading its tiny wings out as it flops forward. The hen jabs again and again at the chick, then at the others as they dart about her. The regular peeping sounds are interspersed with the short piercing trills as the hen keeps pecking and the chicks squeal and flutter, squeal and fall. Several of them now do not move or squeal.

I enter the house and say with some urgency, 'Mama — '

My mother comes with me quickly but without alarm. I am grateful for her speed. She removes the live chicks first, putting them in her apron. Then the others.

Her voice is quiet and matter of fact.

'It was not good, was it,' she says. 'Yoku nakatta ne.' Three words. Good, negation of good in the past tense, agreement with statement. It is not a language that promotes hysteria. There is no blame or pity. I am not responsible. The hen is not responsible. My mother does not look at me when she says this or at the hen. She squats with the live and dead and wounded chicks in her apron.

I think now as I watch Obasan sleeping how like my mother she is. Her eyes also though clouded by age are steady and matter of fact. These are eyes I know well — the eyes of Japanese motherhood, made in Japan. They do not invade and they do not betray. They protect. They are eyes that are directly connected to what is hidden most deeply in the very heart of the child.

Physically, the sensation is not in the region of the heart but in the belly. This that is in the belly is honoured when it is allowed to be, without fanfare, without reproach, without words. Any overt acknowledgement betrays and alters the interior by force. What is there is there."

Is it this attitude of guilt-free acceptance of events that enabled the Japanese in Canada to survive as well as they did and to adapt to the harshness of the social mirroring without an overwhelming inner dis-orientation? When there exists a deep grounding in a sense of worth, a sense of honour, the psychic structure within which the person lives, remains healthy and intact.

The second example is from the beginning of Chapter 5, when the Japanese Canadians are being uprooted — a story with which I am sure you are all familiar. Here the narrator is struggling to define and make sense of the experience. In essence, she judges the particular imagination which existed then and exists now which made that situation possible. Her perspectives are those of the dispossessed whose longing is for home.

Chapter 5.

We descend the shaft. The journey is underground.

The darkness is so dense it is almost solid, circumscribed by the memory of the light. The weight of the darkness is the consciousness of the absence of light.

I am no longer certain whether this is a cluttered attic in which I sit, a waiting room, a tunnel, a train. No clock marks the passing of the hours. There is no beginning and no end to the forest, or the dust-storm, no edge from which to know where the clearing begins. Here, in this familiar density, beneath this cloak, within this carapace, is the longing within the darkness.

Much longing makes the corridor walls break. The journey is multi-directional.

Summer, 1942.

We are leaving the B.C. coast — rain, cloud, mist, an air overladen with weeping. Behind us lies a salty sea within which swim our drowning specks of memory — our small waterlogged eulogies. We are trundling down to middle earth with pick axe eyes, tunnelling by train to the Interior, carried along by the momentum of the expulsion, between paradise and the apocalypse, into the waiting wilderness. We are hammers and chisels in the hands of would-be sculptors, battering the spirit of the sleeping mountain. We are the chips and sand, the fragments of fragments that fly like arrows from the heart of the rock. We are the silences that speak from stone. We are the spaces between subject and object in a dualistic imagination. We are the despised rendered voiceless, stripped of car, radio, camera and every means of communication, a trainload of eyes covered with mud and spittle, sent

328 Visible Minorities and Multiculturalism

to Siloam, the pool called 'Sent'; sent to the sending that we might bring sight. We are the silent watchers, hurled from the land of the blind, sacrificed on the altar of the blind god of the blind. We are the superior and sub-human, the scholarly and the illiterate, the envied and the ugly, the fierce and the docile. We are those pioneers who cleared the bush and the forest with our hands. We are the Findhorn community of Canada with our special strawberry and vegetable gnomes, tending and attending the soil with our tenderness. We are desperate and unrequited lovers, giving gifts to the thieves who steal our land, offering our widow's mite to the Fraser Valley Flood Relief Fund. We are the fishermen who are flung from the sea, to flounder in the dust of the prairies.

We are the *issei* and the *nisei* and the *sansei*, the Japanese Canadians, plundered and ravaged, who disappeared into the future, undemanding as dew. We have gone and we are going with dignity and grace, fragrant as the gardens we once tended, sturdy as the boats we once built, generous and gentle as our thoughtful hands and enduring as the honour that attends our departing.

The quality of our spirit, Minasan, is the measure of our greatness. Omedeto, my people, we have not failed. . . ."

Having once been rendered voiceless, the time is long past for speech and for the arduous task of reconciliation.

The value for me of being here with you, of conferring together with you, of sharing stories, is that we can encourage one another, hear and attend one another, and by being thus visible and audible, we can help to nurture a rich and complex social ecology.

22

Compromise and Self-Expression: Problems of the Third World Writer in Canada

Cyril Dabydeen

In his loneliest days in Europe, the American writer Thomas Wolfe said, "You can't go home again." For many Afro-Asian-Canadian writers and others from the Third World, the same feelings, and sometimes anguish, hold true. In many respects he or she is the writer of exile in Canada. Even if one is born here, one senses the imposition of exile. Why exile? Because the artist is crucially aware that he is part of a minority — an easily identifiable minority — in a country which, it seems, is only symbolically committed to the idea of the cultural mosaic.

How does this perspective affect the Third World writer? What are the possibilities that exist to satisfy his fundamental need for self-expression? For him to act as the spokesman for his tribe? For his self-actualization? For his spiritual growth in Canada, so that he takes his place with integrity and dignity?

In answering these questions one has to look more closely at the concept of nationhood. For too long, it seems, people have been misled into thinking of nationhood primarily in geographical terms — merely as a number of distinctive regional components with equally distinctive physical and climatic characteristics. Canada is also seen as the land of eelgrass and snow; the land of "pristine goodness" as ironically identified by the expatriate poet Patrick Anderson. Closely associated with this view is the quasi-historical one — with all its Anglo-Saxon Protestant ethic underpinnings — suggested, for instance, by Susannah Moodie's pioneering penchant. Nationhood has also embraced elements of the victim/survivor schema due primarily to our proximity with the U.S.A. — as suggested by Margaret Atwood.

Because the concept of nationhood essentially embraces people, the spirit of the multi-ethnic conglomeration that is Canada, the focal point of emphasis should be on the "landscape of the mind" — with all the diverse groups being given adequate opportunities for expression, for the shaping and moulding of "the spirit of the place." As such, there is need for a more expansive, elastic, more fluid definition of nationhood that is more meaningfully representative of the various racial components of this land.

In Canada, there are a significant number of people who have immigrated from outside the traditional European areas. At first there were the Chinese, the Japanese, and other East Asians and Africans — all of whom have made significant contributions to the economic life of this country, a fact which has not been clearly and loudly acknowledged. Perhaps, with more scholarly research, this fact will eventually become more well-known. Traditionally, too, these peoples have been admired for manifesting qualities of dedication, hard work, thrift, the upkeep of the family tradition, and so on.

Significantly, many of these peoples have come from areas with rich cultural backgrounds. These ancestral homelands of China, India, Japan subsist in us whether we are first or third generation Canadians, and still form a substantial part of the psyche. That is, if there has not been assimilation by the mass culture — a fact, if true, makes foolish the whole idea of the cultural mosaic.

Colonization and exploitation have also been, at one time or another, part of the experience of these peoples. Inevitably, residues of these experiences linger and form part of their total make-up. Aligned with this is the constant apprehension that one is never fully accepted here. There is always the question — sometimes stemming from innocence and at other times from malice aforethought — "Where do you come from?" The reminder exists that you are in an environment which could potentially become hostile in a crisis. Witness the Japanese experience during the wars. And then, there are the palpable examples of discrimination against East Asians.

Thus, a feeling of homelessness becomes part of his heritage. His skin pigmentation makes him clearly visible, makes him more prone to attacks, makes him more subject to psychological pressures of a myriad kind. The result of all this is that a series of ambivalences about Canada exist, which are sometimes nurtured, causing turmoil and making restless the human spirit crying for expression.

Bharati Mukherjee, co-author with her husband, Clark Blaise, of the book *Days and Nights in Calcutta,* speaks of the subtle feelings of homelessness; she echoes the thoughts of the internationally-renowned author from the Caribbean, V. S. Naipaul, forever exiled in London. He, more than most, is crucially aware of the inevitability of the Third World writer to emigrate to the metropolis, when he writes about "the absolute impossibility of having a home." The consequence, as Mukherjee rightly puts it, is the falling back on to the world of the imagination; this becomes "the portable home" which one carries in one's head — whether in Canada, America, or Britain.

This "portable home" of the imagination grapples with the ambivalences that I referred to earlier — compounded by the pressure to adapt, to integrate, or even to assimilate, as well as coping with longings and nostalgia. In order to express these conflicts, these writers and artists often fall back on images and metaphors that are derived from Western culture, as well as on those indigenous to themselves and to their ancestral roots. But a further area of conflict exists for these ancestral countries have made considerable contributions to world literature; India, China, Japan, Africa and the Caribbean have produced authors of note. But because of the need to be published, to express what is germane to their spirit, an element of compromise appears, for instance, in relation to the verities of time, place and action.

As Mukherjee said, "A Hindu writer who believes that God can be a jolly, potbellied creature with an elephant trunk, and who accepts the Hindu elastic time scheme and reincarnation, must necessarily conceive of heroes, of plot and pacing and even paragraphing in ways distinct from those of the average American (or Canadian)."

More often than not, these writers are pressured to comply to arbitrary standards dictated by the publishing houses, or else have their work rejected. Instances of character and plot further complicate the matter and sometimes make for an even speedier rejection slip. Of course, this is explainable in terms of the arrant commercialism that sometimes tends to govern the book-publishing industry.

To become published, therefore, a significant compromise takes place. As Mukherjee said, "My aesthetic sense must accommodate a decidedly Hindu imagination with an Americanized sense of the craft of fiction." She becomes, in short, a hybridized writer. She cannot freely create the India of her imagination and forge this as a Bellow or a Malamud can do with America.

If the writer has any integrity, then, he or she must "find a voice that will represent the life that I know," according to Mukherjee, "in a manner that is true to my own aesthetic."

It should be noted that writers with a European background do not face this problem. They can easily fall back on their roots without experiencing the internal conflict that confronts the Afro-Asian-Canadian writer who grapples with his or her integrity and the urge to be authentic — a quality which Morley Callaghan extolls in one of his recent talks on CBC *Anthology*. As an instance, Brian Moore can write of his Irish roots and easily become published; or, the poet George McWhirter, in his most recent book, *A Ship of Fools,* published by Oberon Press, can do the same without being asked to write about Canada per se as a condition for publication.

It is interesting to note that some Canadian writers, like Margaret Laurence, use African motifs to enrich their work; and Dave Godfrey wrote the highly-praised novel, *The New Ancestors,* using Africa as a spiritual force.

Yet non-European Canadian writers are few and far between in this country, partly because, perhaps, they are not given enough encouragement to express themselves, to play their rightful place in shaping and moulding "the landscape of the mind." The absence of this robs Canada of a significant source of richness which, undoubtedly, if corrected, could add a vibrant dimension to Canadian literature and act as a stimulus for experimentation. Ultimately, it could act as a stimulus for the creation of some of the best literature in the world — instead of the elements of parochialism that still pervade this segment of our culture and art.

I would like to call for openness, more so than we have at present. Presses like Anansi, Mosaic, McClelland & Stewart — the few that quickly come to mind — are sometimes moving in the right direction. Given the economic constraints and the entire host of problems that confront the smaller presses in particular, as well as the fundamental question of quality, I still think that more could be done. I suppose it is a question of will; it is also a question of commitment to developing a literature that is representative, in a more meaningful way, of the cultural mosaic that composes this country.

I have identified a number of problems — which I would call structural ones — affecting the growth of such a literature and which directly affect Third World writers:

a) Anglo-American hegemony over book-publishing in this country
b) Editors of publishing houses and the literary magazines are often insensitive to the backgrounds of Third World writers, expecting them, very often, to write as if they should ignore their ancestral roots and background.
c) Editors and publishers, as well as critics, use traditional literary standards, sometimes in an arbitrary manner, to judge works of literature submitted to them for appraisal. For instance, concepts of form, time, and place may be entirely different from Western conception.
d) Publishers may be inclined to say that they do not get quality manuscripts submitted to them. This may be true, but part of the answer lies in the fact that not enough writers of Afro-Asian-Canadian backgrounds are encouraged. With more encouragement, there could possibly be a change in this situation.
e) Canada Council and Provincial Arts grants are sometimes left in the hands of people who, unconsciously, may be supporting an elite system. Perhaps because literature has not reached mass consumption, it immediately lends itself to elitism, which tends to run through literary groups and bodies wherever they exist. These bodies, by the mere fact that they often receive public funding, should be far more representative of the ethnic breakdown of the population.

Very often academics, including their wives and friends, are closely involved in this aspect of culture. Consequently, a certain dry rot sets in after a time; the group should be more flexible so as to infuse in it a certain cultural vibrance and thereby stand the chance of commanding a wider audience.

Moreover, more books will be read as a result, and there will be a greater demand for them in bookstores and libraries.

Next, I would like to point out a number of problems which affect Afro-Asian-Canadian writers. These I would label psychological problems:

1) Lack of self-confidence by Third World artists and writers. This lack tends to grow, causing more insecurities. In a sense, however, these very insecurities can act as a breeding source for literature, which would contain the dramatic potency that is sometimes missing in some of the effete material already produced.
2) These writers could easily fall back on their rich ancestral past

for the cornucopia of myths, symbols and motifs in order to give them the confidence to create important literary works.

3) Of course, some of these Third World writers are hampered by the fact that English may not be their first language; this may not always be a hindrance. Transliteration of works can easily occur; for example, it has been done in Africa, which has added tremendous richness to that continent's literature, especially in relation to the powerful metaphors, images and speech patterns indigenous to those artists' background.

Recommendation: What Needs To Be Done

a) The formation of pressure groups.

b) More emphasis on articulation of the problems facing Third World artists.

c) Symposia — such as this one.

d) Press releases by minority ethnic groups so that their voices can be loudly heard.

e) Public Relations with the general public; more good-will should be fostered.

f) More exposure should be given to the writers already being published by some of the more adventurous presses.

g) Abandon tokenism wherever it exists. The writers should be published because of the recognition of their talent.

h) Ethnic groups should form their own publishing houses and publish their own magazines. *Rikka* is doing this already; so is Austin Clarke. More funding should be given to help them along.

i) The more established literary magazines which receive public funding should be asked to broaden their scope and invite authors of Afro-Asian backgrounds to participate.

j) Bookstores and promotion agents of the publishing houses should make a special effort to see that books written by minority groups are given exposure.

k) And, finally, government bodies — such as Multiculturalism, Wintario, and the Canada Council — should take the initiative in seeing that minority groups artists be given exposure.

23

A Contingency Approach to Ethnic Relations: Lessons From the Japanese Canadian Experience

Ellen Baar
Division of Social Science
York University

Writings focusing on the Canadian experience of Japanese migrants and their descendents have contributed to theoretical development within the field of ethnic relations in two ways. First, these studies focused on the idiographic rather than the nomothetic; that is, they considered issues unique to the Japanese experience rather than considering how general principles of ethnic relations applied to Japanese Canadians.[1] Second, the studies assumed that culture, organization and identity vary with generation and wave of migration.[2] Because of the concern with the idiographic, analysts of the early period were not interested in identifying cultural elements which had been retained or lost, nor were they concerned with ascertaining the degree of identification with and participation in the Japanese community so that the likelihood of full participation in the Canadian community could be assessed. Instead, they were concerned with experiences which seemed unique to the Japanese in Canada. How could one account for the relocation of Japanese-Canadians and the policy of enforced dispersion? Attempts centred about describing and explaining the evolution of competitive relations between Japanese and *hakujin* (white people), identifying the long and short term effects of the resulting competitive relationship, accounting for the reduction of the degree of competitiveness following the Second World War and determining the resulting effects. Because of the issues to be explained, a dynamic rather than a static conceptualization was required. Changes in their environment had to be identified and their effects on the culture, organization and identity of both Japanese and *hakujin* had to be ascertained.

THE IMPORTANCE FOR THEORY CONSTRUCTION OF THE EXTERNAL ENVIRONMENT

During the period of Japanese minority status, the resources outside the community which both Japanese and *hakujin* could mobilize, significantly affected both the pattern of inter and intra-ethnic relations. Implicit recognition of this led analysts to differentiate among five eras, each characterized by different patterns of inter-ethnic relations, forms of organization within the Canadian Japanese community, and relations between generations and degrees of cohesiveness among Japanese in Canada. The era of seasonal migration was differentiated from the era of permanent settlement, the period of the Depression, the war period and the immediate post-war period. During the first era, which lasted until the 1908 Gentlemen's Agreement between Canada and Japan, *hakujin* business emphasized the use of foreign contract labour, and nations such as Japan encouraged their citizenry to emigrate temporarily. Such emigration provided income for steamship and emigration companies, and skills could be acquired abroad as well as foreign capital. Because of the organization of seasonal migration, competitive relations developed between *hakujin* working classes and "the Orientals." It was frequently in the self interest of *hakujin* management to oppose attempts by the *hakujin* working class to use their political power to reduce the threat to their economic security, which they perceived as deriving from the Chinese and Japanese workers.[3] Other segments of the *hakujin* community also employed some of their power to oppose restrictions on the Japanese while favouring restrictions on the Chinese.[4] Japanese in Canada benefited from the willingness of the Japanese government to use its control over emigration permits in the early 1900s to restrict further emigration.[5] This temporarily reduced the degree of competitiveness between Japanese and *hakujin* in British Columbia.

The era of permanent settlement differed from the era of seasonal migration because support from segments of British Columbia's powerful *hakujin* community could no longer be mobilized. Businessmen no longer had a vested interest in limiting restrictions on the Japanese; as permanent settlers the Japanese were perceived to be at least as difficult as the Chinese to convert to British protestant values. Nevertheless, the growing international status of the Japanese government enabled the Japanese Consul to quite effectively mobilize resources on behalf of the Japanese in Canada.[6] During the Depression years, however, Japanese expansion in Asia and Canadian assumption of responsibility for its external affairs left the Japanese community dependent upon its own resources rather than on those mobilized in their behalf by the Japanese Consul. From that period until Japan's remarkable post-war economic recovery, external resources provided because of their ancestry could not be effectively mobilized. As well, the linkage to the Japanese government which had previously been advantageous was now disadvantageous. Throughout the war and the early post-war period, almost all resources had to be mobilized from within the Japanese community, although some churches, the CCF and the Japanese Canadian Committee for Democracy provided some external resources. The era of the Depression, the war and the immediate post-war years are differentiated from one another because these eras varied in terms of the barriers experienced when attempting to mobilize resources from within the community.

Differentiation among the eras of minority status and between the period of minority status and the period of very little oppression, neglect and diminution, implicity recognized the importance of the environment to the pattern of inter and intra-ethnic relations. The Japanese Canadian community never had been a self-contained sociocultural system. As a result, analytically it could not be treated as such or the validity of research would be sharply reduced. The Japanese Canadian socio-cultural system had been immensely affected by its relations with the environment; models of analysis had to take that into account. To account for change within the Japanese Canadian community and between *hakujin* and Japanese, analysts required an open rather than a closed systems perspective. Without such a perspective one could not hope to explain how a classic case of what van den Berghe has termed competitive relations[7] had been replaced by apparently cooperative relations, how a population which had experienced extensive oppression, neglect and diminution had seemingly shed its minority status. Without an open systems perspective the effects on relations among *issei, nisei* and *sansei* could not be understood nor could the generational differences in culture, organization and identity.

THE IMPORTANCE FOR THEORY CONSTRUCTION OF DISAGGREGATING ETHNIC DATA

The concept of generation has provided an important basis of organization within Japanese society. As a result, students of the Japanese Canadian experience were the first ethnic relations specialists to accentuate generational differences, disaggregate their data and treat the nature of inter-generational relations as problematic. Only within the past few years has the importance of disaggregating generational data been appreciated by other students of ethnic relations.[8] With the adoption of this perspective, our understanding of marriage patterns, residential segregation and ethnic identification has changed, and the emphasis is now increasingly on accounting for change rather than stability. With increased emphasis on change, a closed systems model becomes increasingly inappropriate while an open systems model becomes increasingly attractive.

Because the Japanese apply the same term *issei* to all individuals born in Japan who have migrated to Canada, students of the Japanese Canadian experience were among the first to compare and contrast the culture, organization and identity of one set of *issei* with that of another — to undertake to disaggregate data on the basis of the wave of migration.[9] By emphasizing wave, the analyst cannot help but recognize that the culture and norms of one wave differ from those of another. So too do the sources of entropy to which each wave is attuned and the coping mechanisms which each defines as appropriate for limiting entropy. The emphasis on wave sensitizes the analysts to the changing nature of the environment and the effects of environment on culture, organization and identity. Culture no longer is conceptualized as an unchanging set of elements, it becomes living culture rather than museum culture; cultural elements are perceived as responding to their environment, changing rather than remaining static.

The emphasis on wave also makes problematic the nature of relations among waves, the ability of the organizations of one wave to absorb members of other waves, to mobilize the networks of another wave, and to create a single leadership structure defined as legitimate by all waves and generations. The emphasis on generation and wave thus encourages the analyst to make the nature of intra-ethnic relations problematic and to make the nature of such relations as central to the analysis as is the analysis of inter-ethnic relations.

THE PREDOMINANT PERSPECTIVE IN ETHNIC RELATIONS

Traditionally, students of ethnic relations have employed a case study method to establish whether the nomothetic principles developed by other students of ethnic relations apply in the case selected. If not, what modifications are needed to increase the validity of these general principles? The general principles receiving most frequent use direct the analyst's attention to the process of integration of individual migrants into the established social, political and economic institutions.[10] The emphasis on the integration of immigrants evolved because the arrival of immigrants was viewed as potentially disorganizing to the receiving social system. Integration was conceived as a mechanism for salvaging and preserving existing social relationships so that the tendency toward social disorganization would be stemmed. Stated another way, the emphasis on systems maintenance resulted in concern with mechanisms promoting homeostatis. Integration was hypothesized to be one such mechanism.[11]

Because integration was conceived of as a mechanism for maintaining the status quo, integration was defined as having occurred when new members of a social system adopt *in toto* the core beliefs and values of the receiving society, are fully accepted into the formal and informal life of that society and sever all ties with their community of orientation. Integration requires that one all-consuming loyalty be replaced by another so that despite the change in membership, stability can be maintained.

Integration is not always possible. It can only occur when absorption of new members is not perceived as threatening the status quo. If absorption is perceived as impeding systems maintenance, the receiving society will not permit integration and thus individuals may shed their culture, organization and identity yet still be prevented from acquiring new ways of viewing and doing things, new associations and a new social identity.[12] As a result, individuals may become deculturated, and the social system to which such individuals previously belonged will become disorganized.

Because the system maintenance perspective emphasizes the ability of the receiving society to resist socio-cultural disorganization while promoting the disorganization of competing social systems, only two outcomes of contact are posited: the ethnic group either loses or retains its culture, organization and identity. The potentiality for its persistence despite radical change is denied. Attention is not given to the possibility that changes occur in the priority attached to various cultural elements, components of organization and identity, or that some aspects of culture, organization and identity are more "essential to the characteristic mode of operation of socio-cultural systems . . ."[13] while others are less essential to a system's persistence. Because essential characteristics are not differentiated from non-essential variables and since all aspects of culture, organization and identity are either lost or retained, the game is a zero sum one. As well, culture, organization and identity are conceptualized as being fixed, not variable. Any change in their components represents a stage in the inevitable transition toward their total loss.

As a result of the assumptions of the systems maintenance approach, ethnic relations researchers have tended to direct their attention to documenting the degree to which cultural elements, forms of organization and components of identity have radically changed or been lost. In addition, the degree of integration into a new social system — the degree of assimilation — has been a central empirical question. Integration into a new social system has been defined so that an individual with multiple loyalties and memberships has been termed "marginal," in a state of disequilibrium because integration into a new social system has only been partial.[14] Marginality is assumed to exist when individuals occupy a mid-way point in the transition of membership and identity from one socio-cultural system to another. If the transition continues, it is assumed that marginality will be resolved as membership in and identity with the former socio-cultural system is replaced by membership in and identification with the new socio-cultural system. According to this perspective, individuals are only "multicultural" during transition. As well, being multicultural is associated with marginality; it is perceived as being a temporary state which is neither socially nor psychologically healthy.

Ken Adachi's discussion of Buddhists becoming Christians and Buddhist congregations adopting Christian forms of organization provides an example of the implications of adopting a closed systems perspective. In Adachi's view, joining a Christian church indicated rejection of Buddha in favour of Christ, while holding services in an auditorium with pews and hymns is perceived as evidence of irreversible cultural loss. Adachi does, however, recognize that the changes undertaken may not have been major ones in the eyes of those undergoing change, and change of membership in particular may have been an instrumental rather than an affective response. Yet because of his closed systems perspective, Adachi finds it curious that an individual would simultaneously worship both Buddha and Christ. The closed system perspective means that it is inconceivable to analysts such as Adachi that one could accept Christ without rejecting Buddha. Adachi emphasizes the magnitude of differences between the two religions, while the man quoted saw the two religions as compatible and thus continued to practice both; but over time, he assigned a lower priority to the worship of Buddha, and higher priority of the worship of Christ. In his eyes the change in priorities was of little consequence and it certainly did not threaten the ability to maintain the essential variables of a distinctively Japanese community within the critical range:

> I worship Buddha in the morning and Christ in the evening, which order, however, I afterwards reversed to Christ in the morning and Buddha in the evening, relegating to Christ the higher honour of the morning worship.[15]

The change in the God worshipped in the morning is perceived as compatible with retaining one's heritage — morning worship is still viewed as the higher honour, one's relationship to a Supreme Being remains central and thus little of significance is perceived as having changed. Adachi and the man quoted differ in their evaluation of the socio-cultural significance of the change. Adoption of closed systems perspective accentuates the disparity in perspective between the analyst such as Adachi and the individual whose behaviour is being analyzed; each would deny the validity of the other's perspective. Adachi would define the two forms of worship as a temporary stage in the inevitable process of assimilation, while the man studied would view his duel loyalties as persisting, as reinforcing not undermining core Buddhist beliefs, as evidence of his Japanese distinctiveness rather than as evidence of his desire to shed such distinctiveness.

THE PREVAILING PERSPECTIVE: APPROPRIATENESS FOR ANALYSIS OF THE JAPANESE CANADIAN EXPERIENCE

Analysis of Japanese — *hakujin* relationships throughout the period of Japanese minority status could not benefit from use of the prevailing approach because the relations studied were competitive ones, and integration was perceived as certain to produce social disorganization. Competitive relationships evolved to prevent not to promote integration. Because the *hakujin* believed that the Japanese were inherently incapable of acquiring the culture, organization or identity of white British Protestants, social disorganization was perceived as likely unless Japanese could be isolated from *hakujin* so that integration of *hakujin* into the Japanese socio-cultural system could be prevented.[16] A high degree of social distance was considered essential if the *hakujin's* culture, organization and identity were not to be undermined. In addition, social, political and economic control would have to be highly concentrated in the hands of the *hakujin* and Japanese would have to be denied access to all sources of power within Canadian society if social disorganization were to be effectively prevented. Segregation and social control were the mechanisms the *hakujin* adopted to prevent social disorganization. Given the mechanisms selected for preventing social disorganization, analysts of this period of minority relations could not effectively use the predominant ethnic relations perspective.

The prevailing perspective was particularly inappropriate because analysts of the Japanese Canadian experience were not primarily concerned with maintenance of the status quo. Instead, they were documenting change both within and between Japanese and *hakujin* as a result of the mechanisms selected by the *hakujin* to limit social disorganization and the attempts by the Japanese to minimize the restrictions imposed upon them. Change was occurring despite the degree of social control imposed; in fact change was occurring because of it. Instead of maintaining the status quo, the mechanisms designed to promote stability were creating social, political and economic change which were affecting the culture, organization and identity of both Japanese and *hakujin*.[17] The resulting patterns of socio-cultural evolution and their effects on inter and intra-ethnic relations could not be discerned by using the prevailing perspective. That perspective focused attention on stability and continuity not on change. When change did occur it was assumed to promote non-persistence and thus the prevailing perspective was of little use in encouraging analysts to determine whether the evolution occurring within both societies promoted the persistence of one or both or increased the probability of non-persistence.

The prevailing perspective was of little use to those wishing to analyze the period of minority status, but what of its use in accounting for the ability of the Japanese to shed their minority status? The decisions to require dispersion or repatriation and to prevent resettlement in coastal British Columbia in the years immediately following the Second World War were based on the belief that integration was not essential if future threats to systems maintenance from the Japanese were to be prevented.[18] Willingness of *issei* and *nisei* to accept such integration made it politically possible for those who had sought repatriation and then decided to remain in Canada to do so.[19] More significantly, apparent willingness to accept integration was viewed by many *hakujin* as evidence that Japanese were no longer inherently incapable of being integrated. As a result, the degree of threat experienced by *hakujin* was reduced and less emphasis was placed on segregation and social control of the Japanese. Other imposed social distance declined as did the institutionalized barriers to mobility. Shortage of trained personnel provided increased opportunity for Japanese Canadians to acquire the credentials for entry into quickly expanding areas of the economy. The resulting occupational diversification promoted integration into the formal institutions. Their economic success further reduced other imposed barriers to more extensive participation. The decision to promote rather than resist integration did not maintain the status quo. It promoted change in the culture, organization and identity of both Japanese and *hakujin*. Unfortunately the prevailing perspective does not provide direction to those wishing to document such change and establish their importance for inter and intra-ethnic relations. Not only does the perspective not provide such direction, but it is detrimental since it encourages analysts to look for evidence that the traditional Japanese culture, organization and identity has been forfeited in favour of acquisition of a static *hakujin* culture, organization and identity. This encourages analysts to over-emphasize the magnitude of change experienced by the Japanese population and to underemphasize the magnitude of change experienced by the *hakujin* population. In addition, it encourages analysts to view the culture, organization and identity of Japanese as being more affected by integration than by their heritage and as being on the threshold of death rather than undergoing further evolution.

AN OPEN SYSTEMS PERSPECTIVE: WHAT IS IT? WHAT ARE ITS EFFECTS?

Of necessity, some analysts of the early Japanese-Canadian experience implicitly adopted an open systems perspective because it was more appropriate, given their concern with the idiographic and their interest in disaggregating data for generations and waves. An open systems perspective seeks to account for change not stability. It emphasizes relations with the environment not maintenance of the existing internal structure, and focuses on two sources of change. The first derives from the environment, while the second derives from internal allocations of resources by individuals and institutions as part of their efforts to maintain the essential variables of a given social system within the critical range. The open systems approach accentuates the need to focus on changes facilitating systems persistence not the mechanisms promoting homeostasis and systems maintenance.[20] It recognizes that "a system may persist even though everything else associated with it changes continuously and radically."[21] Change is a prerequisite for persistence not an indicator of non-persistence.

> The members must be capable of modifying their ... system, as circumstances dictate, with respect to its scope, its membership, structure and processes, goals or rules of behaviour; or they must be able to manipulate their environment so as to relieve the stress.[22]

Death of a social system occurs when members become insensitive to changes in their environment, unable to adapt and thus to relieve stress. In the process of adaptation, the "goals may be basically and permanently revised. The personnel may be new and inexperienced, and the substantive decision . . . arrived at may be discontinous with the past."[23] Yet the social system may persist, continuing to exist in some form "despite substantial and significant changes in some of its aspects."[24] Changes in the current pattern of operations do not indicate that a social system has failed to persist. In fact, "the destruction of the system type may well be one way of coping with stress so that at least some kind of system may endure."[25]

The open systems perspective makes problematic the number and kinds of resources devoted to maintaining the essential variables within the critical range, the effectiveness and efficiency of the allocations, and their effects on culture, organization and identity. It thus becomes the analyst's job to chart the changes and identify the environmental factors and coping mechanisms which produced the resulting changes. An open systems approach enables one to study ethnicity and its importance not only among newly arrived populations, but among those who have been 'fully integrated' for extended periods of time. High rates of intermarriage such as those found to characterize the *sansei* no longer signify the death of a population; intermarriage represents a change in environment. Its effects on inter and intra-ethnic relations, on group boundaries and boundary maintaining mechanisms, and on culture, organization and identity are problematic. The analyst is no longer a specialist in minority-majority relations, devoid of a task when inter-ethnic social distance declines; the analyst is a student of ascribed characteristics and their effects on culture, organization and identity. The open systems model is appropriate whether self and other imposed social distance is high, moderate or low — it is as appropriate for analyzing the *sansei* as for analyzing the *issei*.

An open systems perspective directs the analyst's attention to the fact that culture, organization and identity are dynamic; they have evolved from earlier forms but their present form differs significantly from those of the same population at an earlier point in time. Over time, different elements of culture, organization and identity have assumed importance. The priority attached to the elements of one's heritage is seen as changing over time. Thus some elements previously accorded great significance may now be peripheral. Their centrality/peripherality is not fixed; it changes in response to the current efforts to maintain what are perceived as being the essential variables of that social system within a critical range. Elements currently viewed as relatively unimportant may in the future assume increased centrality. Aspects of one's heritage which are presently defined as peripheral cannot be assumed to be dead, for environmental changes may once again promote their centrality.

ETHNICITY AS AN INTERMITTENT PROCESS

While those analyzing the Japanese Canadian experience explicitly indicated the need to disaggregate data so that differences among waves and generations could be identified and explained, and implicitly adopted an open systems perspective when focusing on the unique aspects of their experience, there are three additional contributions which have been hitherto overlooked. Analysis of the process, through which minority status was shed, highlights the attitudinal and institutional changes required for such a transition to occur. By better understanding this process, it becomes possible to reanalyze and reinterpret existing data on change of ethnic organization since minority status has been shed. By focusing on *nisei* forms of ethnic organization, it becomes apparent that the ethnic dimension now assumes less centrality than it did prior to the shedding of minority status. In establishing the reason for this and the effects, analysts of ethnic relations are challenged to develop a contingency theory, one which specifies those aspects of the environment upon which a given form of culture, organization and identity are contingent. Such a theory would focus on the living rather than the museum nature of culture, and on change rather than continuity in both the nature of ethnic organization and the nature of identity. Third, by focusing on the peripherality of the ethnic dimension in the lives of the *sansei* and their lower level of ethnic organization, the possibility is raised that when ethnicity assumes a low degree of salience, then a very loose knit network may be all that is required to promote ethnic persistence. In addition, under such circumstances, intermarriage may promote rather than undermine ethnic persistence.

The theoretical importance of the Japanese Canadian experience may be very great for it may force analysts to adapt their theories so that they are appropriate, given Francis's contention that "ethnicity is not a fixed state of affairs but an intermittent process. . . ."[26] If ethnicity is an intermittent process, then culture, organization and identity will be significantly different when ethnicity is central than when it is peripheral. Forms of organization which would be inadequate for assuring persistence when ethnicity is central may be quite adequate when ethnicity is peripheral. If this is so, then a contingency theory is required, one which makes both the form and the efficiency of culture, organization and identity contingent on the centrality of the ethnic dimension and the nature of inter-ethnic relations.

FROM COMPETITIVE TO COOPERATIVE RELATIONS

The change in the pattern of inter-ethnic relations which occurred following World War II has not been explained; change in inter-ethnic relations has been treated as an independent but not a dependent variable. The closed systems perspective has significantly affected the literature dealing with the experience of Japanese Canadians following their compliance with the program of enforced dispersion. In analyzing this period, considerable attention has been devoted to: documenting the declining numbers of resources mobilized within the Japanese community for ethnic activities and organizations; the limited effort to mobilize resources for these activities from outside the Japanese community; the absence of a clear definition of appropriate functions which could be performed by ethnic organizations; and, as a result of a poorly articulated definition of what such organizations should do, the short-lived success of attempts to form new ethnic organizations. One analyst simply concludes that "the Japanese . . . will likely fade as a distinct linguistic and social minority."[27] Because a closed system perspective has been employed, a distinct social system is defined as being on the brink of non-persistence. The prognosis changes, however, if an open systems perspective is employed. So too does the theoretical relevance of the Japanese Canadian experience.

Relations between Japanese and *hakujin* had closely approximated van den Berghe's competitive model. Between 1949 and 1964 the nature of those relationships changed significantly; they increasingly approximated a cooperative model. Understanding the process through which this transition occurred is extremely important because it defines how a population can shed its minority status, a question with significant implications for any theory of ethnic relations. To help understand this process, it is important to begin by more precisely defining the transition which occurred. This requires definition of two models of inter-ethnic relations: the competitive and the cooperative.

As conceptualized by van den Berghe, competitive relations between populations exist when power is concentrated in the hands of an ethnocentric population which views itself as having distinctive positively evaluated characteristics: these differentiate its members from all other members of society and legitimize their claim to greater power, privilege and prestige. Institutionalization of the assumption that access to positions providing power, privilege and prestige can legitimately be granted only to those having the distinctive characteristics means that those lacking such characteristics are systematically denied access to the means of acquiring power, privilege and prestige. A competitive relationship develops when real or imagined size, skill and/or organization of the less powerful creates the perception that the existing forms of social organization are no longer legitimate, and the status gaps that result from those forms of organization are therefore illegitimate. Once those without power are perceived as unwilling to accept the established patterns of role differentiation, then contact between those differing significantly in status is viewed as undermining rather than reinforcing the existing distribution of power. To limit such contact a high degree of restrictiveness is needed; without it the status quo could not be assured. Preservation of majority rights and privileges requires stronger barriers which are more assiduously maintained in order to keep minority members from successfully challenging the legitimacy of the established institutions and the distribution of power, privilege, and prestige resulting from their operation.

Cooperative relationships exist when distinctive populations are free to participate either in alternate or integrated institutions. Integrated institutions are possible because distinctive characteristics, though bases of social differentiation, are not bases of stratification. They are no longer bases of stratification because ethnocentrism has been replaced by cosmopolitanism. With increasing cosmopolitanism, increasing legitimacy is accorded those who differ culturally and organizationally from oneself. This enables them to participate in integrated institutions if they choose and to achieve mobility within such institutions. On the other hand, diversity becomes increasingly acceptable because participation in more than one socio-cultural community is viewed as enriching rather than debasing. Structural pluralism is recognized as an essential prerequisite for cultural pluralism, and multiple memberships and loyalties are now perceived both as possible and appropriate; they no longer threaten the supremacy of one superior culture, form of organization, and identity. As a result, there are alternative channels of mobility which, though distinct from one another, are accorded equivalency; thus facilitating movement between socio-cultural systems.

By differentiating between the two models it becomes clear that the transition from a competitive to a cooperative relationship requires great change in the organization and identity of the majority group and relatively little change on the part of the minority. Although there has been some decline in the degree of ethnocentrism and, some institutions have been reorganized to reflect declining ethnocentrism, the change on the part of the majority within Canadian society has not been of the magnitude suggested. Nevertheless, there have been significant changes in the degree of ethnocentrism and in the organization of Canadian social, political and economic institutions since World War II. These changes constitute important environmental factors which must be more clearly understood if the process through which Japanese Canadians achieved increasing degrees of mobility is to be understood and changes in Japanese culture, organization, and identity are to be more fully understood. The pattern of inter-ethnic relations has a very significant effect on the pattern of intra-ethnic relations. The models delineated above suggest that inter-ethnic relations are affected by the attitudes and institutions of the powerful within the society and by the threat a specific population is perceived as posing for the status quo. The specific threat posed by Japanese Canadians was reduced by the willingness of Japanese Canadians to comply with the policy of enforced dispersion, and to enter occupations experiencing manpower shortages. Reduced visibility of Japanese Canadians as a result of their geographical and occupational dispersion, together with change during the fifties and sixties in the public perception of their country of origin, reduced competitiveness. It was not the first time that these factors had affected the degree of competitiveness of inter-ethnic relations. There had been a significant change in the Canadian perception of Japan between the era of permanent settlement and the Depression period. More specifically, at the first point in time Japan was perceived as an important ally by Britain and Canada, but by the second point in time Japan was perceived as potentially dangerous if unchecked. During the era of seasonal migration, British Columbia businessmen perceived the Japanese as being essential, given manpower shortages, while labourers denied the shortages and resented the arrival of seasonal workers. The surplus of manpower, given the available economic opportunities during the Depression years, and concentration in occupations as a result of restrictiveness during the era of permanent settlement, increased the magnitude of the perceived economic threat of the Japanese in the eyes of British Columbians. The degree of restrictiveness varied with the magnitude of the perceived threat, and thus grew steadily between the period of seasonal migration and the wartime period. As the image of Japan changed and manpower shortages increased, restrictiveness declined. Since the degree of restrictiveness determined the magnitude of oppression, neglect and diminution experienced, public perception of one's country of origin and the perceived availability/scarcity of needed manpower were two variables which recurringly affected the competitiveness of relations, the strength of the barriers and the fervour with which they were maintained.

The change which occurred during the postwar period was not merely a result of decreased competitiveness. In addition, ethnicity assumed less importance, while other bases of differentiation, such as education, assumed increased importance. The cooperative model suggests that declining ethnocentrism was responsible and suggests that ethnocentrism was replaced by cosmopolitanism. Furthermore, it suggests that as cosmopolitanism replaced ethnocentrism, being different culturally and organizationally became increasingly legitimate. In fact, however, it was only later that some indication of greater tolerance of differences developed. Instead, there is considerable evidence that ethnocentrism was replaced by geocentrism not polycentrism.[28] Geocentrism implies that the ethnic dimension becomes less important as a basis of organization. As a result, less emphasis is placed on structural pluralism while more emphasis is placed on integration. Ethnicity is subordinated because it is potentially disruptive, because it threatens the integration required if efficiency is to be maximized. Organization on the basis of ethnicity is alleged to promote conflict, while integration requires consensus. Parochialism must be replaced by anationalism so that the probability of conflict can be reduced. Cosmopolitanism, on the other hand, legitimizes the right to be different and recognizes the need to construct organizations which are responsive to ethnic and national differences. Such differences do not have to be subordinated for the good of the society. Rather than emphasizing the need for integration, structural pluralism is accorded legitimacy and participation in one set of institutions no longer precludes participation in others, since boundaries are permeable and equivalency has been established.

If cosmopolitanism had developed, then the ethnic dimension would have remained central for both Japanese and all other populations in Canada. Instead, during the period 1949 to 1964, ethnicity assumed less centrality not only among Japanese but among most populations within Canadian society. Japanese Canadians were able to shed their minority status not only because the competitiveness of relations had declined but because ethnicity was being de-emphasized. Criteria such as religion continued to be important longer than ethnicity, but over time religion too became less central. The process through which ethnocentrism gave way to geocentrism and the environmental factors, particularly the economic factors, which encouraged this transition need to be more fully understood. Greater attention also needs to be accorded to attempts to increase the degree of polycentrism and cosmopolitanism. Nationalists, minorities seeking liberation and advocates of multiculturalism are all promoting polycentrism. But most importantly, analysts of ethnic relations must recognize that the orientation of the dominant group and the orientation institutionalized within societal-wide institutions will significantly affect culture, organization and identity of populations within that society. As such orientations change, the pattern of ethnic relations will change. In the case at hand, ethnicity became an intermittent rather than a continuous process, it became less central than it was in the past, while other defining characteristics became more central than they had been in the past. Culture, organization and identity have changed; as a result, so have the prerequisites for ethnic persistence. Failure to appreciate this has hindered ethnic analysis. Specialists in ethnic relations have failed to recognize that as a result of such changes, they, like the students of large scale organizations, must now develop contingency theories and nomothetic principles whose applicability is specified to be contingent upon a series of environmental variables and orientations.[29]

THE EFFECTS OF SHEDDING MINORITY STATUS ON ETHNIC ORGANIZATION

One way of identifying the effects of shedding minority status is to compare the culture, organization, and identity of the prewar period with that of the postwar period. Such comparison suggests that when minority status is shed, the degree of institutional completeness declines as do rates of participation in ethnic organizations. Although single purpose institutions were common both before and after the war, the number and variety of them has declined, ethnic leadership has become more concentrated and less dispersed, and more emphasis has been placed on creating a small number of multi-purpose organizations.[30] Traditional patterns of social relations — filial piety, gift giving and the practice of *tanomoshi* — have been de-emphasized as have many other elements of *issei* culture.[31] Close knit ethnically exclusive friendship networks have persisted among the *nisei* but not the *sansei*.

How did the shedding of minority status, the fact that Japanese Canadians have become relatively prosperous and relatively secure economically, and the low degree of other imposed social distance affect these changes? In an era during which Japanese Canadians experienced a hostile environment, a high degree of restrictiveness, widespread scarcity and a high degree of competitiveness in relations with *hakujin*, individuals were dependent upon the collective action undertaken by their fellow ethnics. Such action was the best hope for limiting restrictiveness; it provided ethnic socialization, recreational activities, and social and economic assistance. Recreational activities were needed not only because it was the only way of assuring that some distinctively Japanese activities — *odori, origami, sumie, ikebana* and martial arts — would be made available, but also because restrictiveness limited access to recreational activities outside the Japanese community. It was for this reason that such parellel institutions as sports leagues and dance halls were created. In the era before unemployment insurance, old age pensions and hospital insurance, strong ties with fellow ethnics were necessary. Only through such ties could one hope to achieve a modicum of security. For example, the Fishermen's Benevolent Society and the Japanese Fishermen's Hospital provided services which were absolutely essential.[32] Given restrictiveness, income was almost always in short supply and collective action was needed to provide services which individuals would otherwise be unable to purchase. Most forms of organization which analysts of ethnic relations categorize as being ethnic were adapted to the functions ethnic groups perform when their members are oppressed, neglected and diminished — when they face a high degree of restrictiveness, are economically insecure and possess few organizational alternatives. The closed system perspective has blinded analysts to the possibility that participation in organizations performing these functions may have declined because other institutions, many of them non-ethnic, now perform these functions.

In an era of limited restrictiveness, a benign environment within which considerable social mobility and economic security have been obtained, an unending variety of recreational associations to which one has access, and a government financed system of social services, is there a need for the traditional form of ethnic associations? Are the needs which impelled individual Japanese to affiliate with community associations still unmet? Can organizations of this genre meet those needs of the *nisei, sansei* and *yonsei* which are unmet? Does the failure of the JCCA as a viable national entity, and the rapid death of *sansei* attempts to create appropriate large scale organizations, indicate that ethnicity is no longer important, or do they indicate that organizations have had difficulty defining an appropriate role for themselves, in part because they have emphasized museum culture or attempted to employ organizational forms which were appropriate in the past but not in the present? Creating and promoting a living culture, adapting to the current needs of those of Japanese ancestry has posed a problem which has been poorly understood because of the intellectual framework which still prevails. The failure to develop appropriate forms of organization does not mean such forms will never evolve; the environment, however, has deterred their evolution. In the meantime, ethnicity, particularly among the *nisei,* plays an important role in their interpersonal relations. Fellow ethnics have been defined as attractive and worthy of associating with on a continuing basis, and close social ties among small groups of ethnics have continued to assume considerable importance.[33] These forms of ethnic association have become more important than participation in formal ethnic organizations. It is thus these forms of ethnic association, not community-wide associations, with which analysts must concern themselves. In the main, it appears that these forms of association provide those resources which are scarce despite the fact that minority status has been shed. Today ethnic associations are created and maintained to provide psychological resources for their members; i.e. affectual support.[34] Because this is their primary purpose, such associations are smaller, more closely knit. They more closely approximate social networks than formal organizations. As a result, analysts who focus on measuring the degree of institutional completeness are likely to conclude that Japanese Canadian communities have become disorganized; they are unlikely to recognize a relatively high degree of organization, particularly among the *nisei,* because the form differs so greatly from that upon which the analyst is focusing.

Focusing on the *nisei* suggests that as individuals shed their minority status, the kinds of resources which members seek through collective action change and thus so do the forms of organizations. The ethnic dimension may continue to be an important one, one which significantly affects the organization of social relations, even if very few formal ethnic organizations persist. The absence of formal ethnic organizations within a population may lead analysts to fallaciously conclude that ethnicity is no longer socially significant. Makabe's data indicate that ethnicity is socially significant for the *nisei* although it is considerably less significant for the *sansei.* Eighty-two percent of the former but only twelve percent of the latter reported that their social intimates were of Japanese background.[35] Her data also indicate that participation in all kinds of formal organizations is lower among the *sansei* than among the *nisei.* Thus, in studying the *sansei,* it is even more important than when studying the *nisei* to concentrate on the organization of informal social relationships rather than on institutional completeness. In addition, the effect of perceived other imposed social distance on participation in both ethnic and non-ethnic organizations needs to be considered. Does participation in ethnic and non-ethnic organizations vary directly with the magnitude of perceived other imposed social distance? If it does, can reduced rates of participation in ethnic and non-ethnic associations meaningfully be assumed to be permanent? Or is such participation contingent upon the social environment? If it is contingent, then analysts should direct their attention to specifying those aspects of the environment upon which a given form of organization is contingent. Attempts to develop contingency theory within the field of ethnic relations would assign increased importance to the Japanese Canadian experience because that experience enables the analyst to empirically determine the effects of a low degree of perceived other imposed social distance on culture, organization and identity, thereby getting away from the assumption promoted by a closed system perspective — that if contact with non-ethnics is high and boundaries are permeable, then persistence becomes unlikely.

The *sansei* grew up having limited contact with fellow ethnics and extensive contact with ethnic outsiders. In addition, most *sansei* have experienced a low degree of other imposed social distance. What have been the effects of this combination of experiences on culture, organization and identity, on willingness to devote resources to maintaining the essential variables within the critical range? In formulating the question in this way, the bias of the closed system approach is avoided since the focus is on empirically identifying the forms of culture, organization and identity which evolve within a population experiencing a low degree of self and other imposed social distance, and on the ability to mobilize resources needed to enable persistence. The degree to which a specific socio-cultural system has been successfully maintained is not the empirical question posed. The research concern is not primarily with the idiographic as it was when the *issei* and *nisei* were the central focus of attention; the emphasis is on development of general principles, on the nomothetic. The central research questions become: What are the effects of a low degree of self and other imposed social distance on the centrality/peripherality of the ethnic dimension of culture, organization and identity? Can an ethnic group persist when the ethnic dimension is peripheral rather than central? If so, how? Upon what circumstances is the salience of the ethnic dimension contingent? How does the salience of the ethnic dimension affect persistence? For those wishing to develop a theory of ethnic relations these are critical questions, questions which have assumed less importance than they warrant because of the centrality of the systems maintenance perspective. Furthermore, these questions have become peripheral to the study of ethnic relations, thus inhibiting the development of meaningful theory.

Makabe's data suggest that low rates of participation in all formal organizations and the belief that the ethnic community is irrelevant characterize the *sansei*. They perceive the ethnic dimension as being peripheral and they have few organizational affiliations of any kind.[36] One factor contributing to the perception that the ethnic community is irrelevant is the belief that parallel and alternate structures are not needed. The need for parallel structures has declined as access to existing institutions for Japanese has increased. Because they have shed their minority status, the parallel institutions which evolve when there was a high degree of competiveness in inter-ethnic relations are no longer required. Maintaining such institutions would merely divert resources unnecessarily. The need for alternate structures may also have declined but for different reasons. With the growth of cosmopolitanism within some sectors of Canadian society, some functions previously performed by alternate institutions are being performed within community-wide social institutions. Thus, for example, with expansion in the variety of recreational opportunities provided by the local recreation department and the Y's, instruction in the martial arts, Japanese cooking and flower arranging — recreational activities which previously were only available through ethnic organizations — may now be more generally available. If the ethnic organizations continue to offer activities which previously were only available through the ethnic association, there would be unnecessary duplication. As the need for parallel and alternate institutions declines, so too does the perceived relevance of the ethnic community.

Low rates of *sansei* participation may also be affected by an increasingly complex division of labour, and by an increasing emphasis on specialization and professionalization; all of which encourage both *sansei* and other Canadians to leave the development and implementation of activities to those who are specialists and/or are paid to assume such responsibilities. Such an attitude discourages participation in all voluntary associations, including those which are ethnic.[37] Responsibility for maintaining ethnic relations is shifted from all group members to those groups members who are specialists and/or are paid to assume such responsibilities. For this limited segment of the population, the professional ethnics, the ethnic dimension becomes central, while for most of the rest it becomes peripheral. Increasingly, persistence depends on the ability of the professional ethnics to mobilize the level of resources needed to maintain the essential variables within the critical range. Heretofore, professional ethnics have been *nisei*. Whether some *sansei* will assume the role of professional ethnic and others will provide the resources required to support such a role remains problematic, given the perceived irrelevancy of the ethnic community reported.

If professional ethnics can be recruited, then ethnic persistence may be possible despite low rates of participation in ethnic organizations. To be successful, however, professional ethnics must be able to mobilize resources both from within the group and from without. The number and variety of resources needed at any one time and the number of sources of resources which have to be mobilized may vary considerably. A small number of generous and reliable providers will usually suffice, but there must be a broader network from which support can be mobilized. The required network may be loose knit; attempts to mobilize resources from members of this network can be intermittent, and members of the network need not have continuing contact with one another. In other words, the degree of organization required for persistence is less than is needed for an aggregate to be termed a group, but more than is typically found within an aggregate.

In determining whether the degree of organization within an ethnically defined population is great enough to permit persistence, the nature of the social networks within the population must be understood. Existing data, limited though they are, suggest that as a result of lower rates of contact with fellow ethnics during youth and early adulthood, fewer of the *sansei's* social intimates are Japanese. The *nisei* interacted with one another and developed social ties that persisted despite dispersion, whereas dispersion limited the opportunities *sansei* had for interacting with one another, discovering shared characteristics and recognizing the attractiveness of others of the same background. Sunahara suggests that if presented with opportunities for greater contact, the *sansei* will recognize the attractiveness of fellow ethnics, thus increasing the rate of friendship formation among Japanese.[38] Friendship formation is essential to group persistence because it increases the reachability of the network potentially available to the professional ethnics. Recognizing the attractiveness of fellow ethnics is also important because it can be expected to increase the probability that in those instances when requests for resources are made, the needed resources will be forthcoming. Stated another way, the degree of commitment to fellow ethnics required in order to enable intermittent mobilization of resources is considerably less than that needed to support on-going ethnic organizations. Despite low rates of participation, if individuals with access to considerable resources as a result of mobility achieved can be quickly located through an ethnic network, it is likely that the required level of resources will be forthcoming. Maintenance of such a network is thus a prequisite for ethnic survival.

How is such a network to be maintained, given geographical dispersion, *sansei* disdain for formal organizations, and the perceived irrelevancy of the ethnic community? In recent years, conferences have been one means of linking the *sansei* to an ethnic network.[39] Given the recent availability of government funding for conferences, individuals who are unwilling to join ethnic organizations and pledge continuing support have been able to make contact with fellow ethnics at minimal cost and without obligation. Conferences are an ideal method for making contact because a high degree of commitment is not required before one can attend, and maintaining relations developed at such conferences is voluntary. Contact with those reached through conferences need not be regular or continuous; all that is necessary is the knowledge of how to get in touch. If Sunahara is right that limited contact with other *sansei* defines the *sansei* as personable and attractive, then limited short term contact may provide a high enough degree of ethnic identification to enable mobilization of resources if such mobilization is deemed essential.

While a closed system perspective views intermarriage as indicative of an absence of ethnic identification, the open systems perspective recognizes that a network's reachability can be significantly increased by both intermarriage and the fact that such a high proportion of the *sansei's* social intimates are *hakujin*. The resulting reachability can be expected to facilitate mobilization of resources from outside the group as long as the *sansei* on whom networks are anchored are effectively mobilized and as long as mobilization is infrequently required. The open systems perspective emphasizes the importance of being able to mobilize resources from both within and outside of the group. It suggests that the level of ethnic identification and the degree of organization required for ethnic group persistence, the critical range of support, may be considerably less than previously suggested, particularly when a relatively low degree of importance is assigned by the society to the ethnic dimension. Persistence may occur although the degree of day to day participation in ethnic activities is low and contact among *sansei* is intermittent rather than continuous. Loosely knit networks may be sufficient for persistence when the population is socially mobile and thus both attractive and in a position to mobilize considerable resources. The degree of attractiveness can be expected to affect the probability of positive ethnic identification.

THE CONTINGENT NATURE OF THE PREREQUISITES FOR ETHNIC PERSISTENCE

This conceptualization of the prerequisites for ethnic persistence suggests that less emphasis need be put on measuring institutional completeness and rates of participation in ethnic organizations — measures of the centrality of the ethnic dimension. Instead, attention should be directed toward the professional ethnics, the monitors of the system's essential variables; the reachability provided by the ethnic network; the techniques employed to maintain and increase the degree of reachability; and the frequency with which various degrees of mobilization are undertaken. In other words, ethnicity must be conceptualized as "an intermittent process which is activated solely when ethnic differentiation becomes salient."[40] Once ethnicity is thus conceptualized, the empirical focus establishes when ethnic differentiation becomes salient; what procedures are used for mobilizing some segment or all of the ethnic network; the effectiveness of such procedures; and the changes that occur in procedures used for creating, maintaining and mobilizing the network.

Studies of the *sansei* have been theoretically significant because they have suggested that generations may differ from one another in the degree of importance they assign to the ethnic dimension. The weight assigned to the ethnic dimension will affect rates of regularized participation in ethnic organizations. Such participation may increase the degree of positive ethnic identification and the degree of willingness to regularly commit one's resources to group maintenance. If, however, the ethnic dimension is perceived as being relatively peripheral, a lower level of organization may characterize a given ethnic community; members of that community may have less frequent contact with one another; positive ethnic identification may be less important than other forms of identification; and as a result, individuals may be less willing to commit their resources to group maintenance on a regularized basis. Nevertheless, a loosely knit ethnic network which can be used intermittently to mobilize resources may be adequate for mobilizing enough support from both within and outside the ethnically defined population to permit the essential variables to remain within the critical range — particularly during periods in which ethnic differentiation assumes relatively little salience. As the degree of salience of ethnic differentiation increases, a more closely knit form of ethnic organization may be required for persistence. Analysts of ethnic relations have not recognized that the degree of organization required for ethnic persistence is not a constant; it is a variable contingent upon the salience of ethnic differentiation at a given point in time. When inter-ethnic relations are highly competitive, thus making ethnic differentiation extremely salient, a close knit form of organization may be essential for survival. But, when inter-ethnic relations become increasingly cooperative, a loose-knit form of association may suffice. Because students of ethnic relations have been interested in minority/majority relations, they have studied eras during which the ethnic dimension was central rather than peripheral, during which ethnicity was not only a basis of social differentiation but a basis of social stratification. During such periods, the ethnic dimension was central; it determined one's role signs. As a result, the society required that individuals be unambiguously categorized on the basis of their ethnicity. Individuals could not shed their ethnicity, they could only alter the way in which they were socially categorized. Assimilation was the only way in which one could alter one's ethnic label. As the ethnic dimension became less central and ethnicity increasingly became a basis of social differentiation, not a basis of social stratification, the ethnic dimension became less important as a basis for allocating roles. It became possible for individuals to shed their ethnicity; ethnic affiliation became voluntary, not required. The kinds of functions ethnic associations performed, the sources from which resources could be mobilized to maintain such associations, and the rates of participation in such voluntary associations on the part of ethnic insiders and outsiders have been ignored by analysts of ethnic relations because their models had been designed for the analysis of ethnic relations when ethnicity was a central basis of social stratification. Application of these models to the study of ethnic relations, when the ethnic dimension had become less central, distorted reality and misled those seeking to create appropriate forms of ethnic association. Because the models applied were inappropriate, the role of ethnicity has been misunderstood. So too have the conditions for the persistence of distinctive cultures, organizations and identities. Culture organization and identity all change in response to one's social environment; if they fail to change they become irrelevant. In studying culture, organization and identity the analyst must be concerned with their evolution. The traditional models of ethnic relations, however, have not concerned themselves with the evolution of culture, organization and identity; they have emphasized attempts to maintain elements of culture, organization and identity in the face of environmental change. The focus on maintenance rather than development has de-emphasized the role of the environment but, more importantly, it has suggested that any change in culture, organization or identity constitutes a stage in the process which leads inevitably to their loss. An emphasis on the dynamic nature of culture, organization, and identity results in an understanding that the pattern of evolution is contingent upon the environment. Thus the preconditions for persistence are different when the ethnic dimension is central than they are when it is peripheral. In addition, the degree of centrality/peripherality of the ethnic dimension is variable not fixed. Variation occurs as a result of many changes, two of which include the predominant orientation — ethnocentrism, geocentrism — and the magnitude of the perceived threat to the existing distribution of power, privilege and prestige.

Students of ethnic relations can greatly increase the validity of their analyses, and approach the rate of theory development found in other more dynamic fields within the social sciences, by changing their perspective: adopting an open rather than a closed systems approach;

treating the centrality of the ethnic dimension as variable not fixed; and defining the circumstances upon which a given form of culture, organization and identity is contingent, not the conditions promoting and impeding assimilation.

NOTES

1. This perspective is reflected in the following: Ken Adachi, *The Enemy That Never Was,* Toronto: McClelland and Stewart, 1976, Chapters 1-11; Barry Broadfoot, *Years of Sorrow, Years of Shame,* Toronto: Doubleday, 1977; Helen Redi and Charles Young, *The Japanese Canadians,* Toronto: University of Toronto Press, 1939; Forrest LaViolette, *The Canadian Japanese and World War II,* Toronto: University of Toronto Press, 1948.

2. See for example Adachi, *op. cit.,* especially Chapter 7; Canadian Japanese Association, *Survey of the Second Generation of Japanese in British Columbia,* Vancouver: 1935; and Ellen Baar, "Issei, Nisei and Sansei," in Daniel Glenday, Hubert Guindon and Allan Turowetz (eds.), *Modernization and the Canadian State,* Toronto: Macmillan of Canada, 1978, pp. 335-355.

3. The point is probably most extensively developed in James Morton, *In the Sea of Sterile Mountains,* Vancouver: J. J. Douglas, 1974.

4. *Sessional Papers of the House of Commons,* 1902, 54, "On Chinese and Japanese Emigration," p. 331. Also, Adachi, *op. cit.,* 39-40.

5. Baar, *op. cit.,* 340-342; Adachi, *op. cit.,* 42-45. The inability of the Chinese in Canada to get their government to restrict emigration and the effects are discussed in Chuen-Yan Lai, "Chinese Attempts to Discourage Emigration to Canada," *BC Studies,* Summer 1973, vol. 18, 33-49.

6. *Sessional Papers of the House of Commons,* 1908, 74b.

7. Pierre van den Berghe, *Race and Racism,* New York: John Wiley, 1965, pp. 29-33.

8. See for example two papers by Warren Kalbach, "Propensities for Intermarriage in Canada as Reflected in the Ethnic Origins of Native Husbands and their Wives: 1961 and 1971," presented at the Annual Meeting, Canadian Anthropology and Sociology Association, 1974 and "The Reluctant Ethnics: Generational Persistence of Residential Segregation," presented at York University, March 21, 1979.

9. See a variety of works by K. Victor Ujimoto which deal with post-war *issei* including his Ph.D. dissertation "Post-war Japanese Immigrants in Canada: Job Transferability, Work and Social Participation," University of British Columbia, 1973 and "Contrasts in Prewar and Postwar Japanese Community in British Columbia: Conflict and Change," *Canadian Review of Anthropology and Sociology,* v. 13, p. 80-89.

10. Milton Gordon's *Assimilation in American Life,* New York: Oxford University Press, 1964, Ch. 3, has provided a series of "general principles" which analysts of Canadian ethnic relations have used extensively.

11. The systems maintenance perspective developed by Talcott Parsons includes integration among the four pattern variables. Parsons' perspective was widely adopted in the theories of ethnic relations developed during the 1950s and early 1960s.

12. This point is developed most extensively and effectively by Albert Memmi, *The Colonizer and the Colonized,* Boston: Beacon Press, 1965, pp. 149-153.

13. David Easton, *A Framework for Political Analysis,* Englewood Cliffs: Prentice Hall, 1965, p. 93.

14. The approach denies the possibility that individuals will become 150% men, a concept elaborated upon in Malcolm McFee, "The 150% Man, a Product of Blackfeet Acculturation," *American Anthropologist,* vol. 70, 1968, pp. 1096-1103.

15. Adachi, *op. cit.,* p. 114.

16. This position was made most explicit by the Asiatic Exclusion League at the turn of the century and twenty years later by the White British Columbia League.

17. Patricia Roy, "Educating the 'East': British Columbia and the Oriental Question in the Interwar Years," *BC Studies,* Summer 1973, pp. 57-63. Baar, *op. cit.,* 340-343.

18. Baar, *op. cit.,* pp. 347-349.

19. The Supreme Court of Canada and the Judicial Committee of the Privy Council in London England upheld the right of the Canadian Government to require repatriation. See Adachi, *op. cit.,* pp. 311-317. However, the deportation order was repealed in January, 1947. Many believe that repeal occurred in part because of the willingness of Japanese Canadians to abide by the policy of required dispersion.

20. The difference between an equilibrium model and an open systems model is spelled out in David Easton, "Limits of the Equilibrium Model in Social Research," *Behavioral Science,* volume 1, 1956, pp. 96-104.

21. Easton, 1965, *op. cit.* p. 88.

22. *Ibid.,* p. 87.

23. *Ibid.,* p. 81.

24. *Ibid.,* p. 86.

25. *Ibid.,* p. 98.

26. E. K. Francis, *Interethnic Relations,* New York: Elsevier, 1976, p. 181.

27. Adachi, *op. cit.,* p. 365.

28. Howard Perlmutter, "The Tortuous Evolution of the Multinational Corporation," *Columbia Journal of World Business,* Jan.-Feb. 1969, pp. 9-15. This article differentiates among ethnocentric, geocentric and polycentric orientations in his discussion of corporate forms of organization. The polycentric orientation encourages an area form of organization and the establishment of miniature replicas while the geocentric orientation encourages a product form of organization, the creation of rational branches and the creation of a multinational rather than an international form of business organization. The concept of melting pot suggested one way in which a single culture might evolve. The creation of an anational culture through techniques such as those used to select the term Exxon provides another means of achieving the conditions promoted by geocentrism.

29. One of the best discussions of contingency theory as developed by organization theorists is found in Paul Lawrence and Joy Lorsch, *Organization and Environment,* Homewood, Illinois: Irwin, 1969, Chapter VIII. The emphasis in contingency theory is on "the contingent relationship between the internal characteristics of the organization and the demands of its external environment or its task," (p. 206). The approach emphasizes the fact that there is not one best form of organization appropriate for all organizations. Instead, the appropriate structure and orientation is viewed as being contingent upon two factors: the environmental variables and members' predispositions.

30. See Stanford Lyman, "Contrasts in the Community Organization of Chinese and Japanese in North America," *Canadian Review of Anthropology and Sociology,* v. 5, 1968, pp. 51-67.

31. Adachi, *op. cit.,* pp. 117-121.

32. Daphne Marlatt, *Steveston Recollected,* Victoria: Provincial Archives of British Columbia, 1975, pp. 29-37.

33. Tomoko Makabe, "Ethnic Group Identity: Canadian Born Japanese in Metropolitan Toronto," Unpublished Ph.D. dissertation, University of Toronto, 1976, Chapter 5.

34. This function of voluntary associations is discussed in Nicholas Babchuk and John Edwards, "Voluntary Associations and the Integration Hypothesis," *Sociological Inquiry,* v. 35, Spring 1965, p. 265.

35. Makabe, *op. cit.,* p. 188.

36. *Ibid.,* pp. 213-222.

37. This point is effectively made in the introductory essay by Ivan Illich in Ivan Illich, Irving Zola, John McKnight, Johnathan Caplan and Harlan Shaiken, *Disabling Professions,* London: Marron Boyars, 1977. Despite the title of the book, the central focus is on the debilitating effects of the process of professionalization.

38. David Sunahara, "Alberta Japanese Canadian Youth Conference," *Canadian Ethnic Studies,* Vol. 10, 1978, pp. 124-125.

39. During the decade of the seventies, conferences have been made increasingly possible by decisions of both the federal and provincial governments to provide funding. Such funding minimizes the costs incurred by participants thus reducing the degree of commitment required in order to attend. Two conferences enabling interaction among *sansei* were held in Alberta, one in Lethbridge the other in Calgary. Summaries of the proceedings are contained in *Canadian Ethnic Studies*. See: Sunahara, *op. cit.*, and Ann Sunahara, "The Japanese Experience in North America," *Canadian Ethnic Studies*, 1976, vol. 8, pp. 106-108.

40. Francis, *op. cit.*, p. 181.

24

Income Achievement and Adaptive Capacity: An Empirical Comparison of Chinese and Japanese in Canada*

Peter S. Li
Department of Sociology
University of Saskatchewan

With few exceptions (for example, Royal Commission, 1969; Lanphier and Morris, 1974), data on income disparity among ethnic groups in Canada are lacking, especially with respect to Asian groups. Equally rare is a clear theoretical exposition that would account for such ethnic differences (for exceptions, see Johnson, 1977). This paper examines the 1971 income levels of the Chinese and Japanese in Canada, and attempts to empirically test the theoretical validity of some previous claims that offer explanations of ethnic differential achievements. The analysis is based on a one percent random sample

---

* This study is based on Public Use Sample Data derived from the 1971 Canadian Census of Population supplied by Statistics Canada. The responsibility for the use and interpretation of these data is entirely that of the author.

of individual records from the 1971 Census of Canada,[1] excluding those who were under fifteen years of age, and those who were not in the employed labour force.

Income Disparity

The work of Raynauld, Marion and Beland (Royal Commission, 1969: 23) on the 1961 income structure of Quebec male wage-earners indicates that gross income differences existed among fourteen ethnic groups being considered, and that the "Asiatic" ranked eighth from the top. Since the composition of the "Asiatic" is not known, and the data are confined to one province, little can be said of the income achievements of the Asians.

The 1971 census provides a better basis for analyzing the income levels of the Chinese and Japanese. Table 1 gives the average income of twenty-one ethnic groups, measured in deviations above or below the grand mean, and ranked in a descending order. The figures show that the Japanese had an average income of $937.91 above the national mean, second only to those of Jewish origin. In contrast, the average income for the Chinese was $1025.71 below the national mean, and the group ranked nineteenth among the twenty-one ethnic groups. In view of the fact that both groups were historically mistreated in Canada, and that both groups bear a superficial resemblance in their physical appearance, the Chinese and the Japanese provide an interesting case of comparison.

Some Theoretical Considerations

Despite the many divergent approaches to ethnic stratification (Breton, 1979; Li, 1979a), a number of dominant theories prevail in the literature. Traditionally, the question as to why various ethnic groups have differential socio-economic achievements is explained in terms of the cultural adaptability of ethnic minorities in their competition against the dominant group (Wagley and Harris, 1959). This theme has been developed from a number of perspectives, including the various emphases on the cultural, psychological (Rosen, 1956, 1959) and organizational (Light, 1973) aspects of ethnic adaptations to North America. More recently, status attainment models (Blau and Duncan, 1967; Duncan, Featherman and Duncan, 1972) challenge this traditional approach on the basis of structural inequality, which is manifested in differential opportunities (Jencks, 1973) that lead to unequal distribution of individuals' marketable resources. Other re-

TABLE 1

Mean Income of Ethnic Groups in the Employed Labour Force in Canada*

	Ethnic Groups	N	Mean Income ($)**
1.	Jewish	1,318	+3,543.5
2.	Japanese	185	+ 937.9
3.	Austrian	187	+ 744.4
4.	Russian	255	+ 348.0
5.	British Isles	36,809	+ 293.9
6.	Czech	244	+ 104.5
7.	Slovak	91	+ 83.5
8.	Hungarian	597	+ 56.4
9.	Polish	1,377	− 91.5
10.	Italian	2,951	− 163.8
11.	Scandinavian	1,554	− 195.0
12.	German	5,609	− 223.2
13.	Finnish	242	− 233.7
14.	Other and unknown	3,415	− 324.9
15.	Netherlands	1,759	− 383.6
16.	French	20,008	− 423.5
17.	Ukrainian	2,566	− 642.2
18.	Negro	126	− 918.9
19.	Chinese	501	−1,025.7
20.	West Indian	152	−1,535.6
21.	Native Indian	520	−1,868.1
	Canada	80,466	6,004.7

* Fifteen years of age and over, measured in deviations from the national mean, based on a one percent random sample of the 1971 census of Canada.

** Measured in the number of dollars deviating above (+) or below (−) the national mean income of $6,004.70.

search in this area suggests that unequal market conditions exist for different groups which result in discrimination on the basis of some ascribed factors such as ethnic origin (Duncan and Duncan, 1968; Li, 1978, 1979b), and sex (Connelly, 1976, Armstrong and Armstrong, 1978). Despite the challenge, there are few empirical efforts to verify or falsify the traditional theory of cultural adaptability. This is due in part, to the difficulty in isolating the effects of cultural adaptation on economic achievements, which may be measured indirectly by residual income differences attributed to ethnic or racial origins when effects due to other factors are controlled for. Such differences, however, may also be interpreted as results of unequal market conditions.

The case of the Japanese and the Chinese provides an opportunity to test the theory of cultural adaptability. Given that the two groups are racially homogeneous, one may assume relatively similar market conditions for the two groups,[2] other things being equal. Furthermore, the removal of legislative discriminations against the two groups since the end of the Second World War, and their ethnic proximity to employers are grounds to suggest that the Japanese and the Chinese were probably exposed to similar market conditions in 1971.[3] At the very least, one may presume that residual differences attributed to ethnic origins in this case would reflect more cultural differences in adaptation than unequal market opportunities for one of the two groups, as compared to the other.

The adaptive capacity of minority groups, according to Wagley and Harris (1959: 264-273), determines the groups' socio-economic status, and such a capacity is dependent upon the groups' cultural preparedness. Hence the authors argue, the Jews and French-Canadians are economically more successful than the Indians and blacks because of the high adaptability of the former groups.

In somewhat different terminologies, other authors use a similar argument to explain the economic success or failure of certain ethnic groups. Focusing on the groups with low economic status, Lewis (1959, 1966a, 1966b) proposes, for example, a "culture of poverty" to explain their under-achievement. The argument implies, among other things, that the low adaptability of some groups is attributed to their inability to be rid of a culture of deprivation. In a less tautological way, Rosen (1956, 1959) argues that differential ethnic mobility in North America may be explained by the unequal cultural emphases placed by ethnic groups on what he calls an "achievement syndrome."

Aside from the psychological and cultural dimensions of adaptation, there are those who examine the organizational capacity of ethnic minorities in their adjustment to North America. Kallen (1976), for example, suggests that the Jews are able to maintain strong family ties in Canada, along the lines of the *shtetl* of Europe, and the Jewish family provides the basis through which the achievement-orientation of the next generation is nourished. In a study of ethnic enterprise in North America, Light (1973) argues that the Chinese and the Japanese are more successful in their ethnic business than the blacks because of their ability to maintain the traditional credit rotating associations as means of generating capital for investments. Lyman (1968) suggests, on the other hand, that as a result of different old world cultural influences on the ways the groups construct their ethnic communities overseas, the Chinese follow a pluralist-oriented path, while the Japanese follow an integration-oriented path in their adjustment to the North American society.

These theories suggest that the income disparity between the Japanese and the Chinese is attributed, in part at least, to a difference in their adaptive capacity.

There are obviously other sources of income variation. The literature on income inequality, as indicated earlier, suggests that different groups are exposed to unequal market conditions, such that women (see Connelly, 1976; Armstrong and Armstrong, 1978), ethnic minorities (Royal Commission, 1969; Lanphier and Morris, 1974) and younger people (Johnson, 1977) receive a lower income relative to their counterparts. Part of the income gap between the Chinese and Japanese therefore, may be due to differences in the demographic compositions of the two groups, which were bases of discrimination in the labour market.

The literature also suggests that income is determined by the individuals' marginal productivity to employers, thus workers with more marketable resources are rewarded more (Mincer, 1970).[4] More recently, status attainment models recognize the importance of individuals' marketable resources, especially educational qualification, in the process of stratification (Blau and Duncan, 1967; Jencks, 1973). These resources, however, are interpreted as largely results of previous structural inequality, and not necessarily individuals' human capital investments, as implied in the theory of marginal productivity. Aside from these sources of income variations, the occupational sectors also reward individuals on an unequal basis, over and above differences in educational and other qualifications (see for example, Averitt, 1968; Johnson, 1977).

A Test Model

A multivariate model was developed to test the empirical basis for the theory of cultural adaptation as applied to the case of the Japanese and the Chinese. The income differences between the two groups is seen as resulting from a number of sources, including a difference in cultural adaptation which was measured by residual income differences attributed to the ethnic origins, when variations in other factors were adjusted for. The presence of such a residual difference would provide an empirical basis for claiming a differential adaptive capacity.

The data used in this analysis were based on the individual records of a one percent random sample of the 1971 census. The working sample included those of Chinese and Japanese origins, fifteen years of age and over, who were in the employed labour force of Canada in 1971.[5]

Individuals' total income in the 1971 census[6] was treated as the dependent variable. The independent variables were ethnic origin (Chinese, Japanese), nativity (foreign-born, native-born), sex (female, male), age (interval scale), education (12 categories, ordinal scale), occupation (5 categories, nominal scale) and the number of weeks worked during 1970 (6 categories, ordinal scale). Nativity, sex and age were used to measure the effects of unequal market conditions attributed to these factors. Educational level was treated as a measure of individuals' marketable credentials, and occupation, a crude indicator of industrial sectors. The number of weeks worked during 1970 was used to measure different levels of productivity to employers.

Applying Multiple Classification Analysis (Andrews, et al., 1967) to the data, the gross income difference between the Japanese and the Chinese was analyzed in deviations from the grand mean of the two groups. The other independent variables, measuring the various sources of income variations, were then entered into the regression in a sequential fashion to see how much of the original income difference was attributed to differences in background variables, educational level, and job characteristics. The residual income differences associated with the two ethnic origins, then may be interpreted as attributable to a difference in cultural adaptation.

Findings

Before analyzing the effects of background variables, educational level, and job characteristics on the income levels of the Chinese and the Japanese, it is instructive to examine how the two groups were different along these demographic and socio-economic dimensions. Table 2 provides a summary comparison of the Chinese and the Japanese in the 1971 employed labour force.

The statistics show that there were differences between the two groups. For example, about 75% of the Chinese consisted of postwar immigrants, as compared to 76% of the Japanese who were Canadian-born. A large proportion (28%) of the Chinese were recent immigrants who immigrated to Canada between 1967 and 1971. In contrast, all the postwar immigrants among the Japanese constituted only 17% of the group.

Although there was a slight difference in the distributions of sex between the two groups, greater variations were found in the age structures. The Chinese seemed to be younger in the average age than the Japanese; more than half of the Chinese were under 35 years of age. Furthermore, 20% of the Japanese were between 45-54, as compared to 10% of the Chinese in the same group.

In terms of educational differences, the Chinese had a lower average education than the Japanese, despite an almost identical proportion of those with university educations in both groups. Thirty-six percent of the Japanese, as compared to 23% of the Chinese, completed grades twelve to thirteen. Conversely, 42% of the Chinese, and 36% of the

TABLE 2

Selected Demographic and Socio-Economic Characteristics For Chinese and Japanese in the Employed Labour Force of Canada.†

	Chinese	Japanese	X^2	Gamma
	%	%		
Period of Immigration				
1967-71	27.9	9.2		
1956-66	26.1	7.0		
1946-55	20.6	1.1	199.78*	.71
Before 1946	5.4	6.5		
Canadian born	20.0	76.2		
Sex				
Female	38.5	36.2		
Male	61.5	63.8	.31	.05
Age				
15-24	24.6	21.6		
25-34	26.3	21.1		
35-44	27.7	27.6	13.86*	.12
45-54	10.0	19.5		
55-64	8.6	5.9		
65 and over	2.8	4.3		
Education				
No schooling	8.2	1.1		
Below grade 12	41.5	35.7		
Grades 12-13	23.4	36.2	20.41*	.17
Some university	11.8	11.4		
Completed university or more	15.2	15.7		

Occupation

Professional & Managerial	19.0	19.5		
Clerical & Sales	21.8	27.6		
Skilled & semi-skilled manual**	12.6	18.4	20.99*	.07
Service	27.9	11.9		
Other & not stated	18.8	22.7		

Weeks Worked During 1970

Did not work during 1970	5.0	1.6		
1-13 weeks	6.6	4.3		
14-26 weeks	9.0	8.1		
27-39 weeks	9.2	10.8	7.27	.14
40-48 weeks	16.6	14.1		
49-52 weeks	53.7	61.1		

Total	100.0	100.0		
N =	501	185		

† Fifteen years of age and over, based on one percent random sample of
the 1971 census of Canada.
* $p \leq .05$
** Includes occupations in processing, machining and product fabrication,
assembling and repairing, construction trades, and transport equipment
operating.

Japanese had an education below grade twelve. The Chinese also had
a higher percentage (8%) with no schooling than the Japanese (1%).

With the exception of professional and managerial occupations, there
were clear differences between the two groups in the occupational
categories. Twenty-eight percent of the Japanese were in clerical and
sales occupations, as compared to 22% of the Chinese in the same
occupational group. A higher proportion of the Japanese (18%) were
in the skilled and semi-skilled occupations than the Chinese (13%).
In contrast, the Chinese in service occupations were more than double
that of the Japanese (12%).

There was a small difference between the two groups with respect to
the average number of weeks worked during 1970. A larger proportion
of the Japanese (75%) were employed for 40 weeks or more in 1970
than the Chinese (70%).

Differences in these demographic and socio-economic variables then,
tended to confound the cultural effects of ethnic origins on the income
levels. Table 3 presents the results of the multivariate analyses in which
these effects were statistically controlled for.

Column 2 of Table 3 shows a statistically significant gross income disparity of $1,963.6 between the Japanese and Chinese, before differences in other variables were adjusted for. When nativity, sex and age were introduced to the regression, there was a reduction in the income gap between the groups, suggesting that part of the original differences was attributed to these background variables. As predicted earlier, the coefficients for nativity and sex indicate that the native-born and the male Asians received a higher income than their counterparts. The coefficient for age also suggests that age had a positive effect on income; the younger the age, the less the income.

Adding the variable of education to the equation substantially reduced the income difference from $1,237.9 (column 3, $333.8 + $904.1) to $635.1 (column 4, $171.3 + $463.8), indicating the importance of education to income achievements. The subsequent income gap between the Japanese and the Chinese, however, was no longer statistically significant.

When the variables of occupation and weeks worked were added to the equation (column 5), the income difference between the Japanese and the Chinese was further reduced and remained statistically insignificant. This suggests that the original income disparity associated with the two ethnic groups was accounted for by other variables in the equation, and the relationship between income and ethnic origin was a spurious one. This finding required dropping the variable of ethnic origin in the equation to estimate the correct coefficients for the other variables. Column 6 shows that deleting ethnic origin in the equation basically did not affect the size of the coefficients for other variables. The proportion of variance explained was changed minimally from 34% to 33%, as indicated in the values of R^2 in the two regressions.

Column 6 further shows that relative income advantages for native-born and the male Asians persisted, despite adjusting for the effects of educational attainment and job characteristics. Both age and education have a positive net effect on income; a unit increase in age and in education produced respectively an increase of $70.6 and $219.1 in income. As to be expected, those in the professional and managerial occupations had a net income advantage over the average income earner ($2,855.4 above the average), as compared to those in the service occupations with a net income disadvantage of $1,489. below the average. Those in the white-collar (clerical and sales) and blue-collar (skilled and semi-skilled) occupations had an income slightly below and above the mean income respectively, over and above controlling for other differences. The last set of coefficients indicate that as the number of weeks worked during 1970 increased, so did the income level.

TABLE 3

*Effects of Background Variables, Educational Attainment, and Job Characteristics For Chinese and Japanese in the Employment Labour Force of Canada***

BACKGROUND VARIABLES	N		INCOME			
	(1)	(2)	(3)	(4)	(5)	(6)
Ethnic origin						
Chinese	501	− 529.5	− 333.8	− 171.3	− 169.7	—
Japanese	185	1434.1	904.1	463.8	459.6	—
Nativity						
Foreign-born	445		− 297.6	− 462.2	− 323.6	− 433.8
Native-born	241	—	549.6	853.5	597.4	801.0
Sex						
Female	260		− 2082.3	− 1847.2	− 1851.6	− 1854.4
Male	426	—	1270.9	1127.4	1130.1	1131.7
Age	686	—	68.5	107.5	67.0	70.6
EDUCATIONAL ATTAINMENT						
Level of Education	686	—	—	521.6	203.1	219.1

JOB CHARACTERISTICS

	N	(1)	(2)	(3)	(4)	(5)
Occupation						
Professional & Managerial	131				2893.4	2855.4
Clerical & Sales	160				— 85.8	— 68.6
Skilled & Semi-skilled manual	97				39.7	98.4
Service	162				—1471.4	—1489.0
Other & not stated	136			—	— 961.8	— 966.5
Weeks Worked during 1970						
Did not work in 1970	28				—4171.0	—4192.3
1-13 weeks	41				—3297.0	—3343.3
14-26 weeks	60				—2467.7	—2456.1
27-39 weeks	66				— 530.5	— 487.3
40-48 weeks	109				869.3	837.9
49-52 weeks	382			—	890.7	897.0
GRAND MEAN	686	5508.6	5508.6	5508.6	5508.6	5508.6
R^2		.03	.14	.20	.34	.33

SIGNIFICANCE OF MAIN EFFECTS

	F-Ratio				
Ethnic origin	16.7*	5.3*	1.5	1.7	—
Nativity	—	2.9	7.4*	4.1*	10.2*
Sex	—	65.6*	55.0*	60.9*	61.0*
Age	—	20.4*	48.3*	20.6*	23.6*
Level of Education	—	—	57.2*	6.8*	8.1*
Occupation	—	—	—	12.5*	12.4*
Weeks worked during 1970	—	—	—	14.5*	14.6*

* ≤ .05

** Fifteen years of age and over, based on a one percent random sample of the 1971 Census of Canada.

In summary, the model shows that the gross income disparity between the Japanese and the Chinese in 1971 was due to differences in other variables, such that when variations in the background variables, in educational attainment and in job characteristics were adjusted for, there was no significant income difference between the two groups.

Concluding Remarks

Traditionally, differences in economic achievements of ethnic minorities are explained as differential cultural adaptability. This study fails to provide empirical support for such a thesis. No direct effect of cultural adaptability on income achievements was established, when cultural adaptation was measured indirectly by residual income difference associated with the ethnic origins of Chinese and Japanese, after adjusting for differences in other variables. Variations in income between the two groups were accounted for by a number of variables, including nativity, age, sex, education, occupation, and frequency of employment (weeks worked).

One may argue that cultural adaptation may have an indirect influence on income achievements via other factors so that variations in the demographic structures, educational level and occupational achievement may in fact be consequences of previous adaptation. There are strong theoretical grounds and empirical evidence to suspect, however, that this way of reasoning is contrary to the historical experiences of the Chinese and the Japanese in Canada.

The historical facts show, for example, that prior to the end of the Second World War, the Chinese were subjected to a discriminatory immigration system which sought to exclude them (see Li, 1979a). One of the consequences of such exclusion was to produce a highly unbalanced sex ratio among the Chinese, even long after the legislative control was removed in 1947. This largely delayed the birth of a second generation which did not begin to emerge in sizable numbers until the sixties (Li, 1979d). In contrast, the immigration system permitted the Japanese to bring their wives as early as 1908 (see Adachi, 1976), and this resulted in a much more balanced sex ratio among the Japanese community as compared to the Chinese (Li, 1979d, Table 3). Furthermore, the experience of relocation and subsequent repatriation of the Japanese in Canada resulted in a large drop in population among the Japanese in Canada (Adachi, 1976). The small volume of Japanese immigration to Canada in the postwar years greatly altered the demographic and social characteristics of the Japanese community (Ujimoto, 1976). These historical factors, and not cultural adaptability, are important in understanding the present demographic structures of the Chinese and the Japanese in Canada.

Historically too, the Japanese and the Chinese entered different occupations in Canada, in part because of different opportunities available to the two groups. The heavy concentration of the Chinese in the service industry as laundrymen and restaurant workers, for example, was largely a result of restricted opportunities in the non-ethnic sector (Li, 1979a). The damage to the Japanese ethnic business during the relocation of the Second World War (see Adachi, 1976) probably resulted in many Japanese having to seek employment in other sectors after the war. These historical experiences must be considered in explaining the differences of the two groups in the occupational structure of today.

What is understood as the adaptive capacity of minority groups then, may be no more than different responses under various constrained situations. Ethnic differences in economic achievements in many cases are probably more related to unequal opportunity structures to which these groups are subjected, than to the adaptive capacity of their old world cultures.

NOTES

1. Census of Canada, 1971. Public Use Sample Tape, Individual File.

2. I am not suggesting the presence or absence of discrimination against the Chinese and the Japanese in the Canadian labour market, but rather, a similar market condition for both groups in 1971 because of their racial proximity to employers. Historically, of course, both groups were subjected to rather different conditions.

3. There is evidence to suggest an emergence of prejudice against the East Indians in recent years (see Pitman, 1977; Henry, 1978). Some Canadian regional data also show that the Chinese are perceived more favourably than the East Indians (Li, 1979c). These findings would suggest the likelihood of unequal market conditions for the East Indians, as compared to other Asians in Canada.

4. There is a striking similarity between this argument and that proposed in the functional theory of stratification (Davis and Moore, 1945).

5. The employed labour force is operationally defined by Statistics Canada to include those who: 1) worked for pay or profit in the Armed Forces; 2) worked for pay or profit in the Civilian sector; 3) worked for unpaid family work; 4) with a job but not at work in the Armed Forces; and 5) with a job but not at work in the Civilian sector.

6. This refers to the total income received during 1970. For details, see 1971 Census of Canada, Public Use Sample Tapes, User Documentation, page 4-2-47.

REFERENCES

Adachi, Ken.
  1976. *The Enemy That Never Was: A History of the Japanese Canadians.* Toronto: McClelland and Stewart.

Andrews, F. M., J. N. Morgan, and J. A. Sonquist.
  1976. *Multiple Classification Analysis.* Ann Arbor, Michigan: Survey Research Center, University of Michigan.

Armstrong, Pat and Hugh Armstrong.
  1978. *The Double Ghetto: Canadian Women and their Segregated Work.* Toronto, Ontario: McClelland and Stewart.

Averitt, Robert T.
  1968. *The Dual Economy: The Dynamics of American Industrial Structure.* New York: W. W. Norton and Company.

Blau, Peter M. and Otis Dudley Duncan.
  1967. *The American Occupational Structure.* New York: John Wiley and Sons.

Breton, Raymond.
  1979. "Ethnic Stratification Viewed From Three Theoretical Perspectives." Pp. 270-294 in James E. Curtis and William G. Scott (eds.) *Social Stratification: Canada.*

Connelly, M. P.
  1976. *Canadian Women as a Reserve Army of Labour.* Ph.D. dissertation, Ontario Institute for Studies in Education, University of Toronto.

Davis, Kingsley and Wilbert E. Moore.
  1945. "Some Principles of Stratification." Pp. 64-71 in Joseph Lopreato and Lionel S. Lewis (eds.) *Social Stratification: A Reader.* New York: Harper and Row.

Duncan, Beverly, and Otis D. Duncan.
  1968. "Minorities and the Process of Stratification." *American Sociological Review* 33: 356-64.

Duncan, Otis D., David L. Featherman, and Beverly Duncan.
  1972. *Socioeconomic Background and Achievement.* New York: Seminar Press.

Henry, Frances.
  1978. *The Dynamics of Racism in Toronto.* Research Report, Department of Anthropology, York University.

Jencks, Christopher.
  1973. *Inequality: A Reassessment of the Effect of Family and Schooling in America.* New York: Harper and Row.

Johnson, Leo A.
1977. *Poverty in Wealth: The Capitalist Labour Market and Income Distribution in Canada.* Toronto: New Hogtown Press.

Kallen, Evelyn.
1976. "Family Life Styles and Jewish Culture." Pp. 145-161 in K. Ishwaran (ed.) *The Canadian Family.* Toronto: Holt, Rinehart and Winston of Canada.

Lanphier, C. M. and R. N. Morris.
1974. "Structural Aspects of Differences in Income Between Anglophones and Francophones." *Canadian Review of Sociology and Anthropology* 11: 53-66.

Lewis, Oscar.
1959. *Five Families: Mexican Case Studies in the Culture of Poverty.* New York: Basic Books.
1966a. *La Vida: A Puerto Rican Family in the Culture of Poverty — San Juan and New York.* New York: Random House.
1966b. "The Culture of Poverty." *The Scientific American* 215: 19-25.

Li, Peter S.
1978. "The Stratification of Ethnic Immigrants: The Case of Toronto." *Canadian Review of Sociology and Anthropology* 15: 31-40.
1979a. "An Historical Approach to Ethnic Stratification: The Case of Chinese in Canada, 1858-1930." *Canadian Review of Sociology and Anthropology* 16 (forthcoming).
1979b. "Ethnic Stratification in Toronto: a Reply to Richmond". *Canadian Review to Sociology and Anthropology* 16, (forthcoming).
1979c. "Prejudice Against Asians in a Canadian City." Paper presented at the annual meeting of the Canadian Asian Studies Association, May 25-27, Saskatoon, Saskatchewan.
1979d. "The Chinese Family in Canada, 1885-1971." Paper presented at the annual meeting of the *Pacific Sociological Association,* April 4-7, Anaheim, California.

Light, Ivan H.
1973. *Ethnic Enterprise in America: Business and Welfare Among Chinese, Japanese, and Blacks.* Berkeley and Los Angeles, California: University of California Press.

Lyman, Stanford M.
1968. "Contrasts in the Community Organization of Chinese and Japanese in North America." *Canadian Review of Sociology and Anthropology* 5: 55-67.

Mincer, Jacob.
1970. "The Distribution of Labour Incomes: A Survey With a Special Reference to the Human Capital Approach." *Journal of Economic Literature* 8: 1-26.

Pitman, Walter.
1977. *Now is Not Too Late.* Toronto: Task Force on Human Relations.

Rosen, Bernard C.
1956. "The Achievement Syndrome: A Psychocultural Dimension of Social Stratification" *American Sociological Review* 21: 203-211.
1959. "Race, Ethnicity and the Achievement Syndrome." *American Sociological Review* 24: 47-60.

Royal Commission.
1969. *Report of the Royal Commission on Bilingualism and Biculturalism,* Book IIIa.

Ujimoto, K. Victor.
1976. "Contrasts in the Prewar and Postwar Japanese Community in British Columbia: Conflict and Change." *Canadian Review of Sociology and Anthropology* 13: 80-89.

Wagley, Charles and Marvin Harris.
1959. *Minorities in The New World.* New York: Columbia University Press.

25

Some Issues Regarding Ethnic Relations Research

Gordon Hirabayashi and P. A. Saram
University of Alberta

> *Everybody knows that we like those who re-semble us, those who think and feel as we do. But the opposite is no less true. It very often happens that we feel kindly towards those who do not resemble us, precisely because of this lack of resemblance.*
>
> *Durkheim (1964:54)*

The purpose of this paper is to discuss some issues regarding ethnic relations research and to draw several implications for social science and social policy.[1] The main focus of the discussion will be on a single conceptual category, namely, the definitional component of ethnicity emphasizing a connotation of culture. Following Weber's writings it is suggested that the definitional scope should give greater weight to the political dimension of ethnicity. Though not providing conclusive answers as such, the paper attempts to highlight the implications of such an emphasis for theory, methodology and social policy.

ETHNICITY: A CONCEPTUAL OVERVIEW

Although terms such as, or similar to, ethnicity have come into popular usage in recent times, the conceptual status of such terms has been of continuing interest in the sociological tradition.[2] For example, there have been references to "ethnical" societies as genetic aggregations held together by real or fictitious bonds of blood relationship and a "consciousness of kind"[3] such as in horde, tribe and folk, or ethnic nation (Giddings, 1911: 157-58, 170); "ethnic" as a collective physical type (Durkheim, 1964: 133-34); and "ethnic group" as an aggregation of kinship units claiming their descent either from a common ancestor or ancestors belonging to the same group and whose distinctive social standing in a wider system is symbolized according to biological criteria or a special cultural tradition (Parsons, 1951: 172).

More contemporary writings, especially in North America, portray ethnicity almost essentially in cultural terms (for example, van den Berghe, 1967: 9). A theoretically useful, culturally weighted definition of ethnicity based on a complex set of considerations has been proposed by Isajiw (1974). Several authors have also challenged the usefulness of the concept itself, some implying that it is either a camouflaged (or respectable) label for race or social class, or that ethnic pluralism is in fact an effective ideological counter-current to class consciousness.[4] These concerns notwithstanding, there remains little doubt as to the growing interest in the subject of ethnicity, although what it constitutes and therefore what implications it has for society are not all that clear (Isaacs, 1975).

Canadian writings on ethnicity have traditionally attempted to portray the Canadian social scenario as a "mosaic" in some preference to what has been termed as the American "melting pot." The alleged peculiarities of these two models have been challenged in such well known works as Porter's elaboration of Canadian society as a "vertical mosaic" (1965) and Clement's analysis of ethnic homogeneity in the upper echelons of Canadian society (1975). Similarly writers such as Kennedy have attempted to interpret the American "melting pot" analogy in terms of social mobility, or a homogeneous nation of heterogeneous identities and traditions (1964: 63, 67). More recently Isaacs has argued that an American is an American only as an individual, whereas in terms of basic group identities he or she would belong to distinctive collectivities made up of physical characteristics, names and language, history and origins, religion and nationality (1975: 213-15).

From the standpoint of Canadian ethnic and cultural policy, there seems to be considerable ambiguity as well (Berry, et al., 1977: 3-14). For example, does the term "ethnic" refer to social identity, non-charter groups, origin, or culture? Does the term "culture" refer to aspects of identity, cultural folkways, entertainment and leisure pursuits, or to a fundamental way of thought and life style? Does "multiculturalism" refer to the non-discriminatory accommodation and appreciation of groups despite their diverse identities and cultural backgrounds, or to the importation and active promotion of a diversity of cultures?

If public utterances are some reflections of public opinion, it appears that "ethnic" refers to non-charter groups, namely, native, other immigrant and marginal groups; "culture" refers mainly to those aspects that can be shared, or appreciated hopefully along inter-cultural lines; and "multi-culturalism" refers to a non-discriminatory accommodation and inter-cultural appreciation of groups belonging to diverse ethnic and cultural backgrounds.[5] In this context it is worth noting Read's polemical and politically instructive essay that challenged the uncritical romanticism of finding virtue in every aspect of each and every culture; at least from a humanistic viewpoint, some values he has argued to be more acceptable than others (1941).

WEBER'S CONTRIBUTION

An elaborate analysis of the concept of ethnicity, a contribution not entirely overlooked by contemporary writers including Isajiw (1974), has been offered by the sociologist Max Weber (1968: 302-7, 385-98, 901-40). According to Weber, the distribution of power within a "political community" is organized around the economic variable of "classes," the social honor variable of "status groups" and the social power variable of "parties." Status groups are characterized by specific life styles, especially in the consumption of goods, and maintain their "honor" through varying degrees of social exclusiveness. When the underlying differences between status groups are perceived to be "ethnic" (described below), these groups could become more closed and may develop into "castes." If this development occurs, the respective honor positions of groups become "hierarchical," living becomes "segregational," and the social roles of groups become "politically functional." This sequence, however, is preventable at least in modern societies through status groups acquiring higher "class" positions and perhaps "party" positions as well.

"Conspicuous differences" in physical appearance or life style can give rise to repulsion between groups and a consciousness of kind within groups. These visible differences, however unimportant, serve as indicators of social honor in respective status groups. Almost any kind of conspicuous physical appearance and custom can induce the "belief" in the affinity or disaffinity regarding groups. Sentiments of common "political experience" such as colonization or migration also help to strengthen such beliefs. "Ethnic groups" are human aggregates subscribing to a subjective belief in common descent because of similarities in physical appearance, custom, or both, or because of memories of colonization or migration. Unlike kinship groups, ethnic groups are based on "presumed" identity and also do not constitute actual groups as such, oriented to concrete courses of social conduct. Nevertheless, ethnic groups can facilitate such group formation especially in the political sphere.

In addition to conspicuous characteristics and common political experience, common "language" and "religion" also contribute to the development of ethnicity. Since ethnic differentiation is based primarily on seemingly unimportant yet conspicuous differences, "physical appearance" and the "style of conduct of everyday life" are the crucial indicators of status honor. Repulsion toward certain ethnic traits is not merely symbolic but could also be based on more compelling circumstances. Generally, racial differences by themselves are not particularly conducive to the development of ethnic antipathies. Regardless of the particular features that may have contributed to the formation of specific ethnic identities, it is toward some notion of a "political community," past, present, or future, along with its distributive system of power allocation, that the belief in ethnic identity seems to be oriented. If indeed these aggregates are only "nationalities," or "people" (such as the French Canadians) manifesting what might essentially be politically relevant orientations of whatever nature, the term "ethnic" would have to be abandoned, being unsuitable for rigorous analysis. This in summary is a description of Weber's analysis of ethnic groups.

ETHNICITY: A POLITICAL EMPHASIS

In the context of Weber's writings and using some of his terminology it is possible to attempt a nominal definition of ethnic group. An *ethnic group* is an aggregate of people residing within a wider *political community* and who subscribe to a *common consciousness of identity* regarding their *ancestry,* and perhaps some aspects of *political experience* and *culture,* and segments of whose membership are, or could potentially be, oriented to moving from a *class* and *status group* position to one of *party* as well.

This definition does not recognize that cultural factors are the most important, or that ethnic groups must necessarily adhere to all or any of their cultural-ways beyond that of the consciousness of identity.

Rather, the main thrust of the definition beyond that of identity is that these groups are, or could potentially be oriented to obtaining a better "party" position as to influence the course of political decision-making. These decisions, incidentally, may have to do with such matters as human rights, equality of opportunity, precisely not to be treated as different, redressing old injustices or simply the right to be left alone, rather than matters of cultural development alone. To be sure, culturally based organizations enhance solidarity as they also provide a forum for the exercise of political pressure. Despite the cultural emphasis of Isajiw's discussions of ethnicity, for example, some of the key issues he raises are unmistakably of a political nature (1974: 122; 1975: 83). The general implications drawn by Isaacs are also predominantly political (1975: 217-18).

In North America, ethnic consciousness was also a political consciousness and it led to equal rights and sometimes special rights being bestowed on certain groups. Policies such as positive discrimination and affirmative action are now being challenged by a white ethnic consciousness wanting to redress what it terms as reverse discrimination. All this should not convey the impression that ethnicity is merely a political fact or some kind of political gamesmanship. To be sure, ethnic sentiments provide for group cohesion, pride in one's ancestry, the psychological health of individuals and varieties of partial integration in the wider system. As noted by Parsons, ethnic groups have social "functions" as well, providing a focus of security outside of the family unit to its membership and providing for outsiders an important scapegoat function as targets for displaced aggression (1951: 188). All these and more notwithstanding it cannot be denied that ethnic groups are nationalities living within wider political communities such as nation, nation-state and the like. In states such as Canada, if all groups with the exception of only the charter groups are considered "ethnic", the relationship between these ethnics and the political community surely cannot be underestimated. Isajiw's comment on "centre-periphery" seems precisely to refer to this relationship (1975: 83). A study inquiring into children's views of themselves and of foreign peoples found that national references were not important features of the self-conceptions of English-Canadian and French-Canadian children (Lambert and Klineberg, 1967: 44, 53). Conversely, such references are probably important even to "ethnic" adults as well.

IMPLICATIONS

The *theoretical* implications of a politically weighted definition of ethnicity could be suggested as follows. First, it could help in the construction of ethnic group typologies. For example, it will be possible to view the historical evolution of such types as aboriginal groups, charter groups, guest-peoples, caste groups, status groups and competitive groups. Second, from the stratification perspective of class, status group, and party it is possible to relate the experiences of these diverse groups to one another and to the ideological commitments of the political community. Third, a politically weighted definition would also be helpful toward explaining contemporary trends in ethnicity, ethnic consciousness, cultural cohesion and the dynamics of inter-group relations in Canadian society.

The *methodological* implications of such an approach are equally important. It would provide an additional perspective to that which highlights cultural factors alone. One of the drawbacks of an exclusively cultural perspective is that it portrays ethnic groups purely as "cultural minorities."[6] This could give rise to what might be termed as the "victimological bias" in ethnic relations research, where research inquiry is directed toward learning more of the same about a particular ethnic group which may be perceived at a given time as being "problematic."[7] Such an approach does little or no justice to the subject of ethnic "relations" or to the dynamics of accommodation-adaptation. One learns nothing about the ideological matrices of "host" communities, the kinds of contexts conducive to inter-group tensions and hostilities, or the nature and characteristics of a minority of individuals who actually engage in such hostilities.[8] The ideological matrices of "host" communities are, for example, especially important, for these must surely determine the cognitive guidelines for inter-group relations on the part of individuals. If, as Woods asserts, a hierarchical system of ascribed statuses has been a characteristic feature of the Canadian political tradition in the past (1976: 80-86), the current status of that ideology and how it permeates through society is deserving of some attention.

Second, the cultural bias has perhaps given rise to research questions of the "whom do you hate the most" variety. Such queries fail to tap the factors including the lack of any factors underlying the preferences people make regarding other groups.[9] Purely fictitious groups listed in some questionnaire studies have been rated by respondents as being the most hateworthy. Similarly, as noted by Banton, certain kinds of well intended research conducted in the hope of bringing about inter-group harmony, have provided exactly the opposite result including the subsequent reluctance on the part of authorities to act against what they consider to be mounting public opinion (1970: 17).

Third, from a methodological standpoint, an exclusively cultural approach tends to uncritically adopt the classic prejudice-discrimination-hostility sequence. In other words, prejudice as the primary problem is attributed to ignorance of other cultures. This condition alone may be presumed to lead to discrimination and hostility. On the contrary, prejudice need not necessarily lead to avoidance, discrimination (denial of equal opportunity in employment, housing and services), or hostility (abuse and injury), just as these behavioural manifestations need not necessarily be related to prejudice alone. It is possible that hostility is an indication of the breakdown of discriminatory barriers, just as those who engage in hostility may do so for a variety of reasons including no reason as such, or because other forms of conduct such as discrimination are not within their resources.

Finally, there is the question of how conditions of ethnic tension or hostility might be ascertained. The current practice seems to be confined mostly to journalistic methodologies. To what extent are "incidents" and statements of dislike of others indicative of tension? What kinds of incidents of what frequency committed by how many people belonging to what kinds of socio-economic characteristics constitute tension and hostility? As observed by Berry, et al., their respondents reject explicit ethnic prejudice, racism and bigotry, although the same respondents have varying degrees of like-dislike toward other groups; most types of immigrants were found to be acceptable; those types rated as unacceptable do not belong to specific ethnic or racial categories; and colored immigrants were found to be acceptable (1977: 236, 239, 245). Studies of this nature demonstrate, among other merits, that ethnic relations constitute a far more complex phenomenon than is commonly believed.

The *policy* implications of an emphasis such as suggested in this paper could be described as follows. First, such a perspective de-emphasizes ethnic groups as cultural or culturally-handicapped minorities. It is important that their concerns not be perceived as formally of the same variety of those espousing deviant or counter-cultural causes for social recognition. The preferred emphasis might take the form of equal rights rather than special cultural rights as such. Second, an emphasis of the suggested variety might contribute toward greater social integration (not to be confused with assimilation) and perhaps "party" mobility in Weber's sense. A purely cultural emphasis tends to enhance social isolation rather than promoting inter-culturalism. Also, it could encourage among minorities, a philosophy of "the right to be disliked." Third, with a de-emphasized cultural perspective, ethnic groups are less likely to be perceived as cultural out-groups engaging in varieties of non-criminal deviance and thereby threatening what is vaguely known as the quality of life. Fourth, it could also minimize acts of abuse and injury directed at culturally visible groups. Several of these suggestions do not require the deployment of vast resources or the commitment of large research funds. A mere re-orientation of emphasis, if considered worthwhile, could be brought about through the present efforts of existing resources and the support of ethnic elites.

Fifth, from a legal point of view it would seem reasonable that hostility (abuse and injury) and discrimination be perceived as violations of the law, rather than conduct based on ignorance of other cultures. Like the school system, the family, peer groups and the mass media, the law also is one of the most effective agents of public education. Under a purely cultural definition of ethnicity there could arise a mystification of intent regarding acts of injury, on such grounds as cultural ignorance, culture-shock and misunderstandings regarding the victim. Surely, injury to others attributed to ignorance of their culture can no longer be placed in the same category as criminal acts committed under conditions of insanity and the like.[10] Similarly, the "right to dislike" a group (it is neither practicable, nor consistent with human rights, to be compelled to love everybody) should not be logically extendable to include the right to discriminate, or the right to generate hostility toward individuals, even if there are "objectively" valid grounds for dislike of the group in question.

In conclusion it is necessary to assert that the ideas presented in this essay in no way imply that ethnic groups should not be conscious of, adhere to, or develop and promote their cultures. The essay has attempted to convey two basic points. One is that ethnicity also includes an important political dimension and that this often tends to be submerged by the weight of exclusively cultural considerations. The second theme is that the added complement of the political dimension could have significant implications for both social science and social policy.

NOTES

1. This is a revised version of a paper presented at the session on Asian Canadians, Canadian Society for Asian Studies Meetings, Guelph, Ontario, 26 May 1978.

2. This is not a review of the literature on ethnicity. There are several excellent reviews of this literature and such an endeavour is outside the scope of this paper.

3. In one of his descriptions of "consciousness of kind" Giddings states that it involves a mutual toleration and alliance among unlike individuals, an alliance among like groups, and a non-toleration of unlike groups (1911: 170).

4. For a brief summary of some of these concerns see, for example, Berry, et. al. (1977: 5-14). That the layman often uses the term "race" to describe cultural groups is well known. Media research on ethnic tension and hostilities are also often reported as "racial" incidents. According to some writers, proponents of such doctrines as apartheid present their doctrines as policies of cultural pluralism rather than those of racial discrimination (van den Berghe 1967: 9; Banton, 1970: 29).

5. See Berry, et. al. (1977: 1-15); see also, for example, *Alberta Hansard* (1978: 1055-57).

6. For a discussion of ambiguities in the conceptual use of the term "minority", see Abu-Laban and Abu-Laban (1977).

7. The progress made by native ethnic groups, for example, is disproportionate to the amount of studies done of them.

8. See, for example, Banton (1967) van den Berghe (1967), Rex (1970) and the now-forgotten pioneering essay by Merton (1976: 189-216). Merton's essay is also instructive on varieties of discrimination and modes of "treatment."

9. For another pioneering discussion of facts and fictions in questionnaires and opinionnaires, see Merton (1976: 251-69).

10. Responding to a guilty plea by a youth charged recently with racially motivated assault on another youth, the judge stated that "normally I would have levied a fine or put you on probation immediately for a common assault. However, in view of the fact that there are some racial overtones, I will put this over until ... for thought on sentencing."

BIBLIOGRAPHY

Abu-Laban, Sharon W. and Baha Abu-Laban.
1977. "Women and the Aged as Minority Groups," *Canadian Review of Sociology and Anthropology,* 14/1, 103-16.

Alberta Hansard
1978.

Banton, Michael.
1967. *Race Relations,* London: Tavistock.
1970. "The Concept of Racism," in Sami Zubaida (ed.), *Race and Racialism,* London: Tavistock, 17-34.

Berry, John W. *et. al.*
1977. *Multiculturalism and Ethnic Attitudes in Canada,* Ottawa: Supply and Services Canada.

Clement, Wallace.
1975. *The Canadian Corporate Elite,* Toronto: McClelland & Stewart.

Durkheim, Emile.
1964. The Division of Labor in Society, (George Simpson, *trans.*) New York: Free Press.

Giddings, Franklin H.
1911. *The Principles of Sociology,* London: Macmillan.

Isaacs, Harold R.
1975. *Idols of the Tribe,* New York: Harper & Row.

Isajiw, Wsevolod W.
1974. "Definitions of Ethnicity," *Ethnicity,* 1, 111-24.
1975. "Olga in Wonderland: Ethnicity in Technological Society," Presidential Address, Third Biennial Conference of Canadian Ethnic Studies Association, Winnipeg, October, pp. 77-85.

Kennedy, John F.
1964. *A Nation of Immigrants,* New York: Harper & Row.

Lambert, Wallace E. and Otto Klineberg.
1967. *Children's Views of Foreign Peoples,* New York: Appleton-Century-Crofts.

Merton, Robert K.
1976. *Sociological Ambivalence and Other Essays,* New York: Free Press.

Parsons, Talcott.
1951. *The Social System,* New York: Free Press.

Porter, John.
1965. *The Vertical Mosaic,* Toronto: University of Toronto Press.

Read, Herbert.
1941. *To Hell With Culture,* London: Kegan Paul, Trench, Trubner & Co. Ltd.

Rex, John.
1970. "The Concept of Race in Sociological Theory," in Sami Zubaida (ed.), *Race and Racialism,* London: Tavistock, 35-55.

van den Berghe, Pierre L.
1967. *Race and Racism,* New York: John Wiley.

Woods, John T.
1976. "A Cultural Approach to Canadian Independence," in Wallace Gagne (ed.), *Nationalism, Technology and the Future of Canada,* Toronto: Macmillan, 75-103.

Weber, Max.
1968. *Economy and Society,* (Guenther Roth & Claus Wittich eds.), New York: Bedminster Press.